National Geographic Picture Atlas of

Our Fifty States

National Geographic Picture Atlas of

Our Fifty States

National Geographic Picture Atlas of

Our Fifty States

Published by
The National Geographic Society

Gilbert M. Grosvenor
*President and
Chairman of the Board*

Michela A. English
Senior Vice President

Robert L. Breeden
*Executive Adviser to
the President for Publications
and Educational Media*

Prepared by
The Book Division

William R. Gray
Director

Margery G. Dunn
Senior Editor

Charles O. Hyman
*National Geographic
Book Service*

Staff for this Book

Margaret Sedeen
Editor

Greta Arnold
Linda B. Meyerriecks
Illustrations Editors

David M. Seager
Art Director

Melanie Patt-Corner
Chief Researcher

Charlotte Golin
Designer

Susan C. Eckert
Map Coordinator

Mary B. Dickinson
Catherine Herbert Howell
Edward Lanouette
Writer-Editors

H. Robert Morrison
Melanie Patt-Corner
Jean Kaplan Teichroew
Contributing Writers

Ratri Banerjee
Susan C. Eckert
James B. Enzinna
Patricia F. Frakes
Lise S. Sajewski
Penelope A. Timbers
Anne E. Withers
Editorial Researchers

Karen Dufort Sligh
Jean C. Stringer
Illustrations Assistants

Sandra F. Lotterman
Elizabeth G. Jevons
Karen F. Edwards
Teresita Cóquia Sison
Marilyn J. Williams
Staff Assistants

Richard S. Wain
Production Project Manager

Lewis R. Bassford
Heather Guwang
Production

George V. White
Director
John T. Dunn
Associate Director
Vincent P. Ryan
Manager
and R. Gary Colbert
*Manufacturing and
Quality Management*

Maps by Publications Art
John D. Garst, Jr.
Virginia L. Baza
Sharon M. Atkins
Peter J. Balch
Sven M. Dolling
Gary M. Johnson
Carl Mehler
Joseph F. Ochlak
William T. Spicer

Dianne L. Hardy
Indexer

Sue Appleby Purcell
Educational Consultant

*State Flowers and State Birds
painted by*
Robert Hynes

State Flags painted by
Marilyn Dye Smith
and Robert Hynes

Cover photography:
Michel Tcherevkoff
Eagle photograph:
Tom and Pat Leeson

First edition: 239,000 copies
264 pages, 315 illustrations,
80 maps

Contents

Our Fifty States Map 6

America's
Many Faces 8

The Maps
in Your Atlas 18

The District of Columbia 20

New England 24

Vermont 26
New Hampshire 30
Maine 34

Massachusetts 38
Connecticut 42
Rhode Island 46

Mid-Atlantic States 50

New York 52
Pennsylvania 56
New Jersey 60

Maryland 64
Delaware 68

Appalachian Highlands 72

Kentucky 74
West Virginia 78
Virginia 82

Tennessee 86
North Carolina 90

The Southeast 94

Arkansas 96
Mississippi 100
Alabama 104
Georgia 108

South Carolina 112
Louisiana 116
Florida 120

Great Lakes States 125

Wisconsin 126
Michigan 130
Illinois 134

Indiana 138
Ohio 142

The Heartland 146

North Dakota 148
Minnesota 152
South Dakota 156
Nebraska 160

Iowa 164
Kansas 168
Missouri 172

The Southwest 177

Arizona 178
New Mexico 182
Oklahoma 186
Texas 190

Mountain States 194

Idaho 196
Montana 200
Wyoming 204

Nevada 208
Utah 212
Colorado 216

Pacific Coast States 221

Washington 222
Oregon 226

California 230

Alaska, Hawaii, and Distant Shores 234

Alaska 236
Hawaii 240
Distant Shores 244

Facts at Your Fingertips 248
Population of U. S. Cities
Largest U. S. Metropolitan Areas
More Facts at Your Fingertips 250
Top Products/Top States
Superfacts

Illustrations Credits 251
Acknowledgments 251
Index 252

Our Fifty States

6 a.m.
Hawaii-Aleutian Time

7 a.m.
Alaska Time

8 a.m.
Pacific Time

The fifty United States make up the fourth largest country in the world, both in area and in population. The country's 3,618,770 square miles (9,372,614 sq km) span six time zones and a wide diversity of geography and climate. From the woods of Maine to the mountains of California, from arctic Alaska to tropical Hawaii, almost 250,000,000 Americans form a colorful kaleidoscope of cultures.

Each standard time zone is about 900 miles (1,450 km) wide. Time zones are based on a system that uses lines of longitude as borders. But the borders bend or zigzag so that neighboring areas can share the same time.

Regional colors match the colors of state maps within each regional section of the atlas.

ALASKA

Olympia
WASHINGTON

Salem

OREGON

Sacramento

Carson City
NEVADA

CALIFORNIA

★ Juneau

HAWAII
Honolulu

Hawaii and the Aleutian Islands share the same time zone.

- New England
- Mid-Atlantic States
- Appalachian Highlands
- The Southeast
- Great Lakes States
- The Heartland
- The Southwest
- Mountain States
- Pacific Coast States
- Alaska, Hawaii, and Distant Shores

9 a.m.
Mountain Time

10 a.m.
Central Time

11 a.m.
Eastern Time

MONTANA
★ Helena

NORTH DAKOTA
★ Bismarck

MINNESOTA
St. Paul ★

Lake Superior

MAINE
Augusta ★

VERMONT
Montpelier ★

NEW HAMPSHIRE
★ Concord
★ Boston

Boise ★

IDAHO

SOUTH DAKOTA
★ Pierre

WISCONSIN

Lake Michigan

MICHIGAN

Lake Huron

Lake Ontario

Albany ★

MASSACHUSETTS
★ Providence

WYOMING

Madison ★

Lansing ★

Lake Erie

NEW YORK

Hartford ★
CONNECTICUT

RHODE ISLAND

Salt Lake City ★

Cheyenne ★

NEBRASKA

IOWA

Des Moines ★

PENNSYLVANIA
Harrisburg ★

Trenton ★
NEW JERSEY

UTAH

Denver ★

Lincoln ★

ILLINOIS

INDIANA

OHIO
Columbus ★

★ Dover
DELAWARE

Annapolis
Washington ★⊗
D. C. MARYLAND

COLORADO

Topeka ★

Springfield ★

Indianapolis ★

WEST VIRGINIA
Charleston ★

Richmond ⊛

ARIZONA

Santa Fe ★

KANSAS

MISSOURI
Jefferson City ★

Frankfort ★

KENTUCKY

VIRGINIA

Raleigh ★

Phoenix ★

NEW MEXICO

OKLAHOMA
★ Oklahoma City

ARKANSAS

TENNESSEE

Nashville ★

NORTH CAROLINA

Columbia ★
SOUTH CAROLINA

Little Rock ★

Atlanta ★

MISSISSIPPI

ALABAMA

GEORGIA

TEXAS

LOUISIANA

Jackson ★

Montgomery ★

Baton Rouge ★

Austin ★

Tallahassee ★

FLORIDA

0   KILOMETERS   300
0   STATUTE MILES   300

America's Many Faces

"E Pluribus Unum" is the Latin phrase on the Great Seal of the United States—"From Many, One." When Benjamin Franklin, Thomas Jefferson, and John Adams proposed this motto to the Continental Congress in 1776, they meant that one indivisible nation, the United States of America, was being formed from 13 separate colonies. Today we can see other meanings as well in the words, meanings perhaps undreamed of by those first congressional delegates. From many countries of the world, millions upon millions of immigrants have come to the shores of this country to make one people.

Just as the face of the American people is one of great diversity, so is the face of the land. This essay will present scenes and portraits of both. Wherever we live, to explore the whole expanse of our country brings an understanding of how the American land is part of all of us and how we all are part of the land. Each region of the country offers wonders and surprises and its own particular kind of beauty.

Alaska is a place where you can sense the wildness and spaciousness of much of the land before Europeans arrived. Imagine what it would be like to travel a distance greater than that from New York to the Mississippi River and see mountains, rivers, glaciers, marshes, forests, endless tundra plains, and multitudes of birds and other animals. This is the primeval wilderness that characterizes most of Alaska.

One of the northernmost mountain systems on Earth, the Brooks Range lies within the Arctic Circle and sweeps across Alaska from the Canadian border to the Chukchi Sea. On the North Slope of the Brooks, rolling tundra overlies permafrost that begins from a few inches to a few feet below the surface and reaches down hundreds of feet. Some tundra plants hug the ground to avoid harsh winds. In the briefest of summers, they grow and flower. The tundra and the mountains are migration grounds for moose and caribou herds. Also making their homes on the tundra or on the mountain slopes are musk oxen, Dall's sheep, wolves, arctic foxes, grizzly bears, polar bears, and, in spring and summer, millions of migrant birds.

Thick spruce forests, some perched on high bluffs, line the banks of the Yukon River in its middle stretch. Where the Yukon turns southwestward, leaving behind its canyon walls, it flows through marshy land. The arctic tern, one of the world's champion long-distance commuters, summers here and in autumn migrates as far away as South America and Antarctica.

At a great fan-shaped delta, the Yukon River empties into the Bering Sea. In spring and summer, the delta's thousands of square miles resound with the quacking of ducks, the yodeling of tundra swans, and the calls of millions of other birds. Grizzly bears range through the northern uplands, feasting on salmon and berries. When winter comes, bears sleep in their dens. Quiet descends, except for the rush of the wind, the scratches of moose pawing through the snow for plants to eat, or the low croak of a soaring raven.

To the south, the Aleutian Islands stretch for hundreds of miles in a rampart of windswept, fogbound mountain peaks. Nutrient-rich waters off the Aleutians and other parts of southern Alaska support what may be the greatest concentration of marine mammals in the world. Fur seals, sea otters, sea lions, and walruses thrive here. Humpback whales feed here during the summer, and in the fall head southwestward across 3,000 miles of open ocean to Hawaii.

Being home to humpbacks for half of each year is not all that Alaska and Hawaii have in common. In both states, volcanoes rumble. Both states protect their wildlife populations, but, unlike Alaska's huge refuges, some of Hawaii's are tiny—rocky, sandy islets in the vast Pacific, where seabirds in the tens of thousands nest and raise their offspring, and where the endangered Hawaiian monk seal finds haven.

In the western United States, the Cascade Range, the Sierra Nevada, and the Coast Ranges give this part of the country a high profile characterized by rolling seas of evergreen forest, mountain glaciers and snowfields, rocky cliffs plunging headlong into the ocean, and deep bays and sounds.

Between the Pacific mountain ranges and the Rocky Mountains is the Basin and Range, a region of deserts and plateaus and valleys separated by mountain ranges. Here, on Nevada's high,

In the southern Colorado Rocky Mountains, a frigid lake mirrors mountain peaks once veined with precious ores of gold and silver.

rocky slopes grow groves of bristlecone pines, some of the oldest living trees on Earth. These stunted, gnarled, grotesquely beautiful pines have survived through centuries of storm and drought. Wind-driven ice polishes their wood. The miracle of the bristlecone is its ability to keep a spark of life glowing in a thin strip of bark and a few branches, needles, and roots long after the rest of the tree has died.

In the Grand Canyon, the Colorado River has cut a window into the continent's history. The layers of exposed rock can be read like a book. Once shale lay on top, on the canyon rim. Now eroded, the shale marked the time when dinosaurs ruled the Earth. Today's top layers are limestone, rich in fossils of sponges, fish, and corals that lived in seas some 200 million years ago, when the floating plates of Earth's crust formed the supercontinent of Pangaea. There was no Grand Canyon yet, nor a Colorado River. Where today canyon walls plunge nearly a mile (1.6 km) to the river, the story told by the rocks is one of Earth turning itself inside out in geologic upheavals, faulting, erosion, and sea flooding. The bottom rocks, nearly two billion years old, are themselves the roots of ancient mountains.

Cresting the North American continent, the Rocky Mountains reach from New Mexico to Alaska's Brooks Range. In Wyoming, in the Teton Range of the central Rockies, peaks rise steeply from the valley floor through forests of pine, fir, and spruce, to alpine meadows bright with wildflowers, past glaciers even now shaping the landscape in slow motion, to stark, granite pinnacles. Here, along the banks of the Snake River, aspen and willow provide beavers with their favorite food. River otters, ospreys, and eagles dine on trout. In winter, solitary moose browse in willow thickets, and elk herds graze by night on meadow grasses.

Eastward from the Rocky Mountains, the land slopes down to the plains and prairies of the mid-continent. Little more than a century ago, tallgrass prairie spread for hundreds of miles. Now it has dwindled to a precious few thousand acres, mostly in Kansas.

A tallgrass prairie rolls in waves, like a sea. It rustles in the wind. Its intermingled life-forms weave an intricate web. The plant that dominates is big bluestem, a grass whose total ex-

tent, top to bottom, can be greater than the height of three men. Above the prairie sod, big bluestem can stand ten feet (3 m) in height. Its roots reach down at least twelve feet (3.7 m), finding soil nutrients and protection from harsh weather. From spring to fall, patches of flowers brighten the grassland. Their blossoms lure insects that find meals of nectar or flower parts and help the flowers to reproduce by carrying pollen from one flower to another. Birds and mammals eat the fruits that flowers produce and deposit the undigested seeds where they may sprout into the growth of a new season. Other plants depend on wind to scatter their seeds, and hang on to the seeds until the wind is high enough to carry them away. Still others, with sticky seeds, owe the distribution of their species to animals that accidentally pick up the seeds, carry them off, and later drop them. The seeds may grow, or they may be eaten by birds.

A busy, hidden world thrives under the prairie sod, inhabited by tiny creatures without which the grasses, flowers, shrubs, and animals from deer to mice could not exist here. A kind of microscopic fungus helps the root hairs of plants to absorb nutrients from the soil. In exchange, the plants feed some of their own carbohydrates to the fungus. There are bacteria that live in the root hairs and enable the plants to get the nitrogen essential to growth. Larger creatures such as the larvae of June bugs, cicadas, and click beetles feed on roots. This underground world is a densely populated place, with hundreds of microscopic inhabitants in a handful of soil.

East of the grasslands, past the valleys of the Mississippi and Ohio Rivers, the flanks of the Appalachian Mountains begin their rise. The green-clad Appalachian peaks descend eastward to the Piedmont and the Atlantic Coastal Plain. In these parts of the country, wild places are fewer and smaller than in the West, but their rewards are as great.

In southern Georgia, in the mysterious depths of the Okefenokee Swamp, the bellows of bull alligators can take us back to prehistoric times and remind us of the alligator's ancient

Newborn babies in a Dallas, Texas, hospital take a ride to visit their parents. Every day in this hospital at least 40 new Texans are born.

relative, the dinosaur. Soaring bald cypress trees sink their great knobby roots in thick peat, a legacy of ages of decaying plant life. The swamp water flows slowly, drifting to its outlets, the St. Marys River and the Suwannee River. Waterbirds nest deep in the swamp and often flock to the vast expanses of marsh and water known here as prairies. River otters, black bears, muskrats, bats, bobcats, foxes, and some 40 other species of animals live in the swamp or on the drier uplands of Okefenokee.

Just as there are layers in rock that reveal the geological past, so there are layers in the story of human existence. Those of us alive today in the United States are actors in the latest chapter of a history that began on this continent thousands of years ago. What happened in the first chapter? Who were the first Americans?

Anthropologists and archaeologists debate this question heatedly. For many years, most believed that the earliest humans to enter North America crossed a land bridge between Siberia and Alaska about 12,000 years ago. But in the 1970s, scientists made some intriguing—and still disputed—discoveries. For instance, there are signs that some 16,000 years ago, at a place now called Meadowcroft, in southwestern Pennsylvania, people had made a shelter under a sandstone cliff. These people lived by hunting deer and small animals and by gathering plants to eat and, perhaps, to make baskets. For many generations people used this rock-shelter as a temporary home and as a base camp. Other sites have been excavated in South America where such things as tools, uneaten mastodon meat, a human footprint, and vivid rock paintings suggest that people had ranged that far by 13,000 years ago. Even if this turns out to be true, no one knows how they got there. Did they travel in boats or on rafts? Or did they walk, in small migratory bands, moving southward perhaps a few miles a year all the way from Alaska?

That is exactly what some early Americans did. They trickled, step by step, following mammoths, elephants, bison, caribou, and other beasts. They quarried stone for spearpoints to kill their game and for tools to butcher it. They gathered plants for food, medicine, and clothing. They shared their domain with lions, cheetahs, saber-toothed cats, and huge bears. This was late in the Ice Age, when glaciers still held enough seawater to keep ocean levels low and to expose a vast, ice-free area of Alaska's continental shelf. We call this dry land Beringia or the Bering Land Bridge, but people slowly crossing it from Asia would have had no sense of being on anything like a bridge. At its widest, Beringia covered a thousand miles (1,600 km). It was largely a rolling plain crossed by great rivers and dotted with groves of willow and patches of prairie grasses, sedge, and sagebrush. Spring flowers brightened the tundra then as now.

These hunters, as well as others who may have traveled along the coasts and hunted sea mammals, were the ancestors of the American Indians. They were the first immigrants. They are the people who really discovered America.

In time their descendants fanned out across the continent. When Christopher Columbus sailed into the New World, at the end of the 15th century, there were some two million people—Indians and other native groups—living on the continent north of Central America. Today, five centuries later, the population of the United States alone, at almost 250,000,000, is more than a hundred times greater.

One reason for this growth is that Americans have traditionally been a people on the move. When the first census was taken in 1790, colonists and settlers from Europe made up most of the population. At that time the census counted the number of Americans at a little over 3,900,000. Indians were not included, but historians say that, by then, there were only about 600,000 in the entire area of today's contiguous 48 states. The black population numbered more than 700,000. Most were slaves, tragic and unwilling immigrants, but several thousand were free blacks, many of whom had worked for money as indentured servants. The movement of Europeans to the United States soon took on the proportions of a flood. By 1860 more than five million new Americans had arrived, mostly from western Europe. The greatest growth occurred in the late 19th and early 20th centuries, when more than 22 million newcomers, many from

The energy of big cities everywhere radiates from this special-effects view of New York, the heart of our country's most populous metropolitan area.

southern and eastern Europe, arrived on the shores of America.

The face of our country is always changing. Demographers, people who study the characteristics of populations, tell us that a nation's population changes because of three things: births, deaths, and migration. Demographers can tell us, for instance, that every 8 seconds a baby is born somewhere in the United States. Every 15 seconds someone dies. Every 35 seconds a new immigrant arrives in the United States. And every 3 minutes an American emigrates. A demographic portrait reveals many things—about ourselves, our families, our neighbors, our work, the places we live.

Today we Americans live farther west and farther south than ever before. States in the West and South saw rapid population growth from 1980 to 1990. States in the Northeast and Midwest grew slowly or saw their populations fall. The westward movement of the population center of the 50 states reflects our history. As settlers migrated across the Appalachian Mountains, populated the Midwest, and made homes from the plains to the Pacific coast, the country's population center shifted westward, following them. Today it lies about 95 miles (152 km) southwest of St. Louis, Missouri. (For more information, see pages 172 and 173.)

More than half of the people in the United States live in metropolitan areas of one million or more. This is a group that has grown steadily. In 1950 it was less than one-third of the population. When you include smaller metropolitan areas, you find that almost 80 percent of Americans are dwellers in cities or suburbs.

In 1950, 15 percent of Americans lived on farms. This is a group that has declined steadily, and today includes fewer than 2 of every 100 people. Around the country, rural areas have lost population because of the decline in family farms and because of a loss of mining jobs.

When people give up living on farms or in small towns, where do they go? Most do not go to big cities. They go to the suburbs. City people, too, often choose to move to the suburbs. Today,

The 1,250,000 crushed beverage cans awaiting shipment here testify to a rising American awareness of the importance of recycling our resources.

of all the kinds of places that we Americans live in, it is the outermost fringes of suburban areas that see the strongest growth. Demographers predict that this trend will continue.

When people move, they usually go where the jobs are. The fact that Florida attracts large numbers of retirees means that other people are needed to open and work in stores, dry-cleaning and repair shops, health-care facilities, or restaurants to serve the senior citizens. Where the tourism industry is thriving, such as in Las Vegas, Nevada, that creates jobs in areas from construction to popcorn vending. In Austin, the capital of Texas, employers such as the state government, the University of Texas, and high-tech industries helped to give Texas a 1990 population that was almost 20 percent greater than its 1980 population. But several other states beat that figure: Nevada grew by 50 percent; Alaska, 37 percent; Arizona, 35 percent; Florida, 33 percent; California, 26 percent. Across the United States as a whole, there are at least 10 percent more people than there were in 1980.

Of these some 23 million new Americans, more than a third are immigrants. People have come from China, Korea, the Philippines, India, Iran, Vietnam, and other parts of Asia. They have come from Mexico, Cuba, El Salvador, the Dominican Republic, Guatemala, and Colombia, as well as other Latin American countries. Most of the immigration in the decade of the 1980s was Asian and Hispanic, but newcomers also arrived from Europe, Africa, and Canada.

Another group that has grown in size is the Native American population. Since 1960, the number of people identifying themselves as American Indian has more than tripled. Experts believe that many who once concealed their ethnic identity now proudly call themselves Indian, take a new pleasure in their heritage, and feel optimistic about their future.

The United States has been called a melting pot, a nation of nations, a world nation. One of the strengths of our country has always been its diversity. As we head into the 21st century, we are a people united, yet more diverse than ever.

*"In God's wildness lies the hope of the world,"
wrote naturalist John Muir, an ardent defender of
trees such as these California redwoods.*

The Maps in Your Atlas

An atlas is a collection of maps. Maps show many things, such as where places are, how big they are, and their distance from other places. In your Picture Atlas you will find maps of the fifty United States and the territories, as well as maps of regions. Each map is full of information. Notes on the maps point out places of geographical or historical importance. Some map symbols represent natural features, while others show man-made features.

The state maps in your atlas, like this sample map of Washington, are general reference maps, sometimes called political maps. They present each state as if you were looking straight down on it. These maps emphasize state boundaries and man-made features, such as cities, towns, and highways.

Physical features—mountains, lakes, and rivers—are also shown. Some rivers, such as the Gila in Arizona (page 179), are drawn with dashed and dotted blue lines. This is a cartographer's way of showing that the rivers are intermittent and may dry up in certain seasons. Dashed blue outlines also mark salt lakes and

dry lakes, such as the Bonneville Salt Flats and Sevier Lake in Utah (page 213). A bar scale with each map lets you measure distance in both miles and kilometers.

The maps of regions in your atlas are physical maps. They show features of Earth's surface. Except for Alaska and Hawaii, each region is a group of contiguous states with physical similarities, and sometimes with surprising differences. These maps are also paintings. Because of their three-dimensional quality, as well as the perspective, or angle, from which each region is seen, not everything is visible. A river may disappear behind a mountain, or a city could be hidden by a high peak.

Each state in your atlas has photographs; illustrations of the state flag, flower, and bird; a text article; and a fact box with the state's area and population, the three largest cities with their population, information about the economy, and the date of statehood. The categories of mining, agriculture, and industry appear in order of economic value to that state. Within each category, products are listed in order of value.

This is a pictorial map of the Mid-Atlantic region. Your atlas contains a similar map for each region of the United States. These maps show the main physical features, such as mountains, lakes, rivers, and shorelines. Studying these maps will help you understand the unity and diversity of each region. You can also see that a mountain range can be a barrier or that major cities are often·on rivers or protected bays.

| | 1 | 2 | 3 | 4 | 5 | 6 | 7 | 8 | 9 | 10 | 11 | 12 | 13 | 14 | 15 | 16 | 17 | 18 | 19 |

Point Roberts

NOOKSACK I.R.

NORTH CASCADES NATIONAL PARK

ROSS LAKE NATIONAL RECREATION AREA

Columbia River

Pend Oreille River

A

Ferndale

Bellingham

+ Mount Baker
10,778 FEET
3,285 METERS

NORTH CASCADES NATIONAL PARK

LITTLE PEND OREILLE NATIONAL WILDLIFE REFUGE

B

LUMMI I.R.

MOUNT BAKER N.R.A.

20

21

Cape Flattery

San Juan Islands

Anacortes

UPPER SKAGIT I.R.

Mount Logan +
8,966 FEET
2,733 METERS

Colville

C

SAN JUAN ISLANDS NATIONAL WILDLIFE REFUGE

Skagit River

Mount Vernon

20

LAKE CHELAN NATIONAL RECREATION AREA

COLVILLE INDIAN RESERVATION

KALISPEL I.R.

FLATTERY ROCKS N.W.R.

MAKAH INDIAN RESERVATION

SWINOMISH INDIAN RESERVATION

Oak Harbor

Glacier Peak
10,541 FEET
3,213 METERS

97

Rufus Woods Lake

Franklin Delano Roosevelt Lake

COULEE DAM NATIONAL RECREATION AREA

Newport

D

DUNGENESS N.W.R.

SAUK I.R.

Lake Chelan

OZETTE I.R.

LOWER ELWHA I.R.

PROTECTION ISLAND N.W.R.

SUIATTLE I.R.

395

2

OLYMPIC NATIONAL PARK

QUILEUTE I.R.

Port Angeles

Port Townsend

STILLAGUAMISH I.R.

TULALIP INDIAN RESERVATION

Everett

Lake Chelan

Grand Coulee Dam

SPOKANE INDIAN RESERVATION

E

QUILLAYUTE NEEDLES N.W.R.

JAMESTOWN KLALLAM I.R.

101

Hoh River

Mount Olympus
7,965 FEET
2,428 METERS

GAMBLE I.R.

PORT MADISON I.R.

Lynnwood

Edmonds

Mountlake Terrace

2

Banks Lake

Spokane River

Spokane

F

HOH I.R.

101

Kirkland

Redmond

Davenport

Dishman

OLYMPIC NATIONAL PARK

OLYMPIC MOUNTAINS

Seattle

Bellevue

Mercer Island

2

QUINAULT INDIAN RESERVATION

Bremerton

White Center

Burien

Renton

Cheney

G

PACIFIC OCEAN

COPALIS N.W.R.

SKOKOMISH INDIAN RESERVATION

Des Moines

Kent

21

28

TURNBULL NATIONAL WILDLIFE REFUGE

Shelton

Auburn

MUCKLESHOOT I.R.

Wenatchee

90

SQUAXIN ISLAND I.R.

Tacoma

Puyallup

Ephrata

PUYALLUP I.R.

Parkland

97

Moses Lake

Moses Lake

Ritzville

H

GRAYS HARBOR N.W.R.

Hoquiam

Olympia

NISQUALLY NATIONAL WILDLIFE REFUGE

Potholes Reservoir

COLUMBIA NATIONAL WILDLIFE REFUGE

195

Aberdeen

Tumwater

Lacey

NISQUALLY I.R.

Ellensburg

Columbia River

Westport

12

MOUNT RAINIER NATIONAL PARK

+ Mount Rainier
14,410 FEET
4,392 METERS
Highest point in Washington

82

SADDLE MOUNTAIN NATIONAL WILDLIFE REFUGE

Colfax

J

SHOALWATER BAY INDIAN RESERVATION

Chehalis River

CHEHALIS I.R.

12

Pullman

Raymond

Centralia

395

Chehalis

Yakima

Hanford Site

Snake River

K

WILLAPA NATIONAL WILDLIFE REFUGE

101

JULIA BUTLER HANSEN NATIONAL WILDLIFE REFUGE

Riffe Lake

Cowlitz River

12

Clarkston

5

Toppenish

Yakima

Sunnyside

Richland

L

Columbia

River

Kelso

Longview

Mount St. Helens
8,366 FEET
2,550 METERS

Mount Adams
12,307 FEET
3,751 METERS

YAKIMA INDIAN RESERVATION

TOPPENISH NATIONAL WILDLIFE REFUGE

River

Kennewick

Pasco

McNARY NATIONAL WILDLIFE REFUGE

97

Walla Walla

RIDGEFIELD NATIONAL WILDLIFE REFUGE

PACIFIC CREST TRAIL

CONBOY LAKE NATIONAL WILDLIFE REFUGE

UMATILLA NATIONAL WILDLIFE REFUGE

M

Vancouver

FRANZ LAKE N.W.R.

PIERCE N.W.R.

Camas

Bonneville Dam

14

LEWIS AND CLARK TRAIL

N

STEIGERWALD LAKE N.W.R.

The Dalles Dam

KILOMETERS 60
STATUTE MILES 40

★ state capital

● **Chicago** (page 135) 1 million people and over

● **Seattle** 100,000 to under 1 million people

● Bellevue 50,000 to under 100,000 people

• Redmond under 50,000 people

(65) interstate highways

(72) U.S. highways

(10) state and local highways

national parks, national lakeshores, national seashores, large national recreation areas (N.R.A.), large national monuments (N.M.)

Indian reservations (I.R.)

historic trails

national scenic trails

proposed national scenic trails

□ site symbol: small national recreation areas (N.R.A.) small national monuments (N.M.), national wildlife refuges (N.W.R.), sites of interest

How to Find a Place
Look up Davenport, Washington, in the index. It will say **223** F16. Turn to page 223. Find the letter F on the side of the map and the number 16 at the top. Follow imaginary lines from the number and letter to where they intersect. There you will find Davenport.

District of Columbia

The founders of the United States wrestled with the problem of where the capital of the young nation should be. Finally, in 1790, they agreed on a location somewhere on the Potomac River. They left the exact choice of a site to President George Washington. It is his memory we honor when we call the city Washington, D. C.

George Washington chose a site on the fall line that divides the Piedmont from the Atlantic Coastal Plain. He directed surveyors to lay out a square ten miles (16 km) on each side for the new capital. The city was to stand on both sides of the Potomac at the head of navigation, partly in Maryland and partly in Virginia. Those states ceded the land to the government, but in 1846 Virginia asked for its portion back.

To design the city, President Washington selected Pierre Charles L'Enfant, a French engineer who had served as a volunteer in the Revolutionary War. The chief surveyor, Maryland's Andrew Ellicott, and his assistant, a self-taught black mathematician and astronomer named Benjamin Banneker, used positions of

During World War I, when Woodrow Wilson was President, sheep were put to work cropping the south lawn of the White House to free men for the war effort.

the stars to determine the District's latitude and longitude and to lay out its boundaries.

Today L'Enfant's ideas can be seen in the traffic circles and broad thoroughfares of the city, lined with stately buildings and memorials built in the architectural styles of ancient Greece and Rome. Toward one end of Pennsylvania Avenue stands the domed Capitol Building, toward the other the White House, where Presidents have worked and lived with their families since 1800. During the War of 1812, British troops marched on Washington and set fire to both buildings.

L'Enfant designed the Mall to be a "Grand Avenue . . . bordered with gardens," and so it is. On the Mall stand museums administered by the Smithsonian Institution. These include the Museum of American History, where you can see what life was like in the past. Among the enormous collections here are a green-and-gold 1920s locomotive, gowns of America's First Ladies, one of George Washington's uniforms, and Thomas Edison's phonograph.

George Washington had hoped that the capital city would become part of an important trade route, by way of the Ohio River, to the interior of the country. In 1828 work was begun on the Chesapeake and Ohio Canal to bypass falls and rapids on the Potomac River, but financial prob-

lems and competition from railroads eventually put the canal out of business.

Today government is the chief business of the city. Some 370,000 people, city residents and suburbanites, work directly for the federal government, and hundreds of thousands more work for organizations such as research firms, publishers, and trade associations that want to be near the government. Many Washington workers are lawyers. Their numbers are equal to almost a tenth of the city's population.

Washington is the heart of a metropolitan area of almost four million people, but its status as a federal district makes it unique. It is the only American city whose residents have no voting members of Congress. Congressional committees oversee the District government. Today residents campaign not only for full representation in Congress but also for statehood. The state would be called New Columbia.

For all its grandeur and importance, the District of Columbia is a city on a human scale. There are no skyscrapers. A 19th-century law limited buildings to a height that could be reached by the fire-fighting equipment of the day, and lawmakers have kept the restrictions so as not to dwarf the Capitol. A Washingtonian once remarked that "it's almost as if you could hold the city in the palm of your hand."

Throughout the city are multitudes of parks. In one, Rock Creek Park, a walk through thick native forests can lead your imagination back to the days before European settlement, when Algonquian Indians quarried stone there for tools. If you stand on a street corner just southeast of the Capitol, at a spot where sewer workers unearthed some dinosaur fossils, you might picture the giant creatures that reigned over the area more than a hundred million years ago.

The residents of today's District of Columbia are a varied group. A large number, such as those who work for embassies, are foreign citizens. Immigrants from Africa, Asia, and Latin America have arrived to make the city their home. During the early 19th century, the city was a mecca for free blacks. After the Civil War, former slaves migrated there from the South and, after World War II, so did black farm workers. In those years Washington's black citizens lived isolated and segregated in what one histo-

The map shows the following labels:

H Street · New York Avenue · Massachusetts Avenue · North Capitol Street · Union Station · George Washington University · G Street · Renwick Gallery · Blair House · Martin Luther King Library · Museum of American Art · National Portrait Gallery · Old Executive Office Building · Treasury Department · F Street · Ford's Theatre · Corcoran Gallery of Art · White House · Pennsylvania Avenue · F.B.I. Building · Senate Office Buildings · John F. Kennedy Center · Virginia Avenue · E Street · Department of Commerce · Department of Justice · National Archives · Department of Labor · Department of the Interior · Department of State · Constitution Avenue · 17th Street · The Ellipse · National Gallery of Art · Supreme Court · 23rd Street · Vietnam Veterans Memorial · Museum of American History · Museum of Natural History · 3rd Street · NW · NE · U.S. Capitol · 1st Street · Folger Library · Lincoln Memorial · Reflecting Pool · Washington Monument · THE MALL Smithsonian Institution · Air and Space Museum · SW · SE · Department of Agriculture · Independence Avenue · Library of Congress · Bureau of Engraving and Printing · Department of Energy · NASA · Department of Education · Department of Health and Human Services · House Office Buildings · 3rd Street · Lady Bird Johnson Park · West Potomac Park · Tidal Basin · Department of Housing and Urban Development · Department of Transportation · South Capitol Street · Potomac River · Jefferson Memorial · VIRGINIA

rian has called a "secret city." Their city is secret no longer. Two-thirds of Washington's people are black, and from their ranks come local and national leaders in government, business, medicine, law, and the arts. Every year millions of people in the District of Columbia are not Washingtonians at all, but residents of the fifty states and many foreign countries—tourists who come to experience the living history of the capital of the United States of America.

Area: *69 sq mi (178 sq km)*
Population: *606,900*
Important Economic Activities: *federal government, tourism, printing and publishing*
Founded: *site chosen October 1790; became the United States capital June 1800*

MARYLAND

District of Columbia

Potomac River

Anacostia River

Area enlarged

VIRGINIA

0 KILOMETERS 10

0 STATUTE MILES 5

In the heart of the District of Columbia stand buildings that house the federal government and the nation's treasures.

American Beauty Rose

Wood Thrush

1

2

3

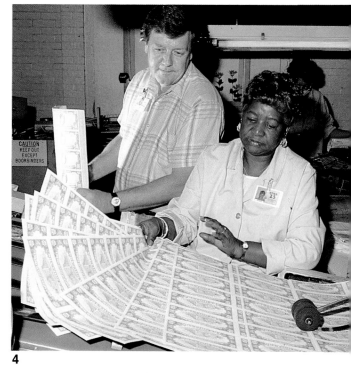

4

District of Columbia

1 *In dusk's soft glow, the 555-foot (169-m) Washington Monument and the domed Jefferson Memorial rise beyond the White House, home to every President except George Washington.*

2 *At the Vietnam Veterans Memorial, a youngster leans forward to kiss the name of his grandfather, killed in action in the Vietnam War.*

3 *The* Spirit of St. Louis, *flown in 1927 by Charles Lindbergh on the first solo flight across the Atlantic Ocean, hangs in the Air and Space Museum.*

4 *Workers at the Bureau of Engraving and Printing examine new sheets of bills.*

5 *Surgeons operate at Howard University Hospital, part of the largest mostly black university in the United States.*

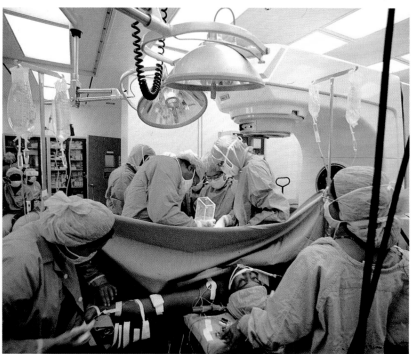

5

New England

The sunlight of a new day first touches the United States mainland on the treeless, mile-high (1.6-km) summit of Mount Katahdin, a solitary mountain of resistant rock called a monadnock that makes up part of the Appalachian Mountains in northern Maine. Lakes and streams glisten near Katahdin's foot. They are part of the Allagash Wilderness Waterway, a 92-mile-long (148-km) run of untamed rivers and lakes that each year lures thousands of canoeists to some of the nation's deepest, wildest woods.

Here, too, with Katahdin as its centerpiece, spreads a remarkable wilderness, a 200,000-acre (81,000-ha) state park bought and donated to the people of Maine by a former governor of the state, Percival Proctor Baxter. Today Baxter State Park serves those who truly savor the wilds. Camping is primitive and strictly regulated. Roads are unpaved. No motorboats, motorcycles, or luxury motor homes disturb the solitude, for this is the lair of the loon and the moose . . . and of those who revel in the lonely splendor of woods and lakes and streams.

Sloping from the mountains toward the ocean, northern New England ends in a burst of bays and inlets and islands, a shoreline as gingerbready as the woodwork on some of the graceful old houses along the coast. There are no deltas here, no great swamps, no sweeps of sandy dune to hint that the ocean waits nearby. The pointed firs march to the very lip of cliffs and headlands that in many places drop sheer to the waves.

Glaciers helped to chisel the shore here, shoving soil and rocks southward. At one time ice covered Mount Washington half a mile (0.8 km) deep. Then, as the glaciers slowly melted and receded, sea levels rose some 400 feet (122 m), transforming Maine's coastal hills into islands and their valleys into myriad fingerlike fjords and deepwater channels.

Whenever the ice paused for any length of time, it piled up sand and soil and boulders along its leading edge, like a giant conveyor belt. You can see here how far south the glaciers reached during the Ice Age. Cape Cod and its island satellites are long, sandy ridges called terminal moraines. They were left behind when the ice began its retreat about 12,000 years ago.

Most New Englanders live near the coast, or along rivers whose flowing waters turned the waterwheels that ran early mills and factories. Today these same rivers produce electric power for homes and industries throughout the region.

In this region the Connecticut River splits the Appalachian Mountains into two major ranges, the White Mountains east of the river and the Green Mountains to the west. In the northwest, the mountains border the fertile pastures and orchards around Lake Champlain. Glaciers were not the only builders of this lake or its valley. Millions of years ago, as Earth's crust shifted, a long, narrow slab of bedrock slipped and tilted toward the west, creating a crease between the Appalachians and neighboring western mountains that filled with water, forming today's sparkling, 107-mile-long (172-km) lake.

Mount Katahdin

Mount Washington

M O U N T A I N S

A N

Portland

Mount Desert Island

Boston

Cape Cod

VERMONT
NEW HAMPSHIRE
MAINE
MASSACHUSETTS
RHODE ISLAND
CONNECTICUT

Vermont

The forested Green Mountains run the length of Vermont and are part of a chain that reaches southward into Massachusetts and north into Canada. The 250-mile (402-km) Vermont range is unbroken, except for deep gaps cut by the Winooski and Lamoille Rivers, and, in Canada, the Missisquoi River.

Streams flowing down the eastern slopes empty into the Connecticut River and help support a rich agricultural valley. The westward-flowing rivers drain into Lake Champlain, which forms part of the border with New York. Vermont is the only state in New England without direct access to the sea, but, at the southern tip of the lake, commercial and pleasure boats work their way to New York City on a canal connected to the Hudson River.

Outdoor Vermont is a year-round asset. Forests cover nearly 80 percent of the state. In fall the leaves flare into brilliance, and thousands of visitors travel the state, admiring autumn's "last hurrah" before the snows descend. When that happens, skiers from near and far swoosh down the powdery slopes or glide along the smooth trails of more than 50 ski resorts.

In the early spring, when the days begin to warm up but the nights are still freezing, sap flows in the sugar maples. From maple groves, called sugar bushes, comes Vermont's sweetest product, maple syrup. A sugar maker, as this kind of farmer is known, boils down the sap of about 4 trees, some 40 gallons, to make one gallon of syrup. Each spring sugar makers tap millions of trees to obtain the half million gallons of syrup Vermont produces every year.

Then, when summer arrives, cool, crisp nights and warm days bring out campers, hikers, and fishermen. Many visitors are French Canadians, and, for them, people in northern Vermont often put up signs in French.

Vermont, with about the same number of people as Boston, Massachusetts, has the smallest population of any state east of the Mississippi River. Montpelier, a regional industrial and insurance center, is the smallest state capital in the United States. Nearly three-quarters of all Vermonters live on farms or in small towns scattered throughout the state. Since 1980, Vermont's population has increased, though not enough to make it a crowded place. Some outsiders are attracted by life in the small communities or by the prospect of employment in a computer factory or another high-tech company around Burlington.

Even though Vermont is rural, it is not agricultural. Only about 15 percent of the land is level and fertile enough for crops. The rest has soil too thin and rocky. Most of the good cropland is in the Connecticut River Valley and around Lake Champlain and its islands.

There are about half as many cows as there are Vermonters, and many herds graze on mountain pastures. Their milk earns more than three-fourths of the state's agricultural income. The state is also famous for its cheese. Manufacturing, too, helps keep the state's economy going. Vermont's extensive forests provide wood for the paper industry and timber for making furniture and toys.

Sons of the superintendent at Bennington's E.Z. Waist Company pose for a 1915 advertisement for knit union suits guaranteed to make "the child happy and comfortable."

Vermont's economy also benefits from its geology. The mountains began to form some 440 million years ago, when the forces of plate tectonics folded, cracked, and thrust the land upward. Molten rock, or magma, slowly cooled and crystallized. Much of the cooled rock became granite. The largest granite quarry in the world is east of Montpelier. Stone for buildings and memorial markers has been sliced from this quarry and polished in nearby Barre for more than a century.

Marble, which forms when limestone crystallizes, is found along the western edges of the Green Mountains and in the world's largest underground quarry, near the town of Danby. The dome, pillars, and walls of the Thomas Jefferson Memorial in Washington, D. C., are made of Vermont's white marble.

Vermonters are grateful for their economic stability, but they worry about endangering the environment. Around 1970 the state government addressed this issue, and Vermont became one of the first states to get rid of roadside commercial billboards and to legislate refunds for can and bottle returns.

The number of Vermont farms is declining. Writer Saul Bellow, a summer visitor to the state, tells of seeing abandoned farms "in the backlands of Vermont," where he discovers "old foundations, heaps of red brick," and "pairs of lilac bushes that once grew beside the driveway." Farming the rocky soil is hard, and the land has become valuable. In some areas farms are taxed on their potential worth as commercial land. But the state has passed laws to help farmers and to help protect its open land. Since 1988, Vermont towns have been required to participate in regional planning.

Area: *43rd largest state, 9,614 sq mi (24,900 sq km)*
Population: *562,758; ranks 48th*
Major Cities: *Burlington, 39,127; Rutland, 18,230; South Burlington, 12,809*
Manufacturing: *electronics, metal products, machinery, paper products, food products, transportation equipment, lumber and wood products, stone, glass, and clay products*
Agriculture: *milk, cattle, hay, maple products*
Mining and Quarrying: *granite, marble*
Other Important Activities: *tourism, printing and publishing*
Statehood: *the 14th state; admitted March 4, 1791*

1 2 3 4 5 6 7 8 9 10 11 12

A

MISSISQUOI N.W.R.
Richford
Lake Memphremagog
Norton

B
Swanton
78
Missisquoi River
Jay Peak
3,861 FEET
1,177 METERS
Newport
Gore Mountain
3,330 FEET
1,015 METERS
114
89

Isle La Motte

C
Saint Albans
Fairfield
108
100
Orleans
105

2

D
South Hero Island
Lamoille River
LONG TRAIL
Hiking path in Vermont from Massachusetts to Canada along crest of mountains
91
114
Granby
102

E
Lake Champlain
15
Smugglers Notch
Mount Mansfield
4,393 FEET
1,339 METERS
Highest point in Vermont
Morrisville
GREEN MOUNTAINS
15
2

Winooski
Burlington
Essex Junction
South Burlington
Stowe
Saint Johnsbury

F
Four thousand years of Indian occupation recorded here
Shelburne
89
Waterbury
Windooski River
2
93

G
7
100
★ Montpelier

H
Vergennes
Waitsfield
Barre
Warren
Northfield
302
91

J
Weybridge
Morgan Horse Farm
First American breed developed here
89
APPALACHIAN MOUNTAINS
Connecticut River

Middlebury

K
30
Salisbury
Strafford

L
7
White River
APPALACHIAN TRAIL
Otter Creek

M
Lake Bomoseen
Proctor
Rutland
White River Junction
Woodstock
Killington Peak
4,241 FEET
1,293 METERS

N
Fair Haven
West Rutland
Plymouth

O
Poultney
Windsor
91

P
30
WHITE ROCKS N.R.A.
Danby
100
Springfield
GREEN MOUNTAINS

Q
Equinox Mt.
3,816 FEET
1,163 METERS
Bromley Mountain
3,260 FEET
994 METERS
11
Grafton

Batten Kill
Manchester Center
Bellows Falls

R
LONG TRAIL
Stratton Mountain
3,936 FEET
1,200 METERS
Townshend

S
7
Mount Snow
3,556 FEET
1,084 METERS
West River

Haystack Mountain
3,420 FEET
1,043 METERS
30
Dummerston Center

T
Bennington
Wilmington
Marlboro
9
Brattleboro

100

U
Whitingham
112
Vernon

Vert mont. The words mean "green mountain" in French and hark back to 1609 when explorer Samuel de Champlain saw the tree-covered hills. The words give the state its name and are a reminder that part of French-speaking Canada is near.

The Long Trail runs the ridges of the Green Mountains. Near Mount Mansfield, Smugglers Notch cuts a gap in the mountains. During the War of 1812, while Britain and the U. S. quarreled, the notch provided a route for Vermonters to trade goods illegally with their British neighbors a few miles to the north.

0 KILOMETERS 30
0 STATUTE MILES 20

Red Clover

Hermit Thrush

1

2

Vermont

1 *Fall colors cast their spell over the village of Grafton. Small towns such as this give rural Vermont an air of tranquillity.*

2 *Children play around the trunk of a sugar maple tree in the Green Mountains. Sap collected in buckets each spring makes maple sugar, syrup, and candy.*

3 *A teacher monitors her class in Granby's one-room schoolhouse. The state constitution, adopted in 1777, requires every Vermont town to have a public school.*

4 *Workers at the Rock of Ages quarry, near Barre, anchor a pulley. Torches have replaced the drills that once cut these blocks.*

5 *Pies for an apple pie festival crowd church pews in Dummerston Center.*

3

5

4

New Hampshire

Every March, on the first Tuesday, citizens in small towns across New Hampshire observe a New England custom that dates back to colonial days, when spring thaws made dirt roads impassable. They hold a town meeting before the mud season sets in, to vote on local laws and decide how much their property taxes will be. They determine what they can pay their teachers and police, how many library books they can buy, and how much salt they can afford to spread over winter's icy roads.

Usually in March, says New Hampshire writer Donald Hall, winter "goes into hibernation, sleeping off the balmy months of peeper-sing until the red leaf wakes it again and the white season returns." But summer is short in the northern part of the state and in the mountains. Winter can last seven months and bring an average of more than eight feet (2.4 m) of snow.

New Hampshire is the most mountainous of the New England states. Mount Washington, the highest peak in the Northeast, looms over the Presidential Range, part of the White Mountains that cut across northern New Hampshire. In warm weather, people hike, drive, or take a historic cog railway to Mount Washington's summit. In winter the trip is like going to the Arctic, with hurricane-force winds frequently pummeling the peak. At such times the crews working at the weather observatory and at the television transmitter are alone.

From the northern mountains flow New Hampshire's most important rivers. The Connecticut begins in a boggy area only a few hundred yards from Canada. After it flows southward through small lakes named for it, it forms the border with Vermont. In the Connecticut and Merrimack River Valleys, dairy cows graze rich pastures below wooded hills.

On a hilltop in the valley of the Merrimack stands the Shaker village of Canterbury, founded in 1792 and now a museum. Leading a self-sufficient, communal, monastic life, Shaker brothers and sisters built a meetinghouse, dwellings, and barns. They cleared rocky fields where they pastured sheep, cattle, and oxen and grew crops. The Shakers believed that their "gift to be simple" was the way to worship God.

With its small towns and covered bridges, New Hampshire looks rural, but it really is high-

Great-granddad's Big Wheel: This monster machine at the 1896 Concord Bicycle Parade weighed in at almost 2,000 pounds (908 kg) and was billed as the world's largest tricycle.

ly industrialized. Manufacturing is the mainstay of its economy. In the early 19th century, Manchester businessmen began to develop the Amoskeag Mills. Amoskeag's massive red-brick mills eventually stretched for a mile and a half (2.4 km) along the Merrimack River below their original power source, the Amoskeag Falls. Amoskeag became the largest cotton textile producer in the world. Every couple of months the mills wove enough cloth to encircle the globe. Immigrants from Canada, Ireland, Poland, and Greece came to work in Manchester.

Once the center of New Hampshire's economy, the mills suffered from competition from other mills, outmoded technology, and a bitter strike over low wages. The mill owners declared bankruptcy on Christmas Eve, 1935.

Grandchildren of people who lost their mill jobs benefited from the development of high-tech industries that produce computers and electronic equipment. Prosperity spread throughout the southeast, particularly around Manchester, Portsmouth, and Nashua. Between 1980 and 1990 the population of New

Hampshire grew by almost 20 percent, more than any other eastern state except Florida. A little more than half of New Hampshire's residents live in urban areas, and about 85 percent of the total live in the southern half of the state. Some people feel that southern New Hampshire is actually a suburb of Boston. Many who live here commute to work in Boston and enjoy the best of both worlds: small-town life with a big-city paycheck and no state income tax.

In northern New Hampshire, cut off from the rest of the state by the White Mountains, small towns depend on the forest products industry. Paper companies own more than a half million acres of land, and Berlin is the only northern industrial city. Workers at its mill have produced paper and pulp for more than a century. Forests of spruce, white pine, ash, birch, oak, and other species cover about 86 percent of New Hampshire. Most of this is second growth. By the early 1900s, most New Hampshire forests had been cleared by farmers or logged by lumber barons. In 1911 conservationists managed to control timber harvesting and establish the White Mountain National Forest, which today covers about one-eighth of the state. In the wild north woods, where they have room to range, live deer, moose, bobcats, and black bears.

New Hampshire's seacoast, only 18 miles (29 km) long, is the shortest in the nation. Portsmouth, with its deepwater harbor, is the state's oldest settlement. Since its founding in 1630, Portsmouth has been known for shipbuilding. There in 1800 the United States Navy opened its first shipyard, the site of the first World War I submarine launching. Today the shipyard builds and repairs submarines.

Area: *44th largest state, 9,279 sq mi (24,032 sq km)*
Population: *1,109,252; ranks 40th*
Major Cities: *Manchester, 99,567; Nashua, 79,662; Concord, 36,006*
Manufacturing: *machinery, scientific instruments, electronics, rubber and plastics, paper products, food products, metal products, lumber and wood products*
Mining and Quarrying: *sand and gravel, granite*
Agriculture: *milk, greenhouse and nursery products, apples, cattle, hay*
Other Important Activities: *tourism*
Statehood: *the ninth state; ratified the Constitution on June 21, 1788*

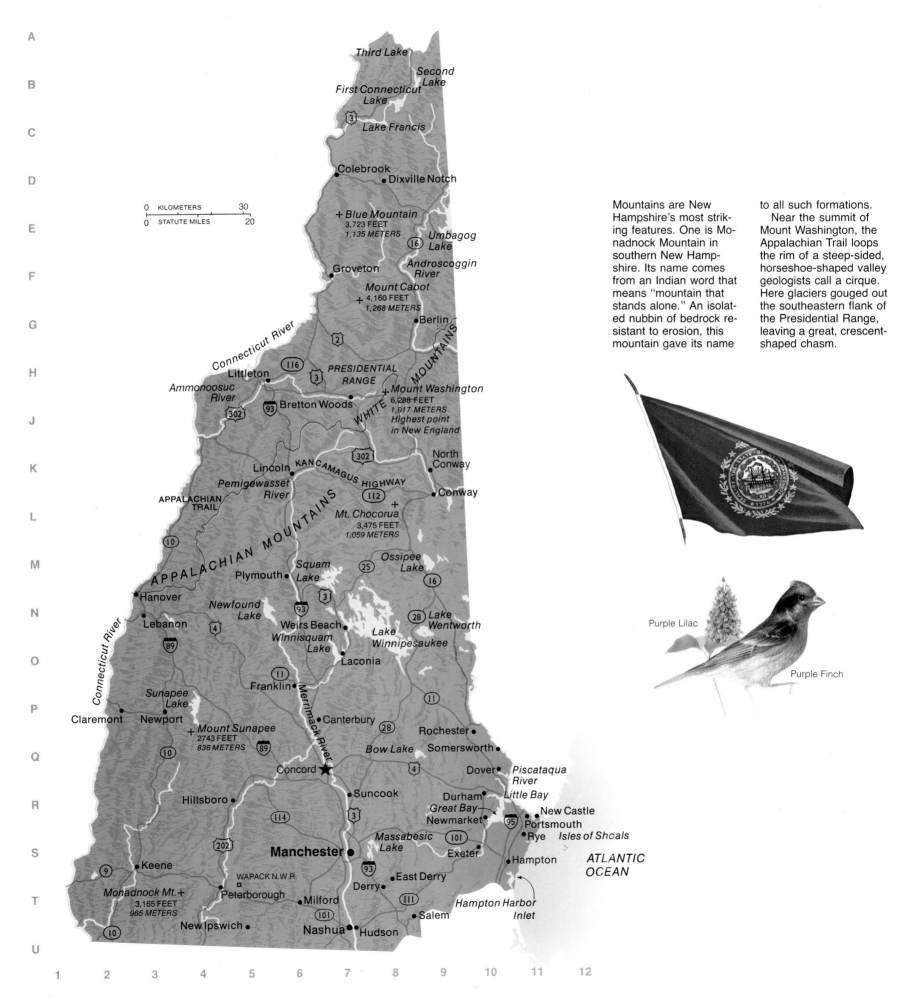

A B C D E F G H I J K L M N O P Q R S T U

Third Lake

Second Lake

First Connecticut Lake

③

Lake Francis

Colebrook
● Dixville Notch

+ Blue Mountain
3,723 FEET
1,135 METERS

⑯ Umbagog Lake

Groveton

Androscoggin River

Mount Cabot
+ 4,160 FEET
1,268 METERS

● Berlin

②

Connecticut River

⑯

PRESIDENTIAL RANGE

WHITE MOUNTAINS

Littleton

⑯

③

Ammonoosuc River

③⓪②

⑨③

Bretton Woods

+ Mount Washington
6,288 FEET
1,917 METERS
Highest point in New England

North Conway

APPALACHIAN TRAIL

Lincoln

KANCAMAGUS HIGHWAY

③⓪②

⑪②

● Conway

Pemigewasset River

Mt. Chocorua
+ 3,475 FEET
1,059 METERS

APPALACHIAN MOUNTAINS

⑩

Squam Lake

③

Ossipee Lake

②⑤

Hanover

Newfound Lake

⑯

Plymouth

⑨③

Weirs Beach

⑤

②⑧

Lake Wentworth

Lebanon

④

Winnisquam Lake

Lake Winnipesaukee

⑧⑨

Laconia

⑪

Franklin

Merrimack River

Sunapee Lake

Newport

⑩

Claremont

Connecticut River

Mount Sunapee
+ 2743 FEET
836 METERS

⑧⑨

Canterbury

②⑧

Rochester ●

Somersworth ●

Concord ★

Bow Lake

④

Dover ●

Piscataqua River

Little Bay

Hillsboro ●

⑪④

Suncook

③

Durham ●

Great Bay

New Castle ●

⑨⑤ Portsmouth ●

Newmarket ●

Rye

Isles of Shoals

②⓪②

Manchester ●

Massabesic Lake

⑩①

Exeter ●

Hampton ●

ATLANTIC OCEAN

⑨

Keene ●

WAPACK N.W.R.

⑨③

East Derry ●

Monadnock Mt. +
3,165 FEET
965 METERS

Peterborough

Derry ●

⑪①

Hampton Harbor Inlet

⑩

New Ipswich ●

Milford ●

⑩①

Salem ●

Nashua ● Hudson ●

0 KILOMETERS 30
0 STATUTE MILES 20

1 2 3 4 5 6 7 8 9 10 11 12

Mountains are New Hampshire's most striking features. One is Monadnock Mountain in southern New Hampshire. Its name comes from an Indian word that means "mountain that stands alone." An isolated nubbin of bedrock resistant to erosion, this mountain gave its name to all such formations.

Near the summit of Mount Washington, the Appalachian Trail loops the rim of a steep-sided, horseshoe-shaped valley geologists call a cirque. Here glaciers gouged out the southeastern flank of the Presidential Range, leaving a great, crescent-shaped chasm.

Purple Lilac

Purple Finch

1

2

3

4

5

New Hampshire

1 *A skier takes wing on Wildcat Mountain. Skiing in winter, hiking in summer, and breathtaking views year-round keep the White Mountains busy in all seasons.*

2 *Mount Washington Observatory, a climate research station, wears a coat of snow and ice. The station lies in the path of some of the world's most ferocious winds.*

3 *Portsmouth, a primary builder of clipper ships in the 1800s, hosts a tall ship, the Simón Bolívar, which hails from Venezuela.*

4 *A technician performs experiments at a microelectronics plant in Nashua, a center of high-tech industry.*

5 *Clean, simple lines in the attic of a Shaker dwelling in Canterbury reflect the religious sect's enduring values of symmetry, order, and painstaking workmanship.*

Maine

On West Quoddy Head, a cape in northeastern Maine, the Algonquian Indians say they "live at the sunrise" because here morning sunlight first strikes the shoreline of the 50 states. West Quoddy Head is just one of hundreds of points of land along the Maine coast. To trace every curve, cove, inlet, and island shore would take a journey of 3,478 miles (5,596 km), farther than from New York City to San Francisco.

Along the coast from Passamaquoddy Bay to Kittery are beaches, rocky cliffs, and bay after bay, cove after inlet after estuary. Rivers that flow into the estuaries are tidal, mixing fresh water and salt water as the ocean tides rise and fall in their ceaseless six-hour rhythm. Tidewater reaches as far inland as Bangor and Augusta, where ships have traveled the Kennebec and Penobscot Rivers since the early 1800s.

Maine's coastline was shaped during the Ice Age. When the glaciers melted, they released water that had been locked away as ice for thousands of years. The ocean began to rise, drowning the coastline. The 1,100 or so coastal islands that, under glaciers, were part of the mainland are now the tops of partly submerged hills. The largest is Mount Desert Island.

Once there were some 20 Algonquian tribes in the Maine region. Today there remain only the Penobscot and the Passamaquoddy, with a population of some 6,000. English colonists settled here in the 1620s. Descendants of those settlers and of Scotch-Irish immigrants make up most of Maine's present population.

The northern half of Maine, bordered by Canada, is home to many French Canadians, the state's next largest ethnic group. In the 18th century, Acadians, people of French descent from Nova Scotia, settled in the valley of the St. John River. Other French Canadians migrated from Quebec after the Civil War to work in the growing lumber and textile industries. Today, throughout much of northern Maine, French is the dominant language and French-Canadian workers have moved south, making Waterville, Lewiston, and other industrial cities bilingual.

Timberlands provide much of the raw material for the state's industries. Maine has more forestland than any other New England state. Pine, birch, maple, and oak cover nearly 90 percent of Maine. Timber companies own almost

Using a spiked wheel gauge, a worker at a logging camp near Flagstaff Lake during the 1930s measures the length of a log. Each revolution of the ten spokes marked five feet (1.5 m).

half the state's woodlands, mostly in the sparsely populated northern region.

White pines were once Maine's greatest forest resource. By the middle of the 19th century most had been cut down to make masts for sailing ships. Today's white pines are mostly second- and third-growth trees. From the forests come paper bags, cardboard boxes, wood pulp, and paper. Canoes, ice-cream sticks, skis, and more toothpicks than from any other state also originate in the north woods.

Northeastern Maine is the richest agricultural area. This is potato country, where 90 percent of the state's most valuable farm crop is grown. Until 1962 Maine produced the greatest number of potatoes in the United States. Today Idaho, Washington, Wisconsin, and Oregon offer strong competition. In 1958 Maine had 26,000 potato farms. In 1990 there were only 700.

Until New England's economic boom of the

1980s took hold, most young adults moved away from Maine to find work. Bygone prosperity is most visible in the inland region, where an abandoned paper or textile mill may be a town's main feature. Increased automation put many workers out of a job, and foreign competition closed many of the mills. Even so, the population of Maine has climbed slowly but steadily.

Since precolonial times most of the people have lived along rivers or where they could reap the bounty of the ocean. Today more than half live on the coast or within a short drive of it. For some, lobstering is a productive occupation, although it can be hard, uncertain work. Maine's yearly catch of some 22 million pounds (10 million kg) is the largest in the country.

Other coastal Mainers grow blueberries. During the short picking season at the end of summer, a grower may need hundreds of temporary workers. Sometimes, if the crop is slow to ripen, schools delay opening so that students can work in the fields. The Passamaquoddies are among the world's leading blueberry packers. During the 1980s other kinds of workers, from cabinetmakers to computer-software designers, helped populate southern coastal towns.

To protect their forests, lakes, rivers, and wetlands from development, the people of Maine have voted millions of dollars to buy land, preserving precious wildlife habitat and wild country. Even today there are places in the state that arouse feelings similar to those of New England writer Henry David Thoreau when he traveled in Maine in the 1840s and 1850s. North of Bangor, he wrote, "the country is virtually unmapped and unexplored, and there still waves the virgin forest of the New World." Most Mainers hope to keep it that way.

Area: *39th largest state, 33,265 sq mi (86,156 sq km)*
Population: *1,227,928; ranks 38th*
Major Cities: *Portland, 64,358; Lewiston, 39,757; Bangor, 33,181*
Manufacturing: *paper products, electronics, transportation equipment, lumber and wood products, leather, food products, machinery, textiles*
Mining and Quarrying: *sand and gravel, stone*
Agriculture: *potatoes, eggs, milk, blueberries, cattle, greenhouse and nursery products, apples*
Other Important Activities: *tourism, printing and publishing, fishing*
Statehood: *the 23rd state; admitted March 15, 1820*

Trees and rocks and water cover most of Maine. Writer Henry David Thoreau thought the state "a damp and intricate wilderness," a place "all mossy and moosey." Thoreau was right. With more than 5,000 streams and rivers and 2,500 ponds and lakes, about a tenth of the state is water—and that's not counting the coastal bays and inlets.

The Appalachian Trail's northern end on Mount Katahdin scrambles over boulders that, to Thoreau, looked "as if sometime it had rained rocks." The mountain's name comes from an Abnaki Indian word meaning "highest land."

Maine

1 *Newly dug potatoes are gathered for storage near Presque Isle. Most Maine potatoes are now harvested mechanically. The result: larger farms and fewer workers.*

2 *Lobster traps crowd a pier on Mount Desert Island. Lobstermen lower the baited traps into coastal waters where lobsters crawl inside to eat the bait of rotting fish. Colored buoys mark the location of the traps and identify their owners.*

3 *A moose and her calf dine on aquatic plants at the edge of a pond in Maine's dense and remote north woods.*

4 *Waving kerchiefs and shaking bells, morris dancers at West Quoddy Head seek to banish winter and wake up the earth.*

5 *A truck in Maine's north woods carries spruce and fir logs destined to become paper and pulp at one of the state's mills.*

1

2

3

4

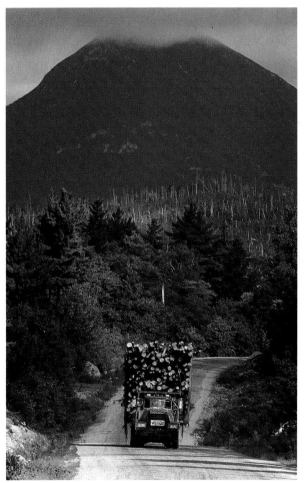

5

Massachusetts

Massachusetts has about 200 miles (322 km) of coastline. But if you count all its bays and inlets and tidal waters, the shoreline is ten times longer. Glaciers from the north shaped

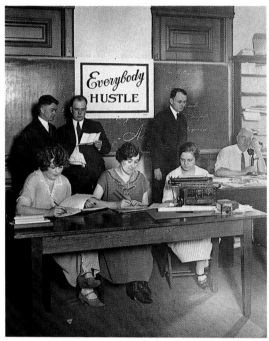

Bostonians of 1902 show off their office equipment: typewriter, telephone, and electric light. Christopher Sholes judged his typewriting invention a blessing, "especially to womankind."

The Puritan settlers of Massachusetts stood at the forefront of education in their new country. To them, literacy was important because "one chiefe project of that ould deluder, Satan [is] to keepe men from the knowledge of the Scriptures." In 1635, five years after establishing the Massachusetts Bay Colony, settlers opened the first public school, Boston Latin. The following year Harvard was founded as the nation's first college. Graduates became clergymen and community leaders and helped spread education throughout Massachusetts. By the mid-1600s, the colony called for all towns with 50 or more families to build an elementary school, and towns with 100 families, a secondary school. This was the first time any government provided education paid for by the citizens.

About a hundred years after it was first settled, Boston had become the largest city in the Colonies and the cornerstone of New England. Today about half of the state's population lives in the Boston metropolitan area, where there are some 68 colleges and universities. The site of Harvard University, Cambridge alone counts 26 bookstores, more per square mile than anywhere else in the country.

In the 19th century, Boston entrepreneurs financed railroads, factories, and ironworks throughout the region. Ships leaving Boston's harbor traded around the globe. Immigrants began to arrive, at first mostly Irish, later French Canadians, and Italians, Germans, and other Europeans. They supplied labor for the textile mills in Lowell, the shoe factories in Beverly, and the sawmills, gristmills, and tanneries that sprang up in towns throughout the state. Even today the population of Massachusetts is ethnically diverse. A third of the people are either foreign-born or are children of at least one parent from another country.

Massachusetts has no coal, oil, or gas, and no metal ores worth mining. When the state's textile and shoe factories closed down and moved south in the 1950s and 1960s, they often were replaced by space research laboratories and electronics companies because Massachusetts had a large pool of skilled, well-educated workers.

Along Route 128, a highway that arcs through Boston's western suburbs, the electronics industry joined forces with universities such as Harvard and the Massachusetts Institute of Technology to develop computers and software products, solar energy devices, and laboratories dedicated to studying artificial intelligence. Researchers in biotechnology companies strive to solve the mysteries of cancer and other diseases, and genetic engineers work to devise advanced medical treatments.

South of Boston a hook of land called Cape Cod reaches 65 miles (105 km) into the Atlantic Ocean. Until around 1850 many towns on the cape, as well as in southeastern Massachusetts and on the islands of Nantucket and Martha's Vineyard, flourished as whaling and trading ports. The largest town was New Bedford. There foresighted merchants built textile mills and factories, making it a successful manufacturing city. Today descendants of the immigrants who worked in New Bedford's factories make up the country's largest community of Portuguese Americans. The whaling industry

declined as whales became scarce and kerosene replaced whale oil as lamp fuel. Tourism and fish processing became the main sources of income. Much of Massachusetts has thin, rocky soil, but sandy bogs in the southeast produce nearly half of the country's cranberries.

West of Boston and the state's coastal lowlands rise rolling mountains threaded by the fertile Connecticut River Valley. Indians had long planted crops alongside the Connecticut River, and 17th-century colonists soon realized that the rich soil and mild climate would make good farming country. The river itself served as a highway. By the early 19th century, vessels hailing from Connecticut River towns carried on a lively trade of crops, lumber products, and farm animals with cities along the East Coast and as far away as the West Indies.

One of the most thinly populated parts of Massachusetts, the Berkshire Hills, is an extension of Vermont's Green Mountains. The Berkshires' the state's many bays. Cape Cod and the offshore islands are terminal moraines, sandy ridges piled along the leading edges of the ice.

Inland, the valleys of the Housatonic and Connecticut Rivers were scoured out and deepened by glaciers. Fertile soils later deposited on the floodplains attracted farmers, and the rivers themselves provided power to run mills.

0 KILOMETERS 25
0 STATUTE MILES 20

Chickadee

Mayflower

ATLANTIC

OCEAN

Pilgrims made their first landfall here in 1620 before continuing on to Plymouth

quiet and solitude appealed to 19th-century writers such as Nathaniel Hawthorne and Herman Melville, who came to live in Pittsfield. Nowadays, one of the Berkshires' summer residents is the Boston Symphony Orchestra. Since 1936 the orchestra has performed nearly every year at the Tanglewood Music Festival.

Area: *45th largest state, 8,284 sq mi (21,456 sq km)*
Population: *6,016,425; ranks 13th*
Major Cities: *Boston, 574,283; Worcester, 169,759; Springfield, 156,983*
Manufacturing: *machinery, scientific instruments, electronics, transportation equipment, metal products, food products, rubber and plastics, chemicals, paper products*
Mining and Quarrying: *stone, sand and gravel*
Agriculture: *greenhouse and nursery products, cranberries, milk, eggs, apples*
Other Important Activities: *tourism, education, printing and publishing, fishing*
Statehood: *the sixth state; ratified the Constitution on February 6, 1788*

Newburyport
Haverhill
Plum Island
PARKER RIVER N.W.R.
Methuen
Lawrence
Ipswich
Cape Ann
Rockport
Gloucester
THACHER ISLAND N.W.R.
Winchendon
Millers River
Athol
Fitchburg
Gardner
Lowell
Merrimack River
Beverly
Salem
Peabody
Marblehead
Leominster
OXBOW NATIONAL WILDLIFE REFUGE
Woburn
Melrose
Lynn
Clinton
Concord
Lexington
Medford
Saugus
Quabbin Reservoir
Wachusett Reservoir
GREAT MEADOWS N.W.R.
Somerville
Malden
Revere
Chelsea
Cambridge
Newton
Boston
Massachusetts Bay
Marlborough
Brookline
Shrewsbury
Wellesley
Needham
Milton
Quincy
Worcester
Framingham
Dedham
Weymouth
Hingham
Scituate
Auburn
Norwood
Randolph
Milford
Charles River
Stoughton
Brockton
Old Sturbridge Village
Duxbury
Southbridge
Webster
Lake Chargoggagoggmanchaugagoggchaubunagungamaug (Lake Webster)
Lake Webster's Algonquian Indian name is said to mean: You fish on your side; I fish on my side; nobody fish in the middle
Provincetown
Truro
CAPE COD NATIONAL SEASHORE
Wellfleet
Plymouth Bay
Plymouth
Plimoth Plantation
Cape Cod Bay
Attleboro
Taunton
MASSASOIT N.W.R.
Taunton River
Assawompset Pond
Sandwich
Cape Cod Canal
CAPE COD
Long Pond
Great Quittacas Pond
Barnstable
Chatham
Fall River
Marion
Hyannis
New Bedford
MONOMOY N.W.R.
Buzzards Bay
Falmouth
Nantucket Sound
Woods Hole
Elizabeth Islands
NANTUCKET N.W.R.
Oak Bluffs
Vineyard Haven
Rhode Island Sound
Edgartown
Chappaquiddick Island
Menemsha
Nantucket
WAMPANOAG INDIAN RESERVATION
MARTHA'S VINEYARD
Siasconset
NOMANS LAND ISLAND NATIONAL WILDLIFE REFUGE
NANTUCKET ISLAND

Massachusetts

1 *Snow dusts the evergreen ridges of Mount Greylock in the Berkshire Hills while autumn lingers on lower slopes and valleys.*

2 *Cranberries spread a crimson carpet on a bog flooded for harvest. Shaken from low-growing vines, the berries bob to the surface and are skimmed into holding pens with long-handled scrubbers.*

3 *Boston's Faneuil Hall stands amid stores, restaurants, and offices overlooking Boston Harbor. A market and meeting place for patriots in Revolutionary times, Faneuil Hall today is a popular gathering spot for tourists and residents alike.*

4 *Commercial fishermen sort through a catch off Cape Cod. Fishing, one of the state's economic mainstays since earliest colonial times, has declined sharply in recent years because of overfishing.*

5 *Cape Cod, named by navigator Bartholomew Gosnold after he explored the area in 1602, presents an arm of glacial sand and gravel to pounding Atlantic waves.*

1

2

3

4

5

Connecticut

While exploring Long Island Sound in 1614, Dutch sea captain Adriaen Block sailed into the wide mouth of the Connecticut River. There he found numerous Algonquian Indians grouped in settlements near the river and along the shore of what is now Connecticut. But it was the English, not the Dutch, who began to settle the area nearly 20 years later. They had been attracted by reports of the Connecticut River Valley's fertility. Today much of the state's tobacco, apples, and potatoes grow there, even though agriculture is not a big source of income for Connecticut. About 21 percent of the state's people live in rural areas, and 79 percent live in and around cities.

The Connecticut River Valley's chief city, Hartford, rises on the fall line at the head of river navigation. Since the 17th century, when the Dutch began trading with the Indians, Hartford has thrived on both industry and business. It has been an insurance center for almost 200 years, first providing financial protection against fires, and later extending coverage to sailing ships and their cargoes. Hartford pioneered in many kinds of insurance that we now take for granted: the first American accident insurance, the first to offer American farmers protection against hail damage, the first American automobile insurance. Today the state is home to more than a thousand insurance companies.

On either side of the Connecticut River Valley rise low hills where the soil is thin and rocky. Glaciers left so many boulders here that, over the years, landowners have fenced their fields and pastures with some 25,000 miles (40,225 km) of stone walls. Crushed stone is an important product for Connecticut, especially because it has no coal or oil or other valuable minerals.

Even without many natural resources Connecticut has developed into a rich industrial state. A knack for making things has been a tradition. Here, in the early 1800s, Eli Whitney devised mass-production machinery and produced muskets with interchangeable parts. Samuel Colt assembled the first successful repeating pistol, and Charles Goodyear succeeded in strengthening rubber by vulcanizing it. Other innovators turned their talents to producing clocks, bicycles, cigars, silk thread, and combs. Over the years Yankee ingenuity replaced dy-

Sailors practice escape maneuvers at the New London Submarine Base in 1938. The diving bell carries them down 100 feet (30.5 m), and they slowly ascend a rope while breathing oxygen from a tank.

ing industries with vital ones. Today high-tech companies that produce computer chips and fiber-optic equipment have taken the place of old brass, rubber, and clothing factories.

Running the length of Connecticut's shore is the coastal lowland. Here the early towns with their spacious harbors enjoyed success with fishing. But it took other maritime activities to make them truly prosperous. Shipbuilding, a major industry at Mystic seaport during the mid-1800s, promoted trade with the rest of the world. During their heyday, Mystic shipyards launched more than 300 vessels. Steamers and clipper ships in turn brought raw materials that spurred Connecticut's growth as an industrializing state. Today Mystic is a re-created seaport, where restored sailing ships recall New England's seafaring past.

Around the 1850s, many of Connecticut's coastal towns thrived on whaling. Chief among

them was New London, near the mouth of the Thames River. The whaling industry declined within a few decades, but New London's importance did not. The United States Coast Guard established its academy there in 1910. Today, in addition, shipyards and major ferry terminals serving Long Island Sound keep New London a busy and important seaport.

One of the most densely populated areas of Connecticut is the coastline along the western reaches of Long Island Sound. Fishing towns on the sound flourished in the mid-1800s as factories grew, demanding more workers. People from agricultural towns flocked to a more lucrative way of life, as did French-Canadian and European immigrants. Today New Haven and Bridgeport have large populations of Italian and Irish ancestry. New Haven is also the home of Yale University, founded in 1701 by Connecticut clergymen. Stamford is a center for corporate headquarters, burgeoning in the 1980s as many companies fled crowded New York City's high prices and taxes.

Connecticut's economy has been linked to warfare and defense since colonial days, when its shipyards built vessels for the British Navy. In more recent years, Connecticut has produced everything from firearms to helicopters and submarines. For most of the 1980s the state's economy boomed, in part because its defense industry did. Now, as the country's defense budget shrinks, thousands of workers may lose their jobs. Some defense contractors, their ingenuity again challenged, are examining ways their specialized skills can be used by other government agencies or in civilian businesses.

Area: *48th largest state, 5,018 sq mi (12,997 sq km)*
Population: *3,287,116; ranks 27th*
Major Cities: *Bridgeport, 141,686; Hartford, 139,739; New Haven, 130,474*
Manufacturing: *transportation equipment, machinery, metal products, scientific instruments, chemicals, electronics, food products, metals, paper products, rubber and plastics*
Mining and Quarrying: *stone, sand and gravel*
Agriculture: *greenhouse and nursery products, eggs, milk, tobacco, cattle*
Other Important Activities: *insurance, printing and publishing, fishing*
Statehood: *the fifth state; ratified the Constitution on January 9, 1788*

Map grid coordinates

1 2 3 4 5 6 7 8 9 10 11 12 13 14 15 16 17 18

A B C D E F G H J K L M N O

Mount Frissell
2,380 FEET
725 METERS
*Highest point
in Connecticut*

• Canaan
• Norfolk
• Lakeville

Bradford Mountain
1,962 FEET
598 METERS

West Branch
Farmington River

*Barkhamsted
Reservoir*

Thompsonville •
• Hazardville
[190]
Stafford
Springs

[32]
[395]

Windsor
Locks
• Enfield

South
Woodstock •

• Putnam

• Sharon
[44]
• Winsted
[202]

Simsbury

[91]

*Shenipsit
Lake*

[84]
Vernon •
• Storrs

[44]
*Natchaug
River*

• Dayville
[6]

[7]
• Cornwall
[8]
*Nepaug
Reservoir*

Bloomfield •
Avon

Windsor •

Manchester •

*Mansfield
Hollow
Lake*

*Quinebaug
River*

Torrington •

APPALACHIAN
TRAIL

• Litchfield

Shepaug River

[202]

Hartford ★
West Hartford •
East
Hartford
[384]

Farmington •
Wethersfield •
• Coventry
[6]
• Willimantic

Willimantic River

Shetucket River

• Windham

• Plainfield

Bantam Lake
[6]
• Bristol
Plainville •
Newington •

Glastonbury •

[32]

Thomaston •

*New
Britain*

Rocky Hill
□ DINOSAUR STATE PARK
Contains dinosaur tracks
made 200 million years ago

[91]

*Pachaug
Pond*

Watertown •

Cromwell •
Portland •

[2]

• New Milford

Southington •

Waterbury
[691]
• Meriden

• Middletown
[66]

Haddam •

*The first English settlers
found Indian tribes living
in this fertile river valley*

Norwich •
[395]

MASHANTUCKET
PEQUOT
INDIAN
RESERVATION
[2]
[95]

New
Fairfield •

• Brookfield

Housatonic River

Naugatuck •
Cheshire •

[15]

Connecticut River

Thames River

*Candlewood
Lake*

[84]

Naugatuck River

• Wallingford

[9]

Chester •

U.S. Coast
Guard Academy

Mystic Seaport •

[202]
Danbury
[6]
• Bethel

Seymour •
Hamden •

[91]

North
Haven •

*Lake
Gaillard*

Essex •

East Lyme •
New
London •
Waterford •
Niantic •

Groton •
• Mystic

• Stonington

[7]
Derby •
• Ansonia

*World's first
nuclear submarine
launched here
in 1954*

*Niantic
Bay*

• Ridgefield

Shelton •

New Haven
East Haven •

Old Saybrook •

Madison •

*Saugatuck
Reservoir*

• Trumbull
[8]
• Orange

West Haven •
*New Haven
Harbor*

Morgan Point

Guilford •
Clinton •
□ SALT MEADOW N.W.R.

*Hammonasset
Point*

[95]

• Wilton
[15]
Stratford •

Milford •

*The
Thimbles*

□
STEWART B. McKINNEY N.W.R.

0 KILOMETERS 20
0 MILES 10

New Canaan •
[124]
Westport •

Bridgeport •
• Fairfield

[95]

□ STEWART B. McKINNEY
N.W.R.
Stratford Point

Long Island Sound

Norwalk •

Stamford •

• Darien
□ *Norwalk
Islands*

STEWART B. McKINNEY
N.W.R.

• Greenwich

Mountain
Laurel

Robin

Connecticut comes from
an Indian word that
means "long tidal river."
The name is appropriate.
New England's longest
river splits the state and
is navigable by ships all
the way to Hartford, 52
miles (84 km) inland.

But why isn't there a
major port at the river's
mouth? And why so few

towns and villages along
its lower reaches?

Glaciers. They blocked
the river's mouth with
sand, making it too shal-
low for large ocean-
going vessels. By the
time channel-clearing
dredges and jetties came
into use, towns and in-
dustries had gone else-
where in the state.

1

2

3

4

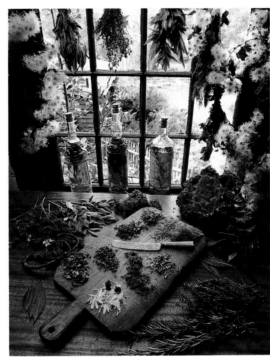

5

Connecticut

1 *A worker checks a jet engine at an assembly plant in Hartford. Connecticut industries today turn out everything from plastic Wiffle balls to submarines.*

2 *A Wampanoag Indian holds his son at a tribal gathering in Portland. Wampanoag helped* Mayflower *Pilgrims celebrate their first Thanksgiving in the New World.*

3 *Cadets drill at the U. S. Coast Guard Academy on the Thames River in New London. Only 300 new students are accepted into the academy each year.*

4 *Oysters are netted by hand near the mouth of the Connecticut River. Connecticut's coastal waters provide an ideal combination of temperature, salinity, and habitat for oyster cultivation.*

5 *Herbs and edible flowers fresh from a farm in Coventry go into salads, vinegars, soups, and breads sold at the farm.*

Rhode Island

The full and official name of the country's smallest state is The State of Rhode Island and Providence Plantations. The state has 35 islands scattered within its largest body of water, Narragansett Bay. The bay's largest island, also called Rhode Island, may have been named for the Greek island of Rhodes. Some people also refer to the island as Aquidneck, an Indian word meaning "longest island."

The Providence Plantations part of the state's name comes from its origin as a refuge for religious dissenters. It was founded in 1636 by Roger Williams, a minister who disagreed with the Puritan government of the Massachusetts Bay Colony. Williams insisted that people should not be persecuted by civil authorities for religious beliefs. He was banished from the Bay Colony, and made his way to Indian friends near Narragansett Bay. Learning the language of the Narragansett, Williams received land from them and became an intermediary between the Indians and the English. He established a farming community on a long arm of the bay, naming it in honor of "God's merciful providence unto me in my distresse." Other settlers followed Williams, and soon the English Parliament granted the colony a charter as "Rhode Island and Providence Plantations." Eventually, Williams drew up America's first document calling for the separation of church and state, one of the nation's guiding principles.

Rhode Island was the first of the 13 Colonies to declare independence, yet, because it feared too powerful a central government, it was last to ratify the U. S. Constitution. Instead, Rhode Island waited to sign until the Bill of Rights was ready to be added in 1790.

Only a few months after Rhode Island became a state, industrialization began. In Pawtucket a 22-year-old English machinist named Samuel Slater designed the first water-powered cotton mill in the United States, a factory in which children worked the spinning machinery. The genius of Slater and other men launched the New England textile industry. Dozens of mill villages sprang up in the valley of the Blackstone River, and the industry spread rapidly. Rhode Island also manufactured textile machinery. Although machinery making and textiles still figure in the economy, other manufactured products have

Six feet (2 m) of seawater flooded downtown Providence after a 1938 hurricane, marooning office workers and submerging automobiles and trolley cars in front of the Biltmore Hotel.

become more important.

Opportunities for factory jobs in the 19th and 20th centuries attracted immigrants from Canada, Europe, the Caribbean, and Southeast Asia, and contributed to Rhode Island's present ethnic diversity. Because the majority of job seekers came from Catholic countries, Rhode Island has the highest proportion of Roman Catholics of any state in the country.

Rhode Island is also the most densely populated state after New Jersey. More than 80 percent of all Rhode Islanders live in urban areas in the east, with about two-thirds living in and around the state capital, Providence.

The least populated parts of Rhode Island are the rocky, forested hills in the west-central and northwest parts of the state. Although very little of this land is farmed now, miles of stone walls in the forests recall a time when it was.

About a third of the state is covered by lakes,

ponds, reservoirs, swamps, and rivers. Eastern and southern Rhode Island are coastal lowlands, with sandy beaches, salt ponds, rocky cliffs, and islands. Narragansett Bay reaches far inland, extending a deepwater channel to Providence.

The state of Rhode Island measures only 37 miles (60 km) from east to west, but it has 400 miles (644 km) of coastline along Narragansett Bay and around the islands. Newport, the site of sailboat races and music festivals, occupies part of the island of Rhode Island.

Before the Revolutionary War, Newport was a major point of entry to the Colonies and one of the busiest ports on the East Coast. Then the British occupied its harbor, ruining the prosperous shipping trade. In the 1730s the town had already become a summer resort as southern plantation owners came north to escape heat and humidity. By the end of the 19th century, industrial titans from New York were summering in Newport and building mansions called "cottages" along the rocky cliffs. One of them, The Breakers, was Cornelius Vanderbilt's grand Italian Renaissance villa, a palace with silver faucets and 70 rooms, 33 of them for servants.

With its reputation for religious tolerance, Rhode Island became a haven for persecuted Quakers and Jews in the 17th and 18th centuries. Touro Synagogue, the oldest Jewish temple in North America, was dedicated in Newport in 1763. It was to this synagogue that President George Washington gave his pledge of religious freedom, stating that the country's new government would give "to bigotry no sanction, to persecution no assistance." This proclamation is read to the congregation every year.

Area: *the smallest state, 1,212 sq mi (3,140 sq km)*
Population: *1,003,464; ranks 43rd*
Major Cities: *Providence, 160,728; Warwick, 85,427; Cranston, 76,060*
Manufacturing: *jewelry and silverware, metal products, scientific instruments, metals, machinery, electronics, textiles, rubber and plastics, food products, chemicals*
Agriculture: *greenhouse and nursery products, milk, eggs, potatoes, apples*
Mining and Quarrying: *sand and gravel, stone*
Other Important Activities: *tourism, printing and publishing, fishing*
Statehood: *the 13th state; ratified the Constitution on May 29, 1790*

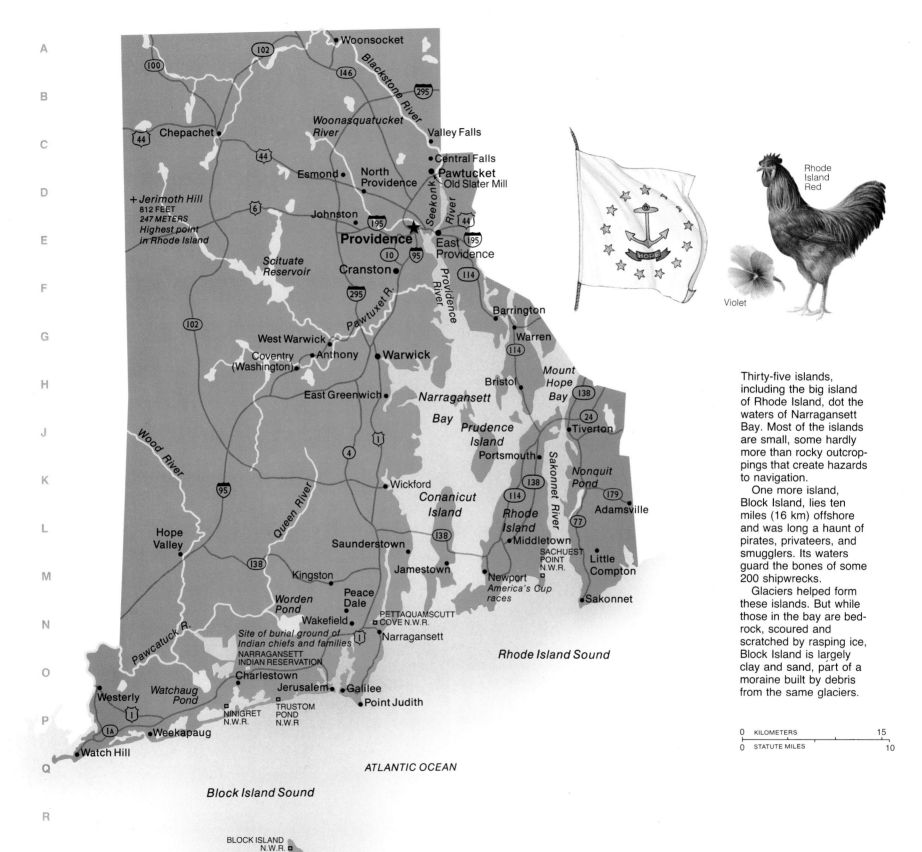

1 2 3 4 5 6 7 8 9 10 11 12 13

A
B
C
D
E
F
G
H
J
K
L
M
N
O
P
Q
R
S
T

Woonsocket

102
100

Blackstone River

146

295

Woonasquatucket River

Chepachet

44

44

Valley Falls

Esmond

Central Falls
Pawtucket
Old Slater Mill

North Providence

Seekonk River

+ Jerimoth Hill
812 FEET
247 METERS
Highest point
in Rhode Island

6

Johnston

195

Providence

East Providence

44

195

Scituate Reservoir

10
95

Cranston

114

295

Pawtuxet R.

Providence River

Barrington

102

Warren

West Warwick

Coventry (Washington)

Anthony

Warwick

114

Mount Hope Bay

138

East Greenwich

Bristol

Narragansett Bay

24

Prudence Island

Tiverton

Wood River

1

Portsmouth

Sakonnet River

Nonquit Pond

4

Wickford

Conanicut Island

138

114

179

Adamsville

95

Hope Valley

Queen River

Saunderstown

138

Rhode Island

77

Middletown

Little Compton

138

Kingston

Jamestown

SACHUEST POINT N.W.R.

Worden Pond

Peace Dale

Newport
America's Cup races

Sakonnet

Pawcatuck R.

Site of burial ground of
Indian chiefs and families

Wakefield

1

PETTAQUAMSCUTT
COVE N.W.R.

Narragansett

Rhode Island Sound

NARRAGANSETT
INDIAN RESERVATION

Westerly

Watchaug Pond

Charlestown

Jerusalem

Galilee

Weekapaug

1

NINIGRET
N.W.R.

TRUSTOM
POND
N.W.R

Point Judith

1A

Watch Hill

ATLANTIC OCEAN

0 KILOMETERS 15

0 STATUTE MILES 10

Block Island Sound

BLOCK ISLAND
N.W.R.

Block Island

Block Island

Thirty-five islands, including the big island of Rhode Island, dot the waters of Narragansett Bay. Most of the islands are small, some hardly more than rocky outcroppings that create hazards to navigation.

One more island, Block Island, lies ten miles (16 km) offshore and was long a haunt of pirates, privateers, and smugglers. Its waters guard the bones of some 200 shipwrecks.

Glaciers helped form these islands. But while those in the bay are bedrock, scoured and scratched by rasping ice, Block Island is largely clay and sand, part of a moraine built by debris from the same glaciers.

HOPE

Rhode Island Red

Violet

1

2

3

4

Rhode Island

1 *Southeast Light crowns the heights of Block Island, a resort of Victorian houses and hotels set amid rolling, treeless moors.*

2 *A silversmith pursues his calling in Providence, where artisans have worked with gold and silver since 1794.*

3 *Spinnaker sails ballooning, sailboats compete in an international race off Newport, a historic seaport and yachting center.*

4 *The Cliff Walk winds past many of Newport's summer "cottages," palaces built by wealthy industrialists during the Gilded Age of the late 1800s. Several are open in season for public tours.*

Mid-Atlantic States

In the Mid-Atlantic region, wooded ridges of the Appalachian Mountains and their foothills, the Piedmont, give way to patterns of farmland along the Atlantic Coastal Plain.

The oldest mountains in North America, the Appalachians began to rise about 300 million years ago. When they were young, they were as tall as today's Rockies, but time and weather have since worn down the Appalachians, smoothing their ragged edges. Rivers on the western slopes, such as the Allegheny, join others and flow eventually to the Gulf of Mexico.

Rivers on the eastern slopes carry eroded rock and soil as sediment to the Atlantic Coastal Plain and into the Atlantic Ocean. Where they cross the Piedmont, the Delaware, Susquehanna, and Potomac Rivers have cut deep, narrow valleys through the hard rock. Waterfalls and rapids mark their passage until they cross a geologic boundary known as a fall line and reach the softer sediments of the Coastal Plain.

At river confluences, such as the site of Pittsburgh, and along the fall line rise some of the country's largest cities, including Baltimore and Philadelphia. On the fall line early settlers found waterpower to run their mills, sheltered inland harbors, and flat terrain to build roads linking the cities together. Today the Mid-Atlantic region is home to some 43 million people, about one-sixth of the nation's population.

MOUNTAINS

Hudson River

Delaware River

New York City

Susquehanna River

Philadelphia

Baltimore

Chesapeake Bay

NEW YORK

NEW JERSEY

PENNSYLVANIA

DELAWARE

MARYLAND

New York

New York has been a major gateway to the United States ever since its earliest days as a Dutch colony. A colonial governor in 1644 claimed to distinguish 18 languages spoken by the inhabitants. Of the millions upon millions of immigrants who have entered the country, many stayed in New York City, transforming it into one of the world's largest and most exciting

Niagara Falls has always attracted more than its share of death-defying daredevils. This tightrope walker balances below the falls around 1890.

cities, a center of commerce and culture.

Other people only paused in New York, passing through the state on their way westward. New York City's deep, sheltered harbor, one of the world's biggest and finest, took in thousands of newcomers each year. Through Ellis Island, within sight of the Statue of Liberty, passed more than 16 million immigrants between 1892 and 1954, when the center closed. One of three Americans today has an ancestor or relative who entered the United States at Ellis Island.

Today New York City is headquarters to a hundred of the nation's 500 largest companies, including giant firms such as Woolworth and RCA. The city's tallest building, the World Trade Center with its twin towers, is home to dozens of corporations. About half a million people work in the city's banks, brokerage houses, and insurance companies. The Wall Street area, a financial center since just after the Revolutionary War, houses the New York and American Stock Exchanges. Here millions of shares of stock in thousands of companies are bought and sold each day. The city is also a leading producer of clothes, books, jewelry, and machinery.

People from all over the world come to New York City to enjoy its art galleries, theaters, concert halls, and museums, including the Metropolitan Museum of Art, the nation's largest art museum. The state has produced hundreds of artists, musicians, and writers, from filmmaker Woody Allen and painter Winslow Homer to the performers who have made Broadway synonymous with show business.

The state's other large population centers include Buffalo, which, thanks to its access to Great Lakes shipping, has huge steel mills, auto assembly and chemical plants, and flour mills. Rochester manufactures optical and photographic equipment, electronic instruments, and copying machines. Syracuse, Utica, and Schenectady, astride the Mohawk Valley transportation corridor, produce electrical machinery and paper products. Albany, the capital, leads in government jobs, and Binghamton assembles computers and business machines.

Almost as varied as New York's people is its geography. The state's terrain ranges from the Great Lakes Lowland to the Adirondack Upland and the great fertile valleys carved by the Hudson and Mohawk Rivers. Much of the state is mountainous and covered by forests. About 135 native tree species grow in the forests. Among them are commercially important trees such as firs, beech, oaks, pines, and sugar maples.

Glaciers left their mark on the state, scooping out and filling the Great Lakes and the long, narrow trenches of the Finger Lakes. As the last glaciers retreated about 10,000 years ago, they left behind a great ridge of rocks and soil that became Long Island. Blocks of melting ice left dimples in the soil that became some of the state's

Niagara River

At the end of the last ice age, melting ice created the Niagara River, which over the ages cut through a high cliff to form Niagara Falls

TUSCARORA INDIAN RESERVATION

IROQUOIS NATIONAL WILDLIFE REFUGE

Lockport

Niagara Falls

Tonawanda

TONAWANDA INDIAN RES.

Cheektowaga

Buffalo

Lackawanna

20

LAKE ERIE

90

Dunkirk

Fredonia

CATTARAUGUS INDIAN RESERVATION

219

OIL SPRING INDIAN RESERVATION

Chautauqua Lake 17

Allegheny River

Jamestown

ALLEGANY INDIAN RESERVATION

8,000 or so lakes. When melting glaciers filled the Great Lakes, the overflow formed the Niagara River and deepened the channel of the St. Lawrence River.

Today New York has about 50,000 farms and is important in the production of dairy products. Large truck farms supply cities with vegetables. Orchards around Lake Ontario, Lake Erie, and the Finger Lakes grow cherries, apples, and other fruit. In the spring, cool air from the lakes delays blossoms, lessening the chances of frost damage. In the autumn, air warmed by the lakes lengthens the growing season, prolonging the ripening process. Wineries in the region produce some of the nation's finest wines from grapes grown in local vineyards.

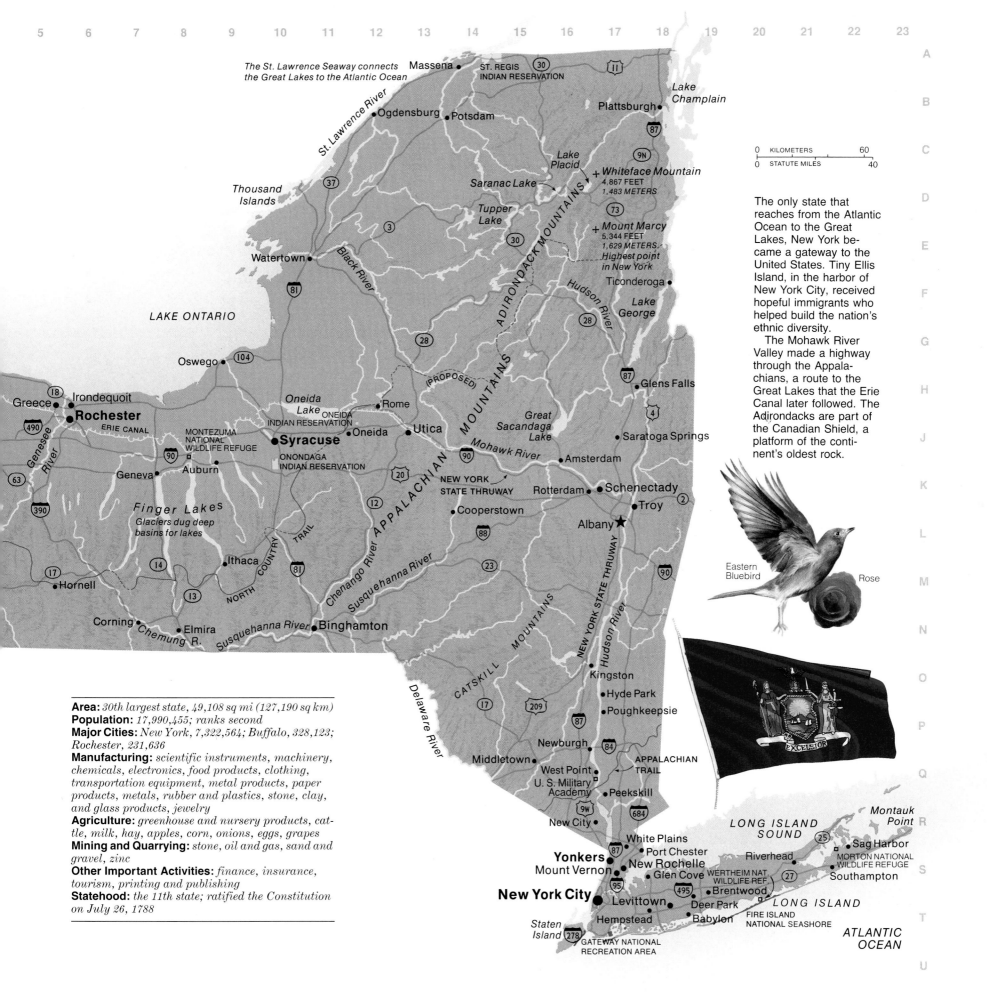

The St. Lawrence Seaway connects the Great Lakes to the Atlantic Ocean

Massena
ST. REGIS INDIAN RESERVATION
30
11
Ogdensburg Potsdam
Plattsburgh
Lake Champlain
87
Thousand Islands
37
9N
Lake Placid
+ *Whiteface Mountain*
4,867 FEET
1,483 METERS
Saranac Lake
73
Tupper Lake
+ *Mount Marcy*
5,344 FEET
1,629 METERS
Highest point in New York
3
30
Watertown
Ticonderoga
Black River
81
Hudson River
28
Lake George
LAKE ONTARIO
28
87 Glens Falls
Oswego 104
4
18 Irondequoit
Greece
Oneida Lake
Rome
Saratoga Springs
Rochester
490
ERIE CANAL
ONEIDA INDIAN RESERVATION
Great Sacandaga Lake
Genesee River
MONTEZUMA NATIONAL WILDLIFE REFUGE
Oneida Utica
Amsterdam
63
90
Syracuse
Mohawk River
90
Geneva Auburn
ONONDAGA INDIAN RESERVATION
NEW YORK STATE THRUWAY
Rotterdam Schenectady
20
Troy
2
390
Finger Lakes
Glaciers dug deep basins for lakes
12
Cooperstown
Albany ★
90
14
88
17 Hornell
13
81
23
Ithaca
(PROPOSED)
NORTH COUNTRY TRAIL
APPALACHIAN MOUNTAINS
Chenango River
Susquehanna River
Kingston
Corning Elmira
Chemung R.
Susquehanna River
Binghamton
CATSKILL MOUNTAINS
Hyde Park
Poughkeepsie
Delaware River
17
209
87
Newburgh
84
Middletown
West Point
U. S. Military Academy
APPALACHIAN TRAIL
9W
Peekskill
New City
684
White Plains
Montauk Point
LONG ISLAND SOUND
87
25
Yonkers
Port Chester
New Rochelle
Riverhead
Sag Harbor
Mount Vernon
MORTON NATIONAL WILDLIFE REFUGE
Glen Cove
95
WERTHEIM NAT. WILDLIFE REF.
27
Southampton
New York City
495
Brentwood
LONG ISLAND
Levittown
Deer Park
Hempstead
Babylon
FIRE ISLAND NATIONAL SEASHORE
Staten Island 278
GATEWAY NATIONAL RECREATION AREA
ATLANTIC OCEAN

The only state that reaches from the Atlantic Ocean to the Great Lakes, New York became a gateway to the United States. Tiny Ellis Island, in the harbor of New York City, received hopeful immigrants who helped build the nation's ethnic diversity.

The Mohawk River Valley made a highway through the Appalachians, a route to the Great Lakes that the Erie Canal later followed. The Adirondacks are part of the Canadian Shield, a platform of the continent's oldest rock.

Eastern Bluebird   Rose

EXCELSIOR

Area: *30th largest state, 49,108 sq mi (127,190 sq km)*
Population: *17,990,455; ranks second*
Major Cities: *New York, 7,322,564; Buffalo, 328,123; Rochester, 231,636*
Manufacturing: *scientific instruments, machinery, chemicals, electronics, food products, clothing, transportation equipment, metal products, paper products, metals, rubber and plastics, stone, clay, and glass products, jewelry*
Agriculture: *greenhouse and nursery products, cattle, milk, hay, apples, corn, onions, eggs, grapes*
Mining and Quarrying: *stone, oil and gas, sand and gravel, zinc*
Other Important Activities: *finance, insurance, tourism, printing and publishing*
Statehood: *the 11th state; ratified the Constitution on July 26, 1788*

1

New York

1 *Visitors don slickers for a spray-filled view of Niagara Falls as it tumbles 182 feet (55 m) over a ledge on the American side of the Niagara River. Water spilling over the limestone rim here eats away the falls at a rate of about an inch (2.3 cm) a year.*

2 *New York City's financial district weaves a carpet of light across Manhattan Island. Twin towers of the World Trade Center (left) rise 110 stories above the Hudson River just north of Battery Park.*

2

3

5

4

3 *Iroquois Indians meet opponents at a lacrosse championship game in Syracuse. Ancestors of these players sometimes substituted the game for war, settling disputes in a contest that could last three days.*

4 *Cider and freshly picked apples and tomatoes prove a mouth-watering temptation to shoppers at a farmers' market in Ithaca.*

5 *Steam wreathes a racehorse after a workout at the track in Saratoga Springs.*

Pennsylvania

Pennsylvania's rivers flow every which way. Nearly 4,500 streams and rivers crisscross the mountains and valleys that make up most of the state. From the mountains near the New York border, streams flow in three directions. Some small ones run northwestward and empty into Lake Erie. Larger streams drain southeastward, emptying into the Susquehanna River and Chesapeake Bay. The waters of still others feed into the Ohio, which joins the Mississippi and ultimately reaches the Gulf of Mexico.

Glaciers advancing and retreating across the landscape thousands of years ago helped set the course of some of Pennsylvania's rivers. They planed away uplands and rerouted rivers by plugging old channels and creating new ones.

Nearly all of Pennsylvania lies in the Appalachian Highlands, a region of plateaus, valleys, and parallel mountain ranges. Corn and hay flourish in the rich soils of southeastern Pennsylvania, as do poultry and dairy farms.

Today most Pennsylvanians live in cities and towns. Philadelphia has ranked as the state's largest city since colonial days. More than a third of all Pennsylvanians live in and around Philadelphia, making it the fifth largest city in the United States after New York, Los Angeles, Chicago, and Houston.

Since its founding by William Penn, Pennsylvania has welcomed people from many lands and many religions. Early settlers included English, Welsh, French, Swedish, and Dutch colonists. Later came Irish immigrants, as well as newcomers from southern and eastern Europe. Some German groups became known as "Pennsylvania Dutch." The word comes from a misinterpretation of *Deutsch*, the German word for "German." Many of them settled in Lancaster County. These Amish and Mennonite farmers maintain neat, prosperous farms. Often these farms are run on religious principles, with horse-drawn equipment and without modern conveniences such as telephones and electricity.

World War II brought the migration of black families from the South in search of factory jobs. Most recently Hispanics and Asians have come, seeking peace, freedom, and a better way of life than was possible in their strife-torn homelands.

Pennsylvania is heavily industrialized. The state counts some 17,000 companies turning out

Young boys were common in coal mines around 1905, before laws were passed to protect children. This youngster worked underground 10 to 12 hours a day, driving mules that pulled coal carts.

300 products ranging from steel rails to nylon bristles. Even so, about three-fifths of its land is forested. Beech, maple, birch, and evergreens flourish in the mountains; hickory, oak, and black walnut in the lowlands. Pennsylvania has more publicly owned parks and forestlands than all the other northeastern states combined.

In the days before railroads and highways, Pennsylvania's waterways served as thoroughfares. Philadelphia, because of its location on the Delaware River some 90 miles (145 km) from the Atlantic, became America's largest freshwater port, shipping food and manufactured goods throughout the eastern states and abroad. Later, Erie became a port vital to Great Lakes shipping. Pittsburgh, a town that grew where the Allegheny and Monongahela Rivers join to form the Ohio River, provided access to the West.

In 1794 Pennsylvania completed America's first turnpike, a stone-paved toll road linking Philadelphia and Lancaster. Travelers paid to travel on the road. The toll collector first received their fee, then turned a pike, or gate, to let them through. A century and a half later, the Pennsylvania Turnpike became the nation's first limited-access highway, a direct descendant of the old Philadelphia-to-Lancaster road.

By the 1850s discoveries of coal, oil, and limestone, and ready access to iron ore shipped across the Great Lakes, had turned Pennsylvania into an industrial powerhouse. In 1859 the nation's first commercial oil well came into production near Titusville, marking the birth of the petroleum industry.

During World War II, Pennsylvania ranked second among the states in industrial production. Pittsburgh's steelmaking furnaces produced so much smoke and soot that motorists drove with headlights on—at noon. Today most of the smog is gone, and the old steel mills are closed. Pittsburgh has a gleaming new downtown laced with parks and promenades. Despite the decline of the steel and coal industries, Pennsylvania still ranks as a major mining and manufacturing state, turning out about a seventh of all the steel made in the United States.

In recent years the state has also diversified its industry, creating jobs in research and high technology. Tourism, too, has become a billion-dollar business. More than 300 lakes, many of them a gift of ancient glaciers, attract boaters and fishermen, and some of the East's most spectacular waterfalls spill down the cliffs and gorges of the Pocono Mountains.

Area: *33rd largest state, 45,308 sq mi (117,348 sq km)*
Population: *11,881,643; ranks fifth*
Major Cities: *Philadelphia, 1,585,577; Pittsburgh, 369,879; Erie, 108,718*
Manufacturing: *food products, chemicals, machinery, metal products, electronics, metals, transportation equipment, paper products, stone, clay, and glass products, scientific instruments, clothing*
Mining and Quarrying: *coal, oil and gas, stone, sand and gravel*
Agriculture: *milk, cattle, greenhouse and nursery products, mushrooms, eggs, broilers, hogs, fruits, hay, corn*
Other Important Activities: *tourism, printing and publishing*
Statehood: *the second state; ratified the Constitution on December 12, 1787*

LAKE ERIE

A — Erie ● 90

B — 19 | Union City Reservoir | ALLEGHENY N.R.A. | Bradford ● | Susquehanna River
6N | Warren | Allegheny Reservoir | 81

C — 6 | Meadville ● | ERIE NATIONAL WILDLIFE REFUGE | ALLEGHENY N.R.A. | 6 | Coudersport | Pine Creek Gorge | 15 | Carbondale ●
Titusville ● | Allegheny River | Delaware River

D — Pymatuning Reservoir | 219 | Canyon 1,100 feet (335 meters) deep, formed thousands of years ago when Pine Creek was a big river → | 220 | Scranton ● Dunmore ● | Lake Wallenpaupack
79 | Oil City ● | Little League baseball founded here, 1939 | 84

E — Shenango River | 80 | West Branch Susquehanna River | Williamsport ● | Wilkes-Barre ● | POCONO MOUNTAINS
Sharon ● | 180 | Nanticoke ● | DELAWARE WATER GAP NATIONAL RECREATION AREA
60 | 380

F — New Castle ● | (PROPOSED) | 80 | Bloomsburg ● | Hazleton ● | Lehigh River
Beaver River | 422 | 220 | 80

G — Allegheny River | MOUNTAINS | State College ● | Schuylkill River | 22 | Easton ●
Ohio River | 119 | 322 | 81 | Bethlehem ●
Kiskiminetas River | APPALACHIAN MOUNTAINS | Kutztown ● | 78 | Allentown ●

H — 76 | Conemaugh River | Lewistown ● | APPALACHIAN TRAIL | 9
Pittsburgh ● Penn Hills ● | Altoona ● | 22 | Juniata River | Lebanon ● | New Hope ●
Meadowcroft Rockshelter | 22 | Monroeville ● | Hershey ● | 422 | Reading ● | Washington Crossing

J — Baldwin ● | McKeesport ● | ALLEGHENY | Johnstown ● | Raystown Lake | Harrisburg ★ | 76 | Pottstown ● | Levittown ●
Bridgeville ● | Bethel Park ● | POTOMAC HERITAGE TRAIL | Mechanicsburg ● | Steelton ● | Lititz ● | Phoenixville ● | Norristown ●
Washington ● | PENNSYLVANIA | Carlisle ● | 15 | Lancaster ● | Valley Forge ● | Upper Darby ● | Bristol ●

K — 70 | Youghiogheny River | Somerset ● | TURNPIKE | 70 | 76 | Susquehanna River | West Chester ● | 30 | Philadelphia ●
Monongahela River | 40 | Chambersburg ● | York ● | Brandywine Cr. ● | 1 | 95
79 | 119 | Uniontown ● | 219 | 220 | 81 | Gettysburg ● | 30 | 83 | Hanover ● | Kennett Square ● | Chester ● | TINICUM NATIONAL WILDLIFE REFUGE

L — (PROPOSED) | Mount Davis + 3,213 FEET 979 METERS Highest point in Pennsylvania | 70 | Waynesboro ●

NORTH COUNTRY TRAIL

---

0 KILOMETERS 60
0 STATUTE MILES 40

The only Mid-Atlantic state that doesn't touch the ocean, Pennsylvania nevertheless has a major port, Philadelphia, on the Delaware River. Colliding continental plates pushed the state's mountains into an S-shaped curve millions of years ago and thrust up a plateau that glaciers and meltwater later carved into a jumble of valleys and flat-topped hills.

Stone Age hunters and gatherers roamed near a glacier in the southwest corner 16,000 years ago, hunting elk and deer and living beneath an overhanging ledge now named Meadowcroft Rockshelter.

Mountain Laurel

Ruffed Grouse

1

Pennsylvania

1   *The seven stallion paddocks of a horse farm wheel across a hilltop near York, along the frozen Susquehanna River.*

2   *Glowing yellow, a railway rail slides from the forge of the Bethlehem Steel mill in Steelton. Completed in 1867, the plant is the nation's oldest steel mill.*

3   *Independence Hall thrusts its belfry above a park in downtown Philadelphia. In this hall, in 1776, the Continental Congress signed the Declaration of Independence, affirming "that all men are created equal."*

4   *A mummer in feathered regalia struts her stuff in a New Year's Day parade, a Philadelphia tradition dating to 1876.*

5   *Chocolate-covered pretzels have long been a Christmas tradition among the Amish and Mennonites. America's first pretzel bakery opened in Lititz in 1861.*

2

4

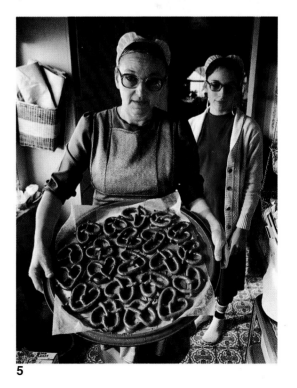

3

5

New Jersey

Tucked between New York City and Philadelphia, New Jersey ranks as one of the nation's most heavily industrialized states, a thriving center of trade and manufacturing that has few equals. Towns and cities, especially in the northern part of the state, crowd close together along the land traversed by America's busiest toll road, the New Jersey Turnpike. Each year the superhighway carries more than 190 million cars, buses, and trucks past railroad yards, tank farms, and industrial sites. Along parts of this corridor live 12,000 people per square mile (4,630 per sq km). The population density of New Jersey varies widely from region to region, but the average is almost 993 people per square mile (383 per sq km). This is higher than in any other state, even higher than in densely populated India or Japan.

Nearly 90 percent of all New Jerseyans live in and around large cities such as Newark, Jersey City, Paterson, and Elizabeth. Each workday thousands of them commute to out-of-state jobs in New York City and Philadelphia. As early as the 1830s some New Jerseyans commuted to New York every day. Today tunnels and bridges link the state to various parts of New York City, and four bridges span the Delaware River to Philadelphia.

New Jersey's farms and factories produce a prodigious outflow of goods—everything from orchids and blueberries to aspirin, trucks, turbines, and telephones. Manufacturing produces a fifth of the state's revenues. Even in colonial days New Jersey's corn, wheat, and vegetables found ready markets in New York and Philadelphia, leading Benjamin Franklin to describe the state as "a cider barrel tapped at both ends."

But this is only part of New Jersey. More than half the state is made up of open land, with farms, woods, marshes, and some of the finest white-sand beaches on the East Coast.

Kittatinny Mountain, a 35-mile-long (56-km) ridge of the Appalachians, lies across the state's northwestern corner. Flanking it is a highland region of low, flat-topped summits largely covered with forests of oak, maple, and ash. Many of the state's 800 or so lakes and ponds nestle in the highlands near Kittatinny Mountain.

Glacial rocks and rubble and steep slopes discourage large-scale vegetable farming here, so

The renowned Diving Horse, a Texas cow pony named Lorgah, is caught in action with two quick flashes. Lorgah made her 1958 plunge to fame from a 40-foot (12-m) tower in Atlantic City.

most farmers stick to dairying and raising poultry. The foothills are horse country, lush, rolling pastures nourished by limestone soils.

The Delaware River forms New Jersey's western boundary. In the north it has cut a dramatic, twisting pathway through Kittatinny Mountain, the Delaware Water Gap. Along its southern reaches, below Trenton, the river is tidal and navigable, and rivals the Mississippi in the amount of commerce it carries.

In the foothills east of the mountain, real estate developers have discovered rural areas close to New York City. Here town-house developments now rub shoulders with dairy farms. Here you can also find towns with white-spired churches and village greens remindful of their early New England settlers.

Across the state, facing the open Atlantic, 127 miles (204 km) of lagoons and barrier beaches reach from Sandy Hook in the north to Cape May on the lower reaches of Delaware Bay. This stretch is known as the Jersey Shore. Beach communities range from comfortable old towns like Bay Head and the exuberant Victorian restorations of Cape May, where Presidents Lincoln, Grant, Pierce, Buchanan, and Harrison vacationed, to the honky-tonk hustle of Asbury Park and Atlantic City's boardwalk, gambling casinos, and Miss America contests. Each year the Jersey Shore draws millions of tourists and vacationers, despite concerns over beaches polluted by industrial and other wastes. And each fall and spring tens of thousands of herons, ducks, terns, and other birds visit Brigantine, Barnegat, and other shoreside areas.

A few miles inland lies the largest tract of protected land between Boston and Washington, D. C., the one-million-acre (405,000-ha) Pine Barrens. Early settlers called the region barren because its sandy soil was not good for farming. Stretching from Cape May north to Toms River, the barrens are made up of swamps and salt marshes, stands of pine, cedar, and oak, cranberry bogs, and tracts of cultivated blueberries. The people of the barrens live mostly in towns and villages, but there are places where the population density is only ten per square mile (four per sq km).

Beneath the Pine Barrens, and nourishing its swamps, streams, marshes, and wildlife, lies a little-known natural wonder, the Cohansey Aquifer. This underground maze of tunnels and caverns is thought to hold the greatest supply of fresh, clean water in the East north of Florida, about equal to a thousand-square-mile (2,590-sq-km) lake 75 feet (23 m) deep.

Between the Pine Barrens and the Delaware River lies the heartland of New Jersey's farming district. The fertile, loamy soils of the region rank among the most productive and valuable in the United States. Almost 60 kinds of fruits and vegetables grow here. Much of the food is trucked to New York City and Philadelphia as well as other eastern cities. Although much farmland has been converted to build offices, shopping malls, and suburbs in recent years, New Jersey still has some 8,300 farms.

Glaciers, in places up to a mile (1.6 km) thick, helped shape the face of New Jersey. Moving south some 20,000 years ago, they covered the northern part of the state, above a line between Phillipsburg and Perth Amboy. They piled up rocks and soil that formed the hills and ridges in the north, and gouged depressions that filled with water. These became lakes and wetlands such as the Great Swamp near Morristown.

Untouched by glaciers, the southern part of New Jersey remains a relatively smooth coastal plain fringed with bays, inlets, and sandbars.

American Goldfinch

Violet

Area: *the 46th largest state, 7,787 sq mi (20,169 sq km)*
Population: *7,730,188; ranks ninth*
Major Cities: *Newark, 275,221; Jersey City, 228,537; Paterson, 140,891*
Manufacturing: *chemicals, food products, scientific instruments, electronics, machinery, metal products, rubber and plastics, paper products, clothing, stone, clay, and glass products, metals, transportation equipment, furniture*
Agriculture: *greenhouse and nursery products, vegetables, milk, blueberries, eggs, soybeans, cattle*
Mining and Quarrying: *stone, sand and gravel*
Other Important Activities: *tourism, printing and publishing, fishing*
Statehood: *the third state; ratified the Constitution on December 18, 1787*

KILOMETERS 30

STATUTE MILES 20

High Point
1,803 FEET
550 METERS
Highest point
in New Jersey

DELAWARE WATER GAP NATIONAL RECREATION AREA

APPALACHIAN TRAIL

KITTATINNY MOUNTAIN

Wanaque Reservoir

Hopatcong
Lake Hopatcong
Dover
Ridgewood
Paramus
Paterson
Clifton
Hackensack
Montclair
Passaic
Bloomfield
Union City
Morristown
East Orange
Hoboken
GREAT SWAMP NATIONAL WILDLIFE REFUGE
Irvington
Jersey City
Newark
Passaic River
Elizabeth
Bayonne

Phillipsburg

Plainfield
Woodbridge

Raritan River

Perth Amboy

Sandy Hook
GATEWAY NATIONAL RECREATION AREA

New Brunswick
Edison
Sayreville

DELAWARE AND RARITAN CANAL

Hopewell
Princeton
Red Bank
Eatontown
Long Branch

Mercerville
Neptune
Asbury Park

Trenton
White Horse
NEW JERSEY TURNPIKE

Lakewood
Point Pleasant
Bay Head

Delaware River

Willingboro

Torms River

Camden
Pennsauken
Cherry Hill
Haddonfield
The first dinosaur skeleton found in North America, 1858
Chatsworth
PINE BARRENS

Barnegat Bay

ATLANTIC OCEAN

Glassboro

ATLANTIC CITY EXPRESSWAY

Mullica River

GARDEN STATE PARKWAY

EDWIN B. FORSYTHE NATIONAL WILDLIFE REFUGE (BARNEGAT)

SUPAWNA MEADOWS NATIONAL WILDLIFE REFUGE

Great Egg Harbor River

Beach Haven

Vineland

Great Bay
EDWIN B. FORSYTHE NATIONAL WILDLIFE REFUGE (BRIGANTINE)

Bridgeton
Millville

PINE BARRENS

Atlantic City
Ventnor City

Maurice River

Ocean City

Delaware Bay

Avalon

Cape May

Every fall millions of migrating birds gather here to cross Delaware Bay

Wildwood

Cape May

A B C D E F G H J K L M N O P Q R S T U
1 2 3 4 5 6 7 8 9 10 11

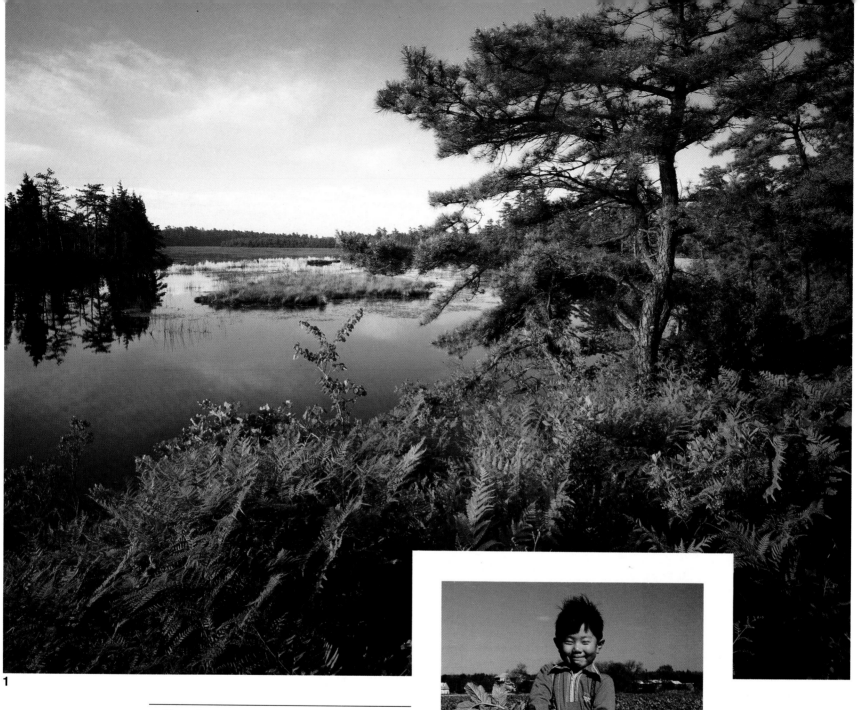

1

New Jersey

1 *A meandering stream reflects a soggy, boggy part of the Pine Barrens. Early settlers mined the region for bog iron to make nails, kettles, and cannonballs.*

2 *Near Vineland, a Korean-American youngster joyfully hefts a whopping radish on his family's vegetable farm.*

2

3

4

5

3 *Planes, trains, ships, and trucks come together in Newark, a major shipping center. Cranes stack truck-size containers on the decks of ships bound for distant ports.*

4 *A worker at a laboratory near Elizabeth examines cancer-fighting interferon. New Jersey has about a thousand plants producing medicines and chemicals.*

5 *A lifeguard team battles the surf to launch a boat near Asbury Park in an annual tournament that draws many contestants, such as these from the Barnegat Bay area.*

Maryland

Chesapeake Bay slices Maryland nearly in two. Hills and mountains rise west of the bay. So do the gentle streams and broad, limestone-rich valleys of the Piedmont. In the foothills lie suburban communities that reach from Baltimore to the nation's capital, Washington, D. C. Just at the edge of the Piedmont, on the Atlantic Coastal Plain, stands the city of Baltimore. East of the bay spreads Maryland's share of the Delmarva Peninsula, a mostly flat, marsh-fringed stretch of land known as the Eastern Shore.

The bay itself is a submerged river valley, or estuary, the United States' largest. It formed after the Ice Age thousands of years ago, as the land gradually sank and sea levels rose, flooding the mouth of the Susquehanna River. Although Maryland has only 31 miles (50 km) of coast on the Atlantic Ocean, the myriad coves, creeks, and indentations on the bay side give the state nearly 4,000 miles (6,440 km) of shoreline.

Chesapeake Bay plays an important part in Maryland life, especially in the Tidewater region surrounding it. More than 2.3 million people live within 20 miles (32 km) of the bay and its tributaries, a number that may reach 12 million by the end of the century.

Despite problems with silting, flooding, and pollution, the bay remains a paradise for boaters, bird-watchers, sport fishermen, and those who like to feast on fish, crabs, and oysters. In a good year the bay provides about 90 million pounds of blue crabs, about half the nation's catch, and nearly all its soft-shell crabs. Tonging and dredging for oysters is hard work and always has been. Soaring expenses, state government regulation, growing competition from Louisiana and Venezuela, and pollution have driven many a waterman from the bay.

Ever since colonial days the bay has served as an avenue of commerce between North America, Europe, and the Caribbean. Colonial planters shipped tobacco, lumber, and livestock to London from sheltered bay-side landings. From the Caribbean came sugar and slaves, sugar to be made into rum, slaves to till the fields of sotweed, as tobacco was sometimes called.

The bay provides direct access to Baltimore, one of the nation's busiest ports and Maryland's most industrial city. Today, as in times past, people of many ethnic backgrounds live in Balti-

Around 1920 a book wagon makes house-to-house deliveries from the Washington County Free Library at Hagerstown. Established in 1902, it was the first county library in the United States.

more. Many Italians live in a 12-block area near the waterfront. Greek families live in a nearby neighborhood, as do Hispanics. Poles and other East Europeans often prefer an eastern part of the city. Brick row houses with gleaming marble doorsteps are a common sight in many of these older Baltimore neighborhoods.

About three-fourths of all Marylanders live in the densely populated corridor between Baltimore and Washington, D. C. Even 30 years ago a newspaper noted that "Baltimore and Washington are reaching out for each other like octopuses, sending out tentacles of freeways, sewage lines, and industrial zones." Those tentacles have long since met and entangled.

Even so, much of Maryland remains rural. Forests cover about 40 percent of the state—spruce, white pine, hemlock, and maple in the western mountains and foothills. Farms and orchards fill the broad, fertile valleys between the mountains. In the lowlands to the east spread forests of yellow pine, cedar, and cypress.

Farmers still grow tobacco on the western shore of Chesapeake Bay. Across the bay raising poultry vies with trapping crabs and harvesting oysters as a way to earn a living. On the ocean side of Delmarva lies Ocean City, a major resort teeming with vacationers and holiday

crowds during the summer months. South of Ocean City lies Assateague Island, a long, thin barrier island with few inhabitants other than nesting shorebirds and wild ponies.

The state capital, Annapolis, hugs the bay. Annapolis's State House, begun in 1772, ranks as the nation's oldest state capitol building in continuous use. And briefly, from November 1783 until the following August, it served as the nation's capitol. The treaty that ended the Revolutionary War was ratified here in 1784.

Birds depend on the bounty of Chesapeake Bay. Thousands of ducks nest and raise their broods in the wetlands fringing the bay. Up to three million Canada geese winter over each year, and bald eagles, protected by law from hunters, have begun to make a comeback.

Area: *the 42nd largest state, 10,460 sq mi (27,092 sq km)*
Population: *4,781,468; ranks 19th*
Major Cities: *Baltimore, 736,014; Rockville, 44,835; Frederick, 40,148*
Manufacturing: *food products, scientific instruments, chemicals, transportation equipment, metals, electronics, machinery, metal products, paper products, rubber and plastics, stone, clay, and glass products, clothing, lumber and wood products*
Agriculture: *broilers, milk, greenhouse and nursery products, soybeans, cattle, corn, vegetables, eggs*
Mining and Quarrying: *stone, coal, sand and gravel*
Other Important Activities: *tourism, printing and publishing, fishing*
Statehood: *the seventh state; ratified the Constitution on April 28, 1788*

8 9 10 11 12 13 14 15 16 17 18 19 20 21 22 23 24 25 26 27

A
B
C
D
E
F
G
H
J
K
L
M
N
O
P
Q

Hancock

Hagerstown

ANTIETAM
NATIONAL BATTLEFIELD
Sharpsburg

Emmitsburg

CATOCTIN
MOUNTAIN
PARK
Camp David

APPALACHIAN TRAIL

Middletown
Frederick
New Market

HARPERS FERRY N.H.P.

Potomac River

CHESAPEAKE AND OHIO CANAL
NATIONAL HISTORIC PARK

Gaithersburg

Monocacy River

Westminster

Liberty
Reservoir

Randallstown

Prettyboy
Reservoir

Lutherville-
Timonium
Towson
Pikesville

Gunpowder
River

HAMPTON
N.H.S.
Parkville

Bel Air
Aberdeen

Susquehanna
River

Havre de Grace

SUSQUEHANNA
NATIONAL
WILDLIFE REFUGE

Elkton

CHESAPEAKE AND
DELAWARE CANAL

Catonsville

Baltimore
Dundalk

Essex

Chester River

Chestertown

Columbia
Glen Burnie

Patapsco River

EASTERN NECK
NATIONAL
WILDLIFE REFUGE

Rockville

Laurel
PATUXENT
N.W.R.

Severna Park

Severn River

Wheaton
Silver Spring
Bethesda

College Park
Bowie

Annapolis
U. S. Naval
Academy

Kent
Island

CHESAPEAKE BAY

EASTERN SHORE

Choptank River

District of
Columbia

Hillcrest Heights
Suitland

Oxon Hill

St. Michaels
Easton

Oxford

Waldorf

Patuxent River

La Plata

POTOMAC HERITAGE TRAIL

Mechanicsville

Wicomico River

(PROPOSED)

Lexington Park

Potomac River

St. Marys City

Point Lookout

Prince Frederick

BLACKWATER
NATIONAL
WILDLIFE REFUGE

Cambridge

Nanticoke River

Salisbury

DELMARVA PENINSULA

Chesapeake Bay
drowns the ancient
valley of the
Susquehanna River

MARTIN NATIONAL
WILDLIFE REFUGE

Smith Island

Pocomoke River

Pocomoke City

Crisfield

Snow Hill

Berlin
Ocean City

ASSATEAGUE
ISLAND
NATIONAL
SEASHORE

Assateague
Island

CHINCOTEAGUE
NATIONAL
WILDLIFE REFUGE

ATLANTIC OCEAN

The nation's largest,
most productive estuary,
Chesapeake Bay ex-
tends about 200 miles
(320 km) between the
Susquehanna River and
the Atlantic Ocean.

A vast mixing bowl,
the bay combines fresh
water flowing from rivers
with salt water from the
ocean. Tidal wetlands
around the edge of the
bay create specialized
environments for many
of the bay's 2,700 plant
and animal species.

Chesapeake water-
men yearly harvest half a
billion pounds of sea-
food, including half the
nation's catch of blue
crabs and more than a
third of its oysters.

KILOMETERS   30
STATUTE MILES   20

Black-eyed
Susan

Northern Oriole
(Baltimore Oriole)

1

2

Maryland

1 *A cook in the town of Oxford prepares a dish of soft-shell clams steamed and dipped in a tangy sauce. Most Maryland clams are shipped to northeastern states.*

2 *Twin spans of the 4.4-mile (7-km) Chesapeake Bay Bridge link the once isolated Eastern Shore with the rest of Maryland.*

3 *Forsaking modern farm equipment, an Amish boy hitches his plow to a four-horse-power team near Mechanicsville. Religious beliefs lead Amish people to seek simplicity in their daily lives and to shun contraptions of the modern world.*

3

4 *Annapolis reaches for the Severn River on radiating streets laid out in 1696. Filling its circle (background), the capitol once housed the Continental Congress. One street runs from Church Circle (foreground) to the green-roofed buildings of the United States Naval Academy.*

5 *Hats aloft! Graduating Naval Academy cadets celebrate by flinging away their "middie" caps at the climax of commencement exercises. No longer midshipmen, they will now wear the hats of commissioned officers.*

5

4

Delaware

Delaware is a small state, "a jewel among states," Thomas Jefferson called it. Only Rhode Island is smaller. The state lies mostly on the Atlantic Coastal Plain, where it forms a flat, low-lying strip of land extending 96 miles (154 km) along the Delmarva Peninsula, which Delaware shares with Maryland and Virginia. Here the land seldom rises more than 80 feet (24 m) above sea level. Only Florida lies lower.

But not all of Delaware is flat. Its northernmost reach, a strip only 10 miles (16 km) at its widest, is an edge of the rolling foothills of the Appalachian Mountains, the Piedmont. Here the Delaware River forms the boundary between New Jersey and Delaware as it flows into Delaware Bay to meet the sea. This part of the state lies along a busy transportation corridor between northern and southern states, and has become heavily industrialized.

Swamps and marshlands rich in plants and insects dot Delaware's Atlantic Coastal Plain, making it a haven for deer, otters, and muskrats, as well as a stopover for migrating ducks and geese. Cypress Swamp spreads across some 30,000 acres (12,150 ha) along the southern border, and contains the northernmost stand of cypress trees in the United States. Salt marshes and estuaries line much of Delaware Bay, providing nesting sites for birds and breeding grounds for mollusks and shellfish. In 1971 Delaware became the first state to enact strict seashore protection laws; they forbid construction of oil refineries, steel mills, and other polluting industries within two miles (3 km) of the coast.

Beyond the mouth of Delaware Bay, from Cape Henlopen to Fenwick Island, lie 28 miles (45 km) of sandy Atlantic Ocean beaches. These are long, thin barrier islands that enclose shallow bays and lagoons. Each summer Delaware's beaches attract vacationers from Washington, D. C., Baltimore, and other eastern cities.

Small as it is, Delaware is almost two states rolled into one, a major commercial and industrial center in the north, where 70 percent of the people live and work, and a thinly populated farming state elsewhere. As a local newspaperman observed: "Delaware is a northern state with a southern exposure. And it's a southern state with a northern exposure."

As to Delaware's northern exposure, it was

In 1935 the world's first synthetic fiber, nylon, was invented in a Du Pont lab. By 1950 Du Pont machines at the plant in Seaford were spinning the sturdy nylon threads by the mile.

along the banks of Brandywine Creek, near Wilmington, that Éleuthère Irénée du Pont in 1802 decided to locate his gunpowder mills. Since then his enterprise has expanded globally and is regarded as one of the world's leading chemical companies. Many other chemical companies operate in Delaware and, with Du Pont, produce plastics, synthetic fibers, and agricultural and industrial chemicals.

Many large companies of all kinds have "paper offices" in Delaware because the state has licensed them to do business, and the legal papers originate in and are stored in Delaware offices. In fact, the incorporation of companies, whether they actually locate in the state or as far away as Asia, has become big business in Delaware. Each year the process brings in about a fifth of the state's income in legal fees and taxes. About half of the largest companies in the U. S. call themselves Delaware corporations. Liberal tax

laws, lawyers and judges experienced in corporate law, and rules that enable businesses to operate without much outside interference have attracted more than 170,000 companies to sign on as Delaware corporations.

In 1981 the state eased credit restrictions and banking regulations, a move that has since spurred an influx of banks, credit card operations, and other financial services.

As for Delaware's southern exposure, commerce gives way to farming in the lower two-thirds of the state. Here the pace of life is slower and more relaxed than in Wilmington. As one writer noted: "This is a small-town state, where peace, quiet, and good neighbors are surplus commodities." The sandy, loamy soil produces abundant corn and soybeans which, in turn, feed the some 217 million chickens that Delaware farmers raise each year.

Delaware gets its name from Lord De La Warre, a governor of colonial Virginia who financed a voyage of exploration along this part of North America's coast. In 1631 the first colonists, from the Netherlands, built a whaling settlement at Zwaanendael ("swan valley"), now Lewes, but Indians massacred the group. In 1638 Swedes arriving near present-day Wilmington introduced log cabins to the New World. The Dutch and the English fought over the territory but eventually England prevailed, and in 1682 the Duke of York gave Delaware to William Penn as part of his Pennsylvania colony. During the Revolutionary War the territory became the "Delaware State."

Area: *the 49th largest state, 2,044 sq mi (5,294 sq km)*
Population: *666,168; ranks 46th*
Major Cities: *Wilmington, 71,529; Dover, 27,630; Newark, 25,098*
Manufacturing: *chemicals, food products, rubber and plastics, paper products, scientific instruments, transportation equipment, electronics, clothing, metal products*
Agriculture: *broilers, soybeans, vegetables, greenhouse and nursery products, corn, milk, eggs, wheat, hogs*
Mining and Quarrying: *sand and gravel, magnesium*
Other Important Activities: *finance, tourism, printing and publishing, fishing*
Statehood: *the first state; ratified the Constitution on December 7, 1787*

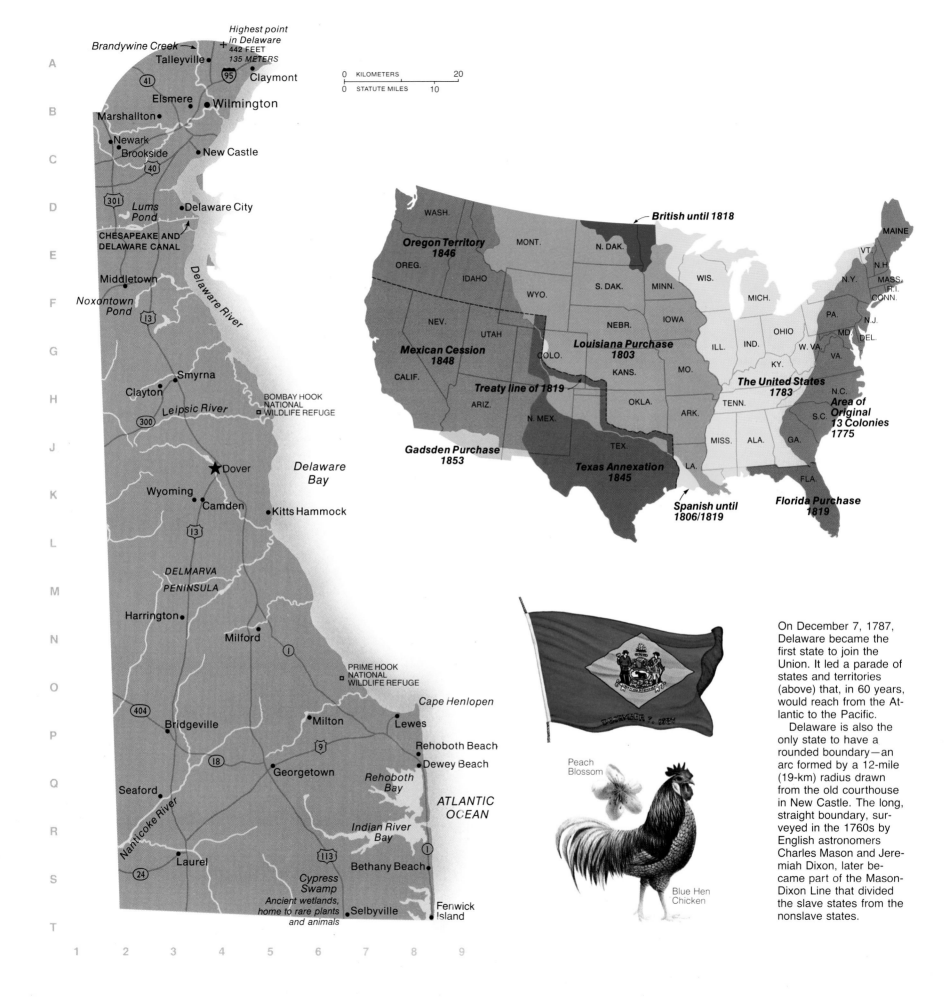

Brandywine Creek

Highest point in Delaware
+ 442 FEET
135 METERS

Talleyville

A

41

95 Claymont

Elsmere

B Wilmington

Marshallton

Newark

C Brookside New Castle

40

D 301 Lums Pond Delaware City

E CHESAPEAKE AND DELAWARE CANAL

Middletown

F *Noxontown Pond*

13

Delaware River

G

Smyrna

H Clayton

300 *Leipsic River*

BOMBAY HOOK NATIONAL WILDLIFE REFUGE

★ Dover

Delaware Bay

J

K Wyoming Camden Kitts Hammock

13

L

DELMARVA PENINSULA

M

Harrington

N Milford

1

PRIME HOOK NATIONAL WILDLIFE REFUGE

O

404 Bridgeville *Cape Henlopen*

P Milton Lewes

9 Rehoboth Beach

Q 18 Georgetown Dewey Beach

Seaford *Rehoboth Bay*

R *Nanticoke River* *Indian River Bay* ATLANTIC OCEAN

113

S 24 Laurel Bethany Beach

T *Cypress Swamp* Ancient wetlands, home to rare plants and animals Selbyville Fenwick Island

1 2 3 4 5 6 7 8 9

KILOMETERS 0 — 20
STATUTE MILES 0 — 10

WASH.

Oregon Territory 1846

OREG.

MONT.

N. DAK.

British until 1818

MAINE

VT.
N.H.
MASS.
R.I.
CONN.

IDAHO

WYO.

S. DAK.

MINN.

WIS.

MICH.

N.Y.

PA.

N.J.

NEV.

UTAH

NEBR.

IOWA

ILL.

IND.

OHIO

W. VA.

MD.

DEL.

Mexican Cession 1848

COLO.

Louisiana Purchase 1803

KANS.

MO.

KY.

VA.

CALIF.

Treaty line of 1819

The United States 1783

N.C.

ARIZ.

N. MEX.

OKLA.

ARK.

TENN.

Area of Original 13 Colonies 1775

S.C.

Gadsden Purchase 1853

TEX.

MISS.

ALA.

GA.

Texas Annexation 1845

LA.

FLA.

Spanish until 1806/1819

Florida Purchase 1819

On December 7, 1787, Delaware became the first state to join the Union. It led a parade of states and territories (above) that, in 60 years, would reach from the Atlantic to the Pacific.

Delaware is also the only state to have a rounded boundary—an arc formed by a 12-mile (19-km) radius drawn from the old courthouse in New Castle. The long, straight boundary, surveyed in the 1760s by English astronomers Charles Mason and Jeremiah Dixon, later became part of the Mason-Dixon Line that divided the slave states from the nonslave states.

Peach Blossom

Blue Hen Chicken

Delaware

1 *Founded by Swedish settlers in 1638, Wilmington today mixes old with new as part of a downtown renewal plan. Delaware's largest city, long a leader in corporate law and the chemical industry, has also become an important credit card center.*

2 *An antique train chugs past Granogue, a du Pont family estate built in 1923. "Château country" is what Delawareans call the rolling countryside northwest of Wilmington dotted with du Pont mansions.*

3

4

3 *Hoisting shellfish from the bottom of Reho-*
both Bay, a clammer grapples with a heavy
bull rake to haul in a load of bivalves
prized for their salty flavor.

4 *Youngsters share a giggle in the Touch and*
Discover Room at Winterthur, a du Pont
estate near Wilmington, now a museum fa-
mous for its gardens and furnishings.

Appalachian Highlands

Like giant ripples on the land, the Appalachian Mountains sweep along the eastern United States for some 2,000 miles (3,200 km) from central Alabama to Maine and on into Canada. Many mountain ranges make up the Appalachian system. Here the Blue Ridge Mountains form the range's eastern front. Behind them, other mountains roll westward to forested interior highlands bordered by rivers.

Along the Blue Ridge, foothills called the Piedmont slope eastward, then step down onto the Atlantic Coastal Plain fringed with low wetlands and long, thin islands. The barrier islands of the Outer Banks, once sand ridges that were flooded when ocean levels rose after the Ice Age, act as a buffer between the mainland and the open ocean. Shallow sounds and lagoons between the islands and the shore also provide food and shelter for fish and wildlife.

Many dams also dot the region. You can see them where rivers widen into long, narrow lakes. These man-made lakes, or reservoirs, attract boaters and fishermen and provide flood control. Water from the lakes spilling through some dams turns turbines that produce electricity for homes and factories in the region.

Ohio River

Louisville

Mississippi River

Nashville

APPALAC

Memphis

Potomac River

Washington, D. C.

WEST VIRGINIA
VIRGINIA
NORTH CAROLINA

KENTUCKY
TENNESSEE

Delmarva
Peninsula

Richmond

Chesapeake Bay

Norfolk

A
P
P
A
L
A
C
H
I
A
N
M
O
U
N
T
A
I
N
S

Raleigh

Outer Banks

Kentucky

Folk musician and maker of musical instruments John Jacob Niles, in his workshop near Lexington around 1940, puts finishing touches on a dulcimer of an unusual shape.

Kentucky is a land of rivers. Much of its border is formed by rivers. This gives the state a shape like a camel trying to get up, one local humorist observed. Kentucky has more than a thousand miles (1,600 km) of navigable waterways for recreation and commerce. Its major cities, located on rivers, were founded in the days when rivers were highways for flatboats and steamboats.

The Appalachian Mountains and the Cumberland Plateau make up much of eastern Kentucky. Here the land is a scramble of heavily forested peaks, ridges, and deep, narrow valleys settled mostly by Scotch-Irish pioneers. Rugged terrain and lack of good roads for many years kept much of eastern Kentucky shut off from the outside world. But such isolation also helped preserve the ballads of the settlers and kept alive skills such as quilting and basketry.

Even though the giant oaks, hickories, and poplars that once grew in Kentucky have long ago been logged, and many mountainsides have been torn apart to dig out coal, the land still retains much of its wild beauty.

Waterfalls tumble from the heights. Cumberland Falls, near Corbin, is one of the largest east of the Rocky Mountains. When the water is high and the moon is full, the mist of the falls creates a moonbow. Kentucky streams have carved cliffs, palisades, and natural bridges. Rivers have gnawed winding passageways called gaps through the mountains. One is historic Cumberland Gap, Daniel Boone's route when he blazed his pioneering Wilderness Road in 1775. Boone and his wife, Rebecca, are buried in a cemetery in Frankfort, the state capital.

Kentucky mines coal and has ever since the 1850s. Today the state ranks as one of the nation's leading producers of soft, or bituminous, coal. Most of it comes from huge deposits in the eastern mountains and in western coalfields near the Ohio River. Geologists estimate that Kentucky and neighboring Tennessee have enough coal to mine for a thousand years.

Nowadays most of the coal is strip-mined, dug out by huge power shovels and bulldozers that tear away the trees, earth, and rocks covering the deposits. Such methods provide cheap coal, but they also pollute streams and destroy farmland, forests, and animal habitats.

A 1977 federal law requires mine owners to reclaim land by restoring its shape and replanting it. But lands stripped before 1977 still lie mostly unreclaimed, giant scars on the land.

In recent years Kentucky has also become a major producer of marijuana. For impoverished farmers and unemployed mine workers of eastern Kentucky, illegal marijuana growing can be tempting. The average tobacco plot earns about $2,000 a year; 50 well-tended marijuana plants can bring in more than $50,000.

West of the mountains lies Kentucky's Bluegrass region, with some of the world's finest horse farms. Gently rolling fields and pastures lie covered with lush grass and laced with white fences. Although bluegrass is really green, it gets its name from the tiny bluish flowers that bloom briefly each May. Limestone bedrock beneath the turf nourishes the rich grass with lime and calcium needed to build strong bones and muscles in fine horses. Farmers in the region also grow large crops of tobacco, corn, and hay.

Lexington serves as the commercial and cultural hub of the Bluegrass region, while Louisville reigns as the site for America's best known horse race, the Kentucky Derby.

Louisville, a major Ohio River port with a waterfront rebuilt in steel, glass, and concrete, turns out trucks, farm equipment, household appliances, and air-pollution equipment. It also produces bourbon whiskey, a leading state export. Factories in Lexington manufacture electric typewriters, paper and food products, and heating equipment.

South-central Kentucky has one of the world's great natural wonders, Mammoth Cave. This longest of all known cavern systems extends some 330 miles (530 km) in five underground levels that have yet to be fully explored. Over millions of years water, seeping through cracks in the limestone bedrock, created a labyrinth of tunnels and chambers. In these dark recesses live fish, shrimp, crayfish, and other creatures. Over the ages these animals have adapted to their environment by losing sight or skin color, or both, and developing sensitive organs on their bodies that help them feel their way around in the blackness.

Kentucky's western tip, the part that jogs south between the Mississippi River and Kentucky Lake, is known as the Jackson Purchase. It was named for Andrew Jackson, who helped buy this bottomland from the Chickasaw Indians in 1818, before he became President of the U. S.

One part of the Purchase can't be reached by road from Kentucky. It's a pom-pom-shaped dot of land barely three miles (5 km) across that a loop of the Mississippi River cuts off from the rest of the state. To get there by car, you have to drive through neighboring Tennessee.

Area: *37th largest state, 40,410 sq mi (104,659 sq km)*
Population: *3,685,296; ranks 23rd*
Major Cities: *Louisville, 269,063; Lexington, 225,366; Owensboro, 53,549*
Manufacturing: *transportation equipment, machinery, electronics, food products, chemicals, metals, metal products, rubber and plastics, paper products, stone, clay, and glass products, clothing*
Mining and Quarrying: *coal, oil and gas, stone*
Agriculture: *horses, cattle, tobacco, milk, soybeans, corn*
Other Important Activities: *tourism, printing and publishing*
Statehood: *the 15th state; admitted on June 1, 1792*

Goldenrod

Cardinal

KILOMETERS 0 — 60
STATUTE MILES 0 — 40

A
B
C
D
E
F
G
H
J
K
L
M
N

Newport
Covington • • Fort Thomas
Florence • Erlanger

BIG BONE LICK STATE PARK
Salt lick attracted prehistoric mastodons, mammoths, ground sloths, musk oxen, bison

Ohio River

71

Maysville
Flatwoods
Ashland
Big Sandy R.

Campbellsburg

Licking River

75

68

64

Louisville • • St. Matthews
Shively
Jeffersontown
Pleasure Ridge Park
Okolona
Valley Station

Frankfort ★
Georgetown
Paris
Morehead

64
Lexington
Versailles
Mt. Sterling
Winchester
Cave Run Lake

23

Ohio River

Tug Fork

AUDUBON PARKWAY

Fort Knox □
Large part of U.S. gold reserve stored here

65

Bardstown

BLUE GRASS PARKWAY

127

402

114

Owensboro •

Harrodsburg
Richmond
Kentucky River

Rough River

Elizabethtown

Danville
Berea

150

80
Pikeville

MOUNTAINS

WESTERN KENTUCKY PARKWAY

BREAKS INTERSTATE PARK □
1,600-foot (488-meter) gorge, deepest east of the Mississippi River

Green River

Campbellsville
Green River Lake

CUMBERLAND PLATEAU

Hazard

APPALACHIAN

Central City •

GREEN RIVER PARKWAY

Nolin Lake

MAMMOTH CAVE NATIONAL PARK
World's longest cave system

CUMBERLAND PARKWAY

DANIEL BOONE PARKWAY

PINE MOUNTAIN

Somerset

65

Glasgow

Lake Cumberland

Corbin

75

Cumberland River

+ *Black Mountain*
4,145 FEET
1,263 METERS
Highest point in Kentucky

Barren River

Bowling Green •

Russellville •

68

Barren River Lake

BIG SOUTH FORK NATIONAL RIVER AND RECREATION AREA

Dale Hollow Lake

25E

CUMBERLAND MTN.

41
65

Franklin •

Middlesboro • □ Cumberland Gap

1

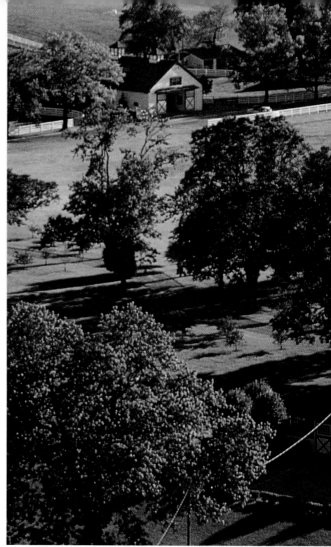

2

Kentucky

1 *Hoofs pounding, nostrils flaring, colts head for the homestretch at Keeneland Race Course near Lexington.*

2 *Rolling pastures surround a gabled barn at Calumet Farm near Lexington. The farm has owned eight Kentucky Derby winners, twice as many as any other stable.*

3 *Seamstresses at an underwear factory near Danville gather around to greet a colleague's new baby.*

4 *Draped along the Levisa Fork of the Big Sandy River, Pikeville presides over the state's richest coal-producing region.*

5 *The Tower, a staircase bathed in light, rises 138 steps to challenge visitors exploring Mammoth Cave's passageways.*

3

4

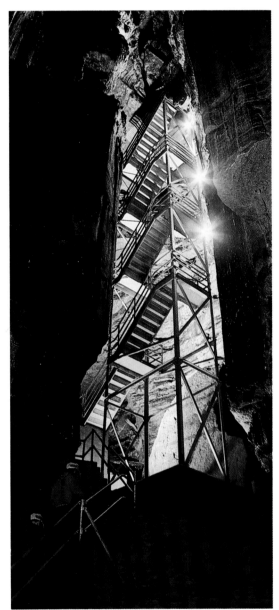

5

West Virginia

West Virginia has its ups and downs. No other eastern state has such rugged land, crisscrossed with hills, mountains, and steep, narrow valleys. Except along river floodplains, very little of its land is flat. West Virginians joke that if you smoothed out the bumps and wrinkles of their state, it would cover more ground than Texas.

West Virginia has quirky boundaries. It has two panhandles and borders that jiggle along rivers and meandering mountain ridges. The skinny northern panhandle resulted when colonial mapmakers, plotting the area of William Penn's Pennsylvania grant from the English king, drew Pennsylvania's western boundary a few miles shy of the Ohio River. The eastern panhandle, reaching to Harpers Ferry, came about during the Civil War, when pro-Union counties in western Virginia broke away from secessionist eastern Virginia in 1861.

Geography had a hand in the breakup. The counties east of the Appalachian Mountains, with their lush fields and plantations worked by slaves, turned east to trade with Europe and the other coastal states. Westerners, on the other hand, could carve out only small, hardscrabble farms amid the thin soils and rough terrain of the mountains. Poor roads and lack of communications left them feeling cut off and ignored by eastern lawmakers. So the westerners turned west to trade, along westward-flowing rivers such as the Ohio and Kanawha. Eventually they grew apart from the flatlanders, quarreling over taxes, slavery, and education.

For a few months the people of West Virginia called their new state Kanawha. The word comes from an Indian term meaning "place of the white stone" and probably refers to the vast salt deposits found in the area. But the name didn't stick, and in 1863 the country's 35th state joined the Union as West Virginia.

Minerals always have been important to West Virginia. Mining and manufacturing today account for nearly half the state's output of goods and services, a bigger percentage than in any other state. Immense seams of soft coal lie under approximately half the state and have been mined since the mid-1800s.

But coal has proved a fickle friend, bringing the state economic bumps and valleys to match its geographical ones. In the peak year, 1949,

In the 1930s, going to the movies could cost a quarter or, on special days, as little as a dime, and helped viewers briefly escape the hardships of the Depression outside the theater doors.

West Virginia's mines produced about 170 million tons of coal and employed 100,000 miners. Then hard times appeared. Some steel mills and factories have shut down, so they don't need coal to stoke their furnaces. Other mills produce steel more efficiently and use less coal. Giant shovels, draglines, and robot rock choppers can rip apart a mountain to get at the buried coal, so there are fewer jobs for miners. Now West Virginia mines produce about the same amount of coal as in 1949 but employ only 25,000 miners.

Underground coal mining is very dangerous. Miners continually face the possibility of explosions and accidents. Black lung disease, caused by long years of inhaling coal dust, kills thousands of miners every year. Worries about acid rain, stream pollution, and ozone holes in the atmosphere caused by burning fossil fuels, such as coal and oil, may also threaten production of high-sulfur coal.

To help weather these economic storms, West Virginia over the last few decades has modernized some of its old steel and glassmaking factories and has also developed new industries. Most of the state's newer jobs, such as banking, insurance, and transportation, are concentrated around its biggest cities. Even so, nearly two-thirds of all West Virginians live in rural areas, on farms and in small communities tucked away in hills and hollows.

Coal is not West Virginia's only important mineral. The state has a lot of salt, too. Long before the first white settlers arrived, Indians hunted deer, bison, and other game attracted to the salt at Great Buffalo Lick near the Kanawha River. Indians traded the salt, and in 1797 Elisha Brooks began selling it to other settlers to make butter and cure meat. Nowadays large chemical companies in the Kanawha and Ohio River Valleys use much of the salt to make chlorine, dyes, paints, plastics, and other products. Charleston, the capital, has a chemical industry that is one of the largest in the United States.

West Virginia also produces oil and gas, and quarries pottery clays. Silica-rich sandstone, found in the eastern panhandle and in several north-central counties, has made the state a major producer of fine glassware. Also, if you have a bag of marbles made in the United States, you can bet they came from West Virginia.

Today about three-quarters of the state is forested. Although the ancient oaks, poplars, and chestnuts have long since fallen to the ax, botanists still consider West Virginia a plant paradise brimming with everything from azaleas and honeysuckles to rarer plants such as coltsfoot, sundew, and bog rosemary.

Area: *41st largest state, 24,232 sq mi (62,758 sq km)*
Population: *1,793,477; ranks 34th*
Major Cities: *Charleston, 57,287; Huntington, 54,844; Wheeling, 34,882*
Mining and Quarrying: *coal, stone, sand and gravel, oil and gas, clay*
Manufacturing: *chemicals, metals, stone, clay, and glass products, metal products, machinery, food products, scientific instruments, electronics*
Agriculture: *cattle, broilers, milk, apples, turkeys, hay, greenhouse and nursery products, hogs*
Other Important Activities: *tourism, printing and publishing*
Statehood: *the 35th state; admitted on June 20, 1863*

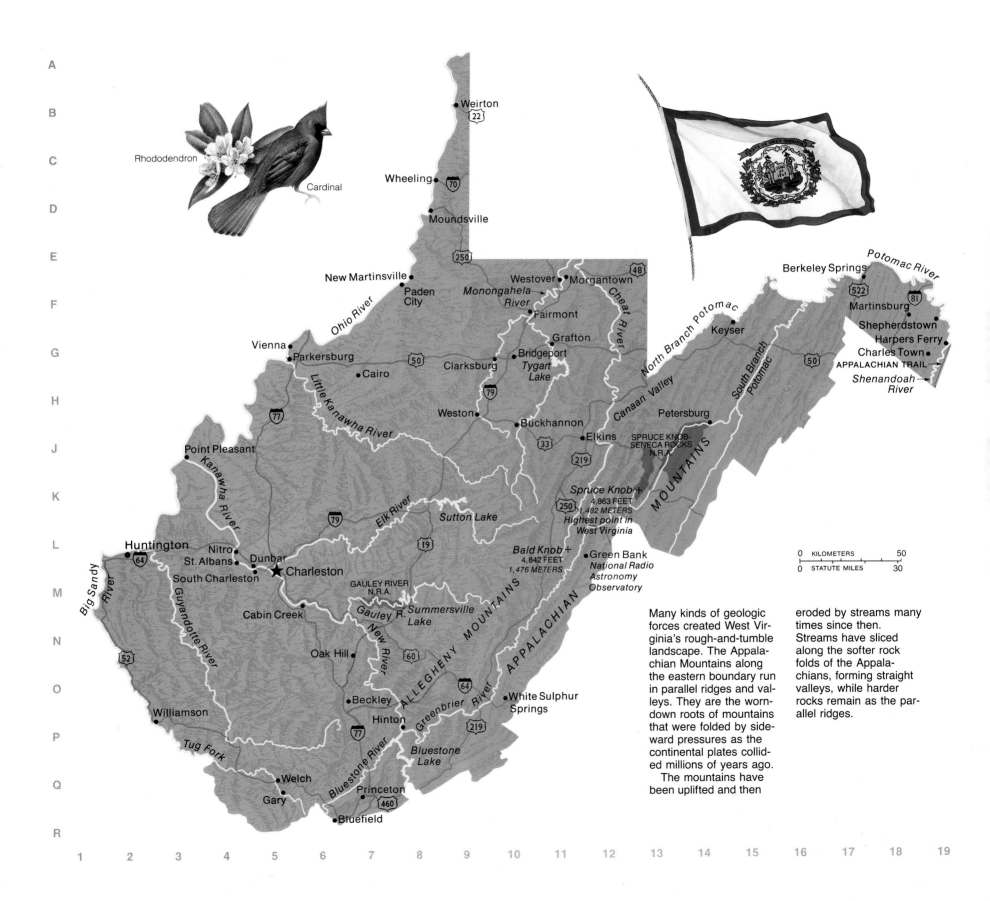

A B C D E F G H J K L M N O P Q R

Rhododendron

Cardinal

Weirton
22

Wheeling
70

Moundsville

250

New Martinsville
Paden City

Ohio River

Vienna
Parkersburg
Cairo

Little Kanawha River

50

Clarksburg

79

Weston

Westover Morgantown
Monongahela River
Fairmont
Grafton
Bridgeport
Tygart Lake

48

Cheat River

Buckhannon

33

Elkins

219

Canaan Valley

North Branch Potomac

Keyser

Petersburg

South Branch Potomac

SPRUCE KNOB-
SENECA ROCKS
N.R.A.

Berkeley Springs   Potomac River

522

Martinsburg
81

Shepherdstown

Harpers Ferry

Charles Town

50

APPALACHIAN TRAIL →

Shenandoah → River

Point Pleasant

Kanawha River

77

Elk River

79

250

Spruce Knob +
4,863 FEET
1,482 METERS
Highest point in
West Virginia

MOUNTAINS

Huntington
64
Big Sandy River
Nitro
St. Albans
Dunbar ★ Charleston
South Charleston

Guyandotte River

Sutton Lake

19

Bald Knob +
4,842 FEET
1,476 METERS

Green Bank
National Radio
Astronomy
Observatory

KILOMETERS   50

STATUTE MILES   30

Cabin Creek

52

Oak Hill

Williamson

GAULEY RIVER
N.R.A.

Gauley R.
Summersville Lake

New River

60

APPALACHIAN MOUNTAINS

ALLEGHENY MOUNTAINS

64

Beckley

Hinton

77

Greenbrier River

White Sulphur Springs

219

Bluestone River

Bluestone Lake

Tug Fork

Welch

Gary

Princeton
460

Bluefield

Many kinds of geologic
forces created West Vir-
ginia's rough-and-tumble
landscape. The Appala-
chian Mountains along
the eastern boundary run
in parallel ridges and valleys. They are the worn-
down roots of mountains
that were folded by side-
ward pressures as the
continental plates collided millions of years ago.

The mountains have
been uplifted and then

eroded by streams many
times since then.
Streams have sliced
along the softer rock
folds of the Appala-
chians, forming straight
valleys, while harder
rocks remain as the par-
allel ridges.

1 2 3 4 5 6 7 8 9 10 11 12 13 14 15 16 17 18 19

1

2

3

4

5

West Virginia

1 *Turning an electronic ear to the stars, radio telescopes along a ridge at Green Bank were among the first to listen, in vain so far, for messages from outer space.*

2 *A miner checks a timber shoring along a coal seam at a mine in Bald Knob while his partner operates a digging machine called a continuous miner.*

3 *Looking much as it did before the Civil War, Harpers Ferry sits amid slopes of the Blue Ridge Mountains at the confluence of the Shenandoah and Potomac Rivers.*

4 *Hot stuff: A worker prepares to tong recycled glass into a furnace at a marble factory in Paden City. West Virginia's three marble factories turn out more than a million of these "glassies" every day.*

5 *Flame azaleas explode into sunbursts of color along a hiking trail in the Allegheny Mountains near White Sulphur Springs.*

Virginia

Without Virginia the United States would be a very different country from the one we know. In 1607 Virginia became the site of the first permanent English settlement in America, Jamestown. Twelve years later the Jamestown settlers established the House of Burgesses, colonial America's first legislative assembly.

As the years rolled by, events crucial to the survival of an independent and united country took place in Virginia: in 1781 the British surrender at Yorktown; in 1865, at Appomattox, the end of the Civil War.

Equally important was the state's contribution of leaders and ideas to a new, young country. Virginians helped lead the American Revolution. They helped draw up the Constitution and the Bill of Rights, upon which the United States government is based. Four of our first five presidents were Virginians: George Washington, Thomas Jefferson, James Madison, and James Monroe.

Virginia is a state of elegant landscapes. In the west are forested mountains and sweeping valleys, in the east, rolling farmlands. Along the coast stretch wild and sandy seashores. The poet Walt Whitman in 1864 wrote: "How full of breadth the scenery, everywhere distant mountains, everywhere convenient rivers."

Four of Virginia's "convenient rivers," the Potomac, Rappahannock, York, and James, flow into Chesapeake Bay. The river mouths made convenient harbors for arriving colonists, and the rivers themselves became convenient highways for shipping tobacco from the flourishing riverside plantations.

The region of the low, sandy plain surrounding the bay is called the Tidewater because its rivers and inlets feel the pull of ocean tides. Much of this area is farming country, with fruits and vegetables trucked to nearby cities.

Hampton Roads, the deepwater harbor formed where the James River empties into the bay, today ranks as one of the country's busiest ports and is home base to almost 150 warships and 110,000 sailors and marines. Cities around the harbor export coal, tobacco, and other goods, while workers at Newport News shipyards turn out vessels ranging from tugboats to nuclear-powered aircraft carriers.

Southside Virginia, as the region south of the

Hampton Institute, founded after the Civil War to educate freed slaves to "lead their people," held classes that ranged from math to bricklaying. Booker T. Washington was a Hampton graduate.

James River is known, also contains the Great Dismal Swamp. George Washington called the 750-square-mile (1,943-sq-km) wetland a "glorious paradise." Now part of it is a wildlife refuge. More than 200 kinds of birds, including hummingbirds, orioles, tanagers, and a dozen warbler species, are found here.

Across the bay lies Virginia's Eastern Shore, part of the Delmarva Peninsula shared with Delaware and Maryland. Much of the peninsula is sparsely populated. Scores of inlets indent the bay side of the Eastern Shore, while on the ocean side barrier beaches, lagoons, and small offshore islands provide a home for wild ponies and snow geese.

West of the Tidewater extends the Piedmont, the rolling foothills of the Appalachian Mountains. A sharp drop-off called the fall line divides the Piedmont from the Atlantic Coastal Plain. Here rivers spill over falls onto the plain. Cities such as Alexandria, Fredericksburg, Richmond, and Petersburg grew along the fall line, where they tapped the power of fast rivers to run mills and factories and served as off-loading points for goods to be moved inland. Richmond,

the state capital, was also the capital of the Confederacy during much of the Civil War.

The Blue Ridge Mountains rise along the western edge of the Piedmont. Roaming the wooded areas are deer and black bears. In the autumn the bears like to raid apple orchards.

Between the Blue Ridge and the Allegheny Mountains lies the Shenandoah Valley. Shenandoah, an Indian word poetically translated as "daughter of the stars," is a fitting name for one of the country's most scenic and fertile valleys. Here farmers raise poultry, livestock, and dairy cattle. Each spring apple blossoms flower over large tracts of land. Limestone makes the valley soil fertile, and water seeping through the limestone bedrock in the nearby mountains has hollowed out caverns and rock formations.

Although Virginia was an agricultural state through most of its history, today its economy depends much less on tobacco and other farm products. Manufacturing and high-tech industries have grown rapidly, because of the state's central location along the eastern seaboard, its extensive transportation network, and the mushrooming growth of the federal government. Many federal facilities are located in Virginia, including the Central Intelligence Agency, centers for space research, and—in the Pentagon building—the headquarters of the Department of Defense and the U. S. Army, Navy, and Air Force. The Pentagon is the world's largest office building, and some 25,000 people work there. Federal and state government agencies account for about a fifth of the state's income.

BREAKS INTERSTATE PARK

Norton

Clinch River

Cumberland Gap

Highest point in Virginia
Mount Rogers
5,729 FEET
1,746 METERS

Bristol

Town is shared with Tennessee

1 2 3 4 5 6 7

Virginia is a state divided by Chesapeake Bay. The Delmarva Peninsula, which fronts on the Atlantic Ocean, is linked at its tip to the rest of the state by a 23-mile-long (37-km) combination bridge and tunnel.

In the west, the Appalachian Trail and Skyline Drive share the crest of the Blue Ridge Mountains overlooking the Shenandoah Valley. Here, near Front Royal, archaeologists have unearthed a Paleo-Indian settlement occupied from more than 11,000 years ago until about 8,500 years ago. Dark spots in the earth show where the Indians built shelters.

Area: *36th largest state, 40,767 sq mi (105,586 sq km)*
Population: *6,187,358; ranks 12th*
Major Cities: *Virginia Beach, 393,069; Norfolk, 261,229; Richmond, 203,056*
Manufacturing: *tobacco products, chemicals, transportation equipment, food products, electronics, scientific instruments, paper products, rubber and plastics, lumber and wood products, clothing*
Mining and Quarrying: *coal, stone*
Agriculture: *cattle, broilers, milk, tobacco, turkeys*
Other Important Activities: *federal government, tourism, printing and publishing, fishing*
Statehood: *tenth state; ratified the Constitution on June 25, 1788*

Flowering Dogwood

Cardinal

KILOMETERS 60
STATUTE MILES 40

Winchester
Shenandoah River
Leesbury
Potomac River
Arlington
District of Columbia
Reston
McLean
Vienna
Fairfax
Annandale
POTOMAC HERITAGE TRAIL
Alexandria
Front Royal
Manassas
Woodbridge
MARUMSCO N.W.R.
MASON NECK N.W.R.
Dale City
FEATHERSTONE N.W.R.
SHENANDOAH NATIONAL PARK
Dumfries
Culpeper
Harrisonburg
SKYLINE DRIVE
APPALACHIAN TRAIL
Rapidan River
Fredericksburg
Potomac River (PROPOSED)
Smith Island
CHINCOTEAGUE N.W.R. AND ASSATEAGUE ISLAND NATIONAL SEASHORE
ALLEGHENY MOUNTAINS
Shenandoah Valley
Staunton
Waynesboro
Lake Anna
Tappahannock
Chincoteague Island
WALLOPS I. N.W.R.
Hot Springs
Charlottesville
Rappahannock River
Tangier Island
DELMARVA PENINSULA
Wachapreague
APPALACHIAN MOUNTAINS
BLUE RIDGE MOUNTAINS
James River
Mattaponi River
Exmore
Covington
Lexington
Pamunkey River
CHESAPEAKE BAY
EASTERN SHORE OF VIRGINIA N.W.R.
Richmond
Bon Air
West Point
York River
ATLANTIC OCEAN
Appomattox River
PRESQUILE N.W.R.
Williamsburg
Yorktown
FISHERMAN I. N.W.R.
APPALACHIAN TRAIL
Lynchburg
Appomattox
Colonial Heights
Hopewell
Jamestown
PLUM TREE N.W.R.
Hampton Roads
CHESAPEAKE BAY BRIDGE-TUNNEL
Salem
Roanoke
Smith Mountain Lake
Farmville
Petersburg
Hampton
Newport News
Blacksburg
Cave Spring
Roanoke River
Smithfield
Radford
Christiansburg
Nottoway River
Norfolk Cape Henry
Pulaski
New River
BLUE RIDGE PARKWAY
Portsmouth
Chesapeake
Virginia Beach
MOUNT ROGERS N.R.A.
Suffolk
BACK BAY N.W.R.
Galax
Martinsville
South Boston
Emporia
GREAT DISMAL SWAMP N.W.R.
Lake Drummond
MACKAY ISLAND N.W.R.
Danville
Buggs Island Lake
Lake Gaston

1

2

3

Virginia

1 *Using a centuries-old technique called pound netting, fishermen of Tangier Island in Chesapeake Bay haul in a catch. Stakes driven into the bottom of the bay hold nets that guide fish into corral-like traps.*

2 *Wisps of fog streak the lowlands of the Shenandoah Valley. Grain fields and apple orchards flourish in this valley, known to Indians, pioneers, and Civil War soldiers.*

3 *A nuclear-powered submarine, looking like a big brother to a flock of balloons, slides down the ways at Newport News.*

4

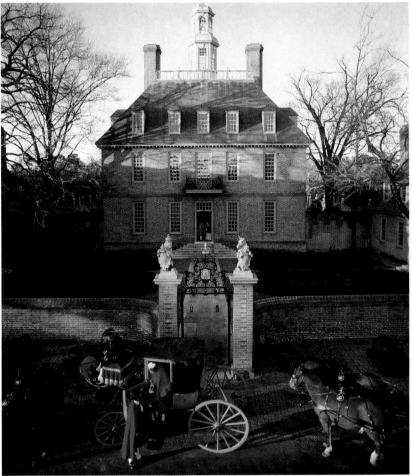

5

4 *A worker checks Smithfield hams hung to cure for six months. These hams are considered delicacies, noted for their robust, tangy flavor.*

5 *The Governor's Palace at Williamsburg, restored to regal splendor after burning to the ground in 1781, was home to seven royalist governors and two elected ones— Patrick Henry and Thomas Jefferson.*

Tennessee

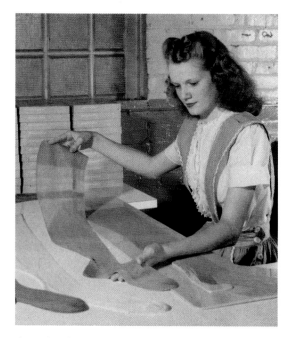

A worker in a Chattanooga hosiery mill in the late 1940s inspects nylon stockings for flaws. During World War II, nylon was used for parachutes, tent fabric, tire cords, and other wartime needs.

Tennessee is three states rolled into one, a long, narrow strip of land reaching from the rumpled ridges of the Great Smoky Mountains to the Mississippi River. Signs near the borders used to welcome motorists to the Three States of Tennessee—East, Middle, and West. That's because geography made each region so different from the other two.

Eastern Tennessee is ruggedly beautiful, a land of mountains row upon row to the horizon. It's hard to imagine, but 300 million years ago these rounded peaks may have thrust as high as the Himalaya. Time and erosion have since done their work, smoothing ragged summits, building soil, and draping slopes and valleys with forests. Each spring a host of trees and shrubs mounts extravagant displays of blossoms.

Amid these mountains, Tennessee shares Great Smoky Mountains National Park with neighboring North Carolina. The 520,004-acre (210,602-ha) park, the nation's most popular, lies within a day's drive of nearly half the people in the United States. The Smokies get their name from the bluish haze that sometimes hangs over the peaks and valleys, wisps of water vapor and evaporating plant oils. Indians knew the region as the Place of Blue Smoke. Black bears roam these mountains, as do deer, skunks, and wild boars.

Valleys and hollows lace the mountains, some of them so hidden and isolated that few people ever visit them. When the U. S. government wanted to make atomic bombs during World War II, it picked a secret site that it named Oak Ridge. Until after the war, very few outsiders ever found out about this town of 75,000 scientists and workers. No map showed it; officially it did not exist. Today people in Oak Ridge work in energy research, in the production of nuclear weapons, and in a multibillion-dollar effort to clean up the hazardous wastes from nearly half a century of nuclear weapons production.

Since the war, industry has grown in East Tennessee because of abundant electrical power created by dozens of hydroelectric dams along the winding Tennessee River and its tributaries. Factories in Alcoa produce and recycle aluminum, while Chattanooga turns out steel and textiles, including yarns, clothing, and hosiery.

There is also a dark side to some of East Tennessee's mountains. Remote, hard-to-reach valleys that once concealed illegal whiskey makers, called moonshiners, now harbor marijuana growers. Today illegal marijuana ranks as Tennessee's largest cash crop.

Middle Tennessee, a large, oval-shaped basin surrounded by a rim of highlands, lies west of the mountains and the Cumberland Plateau. Its principal city, Nashville, presides both as the state capital and world capital of country music. More than 200 music publishing and record companies jam a 14-block area of Nashville known as Music Row. Thousands of songwriters and performers, many working as clerks and waiters, crowd into the city, hoping to strike it rich.

Limestone bedrock underlies much of Middle Tennessee, giving the state some of its most fertile farmland. Tobacco, vegetables, and tomatoes flourish here. So do beef and dairy cattle and the Tennessee walking horse, prized for its smooth, easy-riding gait.

Since 1980 industry has come to Middle Tennessee in a big way with the opening of the General Motors Saturn subcompact car factory in Spring Hill and a Nissan plant in Smyrna. Japanese companies have invested in factories and distribution centers that make and sell everything from auto seats and oil filters to television sets and musical instruments.

West Tennessee, an area of fertile flatlands, lies between the Tennessee and Mississippi Rivers. This is mostly farming country dotted with small towns. Memphis, on the Mississippi River, is the financial and commercial hub of most of the lower Mississippi Valley. It is the world's largest cash cotton market, a producer of furniture and steel, and a center of biomedical research and telecommunications.

During the 1920s, Memphis musicians helped to popularize jazz and the blues. Beale Street is the home of the Memphis blues, based on black folk tunes. The street has been restored, and parks and museums grace the city's riverfront.

In the northwest corner of the state lies

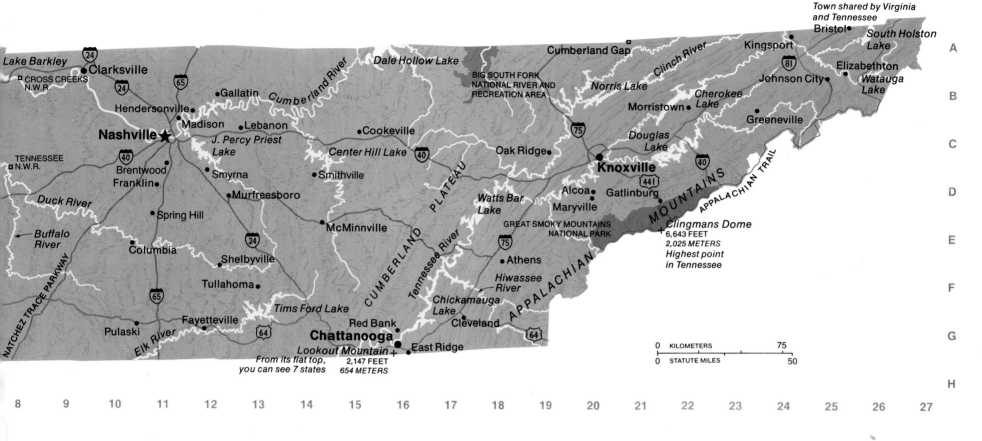

Town shared by Virginia and Tennessee

From its flat top, you can see 7 states

Lookout Mountain
2,147 FEET
654 METERS

Clingmans Dome
6,643 FEET
2,025 METERS
Highest point
in Tennessee

| 0 | KILOMETERS | 75 |
| 0 | STATUTE MILES | 50 |

Tennessee's only large natural lake, Reelfoot. A series of violent earthquakes in 1811 and 1812 created the lake, sloshing water from the Mississippi River into a low-lying area nearby. Today more than 50 kinds of fish swim among the cypress stumps of Reelfoot's shallow water, and the forests around it provide shelter for some 240 bird species, including 200 or so bald eagles that winter here.

Area: *34th largest state, 42,144 sq mi (109,152 sq km)*
Population: *4,877,185; ranks 17th*
Major Cities: *Memphis, 610,337; Nashville, 510,784; Knoxville, 165,121*
Manufacturing: *chemicals, food products, transportation equipment, machinery, electronics, metal products, rubber and plastics, paper products, clothing, stone, clay, and glass products, textiles*
Agriculture: *cattle, milk, soybeans, cotton, greenhouse and nursery products, tobacco*
Mining and Quarrying: *coal, stone, zinc*
Other Important Activities: *tourism, printing and publishing*
Statehood: *the 16th state; admitted June 1, 1796*

Iris

Mockingbird

No, there are not two Tennessee Rivers in Tennessee. It's the same river. But, from its source in the Appalachian Mountains of eastern Tennessee, the river flows out of the state near Chattanooga before turning north and entering western Tennessee.

Almost all of Tennessee's lakes are reservoirs, created by dams built to control floods and to supply power to the turbines that make electricity. Lakes such as Watts Bar and Douglas in eastern Tennessee are easy to see. They are where the rivers widen out behind dams built across their channels.

1

2

Tennessee

1 *Cumberland Gap, here a spillway for clouds beneath Pinnacle Overlook, also provided a route through the Appalachian Mountains for westward-bound settlers.*

2 *A bluegrass band plucks a tune at the Smithville jamboree, an annual country music contest that takes place in July.*

3 *The University of Tennessee's stadium rises beside the Tennessee River in Knoxville. Over 40,000 students attend classes on several campuses throughout the state.*

3

5

4

4 *A white-gloved worker checks the finish on a new car at a Nissan plant in Smyrna. Japan has invested nearly four billion dollars in Tennessee in nearly a hundred facilities that employ about 20,000 people.*

5 *Processing cotton in Memphis, women mix raw cotton in a hopper. A conveyor belt carries it to a ginning machine, an [en]gin[e] that combs out the seeds.*

North Carolina

A girl tending spools in a spinning mill in 1908 was one of more than 1.7 million youngsters from 10 to 15 years of age working in American factories, fields, and mines.

There was "gold in them thar hills," but the hills weren't in California. They were near Charlotte, North Carolina, in the foothills of the Appalachian Mountains that slant across the western part of the state. Here, in 1799, young Conrad Reed found a big, glittery rock that his family used as a doorstop for their cabin. Years passed before the Reeds learned that the glitter in their doorstop was gold. Other people soon found the deposit from which the rock had come, and until 1848, when gold was discovered in California, North Carolina was the country's biggest gold producer.

North Carolina has some 300 different kinds of minerals that were formed millions of years ago. Minerals mined today include mica, used to insulate electrical appliances; limestone for building; lithium, an important ingredient for making glass and aluminum; kaolin clay, used in the manufacture of dishes; and phosphate rock, used in making fertilizers. The state even has rubies, emeralds, and sapphires.

North Carolina has few deep, natural harbors. Most of the rivers trend north to south. In the days before roads, this limited the rivers' usefulness as highways into the interior. Along the coast are extensive swamps and marshy areas that discouraged early settlement.

Such geographic conditions meant that very few colonists came to North Carolina directly by ship from Europe. Most came from other colonies, people looking for new lands to farm. Not until Wilmington was founded in 1730 did North Carolina have a port of any size of its own.

A string of long, thin barrier islands known as the Outer Banks fringes much of North Carolina's Atlantic coast. Points of land called capes jut seaward from the islands on the bulge of the continent. Cape Hatteras, Cape Lookout, and Cape Fear are often swept by storms and hurricanes. Over the years the shifting sands and shoals of the Outer Banks have claimed some 2,000 vessels. In 1903, on the treeless, windswept dunes of the Outer Banks near Kitty Hawk, Orville and Wilbur Wright launched their *Flyer*, the world's first successful airplane.

It was near here, on Roanoke Island, that the famous Lost Colony of English settlers landed in 1587, and disappeared altogether by the time a second expedition reached them. Some historians think the colonists may have become part of an Indian tribe. Today the Lumbee Indians, who have spoken English for at least two centuries, claim that some of their ancestors were members of the missing colony.

Many of the Native Americans living in North Carolina are Cherokee. The Cherokee were among the Indians driven west along the Trail of Tears between 1830 and 1840. Some took refuge in the Great Smoky Mountains, and today their descendants live on a reservation in the western part of the state. A Cherokee myth explains the origin of the Smokies. The Great Buzzard, flying over the land, dipped too close to the ground, where his wings brushed out the valleys and pushed up the mountains.

Between the barrier islands and the mainland stretch broad, shallow expanses of water called sounds. The sounds, the rivers feeding into them, and the edges of the ocean provide food and shelter for shrimp, blue crabs, sea trout, and flounder. The northern part of this area, known as the Tidewater, includes the Great Dismal Swamp, which reaches into Virginia.

Farther inland, on drier ground, lie farms once given over to cotton and now heavily planted in tobacco. Today no other state turns out more tobacco products than North Carolina.

West of the Tidewater lies the Piedmont, a 200-mile-wide (320-km) swath of rolling hills largely covered with oaks, maples, and other hardwoods used to make furniture.

Beyond the Piedmont rise the forested slopes of the Appalachian chain, rugged country that includes the Blue Ridge and Great Smoky Mountains. Most of North Carolina's largest cities are located in the Piedmont, where abundant streams and reservoirs provide hydroelectric power to run mills and factories. In the days before electricity, the same streams powered textile factories run by waterwheels.

In recent years many North Carolina textile plants have shut down because of competition from foreign countries. Even so, the state has some 1,300 textile mills that make about half the nation's hosiery and many of its sheets, towels, and synthetic fabrics. Greensboro has the world's largest mill for weaving denim.

A major road and railroad building effort in

Map Labels

BLUE RIDGE PARKWAY
BLUE RIDGE MOUNTAINS
Yadkin River
Eden
Reidsville
GREAT DISMAL SWAMP N.W.R.
MACKAY ISLAND N.W.R.
Great Dismal Swamp
Roanoke Rapids
John H. Kerr Reservoir
Lake Gaston
CURRITUCK N.W.R.
Elizabeth City
Winston-Salem
Burlington
Henderson
Tar River
Roanoke River
ROANOKE RIVER N.W.R.
WRIGHT BROTHERS NATIONAL MEMORIAL
Kitty Hawk
Albemarle Sound
Roanoke I.
Lenoir
High Point
Greensboro
Durham
Chapel Hill
Rocky Mount
POCOSIN LAKES N.W.R.
ALLIGATOR RIVER N.W.R.
Morganton
Statesville
Thomasville
Lexington
Cary
Raleigh
PUNGO N.W.R.
PEA ISLAND N.W.R.
Hickory
High Rock Lake
Asheboro
Wilson
Salisbury
Sanford
Greenville
MATTAMUSKEET N.W.R.
CAPE HATTERAS NATIONAL SEASHORE
Lake Norman
Kannapolis
Concord
Goldsboro
SWANQUARTER N.W.R.
Shelby
Gastonia
Albemarle
Pee Dee River
Neuse River
Kinston
Pamlico River
Cape Hatteras
Charlotte
New Bern
Pamlico Sound
Ocracoke
Outer Banks
Raleigh Bay
PEE DEE N.W.R.
Fayetteville
CEDAR ISLAND N.W.R.
Monroe
Called Carolina Bays, thousands of shallow, oval depressions, rich in plants such as red bay, dot the Atlantic Coastal Plain
New River
Morehead City
CAPE LOOKOUT NATIONAL SEASHORE
Rockingham
Jacksonville
Cape Lookout
Lumberton
Onslow Bay
ATLANTIC OCEAN
Lake Waccamaw
Cape Fear River
Wilmington
Wrightsville Beach
Green Swamp
Cape Fear

A B C D E F G H J K L

the 1920s helped fuel North Carolina's growth as a modern industrial state. Today five interstate highways link the major cities, and about 20 rail lines haul the chemicals, machinery, and other goods the state produces. And in 1959 three universities, Duke, North Carolina State, and the University of North Carolina, opened a research center in the Raleigh-Durham area to develop and improve technologies in fields such as microelectronics and biotechnology.

Area: *28th largest state, 52,669 sq mi (136,413 sq km)*
Population: *6,628,637; ranks tenth*
Major Cities: *Charlotte, 395,934; Raleigh, 207,951; Greensboro, 183,521*
Manufacturing: *tobacco products, textiles, chemicals, electronics, machinery, food products, furniture, rubber and plastics, clothing, paper products, metal products*
Agriculture: *tobacco, broilers, hogs, turkeys, soybeans, milk*
Mining and Quarrying: *stone, phosphate rock, sand and gravel, clay*
Other Important Activities: *tourism, fishing*
Statehood: *the 12th state; ratified the Constitution on November 21, 1789*

Scale

0 ... KILOMETERS ... 60
0 ... STATUTE MILES ... 40

Cardinal

MAY 20th 1775
N C
APRIL 12th 1776

Flowering Dogwood

North Carolina's biggest rivers originate in the Blue Ridge Mountains in the western part of the state, or on the broad Piedmont, a plateau where most of the state's larger cities are located.

As the rivers flow southeastward, they change. From small, swift-flowing streams that follow narrow courses across the Piedmont, the rivers become wider and slower as they sprawl across the flat Atlantic Coastal Plain on their way to bays, sounds, and the Atlantic Ocean.

1

2

3

4

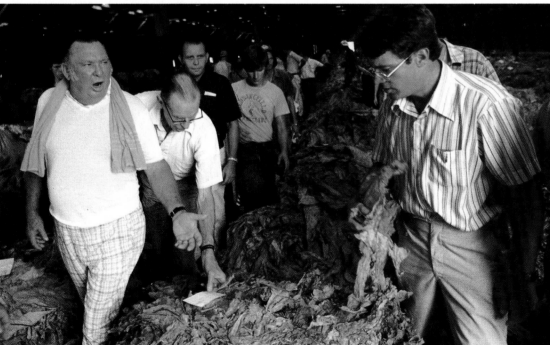

5

North Carolina

1 *Ringed by mountains, Asheville lies within easy reach of two national forests and Great Smoky Mountains National Park. Here its city hall stands in the shadow of the slightly taller county courthouse.*

2 *Preparing for a brain scan by a magnetic imaging machine, a technician at Duke University Hospital in Durham aligns the patient's head with help from a laser beam.*

3 *The nation's tallest lighthouse, with 257 steps to the balcony, stands guard over the shifting sands of Cape Hatteras.*

4 *Framed by a wooden oval, a craftsman near Hayesville uses a wood-shaving tool to shape a headboard. North Carolina's hardwood forests have made the state a major producer of fine furniture.*

5 *Buyers follow the distinctive singsong chant of a roving auctioneer as they bid for tobacco at a warehouse in Wilson.*

The Southeast

Ozark Plateau

Mississippi River

• Vicksburg

Sabine River

New Orleans

Mississippi River Delta

Most of the flat land shown in this painting was not here 600 million years ago. Its roots were attached to an ancestral continental plate known as Gondwanaland. Then, about 350 million years ago, ancestral North America, or Laurasia, and Gondwanaland began to bump together. The slow-motion collision broke or bent or melted rock and thrust up massive mountain ranges, including the Appalachians. When the two plates separated, a chunk of Gondwanaland stayed behind, stuck to North America. That chunk makes up parts of the broad, flat, low-lying Gulf and Atlantic Coastal Plains that swing through the southeastern states from the foot of the Appalachian Mountains—the Piedmont—to the Mississippi River. It also includes the flipper-shaped peninsula we know as Florida.

Part of the Coastal Plains dips beneath the waves and extends out to sea like a massive shelf bordering the continent. Called a continental shelf, the underwater part of the plains was largely dry land during the Ice Age, when sea levels were much lower because more water was frozen in glaciers. Woolly mammoths and saber-toothed cats roamed the continental shelf along Florida's west coast. Sometimes divers and fishermen bring up their bones from offshore, and geologists find their remains onshore.

Florida, a vast limestone peninsula that was once sea bottom, is part of an even larger underwater ledge that in places pops above the waves as islands in the Atlantic Ocean. Much of Florida's limestone is porous and saturated with fresh water, making the state a land of lakes.

South of the biggest lake spreads the Everglades, a vast, shallow sheet of fresh water. The water, only about six inches (15 cm) deep, moves southward so slowly that its flow is barely visible. Modern-day attempts to drain wetlands and control water supply have in some places disrupted the normal water flow, enabling salty seawater to penetrate inland and contaminate sources of fresh water.

A broad ridge of sand along the Atlantic shore, the remains of an old barrier island, provides just enough elevation to lift Miami and other seacoast cities out of the swamps.

Islands and long, thin offshore sandbars fringe much of the coast from north of Savannah to the Mississippi Delta. Yachts and fishing boats thread between the islands and the mainland, protected from storms and ocean waves. Boaters can travel this route, called the Intracoastal Waterway, much of the distance from Texas, through the Florida Keys, to Cape Cod.

Along the Gulf coast, the Mississippi River comes to an end. Sluggish and laden with silt and clay, a broth rich in sediments drained from 31 states and 2 Canadian provinces, the river slows and drops its load in a broad "bird-foot delta" that splays into three main channels as the river empties into the Gulf of Mexico.

Each year the river deposits millions of tons of mud, sand, and grit, enough to bulge Louisiana's shoreline 300 yards (270 m) seaward every year and to weigh it down so that it sinks a bit each year. New Orleans stands on land built up by the river within the last few thousand years—some of the nation's newest real estate. But today, as part of the delta reaches the outer edge of the continental shelf, the Mississippi's land-building days may dwindle as sediments sweep into the deep waters of the Gulf.

The Mississippi Valley, a floodplain varying from 25 to 125 miles (40 to 200 km) wide, merges with the Gulf Coastal Plain in a watery world of salt marshes and sluggish backwaters called bayous. Nearly a fifth of the continent's wild ducks and geese take refuge here in the winter, resting and feeding on a rich assortment of plants and insects. The valley, a downward bend in Earth's crust, is filled with fertile sediments, a gift delivered over the years by the river Indians called Missi Sipi—"father of waters."

APPALACHIAN MOUNTAINS

Atlanta

Montgomery

Savannah

St. Petersburg

Everglades

Miami

Florida Keys

SOUTH CAROLINA

GEORGIA

ALABAMA

FLORIDA

MISSISSIPPI

LOUISIANA

ARKANSAS

Arkansas

An Ozark hill woman during the 1940s makes and sells rag dolls whose faces are inspired by those of people in her community. Other Ozark dolls have heads made of dried apples or carved nuts.

The smallest state between the Mississippi River and the Pacific Ocean, Arkansas shares many characteristics of its neighboring regions. Midwestern Missouri borders the north. Solidly of the South, Louisiana, Mississippi, and Tennessee adjoin the south and east. And Texas and Oklahoma, with their southwestern flavor, border the west.

A diagonal line from the southwest to the northeast corner of Arkansas divides highlands from lowlands. West and north of the line lie the Ozark Plateau and the Ouachita Mountains. To the east and south sprawl the fertile valley of the Mississippi River and part of the wide Gulf Coastal Plain, a region that reaches into Arkansas from Texas and Louisiana and extends eastward to merge with Florida and the Atlantic Coastal Plain.

The Ozark Plateau, often called the Ozark Mountains, is an area of high tablelands eroded into rugged hills and deep valleys by swift streams. Small farmsteads nestle in isolated Ozark valleys. Settlers migrated there from the southern Appalachians in the 19th century. They and their descendants lived a hard, independent existence, farming the thin soil. But now new opportunities have come to the Ozarks. Arkansas has developed the country's largest broiler-chicken industry. Companies supply chicks and feed to farmers on credit. The farmers raise the fowl and then sell them for market.

Today, many tourists and retired people come to enjoy the natural beauty of the Ozarks. Young people often leave for the towns and cities, but Arkansas's population is still heavily rural, with almost half dwelling in the country or small towns and half in urban areas. In the Ouachita Mountains, the parallel ridges are wooded with pine and hardwood. These and other commercial forest areas provide jobs for people such as lumberjacks, pulp-mill workers, furniture makers, and workers who manufacture milk cartons and other paper products.

For thousands of years Indians bathed in the hot water of the many springs that rise in the Ouachitas. The Indians believed that the vapors were the warming breath of the Great Spirit and that their ancestors had been created in the springs. Now their sacred place has become Hot Springs National Park, the smallest and the only urban national park in the United States. At Hot Springs, water from mineral-carrying springs is piped into the town's bathhouses and fountains. Each year more than a million people visit the springs seeking relaxation or relief from arthritis and other aches and pains.

Separating the Ouachitas from the Ozark Plateau, the Arkansas River creates a broad, fertile valley, ideal for growing crops and raising cattle and poultry. Valuable deposits of coal and natural gas lie under the valley floor.

In the 18th century, French explorers from New Orleans traveled the Arkansas River. Near the middle of today's state they found a rocky outcrop on the south bank near a good crossing place. Eventually the landmark became known as *la petite roche*, the little rock. A settlement grew near the ford and took its name from the outcrop. Today Little Rock is the state capital and, with neighboring North Little Rock, a center of business and industry.

Until recently, the Arkansas carried little river traffic because it was prone to floods and to silting and snags that made navigation hazardous. Then, in 1971, with the completion of a system of locks and dams, the river opened to barge traffic that could carry goods such as sand and gravel, chemical fertilizers, or oil from the Mississippi River as far west as Tulsa, Oklahoma.

All river systems in Arkansas drain into the Mississippi. The Mississippi and its tributaries blanket the eastern third of Arkansas with alluvium, rich soil deposited by flowing water. This was cotton country in the 19th and early 20th centuries. Now fields of rice and soybeans create broad swaths of emerald green across the wide, flat valley. Arkansas grows more rice than any other state. Birds flying down the Mississippi Flyway on their fall migrations fatten on the nutritious grain during stopovers.

The western Gulf Coastal Plain possesses much of the state's mineral wealth, including natural gas and petroleum deposits. The sandy soil also supports vast pine forests and good grazing for cattle.

Attracting more industry to the state and expanding tourism will increase the prosperity of Arkansas. Nature has provided magnificent scenery and recreational opportunities, especially in the Ozarks and Ouachitas. Damming rivers for hydroelectricity and flood control has multiplied the number of lakes for fishing and boating. And, once in a while, nature unaided adds to its own bounty: A river will change course, cutting off an old, looping channel to form a new, crescent-shaped oxbow lake.

Area: *27th largest state, 53,187 sq mi (137,754 sq km)*
Population: *2,350,725; ranks 33rd*
Major Cities: *Little Rock, 175,795; Fort Smith, 72,798; North Little Rock, 61,741*
Manufacturing: *food products, electronics, paper products, metal products, machinery, lumber and wood products, chemicals*
Agriculture: *broilers, soybeans, rice, cattle, cotton, eggs, wheat, turkeys*
Mining and Quarrying: *oil and gas, sand and gravel, bromine, bauxite, stone*
Other Important Activities: *tourism*
Statehood: *the 25th state; admitted June 15, 1836*

Arkansas has no foot-hills. The state's high-lands, the Ouachita Mountains and the Ozark Plateau, rise almost with-out warning from plains that are nearly flat. East of the highlands is an alluvial plain, part of a valley formed by the Mississippi River as it shifted its channel over the ages and covered bottomlands with silt.

The state has two types of highlands. The older Ozarks are an up-lifted plateau carved by streams and rivers. The younger Ouachitas, by contrast, are folded sedi-ments pushed into paral-lel ridges by colliding continental plates.

0 KILOMETERS 50
0 MILES 40

1 2 3 4 5 6 7 8 9 10 11 12 13 14 15 16 17 18

A
B
C
D
E
F
G
H
J
K
L
M
N
O
P
Q

71 Bentonville
Eureka Springs
Berryville
65 Bull Shoals Lake
Mountain Home
Norfork Lake
Mammoth Spring
One of the world's largest single springs
St. Francis
Piggott
LOGAN CAVE N.W.R. Rogers
Beaver Lake
62 Harrison
Pocahontas
49
Springdale
Siloam Springs
Fayetteville
Boxley
Buffalo River
Mountain View
White River
Walnut Ridge
Paragould
63
BIG LAKE N.W.R.
Blytheville
62
OZARK PLATEAU
167
Black River
Jonesboro
BOSTON MOUNTAINS
Batesville
Trumann
Osceola
71
Greers Ferry Lake
Newport
55
Marked Tree
Ozark
40 Clarksville
Heber Springs
67
Van Buren
Fort Smith
Lake Dardanelle
7
65
Searcy
Little Red River
Wynne
Saint Francis River
West Memphis
WAPANOCCA NATIONAL WILDLIFE REFUGE
Paris
Russellville
Morrilton
Magazine Mountain 2,753 FEET 839 METERS Highest point in Arkansas
HOLLA BEND NATIONAL WILDLIFE REFUGE
Conway
Lake Conway
Cabot
Jacksonville
Sherwood
CACHE RIVER NATIONAL WILDLIFE REFUGE
Forrest City
OUACHITA MOUNTAINS
Lake Maumelle
North Little Rock
Little Rock
Brinkley
79
270
Blue Mountain 2,623 FEET 800 METERS
Lake Ouachita
Lonoke
40
Marianna
Mena
HOT SPRINGS NATIONAL PARK
70 Benton
Arkansas River
Stuttgart
White River
49
Helena
270
Hot Springs
West Helena
Mississippi River
71 59
70
Lake Greeson
Malvern
De Gray Lake
65
270
Pine Bluff
DeWitt
WHITE RIVER N.W.R.
Murfreesboro
CRATER OF DIAMONDS STATE PARK The diamond mine is the exposed surface of a volcanic pipe millions of years old
Arkadelphia
7
167
Saline River
65
Dumas
1
De Queen
Millwood Lake
Prescott
Fordyce
79
Bayou Bartholomew
Monticello
Ashdown
Red River
30 Hope
Camden
4
Warren
Dermott
Texarkana
The Arkansas-Texas state line runs through the center of this city
Stamps
7
Magnolia
82
El Dorado
Lake Chicot This lake was once a loop of the Mississippi River
71
Lake Erling
FELSENTHAL NATIONAL WILDLIFE REFUGE
Crossett
165
65
OVERFLOW N.W.R.
Eudora

Apple Blossom

Mockingbird

ARKANSAS

1

Arkansas

1 *A country school and a Baptist church share a quiet corner in an Ozark valley. Such serenity appeals to a growing number of tourists and harried city folk.*

2 *Woodcarvers at the Ozark Folk Center in Mountain View preserve a centuries-old craft. People from across the U. S. come here to learn traditional handicrafts, as well as Ozark folklore and music.*

3 *An experiment at the University of Arkansas in Fayetteville envelops a superconductor in wisps of frigid nitrogen. This superconductor can suspend magnets above and below it. In the future such superconductors may be used in electric cables and in trains that speed quietly above their rails on a magnetic cushion.*

2

3

4

5

4 *Rice is harvested near West Memphis in the fertile Mississippi Valley. Arkansas grows one-third of all U. S. rice, some of which goes into cereal, flour, and vinegar.*

5 *Chicks gather around a water dish in a broiler house. Arkansas exports much of its dark meat to the Japanese, who prefer it to the white that most Americans buy.*

Mississippi

Choctaw Indians sit for a portrait in 1908. By 1910 only about 1,000 Mississippi Choctaw remained of the some 20,000 who lived here when Hernando de Soto and other Europeans arrived.

Before the Civil War, King Cotton ruled Mississippi. Steamboats on the rivers were heaped high with bales of the fluffy white fiber. On the plantations, young women in hoopskirts and crinolines sat under shady magnolia trees. Elegant young men galloped on horseback, small dogs yipping alongside. Papa stood on the white-columned porch, surveying his domain.

Such scenes tell only part of the story. They hark back to a time when the social world of Mississippi, as of many other parts of the country, was strictly divided. The lives of plantation owners were very different from the struggles of poor white farmers and black slaves.

The Civil War changed many things, but poor whites and poor blacks still struggled. With slavery abolished, the plantation system became one of tenant farming. Sharecroppers, both black and white, were given land to work, seeds, and tools in exchange for a hefty portion of the harvest owed to the landowner.

The rich, fertile soil that produced cotton was laid down over millennia by the Mississippi River. Each year floods sent tons of alluvium, riverborne sand and silt, over the banks. In time, soil 150 feet (45 m) deep formed on the Mississippi's alluvial plain, or the delta, as the local people call it. Topsoil, the layer from which plants get most of their nutrients, reaches a depth of 25 feet (8 m) in some places.

The alluvial plain, narrow along the state's southwestern border, widens north of Vicksburg to encompass the basin between the Mississippi and Yazoo Rivers. Levees—barriers of earth, sandbags, rock, concrete, or steel—line the banks and usually keep the rivers from overflowing. Delta farmers still raise cotton, but they also grow soybeans, rice, and wheat and have added a new, finny "crop." In purposely flooded old cotton fields, catfish fatten on grain, like livestock, until they are ready to process and ship out. Mississippi leads the country in meeting the demand for this favorite. Many delta families, for whom there often is no other work, can make some money by working in plants that process catfish and rice.

East of the delta lies the eastern Gulf Coastal Plain. Its northern part is a land of gently rolling hills and woodlands. The northeast also contains a stretch of land known as the Black Prairie, an extension of Alabama's black belt. Here corn, hay, and livestock are raised in the rich, dark soil that gives the region its name.

Three major Indian groups once lived in Mississippi: Choctaw, Chickasaw, and Natchez. Today, about 8,000 Indians remain. These are mostly Choctaw, and most of them live on or near their reservation near Philadelphia. Today's Indians are descendants of those who refused to leave their homes when the U. S. government forced the southeastern Indians westward on the march known as the Trail of Tears. One Choctaw who stayed behind gave this reason: "In those aged pines you hear the ghosts of the departed. Their ashes are here, and we have been left to protect them." Not far from Philadelphia are a cave and a mound that Choctaw revere as the birthplace of their tribe.

Jackson, the state capital, sits on the bluffs of the Pearl River and near the Natchez Trace, a wilderness road used by Indians, settlers, and traders. One in eight Mississippians lives in Jackson, and the percentage is growing as manufacturing continues to overtake farming and as people move to urban areas. Even so, Mississippi is a highly rural state, with more than half of its people living in the country or in small towns. Nearly all of Mississippi's residents were born in the United States; 35 percent are black, a higher proportion than in any other state.

About half of Mississippi is forested. Southern pine grows abundantly in the southern part of the Gulf Coastal Plain. By 1930, though, much of the state's timber had been depleted. Since then, reforestation programs and careful harvesting ensure survival of the forest industry and wildlife habitats.

A warm, sunny climate, abundant seafood, and deepwater ports have attracted settlers and vacationers to the coast along the Gulf of Mexico for nearly 300 years. Biloxi, Mississippi's oldest permanent settlement, was founded by the French in 1699 and served for a time as capital of their New World empire. Mississippian Jefferson Davis, the president of the Confederacy, spent his last years here at his estate, Beauvoir, overlooking the Gulf.

The Gulf coast's population is growing rapidly. Jobs in manufacturing, shipping, shipbuilding, and the petroleum industry draw residents from all over the state. The United States military frequently awards large contracts to the shipyards of Pascagoula. Huge catches of seafood are taken from the Gulf, including tons of its famous shrimp. Bananas, melons, coconuts, and pineapples pass through a terminal at Gulfport that is specialized to handle fruit.

Area: *32nd largest state, 47,689 sq mi (123,515 sq km)*
Population: *2,573,216; ranks 31st*
Major Cities: *Jackson, 196,637; Biloxi, 46,319; Greenville, 45,226*
Manufacturing: *food products, transportation equipment, electronics, lumber and wood products, paper products, clothing, furniture, chemicals, machinery*
Agriculture: *cotton, broilers, soybeans, cattle, aquaculture, rice, milk*
Mining and Quarrying: *oil and gas, sand and gravel, clay*
Other Important Activities: *fishing*
Statehood: *the 20th state; admitted December 10, 1817*

Mississippi's western boundary looks like a battle between bedsprings, with twists and curlicues all over the place. Some curlicues, such as Lake Mary and Moon Lake, are oxbow lakes. Both were formed when the Mississippi cut through the narrow neck of a loop and abandoned its old channel, leaving crescent-shaped lakes.

The tattered-looking western boundary results from shifting river channels. These changes, called avulsions, often leave chunks of neighboring states on the wrong side of the river but do not alter ownership of the land.

Mockingbird

Magnolia

Southaven

Corinth

Pickwick Lake

72

Holly Springs

Arkabutla Lake

Coldwater River

Woodall Mountain
806 FEET
246 METERS
Highest point in Mississippi

Booneville

78

Senatobia

New Albany

61

49

Moon Lake

Little Tallahatchie River

Sardis Lake

Oxford

6

Batesville

Pontotoc

Tupelo

Clarksdale

Mississippi River

Enid Lake

55

Amory

A45

61

Tallahatchie River

Grenada Lake

Aberdeen

49W

Yalobusha River

Grenada

Tombigbee River

45

Cleveland

Natchez Trace Parkway

West Point

82

Greenwood

Winona

Columbus

Leland

Indianola

MATHEWS BRAKE NATIONAL WILDLIFE REFUGE

Starkville

Yazoo River

MORGAN BRAKE NATIONAL WILDLIFE REFUGE

NOXUBEE NATIONAL WILDLIFE REFUGE

Greenville

Yockanookany River

Big Black River

Louisville

YAZOO NATIONAL WILDLIFE REFUGE

HILLSIDE NATIONAL WILDLIFE REFUGE

Kosciusko

15

45

PANTHER SWAMP NATIONAL WILDLIFE REFUGE

Yazoo City

MISSISSIPPI CHOCTAW INDIAN RESERVATION

Philadelphia

Giant logs carried here as driftwood by a prehistoric river

Carthage

Pearl River

49

Mississippi Petrified Forest

Canton

16

MISSISSIPPI CHOCTAW INDIAN RESERVATION

Okatibbee Lake

Ridgeland

Ross R. Barnett Reservoir

Clinton

Forest

Meridian

20

59

Vicksburg

Jackson ★

Pearl

20

45

61

Brandon

Natchez Trace Parkway

Crystal Springs

55

Laurel

Waynesboro

84

Washington

Mississippi River

Brookhaven

Ellisville

Natchez

84
98

Homochitto River

84

Chickasawhay River

ST. CATHERINE CREEK N.W.R.

Hattiesburg

Petal

McComb

Columbia

Lake Mary

61

98

Pearl River

Woodville

59

49

BOGUE CHITTO NATIONAL WILDLIFE REFUGE

Only remaining home of endangered Mississippi sandhill crane

98

Pascagoula River

MISSISSIPPI SANDHILL CRANE NATIONAL WILDLIFE REFUGE

Picayune

Moss Point

GRAND BAY N.W.R.

D'Iberville

10

Gulfport

90

Long Beach

Biloxi

Pascagoula

Gautier

Bay St. Louis

Ocean Springs

GULF ISLANDS NATIONAL SEASHORE

Gulf of Mexico

0 KILOMETERS 60
0 STATUTE MILES 40

A B C D E F G H J K L M N O P Q R S T

1 2 3 4 5 6 7 8 9 10 11 12

1

Mississippi

1 *A girl tosses a ball in front of D'Evereux, her family home. Built in 1840, the columned house is one of many Greek Revival buildings surviving in the Natchez area.*

2 *Young men and women in costumes of the Old South waltz at the annual Confederate Pageant soiree in Natchez. The men are dressed as cadets from historic Jefferson College in nearby Washington.*

2

3

4

5

3 *The paddle wheeler* Delta Queen, *built in 1926, docks at Natchez-Under-the-Hill, once a rowdy section of town where rivermen and outlaws drank and gambled.*

4 *A combine harvests cotton along the Yazoo River in the rich delta region. Mechanical pickers can do the work of many people.*

5 *A rooster plays king-of-the-mountain on a henhouse plank after a flood near Vicksburg. The Mississippi sometimes overflows despite levees built to contain it.*

Alabama

In a cave in the northeastern corner of Alabama lie the remains of some of the area's earliest residents. Not only their bones but also their food, pottery, tools, and weapons give us clues to the way these prehistoric hunters and gatherers lived, camping in caves throughout the area in the fall and winter and sometimes year-round. The record of human habitation in Russell Cave is the longest. It was used for some 8,000 years, until, about a thousand years ago, the Indians became farmers and settled down in villages.

Not far from Russell Cave, the space age appears. In 1960 NASA opened the George C. Marshall Space Flight Center in Huntsville. The center's rockets sent the first American astronaut into space, and its Saturn rockets put men on the moon. Unlike other parts of the state, Huntsville draws residents from all over the country to work in its space-related industries.

The Appalachian range extends its southernmost ridges and valleys, with their mineral wealth, into northeastern Alabama. During the Civil War, the area's iron ore went into most of the shells, shot, and rifles used by the Confederacy. The Appalachians also hold coal and limestone which, together with iron, are needed to make steel. The Birmingham region filled with steel mills, creating jobs that attracted many rural Alabamians. Now cheaper iron ore from Venezuela has closed many of the iron mines, and steel has been eclipsed as an area employer by the University of Alabama's medical research center, as well as by government jobs.

Alabama's early wealth was built on enormous cotton crops grown on slave-worked plantations. Central Alabama has the richest agricultural land, a strip of rich, dark soil known as the black belt. But no matter how fertile the soil, a single crop grown season after season eventually depletes the soil's nutrients, and cotton did this. Finally it took the disastrous invasion of the cotton-destroying boll weevil in the early 1900s to convince Alabama farmers to diversify their crops. Cotton remains a major crop, but is now surpassed by peanuts. Cattle and poultry raising have also taken over many cotton fields. So grateful were the people of the town of Enterprise for the lesson taught by the boll weevil that they erected a statue to the long-snouted insect.

More than two-thirds of Alabama is forested, mostly with oak and pine. Tree farming by corporations that own 21 percent of the land replenishes the timber cut for pulp, paper, and lumber. The forest products industry is now the state's chief source of income.

For most of Alabama's history, the northwestern corner was a depressed region. People

---

In 1902 George Washington Carver teaches at Tuskegee Institute, a black college then headed by Booker T. Washington. Carver's pioneering research helped revolutionize Southern agriculture.

there worked hard to raise a few crops and enjoyed few amenities. The creation of the Tennessee Valley Authority by the federal government in the 1930s brought cheap and plentiful electricity to the area by damming the Tennessee River. A side benefit was a multitude of beautiful lakes offering residents and visitors choice fishing, boating, and other water sports.

In 1985 another project was completed. This one linked the Tennessee and Tombigbee river systems so that goods from the interior could reach Alabama's only port, Mobile. The building of the Tenn-Tom waterway moved more earth than the construction of the Panama Canal. It also gave Mobile access to the network of waterways in the eastern United States.

Mobile sits on the low Gulf Coastal Plain at Mobile Bay, an inlet of the Gulf of Mexico. In its architecture, gardens, and street names, Mobile bears witness to its early days of French and Spanish settlement. Today deeply dredged shipping lanes enable oceangoing vessels to berth at Mobile's docks. Cargoes leaving the port include steel, soybeans, lumber, and oil and natural gas from the state's southern region.

More than 60 percent of Alabama's population lives in cities and towns. About one-fourth of the state's residents are blacks. Some of the greatest gains of the civil rights movement of the 1950s and '60s were made in Alabama. It was here that a young Martin Luther King, Jr., led a protest against the law that jailed Rosa Parks, a black Montgomery seamstress, for not giving up her bus seat to a white man. Voting rights for blacks all over the South were won partly as the result of efforts concentrated in Alabama.

Area: *29th largest state, 51,705 sq mi (133,915 sq km)*
Population: *4,040,587; ranks 22nd*
Major Cities: *Birmingham, 265,968; Mobile, 196,278; Montgomery, 187,106*
Manufacturing: *paper products, chemicals, metals, textiles, clothing, machinery, rubber and plastics, food products, transportation equipment, electronics, metal products, lumber and wood products*
Mining and Quarrying: *coal, oil and gas, stone*
Agriculture: *broilers, cattle, greenhouse and nursery products, peanuts, eggs, cotton, soybeans*
Other Important Activities: *federal government, fishing*
Statehood: *the 22nd state; admitted December 14, 1819*

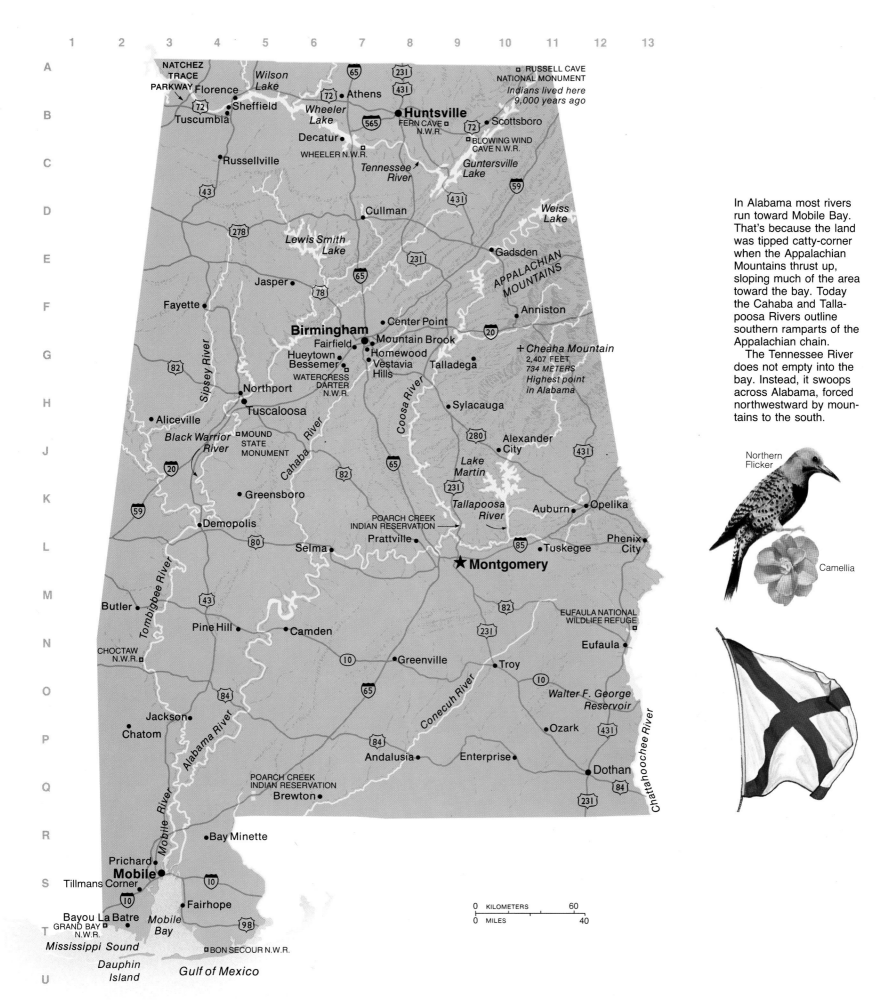

| | 1 | 2 | 3 | 4 | 5 | 6 | 7 | 8 | 9 | 10 | 11 | 12 | 13 |

A

NATCHEZ TRACE PARKWAY · Florence

Wilson Lake

72 · Athens

231

□ RUSSELL CAVE NATIONAL MONUMENT

Indians lived here 9,000 years ago

65

B

72 · Sheffield

Tuscumbia

Wheeler Lake

565

Huntsville

FERN CAVE N.W.R. □

72 · Scottsboro

C

· Russellville

Decatur ·

WHEELER N.W.R.

□ BLOWING WIND CAVE N.W.R.

Tennessee River ↗

Guntersville Lake

59

D

43

278

· Cullman

Weiss Lake

431

E

Lewis Smith Lake

· Jasper

65

231

· Gadsden

APPALACHIAN MOUNTAINS

F

· Fayette

78

· Center Point

· Anniston

20

+ *Cheaha Mountain*
2,407 FEET
734 METERS
Highest point in Alabama

G

Sipsey River

Birmingham
Fairfield
Hueytown · Homewood
Bessemer · Vestavia Hills
WATERCRESS DARTER N.W.R.

Mountain Brook

· Talladega

The Tennessee River does not empty into the bay. Instead, it swoops across Alabama, forced northwestward by mountains to the south.

H

· Aliceville

Northport ·
Tuscaloosa

Black Warrior River

□ MOUND STATE MONUMENT

Coosa River

· Sylacauga

280

J

20

Cahaba River

· Alexander City

431

Northern Flicker

K

59

· Greensboro

82

65

Lake Martin

231

Tallapoosa River

Auburn · · Opelika

L

Demopolis ·

80

· Selma

· Prattville

POARCH CREEK INDIAN RESERVATION →

85 · Tuskegee

Phenix City

Camellia

M

Tombigbee River

· Butler

43

★ **Montgomery**

82

EUFAULA NATIONAL WILDLIFE REFUGE □

N

CHOCTAW N.W.R. □

· Pine Hill · Camden

10

· Greenville

231

· Troy

· Eufaula

O

84

65

Conecuh River

10

Walter F. George Reservoir

P

· Jackson
· Chatom

Alabama River

84

· Andalusia

· Enterprise

· Ozark

431

Chattahoochee River

· Dothan

Q

POARCH CREEK INDIAN RESERVATION
· Brewton

231

84

R

Mobile River

· Bay Minette

S

Prichard ·
Mobile
Tillmans Corner ·

10

10

· Fairhope

T

Bayou La Batre ·
GRAND BAY N.W.R.

98

Mobile Bay

□ BON SECOUR N.W.R.

U

Mississippi Sound

Dauphin Island

Gulf of Mexico

In Alabama most rivers run toward Mobile Bay. That's because the land was tipped catty-corner when the Appalachian Mountains thrust up, sloping much of the area toward the bay. Today the Cahaba and Tallapoosa Rivers outline southern ramparts of the Appalachian chain.

| 0 | KILOMETERS | 60 |
| 0 | MILES | 40 |

Alabama

1 *Shrimp boats in festive bunting gather for the annual Blessing of the Fleet at Bayou La Batre. Sprinkling holy water, the archbishop on the foredeck prays for safe passage and a good catch.*

2 *The fertile fields of Alabama's black belt once lay at the ancient shoreline of the Gulf of Mexico. Ocean oozes enriched with the limy skeletons of tiny marine creatures formed the soil when the sea retreated millions of years ago.*

3 *Upraised porcelain hands at a Dothan factory will give shape to medical gloves when dipped into vats of liquid latex.*

4 *Protected by a welding hood, a student at a Bessemer technical college hones skills that will prepare her for a job in steel production or other manufacturing.*

5 *Upside-down and feeling weightless in a shuttle mock-up, a visitor at the United States Space Camp in Huntsville experiences the free-floating thrill of space flight.*

1

2

3

4

5

Georgia

An Ocmulgee River steamboat takes on cargo at Hawkinsville around 1900. Georgia riverboats carried passengers and freight such as barrels of turpentine, a product of Georgia's pine woods.

The largest state east of the Mississippi River, Georgia is also one of the most varied, physically and economically. The land slopes from the Blue Ridge Mountains in the northeast to sea level in the southeast or, as Georgians say, "from Rabun Gap to Tybee Light." Sparsely populated, the Blue Ridge region provides timber from its vast stands of pine and hardwood; its rivers supply hydroelectric power. Miners quarry the state's granite and the fine, white marble that was used for Abraham Lincoln's statue at the Lincoln Memorial in Washington, D. C.

Also in the north, farmers in the highlands raise poultry. Georgia ranks near the top in egg production—more than a million dozen a day—and in raising broiler chickens. Manufacturing, a growing industry, employs increasing numbers of people, including aircraft assemblers at the Lockheed-Georgia plant in Marietta, the state's largest private employer. There's a good chance that the carpeting in your home or your car was made in factories near Dalton. About half of the country's carpeting comes from this region, and so does much of its cloth.

At the start of the Civil War, Atlanta was a thriving town in the red clay hills of Georgia's Piedmont. Burned to the ground by the Union Army in 1864, Atlanta soon began rebuilding and has never stopped. Today it is the financial, trade, and transportation center of the South, and the world headquarters for Coca-Cola, formulated by an Atlanta druggist more than a century ago. Through the 1980s Atlanta grew rapidly, drawing residents from both inside and outside the state. Two of every five Georgians now live in the Atlanta metropolitan area; two-thirds of those in the city itself are black, as are a fourth of all Georgians. The birthplace of Martin Luther King, Jr., Atlanta became a headquarters for the civil rights movement.

Atlanta's growing population has pushed its suburbs out into an ever widening arc of housing developments, shopping centers, and office complexes, mostly to the city's north. Recently the water needs of all these people have fueled disputes with neighboring states over the resources of shared rivers.

Georgia's rivers become falls and rapids as they tumble from the Piedmont onto the Coastal Plain, the state's largest region. The most fertile farmlands are found in southern Georgia. Once cotton reigned here as the sole source of agricultural wealth. In the early 1900s, after destruction of several cotton crops by the boll weevil, Georgia farmers began to diversify. Farmers in and near the county named Peach, around Fort Valley, grow tons of that fruit. Around the town of Vidalia, farmers grow the sweet onion that can be eaten raw like an apple. Over most of southern Georgia, peanuts thrive. Peanut farmer Jimmy Carter, from Plains, became the 39th President of the United States.

Forests of loblolly, slash, and shortleaf and longleaf pines cover central and southern Georgia. The timber cut in the state makes Georgia the country's leader in pulp production.

Alligators slide through Okefenokee, the country's second largest freshwater swamp. The 700-square-mile (1,820-sq-km) wetland extends into Florida, preserving an ecosystem of swamp, bog, and marsh that shelters some 12,000 gators in addition to 100 other reptile and mammal species and more than 200 bird species.

During the Civil War, when Union Gen. William Tecumseh Sherman left Atlanta smoldering and began his march to the sea, his goal was the city of Savannah. Founded by the British in 1733, Savannah soon became a major international port. Built on a bluff overlooking the Savannah River, the city preserves many beautiful homes that predate the Civil War. Unlike Atlanta and the settlements destroyed all along his march, Sherman spared Savannah, making its surrender a Christmas "gift" to President Lincoln in 1864.

Low-lying barrier islands with densely wooded interiors and sandy beaches protect Georgia's mainland and stretch up and down the coast into South Carolina and Florida. In the late 1700s, plantation owners brought in slaves to clear the islands and tend the indigo, rice, and cotton crops they planted there. Although some of the islands have been developed as resorts, descendants of the slaves remain. Isolation has helped preserve their unique language, called Gullah, rich with the sounds of 17th-century English and West African languages.

Area: *21st largest state, 58,910 sq mi (152,576 sq km)*
Population: *6,478,216; ranks 11th*
Major Cities: *Atlanta, 394,017; Columbus, 179,278; Savannah, 137,560*
Manufacturing: *transportation equipment, textiles, food products, paper products, chemicals, electronics, clothing, machinery, lumber and wood products, stone, clay, and glass products, metal products*
Agriculture: *broilers, peanuts, cattle, eggs, hogs, milk, greenhouse and nursery products*
Mining and Quarrying: *clay, stone*
Other Important Activities: *tourism, printing and publishing*
Statehood: *the fourth state; ratified the Constitution on January 2, 1788*

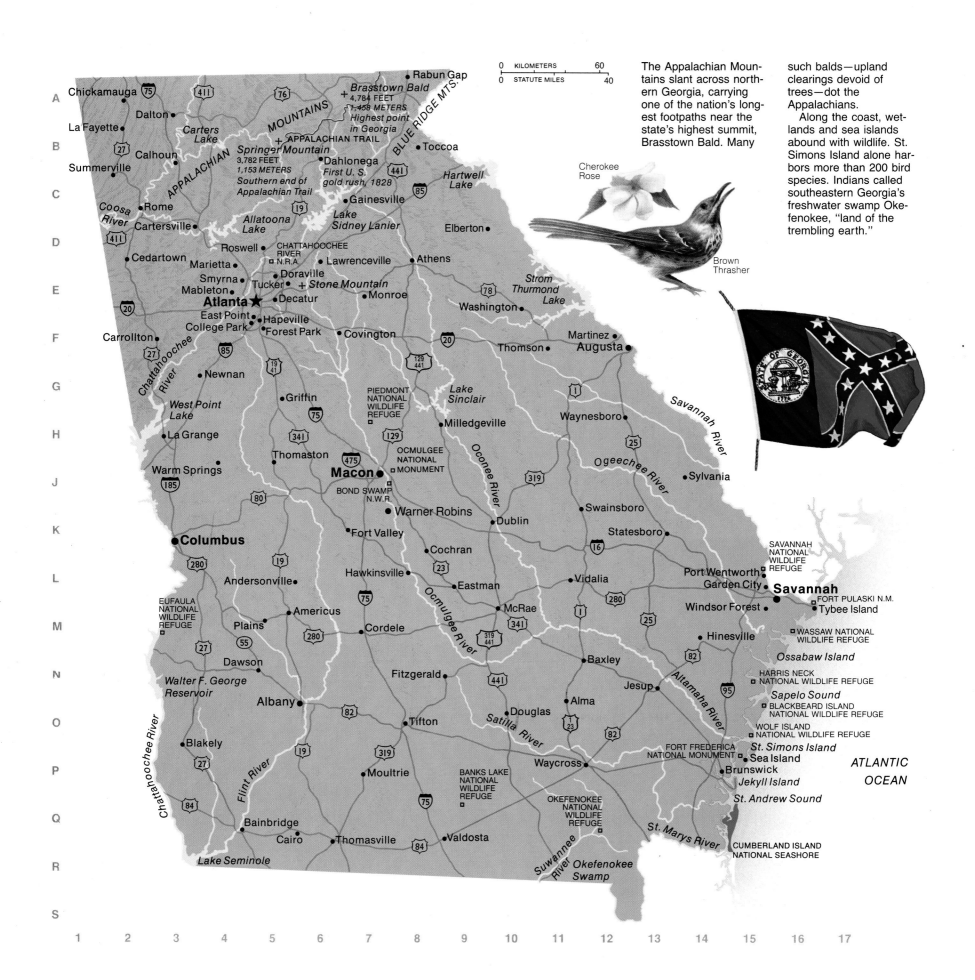

The Appalachian Mountains slant across northern Georgia, carrying one of the nation's longest footpaths near the state's highest summit, Brasstown Bald. Many such balds—upland clearings devoid of trees—dot the Appalachians.

Along the coast, wetlands and sea islands abound with wildlife. St. Simons Island alone harbors more than 200 bird species. Indians called southeastern Georgia's freshwater swamp Okefenokee, "land of the trembling earth."

Cherokee Rose

Brown Thrasher

Map labels

Chickamauga
La Fayette
Dalton
Summerville
Calhoun
Carters Lake
Rome
Cartersville
Cedartown
Roswell
Marietta
Smyrna
Mableton
Atlanta
Decatur
Tucker
Doraville
Stone Mountain
Monroe
East Point
Hapeville
College Park
Forest Park
Carrollton
Newnan
West Point Lake
La Grange
Griffin
Warm Springs
Thomaston
Macon
Columbus
Andersonville
Plains
Americus
Cordele
Dawson
Albany
Blakely
Bainbridge
Cairo
Thomasville
Lake Seminole
Moultrie
Tifton
Fitzgerald
Fort Valley
Warner Robins
Hawkinsville
Cochran
Eastman
McRae
Douglas
Alma
Waycross
Valdosta
Dublin
Swainsboro
Vidalia
Statesboro
Jesup
Baxley
Hinesville
Windsor Forest
Savannah
Port Wentworth
Garden City
Brunswick
Sylvania
Waynesboro
Martinez
Augusta
Thomson
Washington
Milledgeville
Athens
Lawrenceville
Gainesville
Elberton
Hartwell Lake
Toccoa
Rabun Gap
Brasstown Bald
4,784 FEET
1,458 METERS
Highest point in Georgia
Springer Mountain
3,782 FEET
1,153 METERS
Southern end of Appalachian Trail
Dahlonega
First U.S. gold rush, 1828

APPALACHIAN MOUNTAINS
BLUE RIDGE MTS.
APPALACHIAN TRAIL
Allatoona Lake
Coosa River
Chattahoochee River
CHATTAHOOCHEE RIVER N.R.A.
Lake Sidney Lanier
Strom Thurmond Lake
Savannah River
Ogeechee River
Oconee River
Ocmulgee River
Altamaha River
Satilla River
Suwannee River
St. Marys River
Flint River
Lake Sinclair
PIEDMONT NATIONAL WILDLIFE REFUGE
OCMULGEE NATIONAL MONUMENT
BOND SWAMP N.W.R.
Walter F. George Reservoir
EUFAULA NATIONAL WILDLIFE REFUGE
SAVANNAH NATIONAL WILDLIFE REFUGE
FORT PULASKI N.M.
Tybee Island
WASSAW NATIONAL WILDLIFE REFUGE
Ossabaw Island
HARRIS NECK NATIONAL WILDLIFE REFUGE
Sapelo Sound
BLACKBEARD ISLAND NATIONAL WILDLIFE REFUGE
WOLF ISLAND NATIONAL WILDLIFE REFUGE
FORT FREDERICA NATIONAL MONUMENT
St. Simons Island
Sea Island
Jekyll Island
St. Andrew Sound
CUMBERLAND ISLAND NATIONAL SEASHORE
BANKS LAKE NATIONAL WILDLIFE REFUGE
OKEFENOKEE NATIONAL WILDLIFE REFUGE
Okefenokee Swamp
ATLANTIC OCEAN

KILOMETERS 60
STATUTE MILES 40

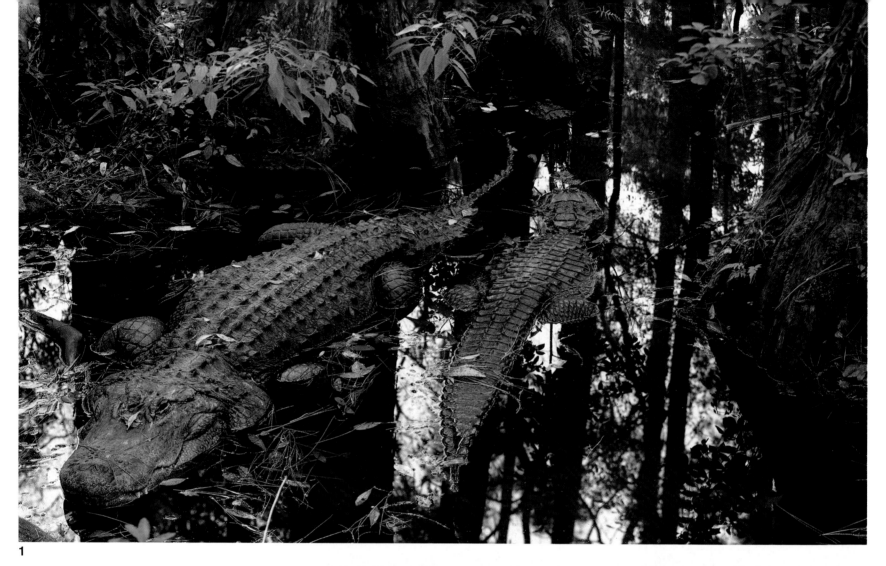

Georgia

1 *American alligators, protected by law from poachers who sell their skins for shoes, purses, and belts, again flourish in the vegetation-stained "black water" of Okefenokee Swamp.*

2 *Delta Airlines mechanics in Atlanta check a jet engine by attaching a "bellmouth" to intensify air intake.*

3 *Enclosed skyways connect shops and hotels at Peachtree Center in downtown Atlanta.*

4 *Peanuts are Georgia's most valuable crop, and more peanuts grow here than in any other state. Sometimes peanut shells are burned for fuel at power plants.*

5 *Quarry workers near Elberton cut granite for buildings, bridges, and monuments.*

3

4

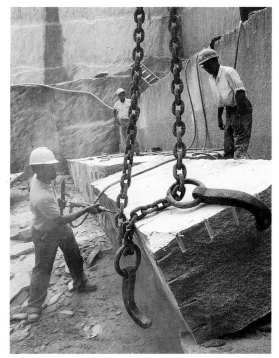

5

South Carolina

"Swamp Fox, Swamp Fox, tail on his hat. Nobody knows where the Swamp Fox's at," began the theme song of a popular 1950s television series. The show portrayed the daring exploits of Francis Marion, a South Carolina Revolutionary War leader whose ragtag band of guerrilla fighters led a Robin Hood-like existence in the state's southern swamps. Marion engaged the British in many skirmishes but never was caught. His ability to melt back into the swamps without a trace earned him the nickname Swamp Fox and his place in history and legend.

Though South Carolina has at least five distinct land regions, for centuries South Carolinians have broadly divided their state into two: the Low Country and the Up Country. Low Country is the Atlantic Coastal Plain, covering two-thirds of the state. Slow-moving rivers flow through the plain, which becomes marshy and swampy near the ocean. A winding shoreline follows bays, peninsulas, and inlets. At the northern end stretch some 60 miles (95 km) of white-sand beaches. To the south a line of lush barrier islands reaches into Georgia and Florida. Known as the Sea Islands, they are densely forested and contain both freshwater and saltwater marshes. Much Sea Islands land is protected nature reserve where wildlife abounds, including alligators and most species of poisonous snakes found in the United States.

Everything not on the Coastal Plain, South Carolinians call the Up Country. The term recognizes the land's gradual rise until it reaches the summits of the Blue Ridge Mountains in the northwestern corner, but other regions lie in between. Columbia, the capital, lies on a band of sandy hills that millions of years ago formed the ocean shoreline. West of Columbia begins the Piedmont, the foothills of the mountains.

The Low Country saw South Carolina's first European settlements. In the 1500s, both the Spanish and the French tried to colonize the coast, but failed. The English succeeded in 1670, establishing Charles Town (named for their king, Charles II) on a peninsula a few miles inland. They were soon joined by French Protestants, called Huguenots, who fled religious persecution in France, as well as by Scots, Spanish and Portuguese Jews, Irish, Germans, and Welsh. The newcomers prospered from trade

The crews of Civil War naval vessels, such as this one off Charleston, included youngsters. This "powder monkey," a boy whose job was to fetch gunpowder for cannons, was paid $8 a month.

with Indians. In time they built airy mansions along the harbor and in their leisure pursued the pleasures of music, dancing, entertaining, and fine dining. After the Revolution they changed the name of their city to Charleston.

Meanwhile, settlers of Scottish and Irish descent moved into South Carolina from highlands to the north. As Up Country farmers, they grew tobacco, corn, and cotton, a crop that was also raised in the Low Country, but with the help of thousands of slaves. Fearing the loss of their wealth if slavery were abolished, Low Country planters led the movement that, on December 20, 1860, made South Carolina the first state to secede from the Union.

The Civil War helped end South Carolina's reliance on cotton as the principal crop, as did the appearance of the destructive boll weevil in the 1920s. Today farmers throughout the state grow soybeans as well as cotton and, mainly in the east, tobacco.

In the late 1800s, South Carolina began to industrialize. The state attracted outside investment because wages were low and unions didn't exist there. Textile factories sprang up in the northwest near Greenville and Spartanburg, along the railroad. Today Interstate 85 parallels the rails through the heart of South Carolina's textile belt.

South Carolina has diversified its industry and now manufactures products ranging from furniture to chemicals for the space program. Investors are diversified as well. Factories representing more than 20 countries, including France, Germany, Japan, and the Netherlands, now operate in several areas of the state.

In September 1989, Hurricane Hugo hit South Carolina's coast. Winds reaching 135 miles an hour (217 kmph) damaged or destroyed thousands of trees lining Charleston's waterfront and tore off the roofs of many buildings and historic mansions.

The storm also ripped through some of the Sea Islands, leaving homeless many descendants of the slaves who once tended the islands' famous long-staple cotton. But even before Hugo, they had seen change come to many of their islands, including Hilton Head, developed as a resort for the rich.

In their isolation over the centuries, the Sea Islanders, who number a third of the state's black residents, developed a distinct culture and language, called Gullah. Most of them still speak this mixture of languages that has donated many words to modern English, such as goober (peanut), gumbo (okra), chigger (small flea), hoodoo (bad luck), and tote (to carry).

Area: *40th largest state, 31,113 sq mi (80,582 sq km)*
Population: *3,486,703; ranks 25th*
Major Cities: *Columbia, 98,052; Charleston, 80,414; North Charleston, 70,218*
Manufacturing: *textiles, chemicals, paper products, machinery, electronics, rubber and plastics, food products, clothing, metal products, transportation equipment*
Agriculture: *tobacco, cattle, soybeans, broilers, milk, eggs, vegetables, turkeys, peaches*
Mining and Quarrying: *stone, clay, sand and gravel*
Other Important Activities: *federal government, tourism*
Statehood: *the eighth state; ratified the Constitution on May 23, 1788*

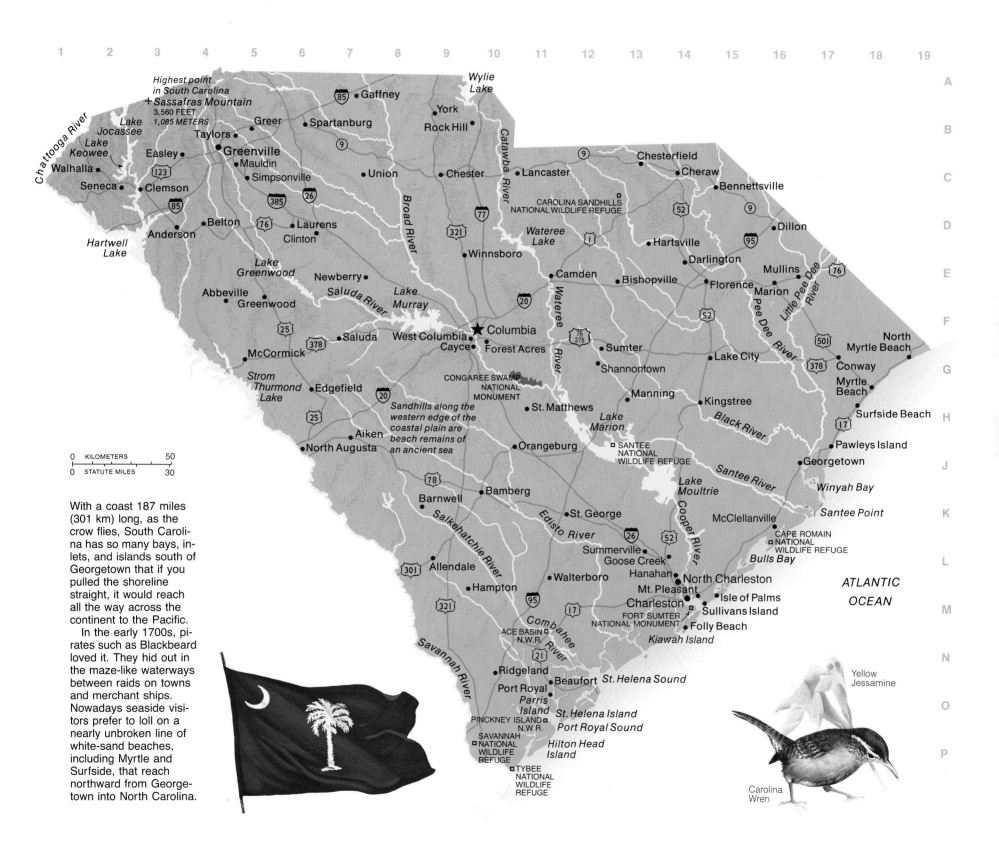

With a coast 187 miles (301 km) long, as the crow flies, South Carolina has so many bays, inlets, and islands south of Georgetown that if you pulled the shoreline straight, it would reach all the way across the continent to the Pacific.

In the early 1700s, pirates such as Blackbeard loved it. They hid out in the maze-like waterways between raids on towns and merchant ships. Nowadays seaside visitors prefer to loll on a nearly unbroken line of white-sand beaches, including Myrtle and Surfside, that reach northward from Georgetown into North Carolina.

1

South Carolina

1 *Pelicans fly over a barrier island near Charleston. Palmetto trees along the beach withstand hurricane-force winds, salt water, and shifting sands.*

2 *Fresh peaches fill market shelves all summer. South Carolina grows more peaches than any state but California.*

3 *From these mansions lining the harbor, Charlestonians watched the shelling of Fort Sumter at the start of the Civil War.*

4 *A family works together to bring in the August tobacco harvest on a farm along the Little Pee Dee River.*

5 *Jumbo shrimp pour from the scale in McClellanville, a fishing town where Gullah, an old, black language, is still spoken.*

2

3

4

5

Louisiana

Louis Armstrong began his jazz career while a teenager in New Orleans. Here, around 1920, he plays cornet with the Fate Marable Orchestra on board the paddle wheeler S.S. Capitol.

Louisiana is in many ways unique. It was founded by the French and governed by both the French and the Spanish before becoming part of the United States. It is the only state whose civil law is based on Roman law as found in French and Spanish sources, rather than on the British common law used by the other states. It is the only state where a quarter of the people speak French, and it is the only one organized into parishes instead of counties, a legacy of Roman Catholic influence during colonial days.

The French settled hot, humid New Orleans in 1718, and set out their neat, perpendicular streets on a wide bend of the Mississippi River. Though the city later spilled out of the bend, the French Quarter, or Vieux Carré ("old square"), is still its heart, attracting visitors from all over the world. They come to stroll beneath wrought-iron balconies draped with flowers and to sample the highly seasoned blend of French, Spanish, and African cuisines known as Creole. Some come to New Orleans to boat and fish on immense, brackish Lake Pontchartrain, crossed by a 24-mile (39-km) causeway, the longest over-water bridge in the world. Each winter, before the season of Lent, the population swells and the city celebrates with the round of parties, parades, and balls known as Mardi Gras.

New Orleans is Louisiana's chief port, and the metropolitan area is home to one-third of the state's population. Oceangoing vessels from Latin America, Europe, Asia, and Africa dock at New Orleans daily. Most of the cargo leaving

Louisiana is made up of corn from states upriver or the riches beneath southern Louisiana and the Gulf of Mexico, vast deposits of oil and natural gas. The banks of the Mississippi from New Orleans to Baton Rouge are lined with refineries and petrochemical plants. Lake Charles in the southwest and Shreveport in northwestern Louisiana also refine and process petroleum, while Lafayette and Morgan City in the south serve as centers for oil and gas drilling.

New Orleans still sends out cargoes of sugarcane and cotton, crops that made it rich more than 150 years ago. Alluvial soil from the Mississippi and its tributaries created fertile land throughout much of the state where other crops, such as soybeans, corn, and sweet potatoes are now also grown. After the rice harvest, farmers in the state's southern prairies often flood their fields to raise crawfish, a Louisiana delicacy, which feed on the stubble.

All along the Mississippi, people must match wits with the river's strength and capriciousness. Natural and artificial levees help keep the Mississippi in its channel. Where natural levees rise very high, from the buildup of sediment over many years, the river contained within them can flow at an elevation higher than its floodplain. In New Orleans, at five feet (1.5 m)

below sea level the lowest point in the state, the river is often higher than the land around it.

Southern Louisiana, where the river forms its delta, is a low-lying land of marshes, swamps, and cypress-studded bayous, slow-moving streams that often mark old river channels. One of the nation's most valuable wetland areas, the delta teems with wildlife, in winter sheltering up to 25 percent of North America's wild ducks and geese. Delta waters also nourish the shrimp and oysters of the seafood industry.

Generally more rural in the north, Louisiana's population is one of the most cosmopolitan in the country. Among its residents are descendants of French and Spanish settlers, former slaves, free blacks from the West Indies, German, English, and Hungarian farmers who settled the Mississippi plain, Irish, Italians, and the Cajuns. The last were French settlers from Acadia, a region of eastern Canada. The Acadians were exiled by the British in the mid-1700s, and many made their way to the bayous and prairies of southern Louisiana. There they lived by farming, fishing, hunting, and trapping. Over time the Acadians became "Cajuns." Today many still work close to the land, while others follow less traditional occupations, from law to the oil industry. Cajuns say that their cultural identity is defined by strong family bonds and a love of life.

"Laissez le bon temps rouler—Let the good times roll" characterizes the leisure time of Cajun Louisiana. On the bayou, spicy food and toe-tapping music make for good times. All it takes is a fiddle, an accordion, a guitar, and a washboard or triangle to keep Cajun feet stomping at a late night dance called a fais-dodo, literally, a "go to sleep"—probably because that's what the small children were supposed to do.

Area: *31st largest state, 47,751 sq mi (123,675 sq km)*
Population: *4,219,973; ranks 21st*
Major Cities: *New Orleans, 496,938; Baton Rouge, 219,531; Shreveport, 198,525*
Mining: *oil and gas, salt*
Manufacturing: *chemicals, food products, petroleum products, transportation equipment, paper products, electronics, lumber and wood products*
Agriculture: *soybeans, cotton, cattle, sugarcane, rice, milk*
Other Important Activities: *tourism, fishing*
Statehood: *the 18th state; admitted April 30, 1812*

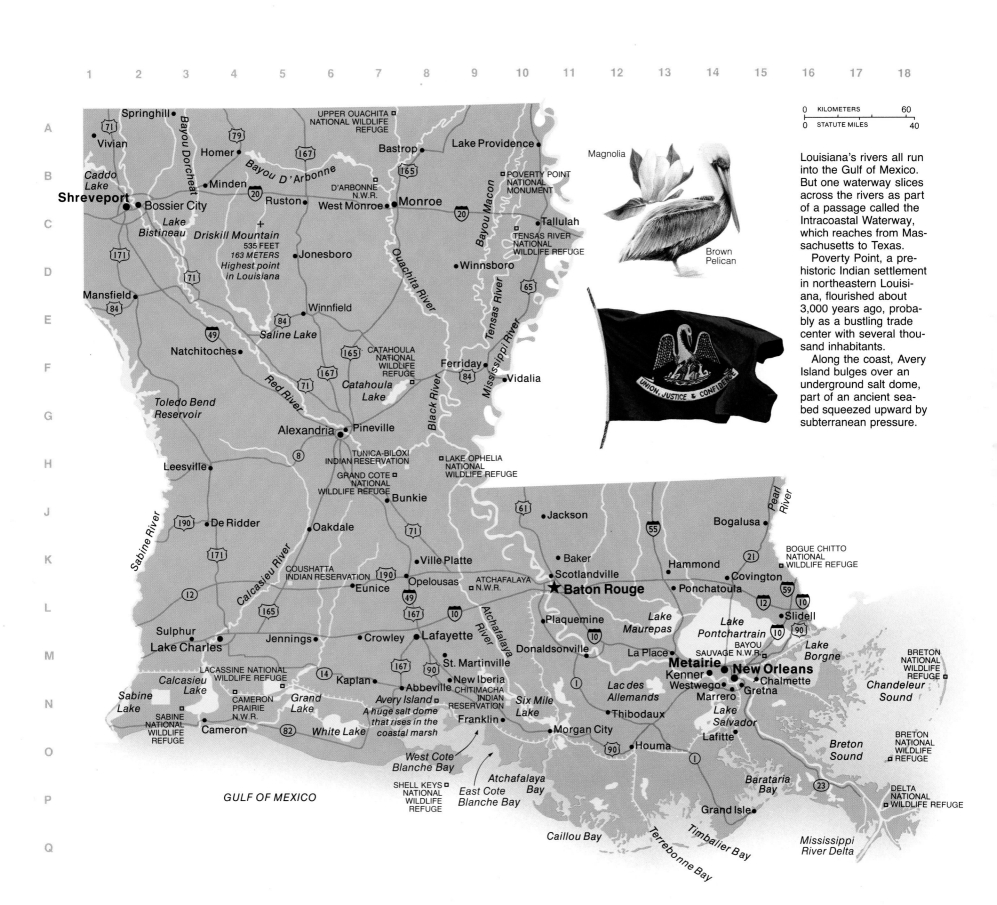

1 2 3 4 5 6 7 8 9 10 11 12 13 14 15 16 17 18

A B C D E F G H J K L M N O P Q

Springhill •
• Vivian
Caddo Lake
Shreveport
• Bossier City
Lake Bistineau
Mansfield •

Bayou Dorcheat

Homer •
• Minden
Ruston
West Monroe

Driskill Mountain
535 FEET
163 METERS
Highest point
in Louisiana

Jonesboro •

• Winnfield

Natchitoches •

Saline Lake

Toledo Bend Reservoir

Red River

Catahoula Lake

Alexandria • Pineville

Leesville •

Sabine River

• De Ridder

Oakdale •

Calcasieu River

Sulphur •
Lake Charles •

Jennings •

Sabine Lake

Calcasieu Lake

CAMERON PRAIRIE N.W.R.
Cameron •

LACASSINE NATIONAL WILDLIFE REFUGE

SABINE NATIONAL WILDLIFE REFUGE

Grand Lake

White Lake

GULF OF MEXICO

UPPER OUACHITA NATIONAL WILDLIFE REFUGE

Bayou D'Arbonne

D'ARBONNE N.W.R.
Monroe

Bastrop •
• Lake Providence

POVERTY POINT NATIONAL MONUMENT

Bayou Macon

• Tallulah

TENSAS RIVER NATIONAL WILDLIFE REFUGE

• Winnsboro

Ouachita River

Tensas River

Catahoula Lake

CATAHOULA NATIONAL WILDLIFE REFUGE

Ferriday •
Vidalia •

Black River

Mississippi River

TUNICA-BILOXI INDIAN RESERVATION

GRAND COTE NATIONAL WILDLIFE REFUGE

Bunkie •

LAKE OPHELIA NATIONAL WILDLIFE REFUGE

• Jackson

• Bogalusa

Pearl River

BOGUE CHITTO NATIONAL WILDLIFE REFUGE

• Ville Platte

COUSHATTA INDIAN RESERVATION

Eunice •
Opelousas •

ATCHAFALAYA N.W.R.

• Baker
• Scotlandville
★ Baton Rouge

Hammond •
• Covington

Ponchatoula •

• Slidell

Crowley •
• Lafayette

Atchafalaya River

Plaquemine •

Lake Maurepas

Lake Pontchartrain

Lake Borgne

BRETON NATIONAL WILDLIFE REFUGE

Kaplan •

St. Martinville •
• New Iberia
CHITIMACHA INDIAN RESERVATION

Abbeville •

Avery Island
A huge salt dome that rises in the coastal marsh

Franklin •

West Cote Blanche Bay

SHELL KEYS NATIONAL WILDLIFE REFUGE

East Cote Blanche Bay

Six Mile Lake

Morgan City •

Atchafalaya Bay

Donaldsonville •

La Place •

BAYOU SAUVAGE N.W.R.

Metairie
Kenner
Westwego

Marrero

Lac des Allemands

• Thibodaux

Lake Salvador

New Orleans
• Chalmette
Gretna

• Lafitte

• Houma

Caillou Bay

Terrebonne Bay

Timbalier Bay

Chandeleur Sound

BRETON NATIONAL WILDLIFE REFUGE

Breton Sound

Baratiaria Bay

• Grand Isle

Mississippi River Delta

DELTA NATIONAL WILDLIFE REFUGE

KILOMETERS 0 ———— 60
STATUTE MILES 0 ———— 40

Magnolia

Brown Pelican

UNION, JUSTICE & CONFIDENCE

Louisiana's rivers all run into the Gulf of Mexico. But one waterway slices across the rivers as part of a passage called the Intracoastal Waterway, which reaches from Massachusetts to Texas.

Poverty Point, a prehistoric Indian settlement in northeastern Louisiana, flourished about 3,000 years ago, probably as a bustling trade center with several thousand inhabitants.

Along the coast, Avery Island bulges over an underground salt dome, part of an ancient seabed squeezed upward by subterranean pressure.

1

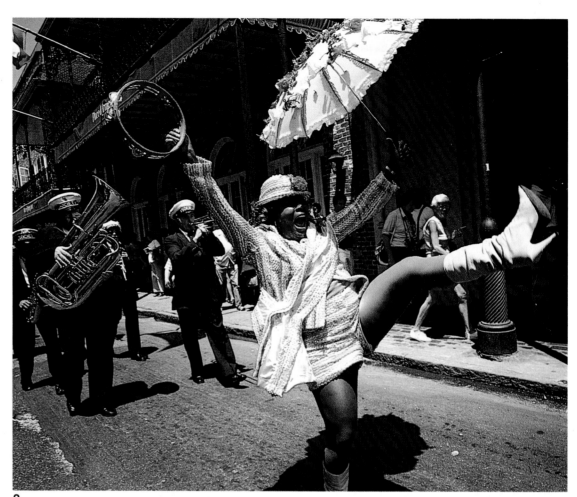

2

Louisiana

1 *An oil rig rises from the Gulf of Mexico off Louisiana. Thousands of drilling platforms dot the offshore waters, where crews work around the clock in a region that produces some 700,000 barrels of oil a day.*

2 *The Andrew Hall Society Brass Band parades through the French Quarter. New Orleans jazz was born around 1900, when black and white musicians combined gospel music, spirituals, dance music, West African rhythms, European harmony, and the beat of brass bands.*

3 *The Mississippi River winds past New Orleans and flows its last 110 miles (177 km) southeast to the Gulf of Mexico. Cargo ships from around the world make the trip by river or artificial channel to trade millions of tons of goods a year.*

3

4 *Swamp red maple and bald cypress trees grow in a swamp along the Pearl River, home to alligators, river otters, bobcats, mink, birds, and crawfish.*

5 *On Avery Island, a worker picks hot peppers. Tabasco sauce made from these peppers has spiced Cajun and Creole dishes, such as crawfish étouffée, chicken gumbo, and shrimp jambalaya, since 1868, soon after the seeds were brought from Mexico.*

Florida

In 1513 Spanish explorer Juan Ponce de León landed in Florida, searching for a legendary spring that would assure him perpetual youth. He did not find the spring and died after fighting Indians on a later trip. Florida may not have the Fountain of Youth, but it does have springs, more than one-third of all the large springs in the United States and many smaller ones. Florida has water of all types, in rivers, bays, lakes, swamps, marshes, creeks, and ponds. Winds from the Atlantic Ocean on the east and the Gulf of Mexico on the west bring moist air and usually plentiful rainfall to the state.

The southernmost of all the states except Hawaii, Florida occupies a peninsula that projects 400 miles (640 km) into the sea. Including all bays, inlets, and offshore islands, Florida has a coastline that totals almost 8,500 miles (13,680 km), longer than that of any other state except Alaska. No part of Florida is more than an hour's drive from tidewater. Off the southern tip of the peninsula, the Florida Keys, a string of limestone and coral islands, trickle westward into the Gulf.

A flat, porous limestone formation underlies the Florida peninsula. Pockets in the limestone store vast quantities of groundwater. The groundwater reaches the surface in some 30,000 lakes, including 730-square-mile (1,890-sq-km) Lake Okeechobee, the largest lake in the southern United States. The groundwater also nourishes springs and streams.

This watery world has many interconnections. One is the complex system of the Everglades. For centuries, lakes in central Florida fed the Kissimmee River, which in turn fed Lake Okeechobee. This inflow and seasonal rains caused Okeechobee to spill over its southern banks, spreading as wide as 50 miles (80 km) to flow slowly 100 miles to Florida Bay. This creeping river is lifeblood to the Everglades. Often only inches deep and brimming with saw grass, it shelters alligators, crocodiles, manatees, multitudes of birds, and the rare and elusive Florida panther. It is an environment unique to Florida and to the world. At the southern tip is Everglades National Park.

From prehistoric Indians to later settlers who fished or dug clams or farmed on mounded islands called hammocks, people have lived in the Everglades for thousands of years. They made few demands on the environment, but today it is people who endanger the Everglades. The Everglades and its sources are channeled by hundreds of miles of canals and dikes to provide fresh water for the farms, cities, and developments that make southern Florida one of the fastest growing areas in the nation. The needs of humans and wildlife often conflict. Now the Everglades is in danger of dying, and this threat has led the state to pay attention to the needs of the "river of grass."

In 1565 the Spanish built the first permanent European settlement in Florida, at St. Augustine. The British and French followed, competing for control of the Gulf of Mexico. In the early 19th century, American settlers streamed in, looking for new farmland. The Seminole Indians owned some of the best land here. The U. S. government forced most of them to move to Oklahoma, all but a small band who escaped into the swamps. Their descendants live today in dis-

The 1890s brought a cycling craze to the United States and gave people a new freedom of movement. Here, cyclists and strollers congregate along the seashore at Palm Beach, a small town in 1895.

tinctive houses on stilts deep in the Everglades.

Settlers pressed southward. By the end of the 19th century, wetlands, including much of the Everglades, were drained. Fertile farmland appeared, but only for a while, since the rich muck soil of the wetlands disintegrates when exposed to air and then blows away. This did not deter developers from draining or settlers from farming. Today two-thirds of the nation's supply of oranges are grown in Florida, as well as three-fourths of its grapefruit. Farmers in southern Florida produce tomatoes, lettuce, celery, green peppers, and other vegetables.

In the late 1800s, two tycoons, both named Henry, raced to develop parts of Florida. They built railroads and many luxurious resort hotels. Henry Flagler completed his east coast railroad to Miami first. Henry Plant built his line from Jacksonville to Tampa.

Today more than four million people live on the east coast from Miami to West Palm Beach, many of them elderly retirees from northern states. St. Petersburg on Tampa Bay has large numbers of senior citizens, too. They used to come just for the winter, but air-conditioning has turned many "snowbirds" into year-round residents. Retirees give Florida the nation's oldest population; 1 in 5 residents is over 65.

No known descendants of the first Spanish colonists remain in Florida, but many newer Spanish-speaking immigrants, mostly from Cuba and other Latin American countries, live in or near Miami. With numerous trade and finance connections to the south, this port city has become a commercial partner of Latin America. Some 70 percent of U. S. trade with Latin America goes through Florida. Illegal drug traffic forms a large part of this trade, and the crime it generates is driving many older residents north along the coast. Even so, every day 800 people move into the state, and its population has grown by one-third since 1980.

Orlando's growing electronics industry has attracted many people. A large number of Floridians work for the federal government, some at military bases such as Pensacola's Naval Air Station. At Cape Canaveral, it's been more than 40 years since the first rocket took off, but launches at Kennedy Space Center still support the aerospace industry and still stop traffic.

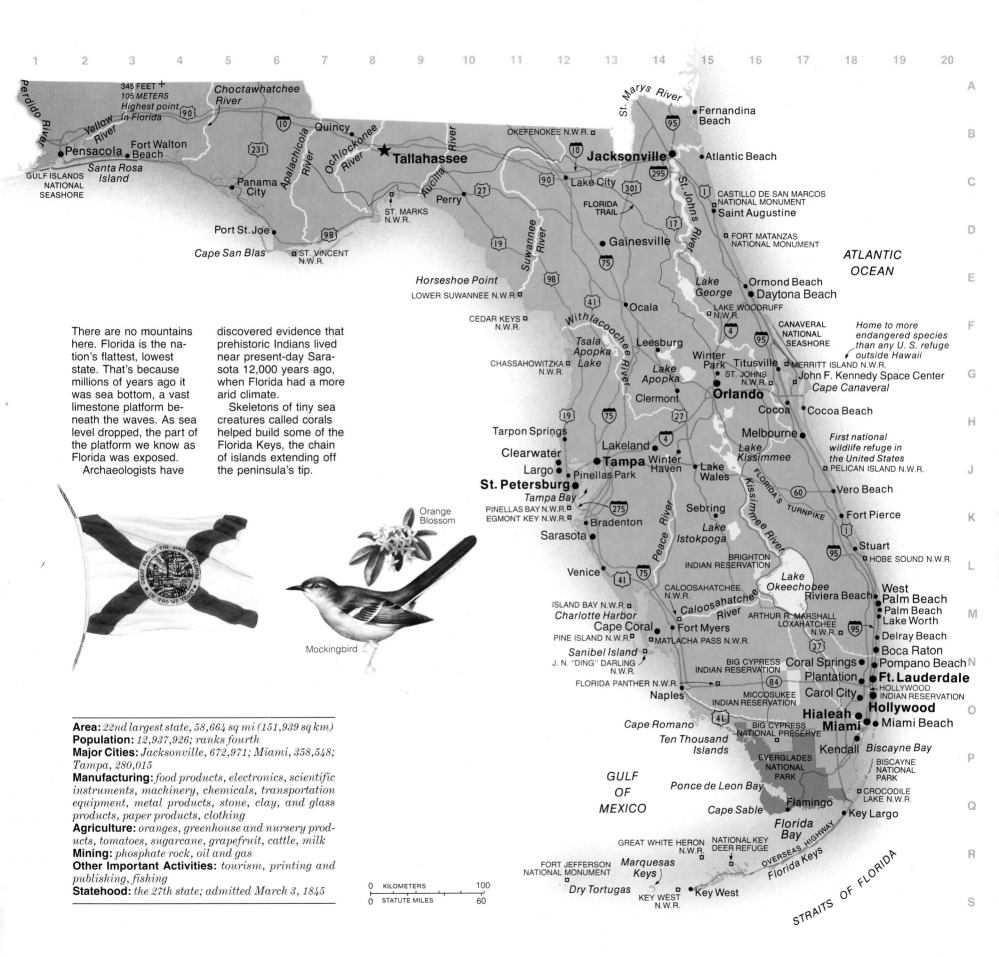

There are no mountains here. Florida is the nation's flattest, lowest state. That's because millions of years ago it was sea bottom, a vast limestone platform beneath the waves. As sea level dropped, the part of the platform we know as Florida was exposed.

Archaeologists have discovered evidence that prehistoric Indians lived near present-day Sarasota 12,000 years ago, when Florida had a more arid climate.

Skeletons of tiny sea creatures called corals helped build some of the Florida Keys, the chain of islands extending off the peninsula's tip.

Orange Blossom

Mockingbird

Area: *22nd largest state, 58,664 sq mi (151,939 sq km)*
Population: *12,937,926; ranks fourth*
Major Cities: *Jacksonville, 672,971; Miami, 358,548; Tampa, 280,015*
Manufacturing: *food products, electronics, scientific instruments, machinery, chemicals, transportation equipment, metal products, stone, clay, and glass products, paper products, clothing*
Agriculture: *oranges, greenhouse and nursery products, tomatoes, sugarcane, grapefruit, cattle, milk*
Mining: *phosphate rock, oil and gas*
Other Important Activities: *tourism, printing and publishing, fishing*
Statehood: *the 27th state; admitted March 3, 1845*

KILOMETERS 100
STATUTE MILES 60

Map Labels

1 2 3 4 5 6 7 8 9 10 11 12 13 14 15 16 17 18 19 20

A B C D E F G H J K L M N O P Q R S

345 FEET +
105 METERS
Highest point in Florida

Perdido River
Yellow River
Choctawhatchee River
Pensacola
Fort Walton Beach
Santa Rosa Island
GULF ISLANDS NATIONAL SEASHORE
Quincy
Panama City
Apalachicola River
Ochlockonee River
Tallahassee
Port St. Joe
Cape San Blas
ST. VINCENT N.W.R.
ST. MARKS N.W.R.
Aucilla River
Perry
Horseshoe Point
LOWER SUWANNEE N.W.R.
CEDAR KEYS N.W.R.
Suwannee River
OKEFENOKEE N.W.R.
Jacksonville
Atlantic Beach
Lake City
FLORIDA TRAIL
CASTILLO DE SAN MARCOS NATIONAL MONUMENT
Saint Augustine
FORT MATANZAS NATIONAL MONUMENT
Gainesville
Ocala
St. Marys River
Fernandina Beach

ATLANTIC OCEAN

Lake George
Ormond Beach
Daytona Beach
LAKE WOODRUFF N.W.R.
CANAVERAL NATIONAL SEASHORE
Home to more endangered species than any U. S. refuge outside Hawaii
MERRITT ISLAND N.W.R.
Withlacoochee River
Tsala Apopka Lake
CHASSAHOWITZKA N.W.R.
Leesburg
Winter Park
Titusville
ST. JOHNS N.W.R.
John F. Kennedy Space Center
Cape Canaveral
Lake Apopka
Clermont
Orlando
Cocoa
Cocoa Beach
Tarpon Springs
Melbourne
First national wildlife refuge in the United States
PELICAN ISLAND N.W.R.
Lakeland
Lake Kissimmee
Clearwater
Tampa
Winter Haven
Lake Wales
Vero Beach
Largo
Pinellas Park
St. Petersburg
Tampa Bay
PINELLAS BAY N.W.R.
EGMONT KEY N.W.R.
Bradenton
Sarasota
Sebring
Lake Istokpoga
Fort Pierce
Stuart
HOBE SOUND N.W.R.
Venice
Peace River
BRIGHTON INDIAN RESERVATION
Lake Okeechobee
West Palm Beach
Riviera Beach
Palm Beach
Lake Worth
CALOOSAHATCHEE N.W.R.
ISLAND BAY N.W.R.
Charlotte Harbor
Caloosahatchee River
ARTHUR R. MARSHALL LOXAHATCHEE N.W.R.
Delray Beach
Cape Coral
Fort Myers
PINE ISLAND N.W.R.
MATLACHA PASS N.W.R.
Boca Raton
Pompano Beach
Sanibel Island
J. N. "DING" DARLING N.W.R.
BIG CYPRESS INDIAN RESERVATION
Coral Springs
Plantation
Ft. Lauderdale
HOLLYWOOD INDIAN RESERVATION
FLORIDA PANTHER N.W.R.
Carol City
Naples
MICCOSUKEE INDIAN RESERVATION
Hialeah
Hollywood
Miami
Miami Beach
Cape Romano
BIG CYPRESS NATIONAL PRESERVE
Kendall
Biscayne Bay
Ten Thousand Islands
EVERGLADES NATIONAL PARK
BISCAYNE NATIONAL PARK
GULF OF MEXICO
Ponce de Leon Bay
CROCODILE LAKE N.W.R.
Cape Sable
Flamingo
Florida Bay
Key Largo
GREAT WHITE HERON N.W.R.
NATIONAL KEY DEER REFUGE
FORT JEFFERSON NATIONAL MONUMENT
Marquesas Keys
OVERSEAS HIGHWAY
Florida Keys
Dry Tortugas
KEY WEST N.W.R.
Key West
STRAITS OF FLORIDA

1

2

3

4

5

Florida

1 *The gleaming hotels that line Miami Beach serve Florida's leading industry, tourism. They stand on land that, a hundred years ago, was a sandbar thick with mangroves and palmettos, and populated mostly by snakes and mosquitoes.*

2 *A picker near Clermont fills a tub with Valencia oranges, Florida's most abundant variety. Today 90 percent of Florida oranges go into making juice.*

3 *White ibises roost on mangrove roots in the Everglades, one of the United States' most threatened areas. Loss of habitat has led to a 95 percent decline in the population of Everglades wading birds. Polluted water from farms flows into the wetlands, daily destroying an area of plant and animal habitat the size of three football fields.*

4 *The space shuttle* Discovery *prepares for lift-off at Kennedy Space Center, the primary site for the launching and landing of the reusable vehicles. In 1981* Columbia *was the first shuttle to take off here.*

5 *Ranch hands round up their herd on the grassy plains near the Peace River. There have been cattle ranches in Florida since the early 1800s. Today Florida is one of the country's top five cattle-producing states.*

Great Lakes States

They are like oceans, these great lakes. French missionaries, gazing across a seemingly limitless horizon of water in the 17th century, thought they had found oceans—"sweetwater seas," they called them. Taken together, the Great Lakes spread some 800 miles (1,290 km) east to west across the continent's interior and hold a fifth of the planet's fresh surface water. If you emptied the lakes across the contiguous United States, their water would cover the land ten feet (3 m) deep. A raindrop falling onto the heavily forested shore of western Lake Superior would take about 215 years to wind its way east through the lakes to the St. Lawrence River outlet at the eastern tip of Lake Ontario.

Created by glaciers that withdrew about 10,000 years ago, the Great Lakes' shoreline extends 8,000 miles (12,870 km) and is sometimes called North America's fifth coast. Along the four lakes shown here cluster the nation's heaviest concentrations of industry, thanks to the region's central location and economical water transportation that brings shipments of iron and coal to lakeside mills and factories.

A quarter of the country's steel pours from furnaces in the Chicago and Gary areas of Lake Michigan. About a third of the cars roll off assembly lines in and around Detroit, and Cleveland's mills, factories, and refineries stretch 65 miles (105 km) along Lake Erie's shore. By value, about a quarter of the country's manufactured goods come from the Great Lakes region.

Beyond the cities spreads the quilt-work pattern of the corn belt, fertile farms and fields that produce about a fifth of the nation's farm income. Level terrain, hot summers, and usually plentiful rain help to produce bumper crops of corn and soybeans year after year. North of the corn belt, between lower Lake Michigan and the Mississippi River, roll the gentle hills and pastures of the nation's dairy belt. East of the lake, peach, apple, and pear orchards flourish because warm winds from the lakes help to prolong their growing season by delaying frosts.

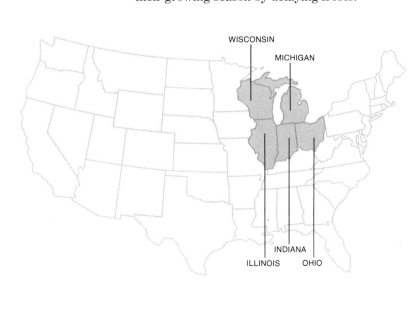

WISCONSIN

MICHIGAN

INDIANA

ILLINOIS   OHIO

Wisconsin

A daredevil leaps a chasm at Stand Rock around 1886 in the forested Dells region of the Wisconsin River. Over the ages the river carved a channel through sandstone, creating these formations.

"As far as a man could go to the north in a day, or a week, or a whole month, there was nothing but woods. There were no houses. There were no roads. There were no people. There were only trees and the wild animals who had their homes among them." In *Little House in the Big Woods*, Laura Ingalls Wilder describes her pioneer childhood in Wisconsin of the 1870s, a life of hunting and trapping and laying in food to last long winters snowbound in a log cabin.

Woods still cover almost half of Wisconsin, but the trees are second-growth hardwoods and evergreens. Not only big woods but also lakes big and small are part of northern Wisconsin. The state has some 14,000 lakes, a legacy of the Ice Age. The largest is Lake Winnebago. Its 215 square miles (557 sq km) teem with fish, including muskie, bass, sturgeon, and trout. Together, lakes and forests beckon thousands of vacationers to this part of Wisconsin each year.

Central highlands blocked the glaciers' path into southwestern Wisconsin and adjoining parts of Minnesota, Iowa, and Illinois. The winding ridges and steep-sloped valleys of this Driftless Area, so-called because it shows no sign of glacial debris, or drift, provide a glimpse of the region's rugged, pre-Ice Age landscape. Streams here cut down through layers of limestone and sandstone and drain into the Mississippi River, Wisconsin's western boundary. Geologists puzzle over the absence of glacial tracks in the area, because they think the ice sheets must have passed through here.

Glaciers did help carve out the Great Lakes, immense reservoirs that hold 95 percent of the fresh surface water in the United States. Two of them, Lakes Superior and Michigan, provide northwestern and eastern Wisconsin with almost 700 miles (1,130 km) of shoreline. In 1634 Jean Nicolet, a French explorer from Quebec looking for a northern passage to China, landed at Green Bay. He donned a colorful silk robe, hoping to impress the Chinese officials he was expecting to meet. Instead, he was greeted by Winnebago Indians, one of three Native American groups that inhabited Wisconsin.

The fur trade soon brought more Europeans to Wisconsin. There was a great market in Europe for gentlemen's top hats fashioned from the glossy pelts of North American beavers. Lead miners numbered among 19th-century settlers, along with farmers who found the rich glacial soil and long growing season of southern Wisconsin suitable for raising wheat.

By the late 1800s, among the green checkerboard fields of the countryside stood buildings that heralded a new era in the state's agriculture: milking barns, with their round silos full of cattle feed. The Swiss were among the Europeans who settled 19th-century Wisconsin, and they brought their cheese-making experience. By 1920, Wisconsin led the nation in dairy farming. With two million cows, it still produces more milk and cheese than any other state.

Placidly grazing cows may support a large part of Wisconsin's economy, but the pounding machines of many factories make manufacturing the state's largest industry. Germans, Poles, Italians, and British were among the Europeans who settled the industrial cities of the southeast, where one-third of Wisconsinites now live. Each group brought customs that are celebrated at festivals in cities of this industrial corner. German beer fests honor the beverage that made Milwaukee the brewing capital of the United States, a title it gained after the Chicago fire of 1871 destroyed that city's breweries.

The same night that Chicago burned, one of the country's most destructive forest fires raged in Wisconsin, laying waste a swath 40 miles (64 km) long and 10 miles (16 km) wide along the shore of Green Bay. In the town of Peshtigo and nearby villages, the fire claimed at least 1,200 lives, four times more than were lost in Chicago, but the news was not reported for days in the national newspapers because Chicago's conflagration had captured the headlines.

Wisconsinites pay high taxes, but these taxes bring them a wealth of social, educational, and community services. Many programs that improve people's lives had their start in Wisconsin. These range from the nation's first kindergarten, opened in Watertown in 1856, to minimum-wage laws, vocational schools, and the first law requiring seat belts in cars.

Wisconsin has a sizable Native American population, numbering about 40,000. Many of these people live on reservations, but by 150-year-old agreements with the federal government, they retain traditional hunting and fishing rights in territories they used to occupy outside. Disputes, both in court and out, have resulted from the exercise of these privileges, such as the right to spearfish out of season. Wisconsin's wildlife bounty now lies at the center of controversy between property owners, sport fishermen, and the area's original inhabitants, with the state striving to mediate their differences.

Area: *26th largest state, 56,153 sq mi (145,436 sq km)*
Population: *4,891,769; ranks 16th*
Major Cities: *Milwaukee, 628,088; Madison, 191,262; Green Bay, 96,466*
Manufacturing: *machinery, food products, paper products, metal products, transportation equipment, electronics, chemicals, scientific instruments, rubber and plastics, metals*
Agriculture: *milk, cattle, hogs, corn, potatoes*
Mining and Quarrying: *stone, sand and gravel*
Other Important Activities: *tourism, printing and publishing*
Statehood: *the 30th state; admitted May 29th, 1848*

LAKE SUPERIOR

APOSTLE ISLANDS
NATIONAL LAKESHORE

*Apostle
Islands*

RED CLIFF
INDIAN
RESERVATION

BAD RIVER
INDIAN RESERVATION

Madeline Island

Superior

(35)

Bois Brule River

(2)

Ashland

(63)

BAD RIVER
INDIAN
RESERVATION

Hurley

(PROPOSED)

NORTH
COUNTRY
TRAIL

Land O' Lakes

LAC DU FLAMBEAU
INDIAN RESERVATION

(53)

Namekagon River

Lake Chippewa

Park Falls

Brule River

(45)

Niagara

(8)

ST. CROIX
INDIAN
RESERVATION

Spooner

LAC COURTE OREILLES
INDIAN RESERVATION

Flambeau River

(13)

POTAWATOMI
INDIAN RESERVATION

(141)

*Washington
Island*

Grantsburg

ST. CROIX
INDIAN RESERVATION

Rice Lake

(8)

Wisconsin River

SOKAOGON CHIPPEWA
INDIAN RESERVATION

Rhinelander

Menominee River

GREEN BAY
N.W.R.

Fish
Creek

GRAVEL I.
N.W.R.

(63)

Amery

Barron

(8)

Timms Hill +
1,952 FEET
595 METERS
*Highest point
in Wisconsin*

ICE
AGE
TRAIL

Merrill

Antigo

Neopit

MENOMINEE
INDIAN
RESERVATION

(141)

Marinette

Peshtigo

St. Croix River

(94)

(53)

Medford

Wausau

Eau Claire River

Rib Mountain +
1,924 FEET
586 METERS

STOCKBRIDGE
INDIAN
RESERVATION

Keshena

(41)

Green Bay

DOOR PENINSULA

Sturgeon Bay

Chippewa Falls

Lake Wissota

(29)

River
Falls

Menomonie

Eau Claire

Chippewa River

Marshfield

*Big Eau Pleine
Reservoir*

Lake Du Bay

(45)

(29)

(10)

Mondovi

Neillsville

Stevens Point

ONEIDA
INDIAN
RESERVATION

Green Bay

De Pere

(43)

Lake Pepin

UPPER MISSISSIPPI
RIVER NATIONAL
WILDLIFE AND
FISH REFUGE

GREAT RIVER ROAD

Black River

WINNEBAGO
INDIAN
RESERVATION

Wisconsin
Rapids

(10)

Appleton

Kaukauna

Menasha

Two Rivers

Mississippi River

TREMPEALEAU
NATIONAL
WILDLIFE REFUGE

NECEDAH
NATIONAL
WILDLIFE
REFUGE

*Petenwell
Lake*

(51)

*Lake
Poygan*

Neenah

Oshkosh

(151)

Manitowoc

Sparta

(90)

(53)

(90)
(94)

*Castle Rock
Lake*

(13)

Fox River

Ripon

*Lake
Winnebago*

(151)

Sheboygan

La Crosse

(61)
(14)

FOX RIVER
NATIONAL
WILDLIFE REFUGE

HORICON NATIONAL
WILDLIFE REFUGE

Fond du Lac

ICE
AGE
TRAIL

UPPER
MISSISSIPPI
RIVER
NATIONAL
WILDLIFE
AND FISH
REFUGE

Wisconsin Dells
*River-carved
sandstone formations*

Baraboo

(16)

Beaver
Dam

(41)

West Bend

(43)

LAKE
MICHIGAN

(35)

(14)

Lake Wisconsin

Columbus

(151)

Watertown

Menomonee
Falls

Mequon

Whitefish Bay

Wauwatosa

*Home of architect
Frank Lloyd Wright*
Taliesin

*Lake
Mendota*

(90)
(94)

Milwaukee River

Brookfield

Milwaukee

West Allis

Prairie
du Chien

Mineral
Point

Madison ★

Monona

Waukesha

New Berlin

South Milwaukee

Greenfield

(18)

(61)

Lake Koshkonong

Whitewater

Rock River

(94)

Racine

Platteville

(151)

Janesville

(14)

(15)

Monroe

Beloit

(14)

(12)

Kenosha

An island of rock surrounded by a sea of ice is how southwestern Wisconsin looked during the Ice Age. Here the glacier divided, flowing around hills rather than riding up over them. Steep-sided valleys and narrow ridges mark this rocky region near the Mississippi River.

Wisconsin's Ice Age Trail, when completed, will trace the glacier's leading edge, enabling hikers and, in some sections, cyclists to take a thousand-mile (1,600-km) tour of glacial features. Much of the trail follows a terminal moraine, the ridge marking a glacier's snout.

WISCONSIN

1848

Robin

Wood
Violet

KILOMETERS   60

STATUTE MILES   40

1

2

3

4

5

Wisconsin

1 *Stepping through a green carpet of duckweed, a white-tailed buck sips from a woodland pond. In a state rich in wildlife, deer are the most numerous large mammals.*

2 *Lush pastures nourish dairy cows grazing on a southwestern farm. Nearly three-fourths of the milk that Wisconsin cows produce is destined for cheese making.*

3 *Lifting a bag of curd from a copper vat of whey, a cheese maker prepares it for molding and curing. Months later, this batch will yield a 200-pound (90-kg) wheel of Wisconsin Swiss.*

4 *At Fish Creek, on the Door Peninsula, hungry bystanders anticipate dinner at a fish boil, said to be a tradition brought by Scandinavian settlers.*

5 *A bold aerialist walks the wing of a 1940 plane at an Oshkosh International Fly-In Convention. More than a half million people and thousands of planes converge annually on Oshkosh to celebrate aviation's colorful history.*

Michigan

A dog barking at a giant mitten. That's one way to describe the shape of the two large peninsulas that make up the state of Michigan. The Straits of Mackinac (pronounced MACK-i-naw) divide the Upper Peninsula, adjoining northern Wisconsin, from the Lower Peninsula, which juts north from Indiana and Ohio.

Michigan's unusual shape goes back to a dispute with Ohio when boundaries were being drawn at the time of Michigan's admission to the Union. Both wanted a strip of territory that contained Toledo. After much squabbling, Michigan ceded it to Ohio, already a state, in exchange for the Upper Peninsula. At the time, some people considered the Upper Peninsula a useless, snowbound wilderness, but its wealth of minerals and forests proved them wrong.

Most of Michigan is surrounded by water. When the first voyageurs paddled into the area around 1620, they met Indians who masterfully plied the lakes and rivers in their birchbark canoes. As white settlers began to harvest Michigan's bountiful resources of timber, copper, and iron, they found transport easiest along the waterways. They enhanced natural routes where necessary. To move iron ore mined in Minnesota and the Upper Peninsula from Lake Superior into Lake Huron, a canal was opened in 1855. Enlarged, the Soo Canals soon ranked among the world's busiest waterways and, during World War II, the most strategic. To ensure the transport of essential raw materials, 20,000 troops protected the Soo Canals from sabotage.

But nothing can protect ships from the fearsome storms that often turn the Great Lakes into watery graveyards. In 1913 alone, Lake Superior claimed 40 ships. A song by Canadian balladeer Gordon Lightfoot about the freighter *Edmund Fitzgerald* records how, in 1975, "that good ship and true" went down with all hands "when the gales of November came early."

The Upper Peninsula (the "U.P." to Michiganders) shares a forested terrain with the northern half of the Lower Peninsula. Although it has 25 percent of the land, the U.P. contains only about 4 percent of the population. Many of its people are descendants of the early Welsh and Scottish copper miners and the Finns who came to cut white pine and then stayed on as dairy farmers when the timber was gone.

The northern half of the Lower Peninsula is sparsely populated. About 90 percent of Michiganders live south of an imaginary line between Muskegon and Bay City. Many of these people, and thousands from other states, head north to vacation among the trees, lakes, and wildlife.

People from New England and New York were the first to settle the southern Lower Peninsula, in the 1820s. Quiet towns centered around a church, a school, and a town hall reflected their Yankee origin. Fertile soils and a climate milder than up north made farming here easier, while the shore of Lake Michigan proved ideal for growing fruit.

To Michigan's Yankee character were added the customs of waves of European immigrants. The Dutch founded the city of Holland, complete with a windmill and tulip festivals. Germans, many of them shopkeepers, settled Saginaw and Ann Arbor, while Irish came to a southern part

---

Newly cut logs are pulled on horse-drawn skids along roads iced to make the journey smoother. This photo was taken in 1893 during a logging boom that depleted Michigan's pine forests.

of the state that reminded them of the green hills of their homeland.

A city on the narrow strait (*détroit* in French) joining Lake St. Clair and Lake Erie attracted the greatest diversity of people, many drawn by its burgeoning industries. As the logging of northern woods encouraged the building of railroads, Detroit began to produce the steel needed for railroad tracks, cars, and bridges. Into this city of promise came Germans, Poles, Hungarians, Italians, Ukrainians, and black Americans from the South. Other groups arrived later, including Mexicans and the largest population of Arab peoples in the United States.

The name "Detroit" is synonymous with the automobile. In 1896 the independent and simultaneous development of a gasoline-powered car by Henry Ford and Ransom Olds transformed Detroit, the state of Michigan, and the world.

A few huge auto companies established factories employing hundreds of thousands of people. With Detroit as its hub, the industry expanded to the suburbs and nearby cities. In recent years hard times hit. Recessions in the 1970s and '80s and consumer preference for more fuel-efficient, foreign-made cars shut down plants and cut back production, leading to 17 percent unemployment in Michigan by 1982.

Now Michigan has learned to diversify its economy. There are thousands of new jobs in small factories, in big companies that study the latest manufacturing technologies such as robotics, and in stores, restaurants, and computer firms. Even so, Michigan still produces more automobiles than any other state.

Area: *23rd largest state, 58,527 sq mi (151,586 sq km)*
Population: *9,295,297; ranks eighth*
Major Cities: *Detroit, 1,027,974; Grand Rapids, 189,126; Warren, 144,864*
Manufacturing: *transportation equipment, machinery, metal products, chemicals, food products, metals, rubber and plastics, furniture, paper products, electronics, stone, clay, and glass products, clothing*
Agriculture: *milk, vegetables, corn, cattle, soybeans, greenhouse and nursery products, fruits*
Mining and Quarrying: *oil and gas, iron ore, sand and gravel*
Other Important Activities: *tourism, printing and publishing*
Statehood: *the 26th state; admitted January 26, 1837*

Map labels

Rock Harbor Lodge
Isle Royale

ISLE ROYALE NATIONAL PARK
Largest island in Lake Superior

LAKE SUPERIOR

Copper Harbor

41 Keweenaw Peninsula

Hancock
Portage Lake
Keweenaw Bay

ONTONAGON INDIAN RESERVATION

□ HURON N.W.R

Mt. Arvon
1979 FEET
603 METERS
Highest point in Michigan

L'ANSE INDIAN RESERVATION

Erosive action of waves, rain, and wind has carved cliffs, caves, and arches in the colorful sandstone

PICTURED ROCKS NATIONAL LAKESHORE

Whitefish Bay
Sault Ste. Marie

Soo Canals
SAULT STE. MARIE INDIAN RESERVATION

GOGEBIC RANGE

28 *Lake Gogebic*

Ironwood

Ontonagon River

Grand Island
Marquette
77

Munising

NORTH COUNTRY TRAIL

Tahquamenon River

28

St. Marys River

BAY MILLS INDIAN RESERVATION

2
45

LAC VIEUX DESERT INDIAN RESERVATION

Brule River

141

Ishpeming

SENEY NATIONAL WILDLIFE REFUGE

Manistique Lake

2

75

HARBOR ISLAND N.W.R.

Drummond Island

Escanaba River

41

Iron Mountain

Escanaba

HANNAHVILLE INDIAN RESERVATION

41

Manistique

Big Bay de Noc

MICHIGAN ISLANDS N.W.R. □

Straits of Mackinac

Mackinac Island

Bois Blanc Island

Cheboygan
Mullett Lake

Beaver Island

Black Lake

Burt Lake

Little Traverse Bay

Menominee River

Green Bay

GRAND TRAVERSE INDIAN RESERVATION

Grand Traverse Bay

Manitou Islands

SLEEPING BEAR DUNES NATIONAL LAKESHORE
Glaciers pushed rock, sand, and silt from the north to create huge dunes, some as high as 460 feet (140 meters)

22

Traverse City

Torch Lake

Elk Lake

Kalkaska

Grayling

Hubbard Lake

75

23

Alpena

□ MICHIGAN ISLANDS NATIONAL WILDLIFE REFUGE

LAKE HURON

Au Sable River

Oscoda

KILOMETERS 0 — 80
STATUTE MILES 0 — 40

31

Manistee River

Cadillac

Houghton Lake

Houghton Lake

Higgins Lake

Manistee

NORTH COUNTRY TRAIL

131

Ludington

Pere Marquette River

Muskegon River

10

ISABELLA INDIAN RESERVATION

ISABELLA INDIAN RESERVATION

Saginaw Bay

Harbor Beach

25

LAKE MICHIGAN

31

Big Rapids

Midland

Bay City

Cass River

Fremont

Mt. Pleasant

Saginaw River

Saginaw

Muskegon Lake
Norton Shores Muskegon

SHIAWASSEE NATIONAL WILDLIFE REFUGE

27

23

Flint River

96

NORTH COUNTRY TRAIL (PROPOSED)

Owosso

Flint Burton

Sterling Heights

69

Grand Haven

96

Grand Rapids

Grand River

75

Holland

Kentwood
Wyoming

Lansing ★ East Lansing

Pontiac

Troy

Roseville

94

St. Clair River

Port Huron

Lake Saint Clair

Warren

196

Kalamazoo River

69

127

Royal Oak

Livonia

96

St. Clair Shores

East Detroit

Detroit

South Haven

Battle Creek

Dearborn Heights

Dearborn

Kalamazoo

94

Portage

Albion

Jackson

Ann Arbor

Ypsilanti

Trenton

Wyandotte

□ WYANDOTTE N.W.R.

Benton Harbor
St. Joseph

131

St. Joseph River

12

Adrian

Raisin River

Monroe

LAKE ERIE

Coldwater

Detroit River

Niles

12

Apple Blossom

Robin

Michigan, like Florida, is a peninsula state, surrounded by water on three sides. But, unlike Florida, Michigan is *two* peninsulas, an upper one and a lower one. Four of the five Great Lakes lapping against the state's shores make this so.

Michigan is also the only state in the lower 48 where you have to drive *south* to get to Canada—if you're going from Detroit across the Detroit River into Canada.

Scientists believe that the Keweenaw Peninsula and Isle Royale in northwestern Michigan are the upturned edges of a giant trough that forms the basin of Lake Superior.

TUEBOR

Michigan

1 *Fireworks burst over the Detroit skyline and the narrow strait that separates the city from its Canadian neighbor, Windsor, Ontario. Each year the two cities jointly celebrate their countries' independence.*

2 *Shiny cars of many makes and vintages illustrate the evolution of the automobile at the Henry Ford Museum in Dearborn.*

3 *Birch trees frame Mackinac Bridge, a five-mile-long (8-km) span connecting Michigan's Upper and Lower Peninsulas.*

4 *Modern Paul Bunyans push-pull a saw through a wooden beam in record time. Annual competitions such as this jamboree commemorate the logging history of the Upper Peninsula.*

5 *A research scientist in Midland arranges slides showing a rat's rate of absorption of a new chemical compound. Big business in Michigan, chemicals undergo testing before they are put on the market.*

1

2

3

4

5

Illinois

In 1933, six bridges raised in Chicago let barges pass into Lake Michigan. This is the end of a long gulf-to-lake trip up the Mississippi and connecting waterways from New Orleans.

From the shores of Lake Michigan, the bustling, teeming city of Chicago fans out to the Illinois prairie. By far the largest part of Illinois is prairie, pancake flat, with farms, small towns, and medium-size cities. Across the southern part of the state runs a strip of rocky, wooded hills, a bit of the Ozarks that reaches into Illinois from Missouri. The southernmost tip of the state is flat and belongs to the Gulf Coastal Plain.

Illinois marked the southern edge of glacial advance in North America. The ice sheets that descended here ground down landforms and left behind a thick blanket of dark, rich soil. Uplands appear only in the northwestern corner, a spot the glaciers skipped or touched lightly, and areas in the south and west of the Illinois River, where they never reached.

Chicago is part of Illinois only because of a proposal by territorial delegate Nathaniel Pope. At the time statehood was granted in 1818, Pope

petitioned Congress to add a strip of land on the north that included some 60 miles (97 km) of Lake Michigan shoreline. Otherwise, the state's northern boundary would have ended at the tip of the lake and Chicago would be in Wisconsin.

Chicago, the country's third largest city and hub of air, rail, land, and water transportation, had its beginning in the late 1770s. Jean Baptiste Pointe du Sable, a black trapper and trader, built a cabin on marshy land along a river the Illiniwek Indians called Checagou. Chicago would undergo several transformations, including one as an army post, before a surge of growth that began in the 1860s. By then a canal had been dug that connected the city and the Great Lakes with the Mississippi River system. Chicago stood in the key spot where these important waterways linked up. A century later the completion of the St. Lawrence Seaway extended this route to the Atlantic Ocean.

From the 1860s on, Chicago offered the promise of jobs in factories, stockyards, lumberyards, and on the docks to Europeans fleeing violence or poverty at home. Southern blacks came too; today blacks make up 40 percent of Chicago's population. Migrations continue, bringing Asians, Puerto Ricans, and Mexicans as well. The city and its ever expanding suburbs are home to more than half of all Illinoisans.

Three-fifths of the factories in Illinois are in the Chicago area. The city's steel mills remain among the world's most productive. Chicago's mail-order businesses and grain exchange are the largest in the U. S., its O'Hare International Airport the world's busiest. Three of the tallest buildings in the world tower over downtown Chicago. The nation's first skyscraper rose there on a frame of steel in 1884, as part of the rebuilding after the Great Fire of 1871 destroyed the earlier wooden structures, taking 300 lives.

Some 500 rivers drain the state. The Illinois River flows 273 miles (439 km) to the Mississippi River, the western boundary. The Wabash and the Ohio form the borders on the south and southeast. The city of Cairo, where the Mississippi and the Ohio converge, was an important cotton port more than a hundred years ago. Farmers here grew cotton until the 1960s, before switching to more profitable soybeans.

This part of Illinois has a southern heritage.

The first settlers here were from states to the south or southeast. Illinois pioneers included a poor farm family from Kentucky named Lincoln. They settled near Springfield, the state capital, where young Abe held a number of jobs and read law before beginning his career in politics.

After the Erie Canal was finished in 1825, providing an easy route across the Appalachians, settlers from the East and from Europe joined the southern immigrants or moved into central or northern Illinois, where they discovered the prairie, covered with tall, waving green and purplish grasses.

Prairie sod was thick and gummy, and did not yield to wooden or iron plows. But in 1837 a blacksmith named John Deere invented a self-polishing steel plow that cut through the sod with ease. Opening a factory in Moline, Deere made his fortune. The company he started still manufactures farm machinery, one of the state's largest exports.

In a state where more than 80 percent of the population lives in urban areas, a surprising 80 percent of the land is farmed. Much of the fertile glacial soil, up to 75 feet (23 m) thick in some places, supports crops of corn and soybeans. The corn in turn fattens some 4.4 million Illinois hogs that are sent to market each year.

In the ground are some of the largest coal reserves in the U. S. When burned, this mostly bituminous, or soft, coal produces more pollution than hard coal. But as cleaner methods for burning are developed, this Illinois resource could help solve the country's energy problems.

Area: *24th largest state, 56,345 sq mi (145,934 sq km)*
Population: *11,430,602; ranks sixth*
Major Cities: *Chicago, 2,783,726; Rockford, 139,426; Peoria, 113,504*
Manufacturing: *machinery, food products, chemicals, metal products, electronics, transportation equipment, metals, rubber and plastics, scientific instruments, paper products, stone, clay, and glass products, furniture, clothing*
Mining and Quarrying: *coal, oil and gas, stone, sand and gravel*
Agriculture: *soybeans, corn, hogs, cattle, milk, wheat, hay, greenhouse and nursery products*
Other Important Activities: *finance, transportation, tourism, printing and publishing*
Statehood: *the 21st state; admitted December 3, 1818*

1 2 3 4 5 6 7 8 9 10 11

A

B

C

D

E

F

G

H

J

K

L

M

N

O

P

Q

R

S

T

Charles Mound
1,235 FEET
+ 376 METERS
Highest point
in Illinois

*The northwest corner
of Illinois shows no
evidence of glacial action*

Zion

Waukegan
North Chicago

Rockford
Machesney Park

Freeport

Highland Park *LAKE*
Wilmette *MICHIGAN*

Arlington Heights
Schaumburg
Evanston
Oak Park

UPPER MISSISSIPPI RIVER
NATIONAL WILDLIFE
AND FISH REFUGE

De Kalb
Elgin
Des
Plaines

Sterling
Dixon
Elmhurst
Chicago
Naperville
Cicero

Rock Island
Aurora
Downers
Grove
Oak Lawn

Moline
HENNEPIN
Harvey
Calumet City

MARK TWAIN
NATIONAL
WILDLIFE
REFUGE
CANAL
Joliet
Chicago Heights

Kewanee
Morris
Park
Forest

Ottawa
Seneca

Streator
Kankakee

Monmouth
Galesburg
Pontiac

Peoria
Pekin
Normal

Nauvoo
Bloomington
Rantoul

Macomb
Dickson
Mounds
CHAUTAUQUA
NATIONAL
WILDLIFE
REFUGE

Danville

MARK TWAIN
NATIONAL
WILDLIFE
REFUGE
Lincoln
Champaign
Urbana

Quincy
Beardstown

Springfield
Decatur

Jacksonville
Sangamon River

MARK TWAIN
NATIONAL
WILDLIFE
REFUGE
Lake Shelbyville
Charleston

Mattoon

Mississippi River

Effingham

Alton
Lawrenceville

MARK TWAIN
NATIONAL
WILDLIFE
REFUGE
Edwardsville
Carlyle Lake
Little Wabash River

East St. Louis
Collinsville

Belleville
Centralia

Mt. Vernon

Big Muddy River
Rend Lake
Carmi

Du Quoin

Kaskaskia

Crab Orchard Lake

Carbondale
Marion
Shawneetown

CRAB ORCHARD
NATIONAL WILDLIFE REFUGE

*Southern limit of
North American
glaciation*

CYPRESS CREEK
NATIONAL
WILDLIFE REFUGE

Ohio River

Cairo

GREAT RIVER ROAD
Rock River
Fox River
Kankakee River
Illinois River
Spoon River
Kaskaskia River
Wabash River

KILOMETERS 80
STATUTE MILES 40

The Mississippi River
forms the entire western
boundary of Illinois, or at
least it did until the flood
of 1881. In April of that
year, the raging Missis-
sippi broke through a
narrow-necked peninsula
that separated it from the
mouth of the Kaskaskia
River. Kaskaskia, a
village that had been settled by Indians and
French traders and had
served as a territorial
and state capital, found
itself a 10,000-acre
(4,050-ha) island.

Eventually the Missis-
sippi abandoned its old
channel, and Kaskaskia
became a piece of Illi-
nois on the Missouri side
of the river.

ILLINOIS

Violet

Cardinal

1

2

3

4

5

Illinois

1 *Antenna repair atop Chicago's Hancock Center requires steel nerves. Lesser high rises march along Lake Michigan's shore.*

2 *The Ohio (at right) meets the Mississippi River at Cairo. Flatlands like Egypt's Nile Delta suggested the city's name.*

3 *Steel bins store 260,000 bushels of corn on an Illinois farm. The state vies yearly with Iowa as top corn producer.*

4 *Sleeping on the job, a dummy fitted with electronic sensors tests mattress comfort at a Chicago factory.*

5 *A scientist at Fermilab, near Chicago, examines a glass-and-wire device that detects the pion, a subatomic particle. Enrico Fermi and his University of Chicago colleagues produced the world's first self-sustaining nuclear chain reaction in 1942.*

Indiana

A fertile valley of Indiana's Wabash River witnessed two attempts to form a utopia, or ideal society. The first community, named Harmonie, was founded in 1814-15 by a group of Lutheran separatists (called Harmonists) fleeing persecution in Germany. They settled in Pennsylvania before moving to Indiana. Harmonie lasted only ten years, time enough to build a village and plant fields, vineyards, and orchards; then the Harmonists returned to Pennsylvania. The second community, New Harmony, drew artists and scholars from eastern states. These pioneers came to the village in 1825 to pursue knowledge in an atmosphere of equality and independence. Their experiment lasted only two years, but the town of New Harmony remains a source of artistic creativity in modern Indiana.

The state has produced many writers whose works are regarded as American classics. Generations of schoolchildren have memorized the verses of 19th-century poet James Whitcomb Riley, including his *Little Orphan Annie*. A native of Terre Haute, Theodore Dreiser wrote the novels *An American Tragedy* and *Sister Carrie*. High school and college literature classes often read the books of Indianapolis-born Kurt Vonnegut, Jr., author of *Slaughterhouse Five* and *Cat's Cradle*.

Indiana bears the marks of glaciers over five-sixths of its terrain. In the north, glaciers left behind moraines, deposits of rocks and debris, and depressions that filled with water to form kettle hole lakes. Along part of the Lake Michigan shore, winds have piled immense hills of sand called the Indiana Dunes. The largest dune, Mount Baldy, is bare of vegetation, and is called a "live" dune because prevailing winds move it slowly away from the lakeshore. Older dunes, stabilized by a covering of soil, grasses, and trees, lie farther inland.

On the western end of the Lake Michigan shore stands a group of industrial cities, midway between sources of materials needed by the steel industry: the iron ranges of Minnesota and the coalfields of southern Indiana and Illinois.

In the early 20th century one of the world's largest steel mills was built in Gary. Like Chicago, and unlike the rest of Indiana, the area drew large numbers of Poles, Hungarians, Czechs, Italians, and other European immigrants, as

By the early 1900s, roads like this had been improved to ease the farmer's trip from farm to market. Smooth roads did nothing to improve the behavior of these wayward hogs.

well as blacks from southern states. Even after suffering severe economic problems, northern Indiana remains the country's largest steel producer. But the people pay a price. Smokestacks spew out pollutants that, despite attempts to control them, can darken the sky at noon.

Central Indiana is covered by till plains that create a gently rolling landscape. Till, or glacial debris, is a mixture of rocks, clay, sand, and other sediment deposited by glaciers. The deep, rich soil of the till plains provides the state's best farmland. Pioneers of the early 19th century flocked to this part of Indiana to buy farms from the federal government at low rates.

The glaciers stopped short of south-central Indiana, leaving there a more rugged terrain of steep hills interspersed with lowlands. Large deposits of coal and petroleum underlie the area. So does a valuable outcrop of limestone that "cutters," generations of quarry workers from Bloomington and nearby towns, have carved up to build landmarks such as the Empire State

Building and Rockefeller Center in New York City, the Pentagon in northern Virginia, and the U. S. Treasury in Washington, D. C.

A road map of Indiana shows at its center a ring around the state capital, Indianapolis. Of the 91,395 miles (147,055 km) of roads in the state, many converge on Indianapolis. Among them are U. S. 40, once called the National Road, a wide, bumpy track that took pioneers to the western frontier.

The state was an early center of the automobile industry, producing some 200 makes of cars before being eclipsed by Michigan's carmakers. Today, Indiana-made Stutzes, Duesenbergs, and Maxwells rank among the antique autos most prized by collectors. Each year, on Memorial Day weekend, Indianapolis resumes its place as automotive capital with the running of the Indianapolis 500. Drivers in state-of-the-art cars circle the Indy track 200 times, hoping to win the prize of more than three million dollars that is awarded for the fastest time.

As a transportation hub, Indianapolis became a center for the processing and distribution of farm products. The manufacturing of medicines, cars, aircraft parts, and electrical goods also made the city an industrial center. When hard times hit the auto industry in the 1970s and '80s and other factories began to close, the leaders of Indianapolis looked for new ways to help the city prosper. Sports was one solution, suggested by the popularity of the Indy 500. The city built the 61,000-seat Hoosier Dome. Newly constructed facilities for swimming, bicycle racing, tennis, and track-and-field have turned Indianapolis into a world-recognized center for amateur and professional sports.

Area: *38th largest state, 36,185 sq mi (93,720 sq km)*
Population: *5,554,159; ranks 14th*
Major Cities: *Indianapolis, 731,327; Ft. Wayne, 173,072; Evansville, 126,272*
Manufacturing: *metals, chemicals, transportation equipment, electronics, machinery, food products, metal products, rubber and plastics, scientific instruments, furniture, lumber and wood products*
Mining and Quarrying: *coal, limestone, sand and gravel, oil and gas*
Agriculture: *soybeans, corn, hogs, cattle, milk, eggs*
Other Important Activities: *printing and publishing*
Statehood: *19th state; admitted December 11, 1816*

Indiana is mostly flat. As the drainage pattern of the rivers shows, it also slopes to the southwest. Most of the rivers flow toward the Wabash River, which marks the southwestern border.

Some southern parts, untouched by glaciers during the Ice Age, are hilly and wooded. Here, towns with names such as Stoney Lonesome and Beanblossom attract artists and artisans.

Quarries south of Indianapolis produce some of the nation's finest limestone, formed from the skeletons of tiny sea creatures that lived here when ancient oceans covered the area.

Cardinal

Peony

0   KILOMETERS   60

0   STATUTE MILES   40

LAKE MICHIGAN

INDIANA DUNES
NATIONAL
LAKESHORE

Michigan City

East Chicago
Hammond   Gary
Munster
Highland
Merrillville
Crown Point
Portage
Hobart
Valparaiso
La Porte

Elkhart
South
Bend   Mishawaka
Goshen
Angola

Kankakee River
Plymouth
Warsaw
Tippecanoe River
St. Joseph River
Maumee River

Fort Wayne
St. Marys River

Lake Shafer
Twelve Mile
Logansport
Wabash
Peru
Huntington
Huntington Lake
Wabash River

Lake Freeman
Salamonie Lake

Mississinewa Lake
Salamonie River

West Lafayette
Lafayette
Kokomo
Marion
Mississinewa River

Frankfort
231
Sugar Creek
Morse Reservoir
Muncie
Highest point in Indiana 1,257 FEET 383 METERS

Crawfordsville
Lebanon
Noblesville
Anderson
New Castle

Carmel
Geist Reservoir

Brownsburg
Lawrence
Richmond
Indianapolis
Greenfield
Connersville
Plainfield
Beech Grove
Brookville Lake

Cecil M. Harden Lake
Eel River
Greenwood

Terre Haute
Cataract Lake
Franklin
Shelbyville
Martinsville
Whitewater River

Beanblossom
Stoney Lonesome
Columbus

White River
Gnaw Bone
Muscatatuck River
Lawrenceburg

Bloomington
Monroe Lake
Seymour

Bedford
MUSCATATUCK NATIONAL WILDLIFE REFUGE
Patriot

Madison
Ohio River

Vincennes
Washington
Salem
Pumpkin Center

Wabash River
Patoka Lake
Patoka River

New Albany
Clarksville
Jeffersonville

New Harmony
Santa Claus

Evansville
Tell City

Ohio River

Indiana

1 *A craftsman polishes a saxophone at a factory in Elkhart. The city is one of the world's chief producers of band instruments.*

2 *Sitting on some of the lowest land in Indiana, the town of New Harmony overlooks the Wabash River as it flows southward to its confluence with the Ohio.*

3 *Skilled nurses attend a patient at a children's hospital in Indianapolis. The capital has become a regional center for advanced medical care.*

4 *Home to pro football's Colts, the Hoosier Dome symbolizes Indianapolis's commitment to sports. In 1984 the city used the 61,000-seat stadium to entice the team to leave Baltimore, Maryland.*

5 *Polluting smoke billows from a steel mill in northwestern Indiana. Foreign competition, automation, and other kinds of new technology mean fewer jobs for residents of this industrial region.*

1

2

3

5

4

Ohio

In Harriet Beecher Stowe's 1852 antislavery novel, *Uncle Tom's Cabin*, the slave Eliza and her baby made a daring winter escape across the Ohio River from Kentucky, leaping from one floating raft of ice to another, "till dimly, as in a dream, she saw the Ohio side, and a man helping her up the bank."

During the mid-1800s, Ohio abolitionists, with antislavery workers in other states, provided sanctuaries called stations along the Underground Railroad, a network of escape routes for slaves from the South. The fugitives usually moved at night on foot, often alone, but sometimes sheltering in the homes of sympathizers across the state, until they could board boats and cross Lake Erie to freedom in Canada.

About 2,000 years ago, Indians hunted, fished, and farmed in the river valleys of central and southern Ohio and traded for raw materials from the Rocky Mountains to the Gulf of Mexico. They left evidence of remarkable engineering ability: thousands of hand-built earthen mounds, many of them immense and often made in geometric or animal shapes. These Mound Builders were gone, and other Indian cultures had taken their place, when the first white explorers arrived in the 17th century.

At the end of the Revolutionary War, parcels of land in Ohio were awarded or sold to war veterans and others who wanted to start new lives on the frontier. In 1788 a group from Massachusetts and Connecticut sailed down the Ohio to its confluence with the Muskingum River. Their community, Marietta, opened Ohio to permanent white settlement and became the first of many prosperous ports along the river.

The most famous is Cincinnati, which sits on a graceful bend of the Ohio in a low basin backed by seven hills. In the early 1800s, the port moved the grain, produce, and livestock of central Ohio farmers, first on flatboats and then on steamboats. Early settlers from New Jersey, Virginia, and New England were soon joined by Germans, who worked in the slaughterhouses and sausage factories. Today many people help manufacture soap products and machine tools—machines that shape metal for making parts for automobiles, refrigerators, and other products. Residents of Ohio, Indiana, and Kentucky head to cosmopolitan Cincinnati, shopping lists in

Around 1895 an elementary school teacher maintained authority with a pointer and a stern manner. Fractions on the blackboard signify a typical, fact-oriented education based on the three R's.

hand. The Ohio River still moves the state's resources, often in lines of 20 barges, each loaded with thousands of pounds of coal, oil, iron ore, chemicals, metals, salt, sand, or gravel.

In 1796 New Englanders arrived on the shores of Lake Erie, shallowest of the Great Lakes. By the mid-1800s, Cleveland was one of the fastest growing cities in the third most populous state in the country. Cleveland became home to the largest assortment of ethnic groups in Ohio. Germans, Irish, Poles, Italians, Czechs, Russians, southern blacks, and Greeks number among the dozens of different groups who came, especially after the Civil War. They worked in the iron and steel mills, oil refineries, and other factories that line Lake Erie and the Cuyahoga River. By the early 1900s, Ohio was an industrial state, three-fourths of whose people would eventually live in urban areas. Throughout most of the state, large cities and towns punctuate vast spreads of corn, wheat, and cattle pasture.

Other factory towns face Lake Erie. Toledo makes glass and automobile parts, and serves as a regional coal distribution center. Lorain makes steel, as well as cars, trucks, and buses.

Akron used to make more bias-ply rubber tires than any city in the world. But foreign competition, the popularity of longer wearing radial tires, and the moving of factories south and west forced Akron's rubber plants to close. Thousands of people lost their jobs. Now city leaders look for ways to restore prosperity. One hope is the Thomas Edison Program, a state project that brings together Ohio companies, up-to-date technologies, and the financing that makes industrial development possible.

Columbus, Ohio's capital and largest city, has mostly light industry. But what it has more of than any other U. S. city except Washington, D. C., is data base information. Enormous quantities of data are stored at Ohio State University and at labs, research institutes, scientific information services, and computer libraries.

The landscape of southeastern Ohio is steep, rugged, and heavily wooded, part of the Appalachian Plateau that also extends into Pennsylvania and West Virginia. Rich natural resources including coal, clay, oil, salt, and natural gas provide mining jobs for the area's residents.

For more than a century, Ohio's industries grew unchecked. Factories belched out smoke and sent chemical waste into rivers and lakes. In the 1960s, Lake Erie was declared "dead" from pollution, and recreational uses of the lake were banned. Since then, laws passed to clean up the lake by limiting industrial waste have paid off, although toxic sediments still cause concern. Swimming beaches are now open, and walleye by the million again await fishermen's lures.

Area: *35th largest state, 41,330 sq mi (107,044 sq km)*
Population: *10,847,115; ranks seventh*
Major Cities: *Columbus, 632,910; Cleveland, 505,616; Cincinnati, 364,040*
Manufacturing: *transportation equipment, machinery, metal products, chemicals, metals, food products, electronics, rubber and plastics, stone, clay, and glass products, paper products, scientific instruments*
Mining: *coal, oil and gas*
Agriculture: *soybeans, milk, corn, cattle, hogs*
Other Important Activities: *printing and publishing*
Statehood: *the 17th state; admitted March 1, 1803*

Prehistoric Indians lived along waterways such as the Ohio River, which today forms much of the state's eastern and southern borders. Some of the mounds they built still exist, linked by a national scenic trail.

Dashed red lines on the map show unfinished parts of the North Country Trail, planned as the nation's longest marked footpath. When completed, the trail will extend 3,200 miles (5,150 km) from North Dakota to New York. Ohio's section will link archaeological sites along the Little Miami River to Great Serpent Mound and Mound City near Chillicothe.

KILOMETERS 60
STATUTE MILES 30

1 2 3 4 5 6 7 8 9 10 11 12 13 14 15

A B C D E F G H J K L M N O P Q R

LAKE ERIE

CEDAR POINT NATIONAL WILDLIFE REFUGE
WEST SISTER ISLAND NATIONAL WILDLIFE REFUGE
OTTAWA NATIONAL WILDLIFE REFUGE
Kelleys Island

Ashtabula
Painesville
Willoughby
Mentor
Euclid
Wickliffe
East Cleveland
South Euclid
Cleveland
Cleveland Heights
Lorain
North Olmsted
Lakewood
Shaker Heights
Garfield Heights
Parma
Mosquito Creek Lake
Warren
Niles
Austintown
Youngstown
Boardman
Struthers
Alliance
North Canton
Canton
East Liverpool

Toledo
Oregon
Maumee
Bryan
Defiance
Bowling Green
Fremont
Sandusky
Norwalk
Elyria
Strongsville
Brunswick
CUYAHOGA VALLEY NATIONAL RECREATION AREA
Cuyahoga River
Cuyahoga Falls
Kent
Akron
Barberton
Wooster
Massillon
Tuscarawas River
New Philadelphia
Atwood Lake
Leesville Lake
Steubenville

Maumee River
Van Wert
Fostoria
Tiffin
Shelby
Ashland

Blanchard River
Findlay
Sandusky River
Mansfield

Lima
Ottawa River
Kenton
Marion
Olentangy River

Celina
Grand Lake
Wapakoneta
NORTH COUNTRY TRAIL
Indian Lake
Scioto River
Campbell Hill 1,550 FEET +472 METERS Highest point in Ohio
Delaware Lake
Mt. Vernon
Mohican River
Coshocton
Martins Ferry

Sidney
Bellefontaine
Marysville
Delaware
Alum Creek Lake
Hoover Reservoir
Newark
Cambridge
New Concord

Piqua
Great Miami River
Upper Arlington
Worthington
Dillon Lake
Zanesville
Senecaville Lake (PROPOSED)
NORTH COUNTRY TRAIL

Greenville
Troy
Springfield
Columbus
Whitehall
Reynoldsburg
Buckeye Lake
Muskingum River

Huber Heights
Fairborn
Beavercreek
Dayton
Kettering
Xenia
Washington Court House
Lancaster

Middletown
Wilmington
Circleville
Ancient Indians shaped mounds from the earth to cover their dead
MOUND CITY GROUP NATIONAL MONUMENT
Chillicothe
Athens
Marietta
Belpre

Hamilton
Fairfield
North College Hill
Cheviot
Sharonville
Reading
Norwood
Cincinnati
Rocky Fork Lake
GREAT SERPENT MOUND
Jackson
Paint Creek
Scioto River

Ohio River
Portsmouth
Gallipolis
Ironton

Ohio River

Little Miami River

Cardinal

Scarlet Carnation

1

2

Ohio

1 *Lighted buildings old and new illuminate downtown Cleveland. In the background flows the Cuyahoga River.*

2 *Native Americans built this earthen coiled serpent more than 1,500 years ago. The Great Lakes region has thousands of these mounds, used for rituals or burials.*

3 *Pitching straw is all in a day's work at a county fair. Rural traditions remain strong in largely industrial Ohio.*

3

4

4 *In a lab near Cincinnati, researchers sample the breath of people testing the effectiveness of toothpaste and mouthwash.*

5 *Young racers in engineless cars burn up the track at the All-American Soap Box Derby, held each August in Akron. Children from around the world bring homemade cars to compete in the downhill race.*

5

The Heartland

When pioneering settlers rolled westward across the heart of the continent, they found themselves adrift on a sea of grass that seemed to stretch onward endlessly. It could be unnerving, especially for those who had lived all their lives in the comforting shade of eastern forests. For now they were venturing into a new land, a place of endless open sky and sun and wind, a realm of rolling prairies with only widely scattered hills and highlands. What trees grew here stood mainly along rivers and in upland areas such as the Black Hills, the Ozark Plateau, and along Lake Superior.

In the eastern part of the prairie rainfall was usually plentiful. Here the Indian grass and big bluestem grew up to eight feet (2 m) tall. The land was fertile, but so thickly and tightly matted with grass roots that it took as many as 20 draft animals to drag a wooden or cast-iron plow through the sod. It wasn't until John Deere's Prairie Queen plow of self-polishing steel came into widespread use in the 1850s that a farmer working alone could break through the sod and turn the fertile glacial soil beneath.

Farther west, pioneer families found that the land gradually grew drier and the grasses grew shorter. On the Great Plains—the western part of the prairie—they encountered what was at first thought to be the Great American Desert, a semiarid expanse of short, bunched grasses best suited to raising cattle. But the plains, though dry, were fertile. What they needed was water. Under large areas of the land lay a layer of sand and gravel so vast that it could hold enough water to fill Lake Huron. Windmills that drew water out of the ground made parts of the high plains ideal for growing wheat—spring wheat in the colder north, and winter wheat in the milder south.

This heartland region, with less than 15 percent of the land in the United States, raises more corn than all of Europe, more wheat than South America, and more cattle than Australia. Cities from Minneapolis and St. Paul to Wichita and St. Louis rose to prominence as transportation and processing centers to serve farmers and cattlemen. Although they have since branched into other businesses, they still thrive as centers of agribusiness, the modern farming industry that finds its roots deep in heartland soil.

Lake Superior

Duluth

St. Paul
Minneapolis

Omaha

Kansas City

St. Louis

Mississippi River

Ozark

Plateau

NORTH DAKOTA
SOUTH DAKOTA
MINNESOTA
IOWA

NEBRASKA
KANSAS
MISSOURI

North Dakota

Geographically, North Dakota is right in the middle of it all. A stone monument near the town of Rugby marks the dead center of the continent. From there it is about 1,500 miles (2,400 km) to the Atlantic Ocean, Pacific Ocean, Arctic Ocean, and the Gulf of Mexico.

North Dakota has endless prairie horizons and few people. Only half of North Dakotans are urban dwellers and about 15 percent live on farms or ranches. In the 1980s North Dakota faced a population drain. Near the Montana line a billboard pleaded, "Stay in North Dakota—Custer was healthy when he left." Now there are predictions that the state's oil reserves may need new workers and that the population may rise a little.

North Dakota's wild and woolly weather contributes to its loneliness. Dust storms, raging blizzards, and some of the hottest and coldest temperatures ever recorded on the continent help "keep the riffraff out," as one hard-bitten Dakotan explained. North Dakota lies far from the moderating influences of oceans and large lakes. It has no mountains and few trees to blunt the winds that race across its open expanses.

For those who tough it out, there are compensations. The valley of the Red River of the North has some of the world's best cropland, black soil rich in humus, decomposed plant and animal matter. These bottomlands are the bed of a glacial lake that drained away when the ice retreated about 10,000 years ago. The fertile topsoil, combined with long summer days and adequate rainfall, produces bumper crops. Huge farms, typical of today's agribusiness, are not new to North Dakota. In the 1870s, speculators bought hundreds of thousands of acres of cheap land and created what were called "bonanza farms" to grow wheat and attract settlers as workers.

West of the Red River Valley, at a steeply pitched slope called an escarpment, the gently rolling Drift Prairie steps upward. The prairie gets its name from drift, rock debris carried here by glaciers. Over thousands of years, with weathering and the addition of organic matter, drift becomes soil.

The Drift Prairie is dimpled by thousands of kettle hole lakes and ponds that occupy depressions formed by the melting of large chunks of buried glacial ice. Today the kettle hole regions are a haven for millions of migrating ducks and geese, as well as for resident pheasants, grouse, partridges, and meadowlarks.

Farmers here grow wheat, a lot of it. No other state grows more spring durum wheat, used to make spaghetti and other pasta. Nor does any other state grow more barley, or flaxseed, used to make linseed oil for paint, or sunflowers, whose seeds are pressed for high-protein vegetable oil.

Near the northern part of the Drift Prairie,

On a day in 1905 the citizens of Mott turn out to await the arrival of the stagecoach and the mail. This settlement on the Great Plains was established as a trading center on the Cannonball River.

along the border with Canada, rises a cluster of low, lake-studded hills called the Turtle Mountains. This is one of the state's few forested areas. It is also the site of a summer camp for artists and musicians, and a spectacular international garden that commemorates the years of peace between Canada and the United States.

The Great Plains rise west of the Drift Prairie. North Dakotans call this region the Missouri Plateau, for the river that curves across the western part of the state. On the east bank of the Missouri the state capital, Bismarck, serves the surrounding region with agriculture-related industries such as food processing, the manufacture of farm machinery, and shipping. A two-mile-wide (3-km) dam across the river, the nation's largest earthen dam, creates Lake Sakakawea, named for the Indian woman who accompanied explorers Meriwether Lewis and William Clark on their trek across the continent in the early 1800s. The plateau is hilly, stony country wrinkled by gorges and ravines. Rain is sparse here, and cattle graze the shortgrasses.

Here, too, are found oil and lignite, a soft, brownish coal that fuels local power plants. The lignite lies close to the surface. Huge shovels and draglines gouge it out of the earth, often scarring the countryside.

The Indians who lived in the western Dakotas knew a section of the Missouri Plateau as Mako Sica—"land bad." We know this jumbled maze of hills and pinnacles carved by the Little Missouri River as the Badlands. It was here that Theodore Roosevelt ranched during the 1880s, before he became President of the United States. Today his Elkhorn Ranch makes up part of North Dakota's only national park, a place where bison roam and coyotes prowl.

Area: *17th largest state, 70,703 sq mi (183,121 sq km)*
Population: *638,800; ranks 47th*
Major Cities: *Fargo, 74,111; Grand Forks, 49,425; Bismarck, 49,256*
Agriculture: *wheat, cattle, barley, sunflowers, sugar beets, milk*
Mining: *oil and gas, coal*
Manufacturing: *food products, machinery, transportation equipment, stone, clay, and glass products, chemicals, metal products*
Other Important Activities: *tourism, printing and publishing*
Statehood: *39th state; admitted November 2, 1889*

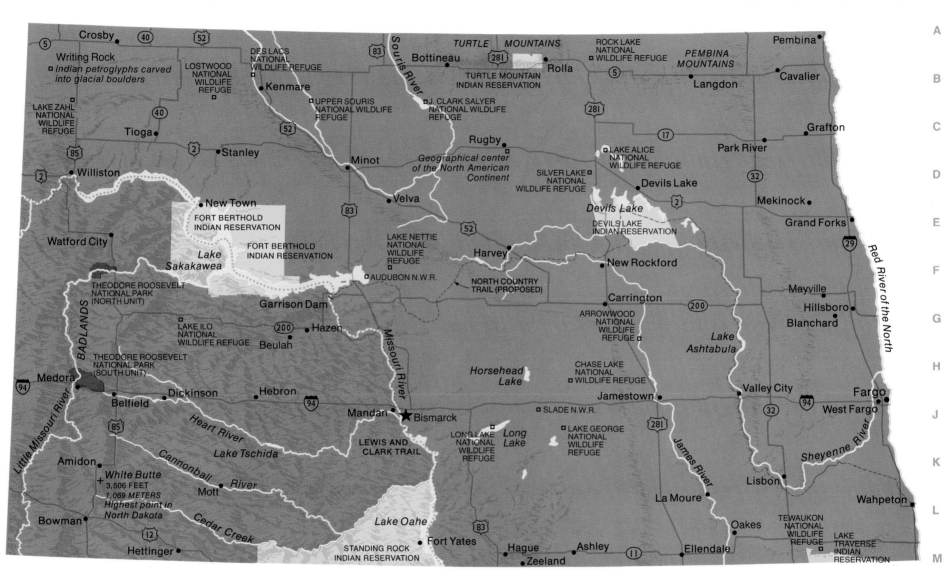

1 2 3 4 5 6 7 8 9 10 11 12 13 14 15 16 17 18 19

A B C D E F G H J K L M

Crosby
Writing Rock
□ Indian petroglyphs carved
into glacial boulders
LAKE ZAHL
NATIONAL
WILDLIFE
REFUGE
Tioga
Williston
Watford City
BADLANDS
THEODORE ROOSEVELT
NATIONAL PARK
(NORTH UNIT)
THEODORE ROOSEVELT
NATIONAL PARK
(SOUTH UNIT)
Medora
Belfield
Amidon
White Butte
3,506 FEET
1,069 METERS
Highest point in
North Dakota
Bowman
Hettinger

LOSTWOOD
NATIONAL
WILDLIFE
REFUGE
Kenmare
Stanley
New Town
FORT BERTHOLD
INDIAN RESERVATION
FORT BERTHOLD
INDIAN RESERVATION
Lake
Sakakawea
LAKE ILO
NATIONAL
WILDLIFE REFUGE
Beulah
Hazen
Garrison Dam
Dickinson
Hebron
Heart River
Lake Tschida
Cannonball
River
Mott
Cedar Creek

DES LACS
NATIONAL
WILDLIFE REFUGE
UPPER SOURIS
NATIONAL WILDLIFE
REFUGE
Minot
Velva
LAKE NETTIE
NATIONAL
WILDLIFE
REFUGE
AUDUBON N.W.R.
NORTH COUNTRY
TRAIL (PROPOSED)
Missouri River
LEWIS AND
CLARK TRAIL
Mandan
Bismarck
Lake Oahe
STANDING ROCK
INDIAN RESERVATION
Fort Yates

Souris River
TURTLE MOUNTAINS
Bottineau
TURTLE MOUNTAIN
INDIAN RESERVATION
J. CLARK SALYER
NATIONAL WILDLIFE
REFUGE
Rugby
Geographical center
of the North American
Continent
Harvey
New Rockford
Carrington
ARROWWOOD
NATIONAL
WILDLIFE
REFUGE
Horsehead
Lake
CHASE LAKE
NATIONAL
WILDLIFE REFUGE
Jamestown
SLADE N.W.R.
LONG LAKE
NATIONAL
WILDLIFE
REFUGE
Long
Lake
LAKE GEORGE
NATIONAL
WILDLIFE
REFUGE
La Moure
Hague
Zeeland
Ashley
James River

ROCK LAKE
NATIONAL
WILDLIFE REFUGE
Rolla
SILVER LAKE
NATIONAL
WILDLIFE REFUGE
LAKE ALICE
NATIONAL
WILDLIFE REFUGE
Devils Lake
Devils Lake
DEVILS LAKE
INDIAN RESERVATION
Lake
Ashtabula
Valley City
Lisbon
Oakes
TEWAUKON
NATIONAL
WILDLIFE
REFUGE
Ellendale

PEMBINA
MOUNTAINS
Pembina
Langdon
Cavalier
Grafton
Park River
Mekinock
Grand Forks
Red River of the North
Mayville
Hillsboro
Blanchard
Fargo
West Fargo
Sheyenne River
Wahpeton
LAKE
TRAVERSE
INDIAN
RESERVATION

KILOMETERS
0   80
STATUTE MILES
0   40

Glaciers helped shape much of North Dakota. Moving sheets of ice reached almost to the present-day Missouri River. Ice blocked preglacial rivers from their old channels and forced them to cut new southerly courses. Several combined to form the Missouri.

South and west of the river, the land is rough and hilly, slashed and carved by erosion. No glacier smoothed the land here. East of the river the land is mostly flat to gently rolling, and twice drops down toward the north-flowing Red River of the North, the state's eastern boundary.

Wild
Prairie Rose

Western
Meadowlark

North Dakota

1 *A young brave takes part in the Grass Dance at a powwow held each July near Lake Sakakawea. "It is a time," according to one participant, "to teach children to share in our culture." The dance recalls past hunts and memorable deeds.*

2 *A country churchyard greens checkerboard farmland in the Red River Valley. Land now lush with wheat fields reaching to the horizon once lay at the bottom of ancient glacial Lake Agassiz.*

3 *Beneath a brooding sky, six-foot-tall (2-m) sunflowers face the sun near an old grain elevator in the Red River Valley. Heads containing up to a thousand protein-rich seeds produce high-quality oils for cooking and making margarine.*

4 *Technicians check a Minuteman missile, one of 300 buried in steel silos beneath the state's prairies. This one, at Grand Forks Air Force Base, is used for training.*

5 *A baby pelican begs a meal from its parent. These white pelicans, and half the wild ducks in the lower 48 states, are among the 353 bird species found in North Dakota.*

1

2

3

4

5

Minnesota

Minnesota has some 22,000 lakes, wetlands, and ponds, more than any other state except Texas and Alaska, thanks mostly to glaciers that left behind hollowed-out places that filled with water. One of them, Lake Itasca, is the source of the Mississippi River. Minnesota's rivers and streams extend 92,000 miles (148,000 km) and flow in three directions. The Mississippi drains southward into the Gulf of Mexico, while rivers in the northern part of the state flow north into Hudson Bay or east into Lake Superior.

Water has helped make Minnesota a transportation and commercial center for the upper Midwest. Duluth, with its neighbor, Superior, Wisconsin, is the world's busiest freshwater port. From the western end of Lake Superior, Duluth has access to the Atlantic Ocean through the Great Lakes and the St. Lawrence Seaway. Ships from Duluth carry grain and iron ore overseas or to factories near the Great Lakes.

Frontiersmen and trappers could travel up the Mississippi as far as the Falls of St. Anthony without stopping to portage their goods. Indians camped near the falls, fur traders set up posts, and in the 1820s the U. S. Army built an outpost there. Settlers arrived, and the twin cities of Minneapolis and St. Paul grew up on either side of the river. Minnesota's capital, St. Paul, was briefly known in its earliest days as Pig's Eye, after a voyageur who lived there. It became St. Paul when a Roman Catholic priest built a chapel near the river, dedicating it to the saint. The Falls of St. Anthony provided power for milling grain and cutting wood, activities that in time became giant industries. Today electronics and other high-tech industries are also economically important to both cities.

About half of all Minnesotans live in and around the Twin Cities, an area that includes 1,650 parks and 650 lakes. In summer, people swim and sail. They canoe from lake to lake. Winter finds them skating, ice fishing, and even playing softball on ice.

Minneapolis has rebuilt much of its downtown. An elevated network of glass-enclosed, climate-controlled walkways, called skyways, links buildings in a large area of downtown Minneapolis. The skyways shelter pedestrians from cold, snowy winters and summer heat.

In the early days Minnesota's great forests of white and red pine supplied much of the lumber used to build towns and cities across the Great Plains. The northern third of the state still is wild and woodsy, a haven for deer, moose, bears, and birds. Waterfowl find food and shelter in bogs and marshes. Along the border with Canada spreads the Boundary Waters Canoe Area Wilderness, a thousand lakes in a million acres. Through this watery maze paddled Indians, explorers, and voyageurs. Today it is the country's only national canoe area, a haven that

In costumes white as snow and sparkly as ice, Minneapolis children present a winter pageant in 1925. Minnesota residents traditionally enliven winter with festivals and seasonal sports.

shuts out most intrusions of the modern world.

Minnesota's rich glacial soils, covering the western part of the state, attracted throngs of farmers from eastern states and from Germany, Scandinavia, and other parts of Europe. Sprinkled with lakes and streams, the rolling farmlands of the region are home to the dairy cattle that make Minnesota a leading producer of milk, butter, and cheese.

In 1865 a geologist discovered rich deposits of iron ore in the northeastern wedge of the state known as Arrowhead Country. Soon other rich deposits turned up in the Mesabi Range. Glaciers had nearly exposed these deposits, leaving only a thin layer of drift soil to cover them. They were easily mined by stripping away the topsoil and digging giant pits to get the ore out of the ground. By the beginning of the 20th century more than 100 open-pit mines dotted the Mesabi Range. Mining camps such as Hibbing, Virginia, and Gilbert grew into prosperous towns.

Minnesota provides about 80 percent of the nation's iron ore, but most of the richest deposits have been depleted. The chief ore mined now comes from a hard rock called taconite. The taconite is processed to extract the ore, which is made into pellets and shipped to steel mills around the Great Lakes.

The processing of taconite produces tailings, or waste materials, that carry cancer-causing asbestos. Controversy began to flare in the 1960s over the dumping of these tailings into Lake Superior by a plant near Duluth. Some of the fibers were entering the city's water supply. In 1976, after years of arguments, a federal judge ordered the dumping halted. Now the tailings are deposited in a huge, specially built basin on land where they no longer pose a threat.

Area: *12th largest state, 84,402 sq mi (218,601 sq km)*
Population: *4,375,099; ranks 20th*
Major Cities: *Minneapolis, 368,383; St. Paul, 272,235; Bloomington, 86,335*
Manufacturing: *machinery, food products, metal products, scientific instruments, electronics, paper products, transportation equipment*
Agriculture: *milk, soybeans, cattle, corn, hogs, turkeys, wheat*
Mining and Quarrying: *iron ore, sand and gravel*
Other Important Activities: *shipping, tourism, printing and publishing*
Statehood: *the 32nd state; admitted May 11, 1858*

Part of Minnesota jogs into Canada, cut off from the rest of the state by the waters of Lake of the Woods. That's because after the American Revolution, when diplomats drew up the new nation's boundaries, they tried to include the headwaters of the Mississippi River. But it wasn't until nearly 150 years later that the river's real source, Lake Itasca, was identified. Thus the Northwest Angle is an enclave, a piece of American territory surrounded by a foreign country.

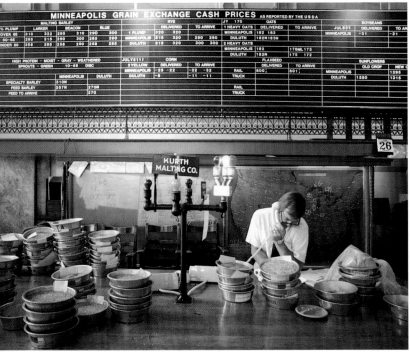

1

Minnesota

1 *A trader fills orders at the Minneapolis Grain Exchange, the nation's largest cash grain market. Tins hold grain samples ranging from barley to soybeans. Minneapolis, settled by European immigrants in the 1800s, ranks among the world's leading grain and flour centers.*

2 *Contour plowing protects a field near Rochester. Rows of corn and alfalfa weave across slopes, rather than up and down, to help keep the soil from washing away when it rains.*

2

3

4

5

3 *Blanket tossers loft a girl into the air as part of St. Paul's Winter Carnival, a two-and-a-half-week-long midwinter celebration that dates back to 1886. One of the carnival's oldest features, blanket bouncing is a traditional northland sport.*

4 *Dusted with snow, a gray wolf roams the forests of northern Minnesota. Deep woods, although heavily logged in the past, still cover about a third of the state and shelter some 1,400 wolves.*

5 *Split Rock Lighthouse, a beacon for sailors since 1910, crowns a cliff along the shore of Lake Superior near Two Harbors. For more than half a century the landmark light warned ore ships and other vessels away from submerged reefs and ledges.*

South Dakota

In about the middle of South Dakota, the Missouri River divides the state into two very different parts. The river marks the leading edge of glacial ice that had retreated by 10,000 years ago. The river and the rich, loamy soils and gently swelling hills of eastern South Dakota are its legacy. To the west of the river spread the grasslands of the Great Plains and rugged land carved into hills and canyons by wind and water.

Glaciers also created thousands of kettle hole lakes and ponds across eastern South Dakota. Once farmers drained the wetlands in their fields because they were a nuisance to plow around and they took up space that could be used for crops. But draining led to a declining duck population; the soil began to dry out as water tables dropped; and without the ponds to hold excess water, floods sometimes occurred.

Today water holes are being preserved or restored, many with money raised from the sale of state and federal duck stamps to hunters and collectors. Some farmers stock the ponds with fish. Others rent them in season to duck hunters. During dry spells, grasses sprout for animal pasture. "Early settlers found wetlands dotting the landscape," observes one soil expert, "and valued them for their water, hay, and fire protection." Now they are valued again.

West of the Missouri River, ranchers graze sheep and cattle. Not many trees grow in western South Dakota except on the weathered granite pinnacles and ridges of the Black Hills. Their name comes from thick stands of pondero-

Each fall in the 1890s, Indian children were transported to boarding schools where they were required to dress and act like whites, to study in English, and to take an English name.

sa pine, aspen, and spruce that make the hills appear darker than the surrounding land.

East of the Missouri, rainfall is usually adequate, and farmers grow crops and operate feedlots to fatten cattle shipped from western parts of the state. With 91 percent of its land devoted to agriculture, South Dakota earns about 12 percent of its income from farming and ranching, a higher percentage than any other state.

The eastern half is the most heavily populated. Nearly two-thirds of all South Dakotans live here, most on farms or in small rural communities. Sioux Falls is a center for meat-packing and other agriculture-related businesses. Computer industries have come to the city, and banks and insurance companies process information there.

Native Americans make up more than 7 percent of South Dakota's population, a greater proportion than in any other state except Alaska, Oklahoma, and New Mexico. Most live on huge reservations where poor land makes farming and ranching difficult. But the Pine Ridge Reservation has begun to experiment with farming methods such as drip irrigation and wind fences to protect crops. The reservation has a radio station that broadcasts in the Lakota Sioux language. Young leaders are

working to build new pride in a people who have suffered a hard life.

The Sioux regarded the Black Hills as sacred, the center of their spiritual world, "the heart of everything that is." In the Black Hills they found bountiful hunting grounds filled with streams and lush meadows grazed by deer, elk, pronghorns, and bison. When gold was discovered there in 1874, miners and settlers swarmed into the hills, onto land that the government had given to the Indians and eventually took back. The invasion touched off a series of skirmishes that led to Lt. Col. George A. Custer's defeat in nearby Montana Territory.

Gold still comes from the Black Hills. Near the town of Lead (pronounced Leed, from the miners' term for the ore deposit) is the Homestake Mine. The country's oldest gold mine in continuous operation, Homestake produces about 160 million dollars' worth of gold a year and ranks in production second only to Nevada's Carlin Mines. The Indians still battle for the return of their sacred hills, but now the struggle takes place in courts and in Congress. In 1985 Sioux leaders won the right to set up a community in the Black Hills near Rapid City, where they practice and teach religious traditions.

Tourism is an important source of income for South Dakota, ranking right behind agriculture. Each year, from spring to fall, more than two million visitors come to the Black Hills to see the immense faces of Presidents Washington, Jefferson, Lincoln, and Theodore Roosevelt carved out of Mount Rushmore. But when winter comes, snow whitens the granite heads and, except for the sweep of cold wind, quiet descends on the Black Hills.

Area: *16th largest state, 77,116 sq mi (199,730 sq km)*
Population: *696,004; ranks 45th*
Major Cities: *Sioux Falls, 100,814; Rapid City, 54,523; Aberdeen, 24,927*
Agriculture: *cattle, hogs, soybeans, corn, milk, wheat*
Manufacturing: *food products, machinery, electronics, lumber and wood products, metal products, stone, clay, and glass products, transportation equipment, jewelry*
Mining: *gold*
Other Important Activities: *tourism*
Statehood: *the 40th state; admitted November 2, 1889*

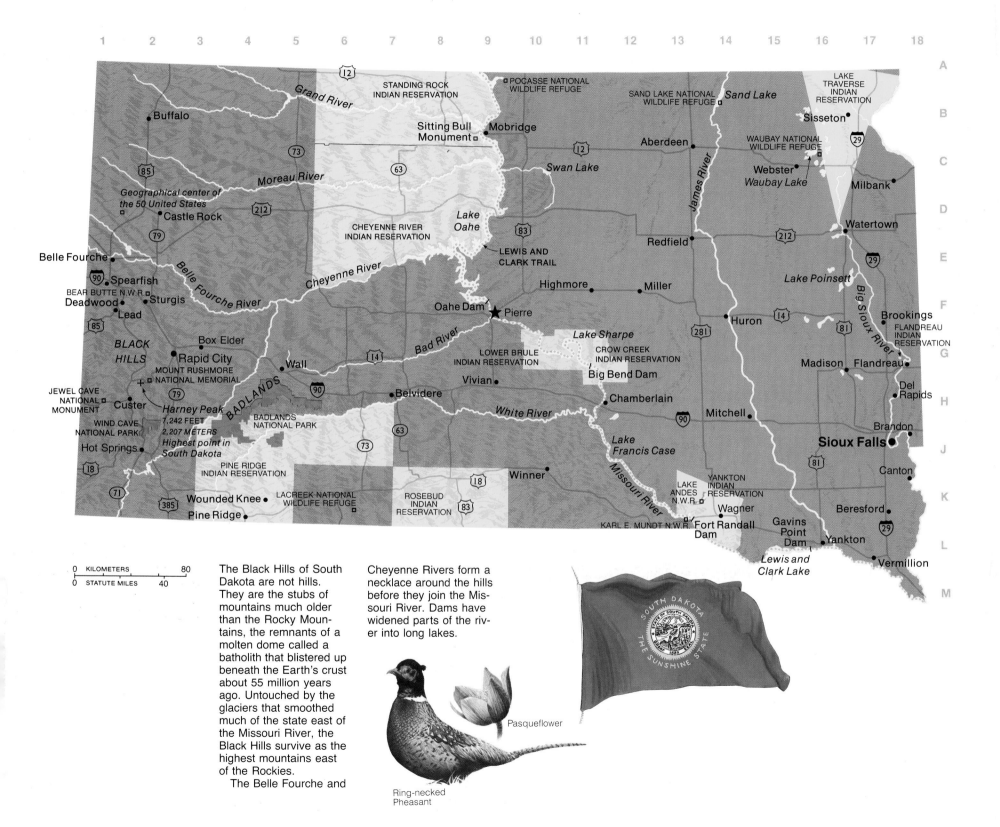

1 2 3 4 5 6 7 8 9 10 11 12 13 14 15 16 17 18

A

B

C

D

E

F

G

H

J

K

L

M

LAKE TRAVERSE INDIAN RESERVATION

POCASSE NATIONAL WILDLIFE REFUGE

SAND LAKE NATIONAL WILDLIFE REFUGE

Sand Lake

STANDING ROCK INDIAN RESERVATION

Grand River

Buffalo

Sitting Bull Monument

Mobridge

Aberdeen

WAUBAY NATIONAL WILDLIFE REFUGE

Sisseton

Webster
Waubay Lake

Swan Lake

Milbank

Moreau River

Geographical center of the 50 United States

Castle Rock

CHEYENNE RIVER INDIAN RESERVATION

Lake Oahe

James River

Redfield

Watertown

LEWIS AND CLARK TRAIL

Belle Fourche

Belle Fourche River

Cheyenne River

Highmore

Miller

Lake Poinsett

Spearfish

BEAR BUTTE N.W.R.

Deadwood

Sturgis

Lead

Oahe Dam

Pierre

Huron

Big Sioux River

Brookings

FLANDREAU INDIAN RESERVATION

BLACK HILLS

Box Elder

Bad River

Lake Sharpe

CROW CREEK INDIAN RESERVATION

Madison

Flandreau

Rapid City

MOUNT RUSHMORE NATIONAL MEMORIAL

Wall

LOWER BRULE INDIAN RESERVATION

Big Bend Dam

Del Rapids

JEWEL CAVE NATIONAL MONUMENT

Custer

BADLANDS

Vivian

Belvidere

Chamberlain

Mitchell

Brandon

Harney Peak
7,242 FEET
2,207 METERS
Highest point in South Dakota

BADLANDS NATIONAL PARK

White River

Lake Francis Case

Sioux Falls

WIND CAVE NATIONAL PARK

Hot Springs

PINE RIDGE INDIAN RESERVATION

Canton

Wounded Knee

LACREEK NATIONAL WILDLIFE REFUGE

ROSEBUD INDIAN RESERVATION

Winner

Missouri River

LAKE ANDES N.W.R.

YANKTON INDIAN RESERVATION

Beresford

Pine Ridge

Wagner

Gavins Point Dam

Yankton

KARL E. MUNDT N.W.R.

Fort Randall Dam

Lewis and Clark Lake

Vermillion

The Black Hills of South Dakota are not hills. They are the stubs of mountains much older than the Rocky Mountains, the remnants of a molten dome called a batholith that blistered up beneath the Earth's crust about 55 million years ago. Untouched by the glaciers that smoothed much of the state east of the Missouri River, the Black Hills survive as the highest mountains east of the Rockies.

The Belle Fourche and Cheyenne Rivers form a necklace around the hills before they join the Missouri River. Dams have widened parts of the river into long lakes.

Pasqueflower

Ring-necked Pheasant

KILOMETERS 0 — 80
STATUTE MILES 0 — 40

SOUTH DAKOTA
THE SUNSHINE STATE

1

2

3

4

5

South Dakota

1 *The bones of a rhinoceros-like titanothere rise at a museum in Rapid City. The now parched Badlands, rich in fossils, were lush and green when titanotheres lived here some 25 million years ago. Indians, who first found the huge skulls, called the fearsome beast Thunderhorse.*

2 *A high-school band performs in the Black Hills beneath the stony gaze of Presidents Washington, Jefferson, Theodore Roosevelt, and Lincoln. Carved from the granite flanks of Mount Rushmore, each head is as tall as a six-story building.*

3 *Beneath grassy plateaus, the ridges and canyons of the Badlands reveal layers of time. The whitish band near the top was formed by ash from volcanoes to the west or southwest, ejected some 25 million years ago. Streams gradually gnawed away at the plateaus, exposing layers of pinkish siltstone, clay, sand, and the lowest and oldest—65-million-year-old black shale that formed the bottom of an ancient sea.*

4 *A bearskin, the heads of elk and a bighorn sheep, and other Wild West memorabilia adorn the walls and rafters of an old-style saloon in Deadwood.*

5 *A black-tailed prairie dog in Wind Cave National Park near Custer throws its head back to shrill an "all clear" signal. Some 350 bison and 18 prairie dog villages share this remnant patch of America's once vast interior grasslands.*

Nebraska

Some people thought Nebraska was a desert. Its hills and grasslands rolled on as far as the eye could see. What trees there were grew only in draws and along riverbanks. How could crops grow here? "Almost wholly unfit for cultivation," reported Maj. Stephen Long, who led an expedition along the Platte River in 1820.

Major Long was mistaken. He was traveling in a year of drought more severe than the Dust Bowl years of the 1930s. Almost from the day it became a state, in 1867, Nebraska has ranked as a leading farm state. Beef, corn, and dairy products are important income producers, and the state vies with Indiana as the top grower of the hard-kerneled corn used for popcorn.

Farms and ranches take up about 96 percent of Nebraska's land, a greater percentage than in any other state. In eastern Nebraska, where rainfall is usually sufficient, corn and soybeans are the big crops. Oats grow there, too, and wheat, alfalfa, and a feed grain called sorghum. Farmers also raise corn-fed hogs and poultry.

Most of the rest of the state lies in the Great Plains, rolling terrain that slopes gradually upward toward the west. Rainfall here is usually sparse, but by irrigating their fields farmers can grow bountiful crops. Only Texas raises more beef cattle than Nebraska. A writer once described this part of the state as a land of "broad fields, deep skies, wind, and sunlight; clouds racing over prairie swells; herds of cattle grazing on the sandhills; red barns and white farmhouses surrounded by fields of tasseling corn and ripening wheat."

The Missouri River runs along Nebraska's eastern boundary. The Platte River, "a mile wide and an inch deep" in pioneer days, cuts across the state from west to east and joins the Missouri near Omaha. Nebraska's central location and the route along the Platte Valley made Nebraska a funnel for transcontinental travelers. Steamboats traveled the Missouri, and the lush Platte floodplains provided water and fodder for wagon trains, stagecoaches, and the Pony Express. During the 1840s and 1850s hundreds of thousands of pioneers bound for Utah, Oregon, or California rumbled through the state in their covered wagons. In places their wheels wore ruts that can be seen to this day.

In time the Platte became the route followed

On trial in 1879 for leaving his reservation without government permission, Ponca chief Standing Bear, shown here with his friend Julius Meyer, won acquittal and recognition that an Indian "is a person" in the eyes of the law.

by the nation's first transcontinental railroad, as well as by Interstate 80, the most heavily traveled east-west highway. Today the Platte, much less than a mile wide and far more than an inch deep, is regulated, its water released from reservoirs to meet the needs of irrigation, recreation, flood control, and power generation.

Nebraska's two biggest cities, Omaha and Lincoln, the capital, are near the Missouri River. Omaha, once known mainly for meat-packing and food processing, is now a center for finance, insurance, telecommunications, and the transportation and distribution of goods. Offutt Air Force Base, a few miles south of the city, serves as headquarters for the Air Force's Strategic Air Command and provides thousands of jobs.

Omaha is one of the country's largest processors of meats and meat products. Hogs, for example, supply not only pork and bacon for the

table but also heart valves for human use, insulin for diabetics, and skin to help treat burn victims. Other towns, such as Fremont and Lincoln, also have large meat-packing plants. Mills in central and western Nebraska produce large quantities of food for livestock.

Nebraska's Sand Hills cover about 20,000 square miles (51,800 sq km) of the plains in the north-central part of the state. These low, undulating hills are dunes covered with grass, the largest dune area in North America. The sand, blown here from dry river bottoms within the last few thousand years, acts like a sponge, absorbing and holding much of the rain that falls here. Some scientists believe that the grass that now holds the dunes in place began to grow here only a few hundred years ago.

Hundreds of small lakes and ponds glitter among the Sand Hills and provide food, shelter, and nesting sites for trumpeter swans, geese, and ducks. But the lakes are not the only source of water. The Sand Hills lie on top of one of the nation's largest underground water supplies, the Ogallala Aquifer. Water seeping from this 2,000-square-mile (5,180-sq-km) underground reserve keeps the Loup and Elkhorn Rivers flowing year-round. The aquifer also supplies abundant fresh water for cattle and crops. Farmers have tapped the aquifer with some 73,000 wells to irrigate more than 8 million acres (3 million ha), more land than in any other state except California. Now some people worry that the water may someday run out.

To help save water, many plains farmers practice dry farming. They leave some of their land unplanted for a season or so, enabling it to conserve moisture from melting snow. At planting time they till the soil in shallow grooves, rather than plowing it deeply. This helps reduce evaporation by exposing less soil to the air.

Many farmers also leave dead stalks and stubble in the fields after harvesting a crop. The stalks catch and hold snow in the winter, and in the spring they help shield the moist soil from drying sun and wind. Contour plowing, across a slope rather than up and down, is another dry farming technique used by many Nebraska farmers; so is planting hardy, frost-resistant crops such as barley and wheat that can be harvested ahead of the blazing heat of summer.

TOADSTOOL PARK □
Huge rocks carved by erosion; fossils and rare agates

Chadron
Gordon
FORT NIOBRARA N.W.R.
Valentine
Niobrara River
KARL E. MUNDT NATIONAL WILDLIFE REFUGE

PINE RIDGE N.R.A.
Bassett
SANTEE SIOUX INDIAN RESERVATION
LEWIS AND CLARK TRAIL
South Sioux City

AGATE FOSSIL BEDS NATIONAL MONUMENT □
Fossils of extinct mammals that lived here about 20 million years ago
Alliance
NORTH LOUP RIVER
VALENTINE NATIONAL WILDLIFE REFUGE
O'Neill
Elkhorn River
WINNEBAGO INDIAN RESERVATION
Wayne
OMAHA INDIAN RESERVATION

SAND HILLS
Calamus River
Norfolk
Missouri River

NORTH PLATTE N.W.R.
Scottsbluff
Gering
CRESCENT LAKE NATIONAL WILDLIFE REFUGE
Halsey
Middle Loup River
Columbus
Fremont
Blair
DESOTO N.W.R.

SCOTTS BLUFF NATIONAL MONUMENT
Chimney Rock
North Platte River
Lake McConaughy
South Loup River
Loup River
Schuyler
Omaha
Ralston
La Vista
Papillion
Bellevue

OREGON AND PONY EXPRESS TRAILS
Kingsley Dam
Ogallala
North Platte
MORMON TRAIL
Grand Island
Platte River
Seward
Plattsmouth

5,426 FEET 1,654 METERS
Highest point in Nebraska
Sidney
South Platte River
Cozad
Lexington
York
Big Blue River
Lincoln

Kearney
Hastings
MORMON TRAIL
Crete
Nebraska City

Holdrege
OREGON AND PONY EXPRESS TRAILS
HOMESTEAD NATIONAL MONUMENT OF AMERICA □
Beatrice
IOWA INDIAN RESERVATION

McCook
Little Blue River
Fairbury
Falls City
SAC AND FOX INDIAN RESERVATION

Republican River

Goldenrod

Western Meadowlark

0 KILOMETERS 80
0 STATUTE MILES 60

Area: *15th largest state, 77,355 sq mi (200,350 sq km)*
Population: *1,578,385; ranks 36th*
Major Cities: *Omaha, 335,795; Lincoln, 191,972; Grand Island, 39,386*
Manufacturing: *food products, electronics, machinery, chemicals, transportation equipment, metal products, rubber and plastics, metals*
Agriculture: *cattle, corn, hogs, soybeans, wheat, sorghum, milk*
Mining and Quarrying: *oil and gas, sand and gravel, stone*
Other Important Activities: *printing and publishing*
Statehood: *the 37th state; admitted March 1, 1867*

Dinohyus, the "Terrible Pig," was a ferocious, heavily tusked animal that at the shoulder stood taller than a man. About 20 million years ago it roamed the wilds of what is now western Nebraska. So did other long-gone creatures—Menoceras, a small rhinoceros; Moropus, a clawed early relative of the horse; and alligators and other animals that lived here even earlier, when much of the region was a tropical swamp.

Today rainfall is scarce in western Nebraska. But over the years what moisture does fall has carved the land into hills and gullies, exposing a wealth of fossils. Many such treasures can be seen at Agate Fossil Beds National Monument and at Toadstool Park, where erosion has also carved hills and rocks into wonderful shapes.

1

2

3

4

5

Nebraska

1 *This western Nebraska farm family keeps track of costs and prices on a computer. Today many farmers are university educated and use the latest technology.*

2 *Checking the gears of a windmill, a cattle rancher near Alliance draws water from the Ogallala Aquifer, an underground layer of sand and gravel that provides fresh water to parts of seven states.*

3 *Ripening wheat spreads a golden blanket on this Great Plains farm near Scottsbluff.*

4 *Chimney Rock, 325 feet (99 m) high and visible for 30 miles (48 km), became a beacon for westward-bound pioneers as they followed the Oregon and Mormon Trails.*

5 *Heralds of spring, sandhill cranes pause to rest and feed along the shallow Platte River on their northward journey from Mexico to Arctic nesting grounds.*

Iowa

If you set out to invent a farming state, you couldn't do much better than to come up with Iowa. For one thing, the state lies between two great rivers, the Mississippi, which forms its eastern border, and the Missouri, which defines most of Iowa's western boundary. In the days before roads and railways, these rivers served as ready-made highways for canoes, flatboats, and paddle-wheel steamboats carrying citizens and products of a young nation. Today tugs churn along these rivers, hauling barges of grain, coal, and other goods, a relatively inexpensive way to move bulky cargoes.

For another thing, glaciers overran the land, smoothing off hilltops and filling in valleys with glacial drift, a mixture of clay, sand, gravel, and boulders that weathers over millions of years to become soil. In some places Iowa soil is as deep as 600 feet (183 m) and contains a rich mixture of humus. Then, after the glaciers receded, winds blowing across the open plains laid down layers of powdery soil called loess. Farmers like loess because it has no rocks or boulders in it to break a plow.

Fertile soil is Iowa's greatest treasure. Farms cover about 92 percent of the state and supply the entire United States with about 7 percent of its food, even though only 4 percent of all Iowa workers are farmers. Iowa's farmers grow great quantities of corn, soybeans, oats, and hay, and raise about a third of the nation's hogs, more than any other state.

Before white settlers arrived, western Iowa's gently rolling prairie lands grew grass as tall as a rider on horseback, a sea of grass that reached to the horizon in all directions. Most of the grass is gone now, although patches of it survive on old floodplains, along streams and railroad rights-of-way, and in forgotten corners of pioneer graveyards. Today, great rectangular fields glow with ripening grain. Distant towns signal their presence with sheltering trees, church steeples, and tall grain elevators.

Its growing season with many long, sunny summer days helps to make Iowa a leading farm state. Although there can be times of drought, deep winter snows and up to 36 inches (91 cm) of rain during the growing season usually result in bumper crops year after year.

Sometimes crops are too plentiful. When that

Ready to race, with boots, goggles, and number patch on his back, a Cedar Rapids motorcyclist of the early 1900s shows that early motorcycles were little more than bikes with engines attached.

happens, prices drop. Also, land values and interest rates rise and fall. A farmer who goes heavily into debt to buy expensive land and equipment can have a hard time paying off his loans. Then, if the bank takes over the property, the farm may be lost, and the family may move away to find work in town or in another state.

Over the years hard times have hit Iowa and other farming states several times, most recently in the 1980s. Between 1980 and 1989, some 208,000 Iowans, many of them young people, moved to other states. As small farmers have sold out to richer neighbors and agricultural corporations, farm sizes have increased even as the number of farms has dropped. And bigger, more efficient farms mean bigger, costlier machines, with fewer jobs for individual farmhands.

When farms fail, the small towns that depend on farmers' business find themselves in trouble, too. Car dealers, small banks, and sellers of farm implements often find that they can't keep going. Grocery stores and coffee shops lose customers. Small schools close and students must transfer to larger ones nearby. Townspeople who want to stay often commute to city jobs. Bad times threaten traditional small-town life.

In trying to hold on to its people and prevent the wide swings between good times and bad, Iowa has sought to attract nonfarm industries.

Des Moines, home to more than 50 insurance firms, ranks as one of the nation's leading insurance centers. In recent years Cedar Rapids and other towns have expanded into computers, fiber optics, and other high-tech businesses.

The number of such industries is growing, but most of Iowa's businesses still are related to agriculture. Waterloo has a large meat-packing industry and manufactures farm equipment. Cedar Rapids and Keokuk have cereal mills. Sioux City has the world's largest popcorn factory, and several cities produce large quantities of corn oil, cornstarch, and dairy products. Cedar Rapids has attracted a facility that will develop and produce enzymes, or proteins, for human and animal nutrition.

Many people think of Iowa as flat, but it is mostly hilly; there is rugged terrain in the northeast corner, which was ice covered only in an early period of glaciation, more than half a million years ago. Here the exposed bedrock has been cut by streams into deep valleys with steep bluffs. On the other side of the state rise the loess hills of the Missouri River Valley. Wind has piled up these thick deposits, which water has eroded into sharp-ridged hills, crests, and ravines, making a rumpled landscape.

Mound Builders lived in Iowa as long ago as 1000 B.C. In the northeastern part of the state these prehistoric Indians made their homes along bluffs overlooking the Mississippi River. About 2,500 years ago they built many earthen mounds, some in the shape of birds and other animals. Animal-shaped mounds are called effigy mounds. One group consists of the figures of ten marching bears. Some mounds held the bones of people buried with jewelry or weapons or the teeth of bears.

Area: *25th largest state, 56,275 sq mi (145,753 sq km)*
Population: *2,776,755; ranks 30th*
Major Cities: *Des Moines, 193,187; Cedar Rapids, 108,751; Davenport, 95,333*
Manufacturing: *food products, machinery, electronics, chemicals, metal products, rubber and plastics, transportation equipment*
Agriculture: *hogs, soybeans, cattle, corn, milk*
Mining and Quarrying: *stone, sand and gravel*
Other Important Activities: *insurance, printing and publishing*
Statehood: *the 29th state; admitted December 28, 1846*

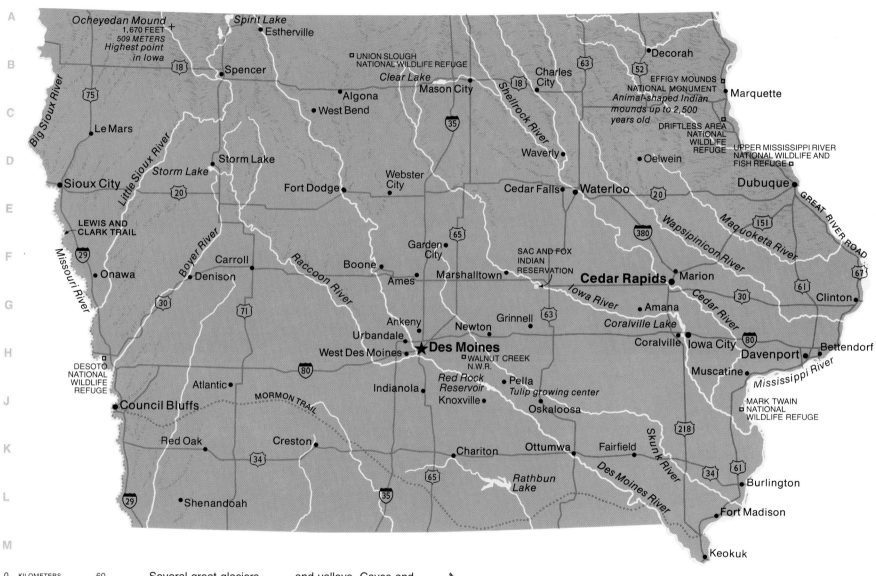

Several great glaciers shaped Iowa over the past two million years, smoothing the land by covering the bedrock with varying thicknesses of glacial drift. In the northeastern corner, around Decorah, erosion wore away the drift, exposing the bedrock, which has since been cut by streams into ridges and valleys. Caves and caverns developed where groundwater dissolved parts of the limestone bedrock.

Swamps and lakes dot the state's north-central region. They serve as headwaters for several rivers, including the Raccoon, Skunk, and Iowa, and provide habitat for ducks and geese.

Wild Rose

American Goldfinch

IOWA

1

2

3

4

Iowa

1 *Its dome gleaming like Iowa's golden corn, the state capitol, at Des Moines, has served as the seat of government since 1884.*

2 *A barn peeps between corn tassels. Hybrid corn, pioneered in the state, has helped double and redouble yields since the 1930s.*

3 *Bicyclists take a refreshing watermelon break in West Bend, partway through the annual back-road jaunt across the state sponsored by the* Des Moines Register.

4 *Garden City, a town near Ames, springs like a prize crop from soil that is a glacial legacy, enriched by the prairie grasses that once grew here.*

5 *"Berry Patch Kids," the grandchildren of dairy farmers, coax a hesitant calf at the state fair in Des Moines. Iowa families have enjoyed the August fair since 1854.*

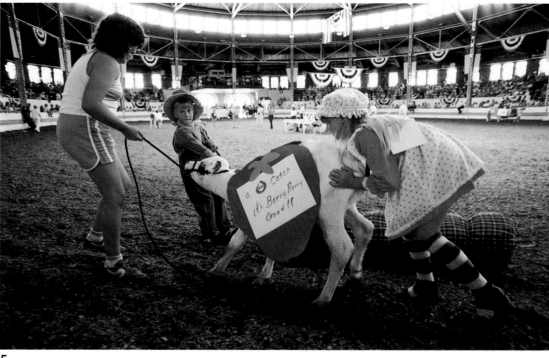

5

Kansas

"No matter where you deliver an airplane from Wichita, you're already halfway there." So said Walter Beech, founder of the Beech Aircraft Corporation. Behind Beech's joke is the fact that Kansas lies exactly in the middle of the lower 48 states. A limestone column in a pasture near Lebanon marks the spot.

Kansas's central location and its extensive transportation network haven't gone unnoticed by businesses. Some 4,000 manufacturing and processing plants are located throughout the state, among them many meat-packing and flour-milling plants. Since 1952, industry has surpassed agriculture as a source of income. In Wichita alone, four large aircraft manufacturers turn out nearly two-thirds of the world's private and commercial airplanes and give jobs to more than 36,000 skilled workers.

Other Kansas enterprises include the manufacture of camping equipment and greeting cards. At Hutchinson, one company stores everything from Hollywood films to government documents in parts of a salt mine deep beneath the town, where constant temperature and low humidity make a good place to keep valuable objects. The salt was left behind by shallow seas that washed over the middle of the continent millions of years ago, then evaporated. The salt was covered by sediment. Thick salt deposits underlie parts of central and western Kansas.

Kansas also produces a lot of oil, gas, and coal. It is one of the few sources for helium, the gas used to lift balloons. Some 60,000 wells pump oil and gas from beneath the state's prairies. In southeastern Kansas, one of the world's largest electric coal shovels, a 16-story-high monster known as Big Brutus, for many years dug dirt and rocks to expose surface coal seams for strip miners. Big Brutus was retired in 1974.

Kansas is a leading agricultural state, too. Most of the land has fine loess soil. Kansas produces some 17 percent of the nation's wheat, usually more than any other state. In most years, the harvest would fill a train reaching from western Kansas to the Atlantic Ocean. Much of this wheat is hard red winter wheat, a hardy grain planted in the fall and harvested the following spring. It was developed from Turkey Red, a type of wheat introduced into Kansas in the 1870s by Mennonite settlers who had fled religious persecution in Russia. Kansas farmers also grow bumper crops of corn, milo, soybeans, and other feed crops eaten by the more than six million beef cattle that go to market each year.

In the drier regions of western Kansas, farmers irrigate their fields with water from a vast underground supply, the Ogallala Aquifer, a thick layer of waterlogged sand and gravel. But farmers have been using the water faster than rainfall can replenish it, and some geologists now warn that parts of the aquifer could run dry.

In the days before white settlers came, head-high bluestem grass blanketed the prairies, providing forage for enormous herds of bison. Maj. Richard Dodge in 1871 reported riding 25 miles through a single herd of bellowing bison, which he said took "about five days passing a given point." When railroads reached Kansas after the Civil War, cowboys herded cattle from Texas to railroad towns such as Abilene, Wichita, and Dodge City. Here the cattle were fed and loaded aboard trains to be shipped east. These were rough-and-tumble times that gave rise to legendary lawmen and gunslingers such as Wyatt Earp, Bat Masterson, and Doc Holliday.

Cattle still come to these and other Kansas towns, but now they stay in large, scientifically run feedlots where computers measure out fattening diets of grains and vitamins.

Many people think of Kansas as a flat, featureless place where a girl named Dorothy tangled with a tornado that swept her off to a storybook land named Oz. Actually, Kansas is not particularly flat. Low hills wrinkle much of the state, and eastward-draining rivers cross the sloping plains and prairies. East of Wichita the Flint Hills, mostly too stony to plow, preserve a 50-mile-wide (80-km) swath of the tallgrass prairie that extends from northern Kansas to Oklahoma. Here bluestem and Indian grasses, sprinkled with wildflowers in the spring, carpet the land as far as the eye can see.

In southern Kansas the flat-topped mesas and buttes of the Red Hills get their name from reddish rock and soil that contains iron oxide, or rust. The Smoky Hills stand in the north-central part of the state. Largely limestone and sandstone deposits laid down by ancient seas, they contain fossil seashells and sharks' teeth, as well as castle-like formations carved by rivers and streams. Trees here are few and far between. Wood was so scarce for the early settlers that they quarried and cut limestone for fence posts. Examples of their handiwork, a hundred years old, still stand, marking off old fields.

Separating grain from straw, a 1930s steam threshing machine pours out smoke from its coal fire. To bring in the wheat harvest, neighbors worked together in crews of 12 or more.

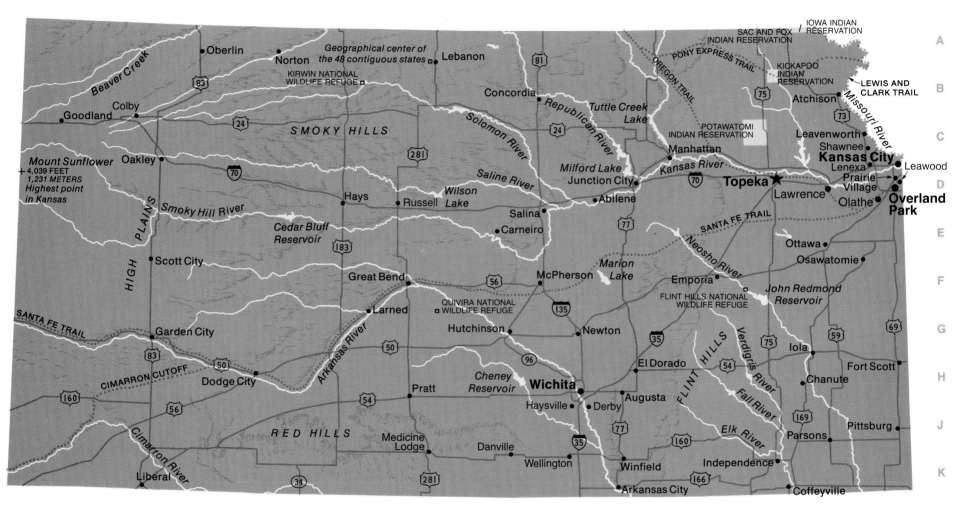

**Map labels:**

Beaver Creek · Oberlin · Norton · Geographical center of the 48 contiguous states · Lebanon · IOWA INDIAN RESERVATION · SAC AND FOX INDIAN RESERVATION · PONY EXPRESS TRAIL · OREGON TRAIL · KICKAPOO INDIAN RESERVATION · LEWIS AND CLARK TRAIL

KIRWIN NATIONAL WILDLIFE REFUGE · 83 · 81 · 75 · Atchison · Missouri River · 73

Goodland · Colby · SMOKY HILLS · Concordia · Republican River · Tuttle Creek Lake · POTAWATOMI INDIAN RESERVATION · Leavenworth · Shawnee · Kansas City

24 · Solomon River · 24 · Manhattan · Lenexa · Prairie Village · Leawood

Mount Sunflower · +4,039 FEET · 1,231 METERS · Highest point in Kansas · Oakley · 281 · Milford Lake · Kansas River · Topeka · Overland Park · Olathe

HIGH PLAINS · 70 · Saline River · Junction City · 70 · Lawrence

Smoky Hill River · Hays · Russell · Wilson Lake · Abilene · 77

Cedar Bluff Reservoir · Carneiro · Salina · SANTA FE TRAIL

SANTA FE TRAIL · 183 · Scott City · Great Bend · McPherson · Marion Lake · Emporia · Neosho River · John Redmond Reservoir · Ottawa · Osawatomie

56 · QUIVIRA NATIONAL WILDLIFE REFUGE · FLINT HILLS NATIONAL WILDLIFE REFUGE

Garden City · Larned · 135 · Hutchinson · Newton · 69

Arkansas River · 50 · 50 · 35 · Verdigris River · 75 · Iola · 59 · Fort Scott

CIMARRON CUTOFF · Dodge City · 96 · El Dorado · 54 · FLINT HILLS · Chanute

160 · 56 · Pratt · Cheney Reservoir · Wichita · Augusta · Fall River · 169

Cimarron River · 54 · Haysville · Derby · Elk River · Parsons · Pittsburg

RED HILLS · Medicine Lodge · Danville · 77 · 160 · Independence

Liberal · 34 · Wellington · 35 · Winfield · 166 · Coffeyville · 281 · Arkansas City

---

Area: *14th largest state, 82,277 sq mi (213,098 sq km)*
Population: *2,477,574; ranks 32nd*
Major Cities: *Wichita, 304,011; Kansas City, 149,767; Topeka, 119,883*
Manufacturing: *transportation equipment, food products, chemicals, machinery, electronics, paper products, petroleum and coal products, stone, clay, and glass products, metal products*
Mining: *oil and gas*
Agriculture: *cattle, wheat, sorghum, soybeans, corn, hogs, milk*
Other Important Activities: *printing and publishing*
Statehood: *the 34th state; admitted January 29, 1861*

There used to be sharks in Kansas . . . and flying reptiles with wingspans close to 20 feet (6 m). But that was millions of years ago, when much of the continent lay at the bottom of a great shallow sea. When these animals died, marine oozes covered them and later hardened into layers of sedimentary rocks. Today their fossil skeletons turn up in chalk beds in the Smoky Hills.

East of the Flint Hills lie coal deposits formed millions of years ago, when rotting vegetation was buried and compressed beneath layers of sediments laid down by encroaching seas.

KILOMETERS 80 / STATUTE MILES 40

Western Meadowlark

Sunflower

KANSAS

1

2

3

4

Kansas

1 *Grain elevators and a church stand side by side in Danville, a small town whose population soars on Sundays and at harvesttime.*

2 *High-school football teams in sparsely populated western Kansas play with squads of eight, rather than the regulation eleven. And on a frosty October evening, fans are also scarce.*

3 *Kansas City, long a low-rise industrial town, displays a new skyline of office buildings along the Missouri River.*

4 *Where's the beef? Right here in a western Kansas packing plant, speeding along a line to become steaks and hamburger.*

5 *Merry maidens perform a 16th-century English country dance at a Renaissance festival near Kansas City.*

5

Missouri

"Meet me in St. Louie, Louie," at the 1904 World's Fair in St. Louis, where ice-cream cones were first sold. They were invented, the story goes, by a salesman packing ice cream into rolled-up waffles.

If all the people of the United States, standing exactly where they live, were balanced on a giant seesaw shaped like a map of the country, the seesaw would center in Missouri. The national census, ever since the first in 1790, has shown that, as our country expanded, the geographical center of the population moved steadily westward and a little southward. It now lies at a point southwest of St. Louis.

Missouri is central in other ways, too. In the heart of the country, it has geographical features like those of many areas around it, north, south, east, and west. Within Missouri's borders you can find low forested mountains, fertile farmlands built by glaciers, cotton-growing bottomlands like those of the Deep South, and the Big Sky plains and prairies of the West.

Also, two of the continent's mightiest rivers, the Mississippi and the Missouri, have their confluence near St. Louis. This has helped to make the state a key transportation center since the earliest days. Fur trappers, traders, gold seekers, and tens of thousands of settlers arriving by riverboat at St. Louis and other river ports outfitted themselves for the long westward trek along the Oregon and Santa Fe Trails. Near St. Louis, explorers Meriwether Lewis and William Clark began their epic journey to the Pacific Ocean. On the Missouri River, Pony Express riders headed west from St. Joseph on a ten-day gallop to California. Mark Twain, who spent his boyhood in Hannibal, apprenticed at the age of 22 to learn the trade of a steamboat pilot. His adventures appear in his autobiographical *Life on the Mississippi*.

Some 20 rail lines, 300 airports, and 109,000 miles (175,000 km) of highways have turned the state into a leading trucking and shipping center. Boats and barges on the Mississippi and Missouri make St. Louis and Kansas City two of the nation's busiest inland ports.

Today the Gateway Arch, a gleaming curve of stainless steel, rises above St. Louis to honor the city's position as a portal between East and West. Designed by architect Eero Saarinen and completed in 1965, the 630-foot (192-m) arch can be seen from miles away and is judged to be a marvel of modern engineering. It arcs across a stretch of riverfront where the early travelers came ashore to do business. The arch itself tapers to an observation room at the top and is designed to withstand winds of up to 150 miles an hour (240 kmph). Its curve, called an inverted catenary, like the upside-down curve of a loose-hanging chain, thrusts its weight downward onto feet anchored to bedrock.

Because of their strategic riverside locations, St. Louis and Kansas City have become important manufacturing centers. More than half the state's 8,700 factories are located in and around the two cities. Missouri factories employ about a quarter of the state's workers, many of whom turn out transportation equipment: autos, barges, bus and truck bodies, railroad cars, airplanes, and aerospace equipment.

The state's varied geography contributes to a wide variety of crops, from corn and soybeans, grown in the glacial soils north of the Missouri River, to fruits and vegetables in the Ozark region and cotton along the Mississippi River.

Forests once covered nearly two-thirds of Missouri, but long ago fell to loggers' axes. Now most of the state's forests blanket the rugged hills and valleys of the Ozark Plateau. Today their oak, hickory, and pine make the state a leading producer of charcoal and barrel staves.

Ages ago, the Ozarks were a region of volcanic peaks. As volcanism subsided, the land sank and was flooded by shallow seas into which sediments washed from surrounding highlands. The sediments slowly became bedrock, and eventually the sea bottom was pushed upward to become dry land. Soon, swift-flowing streams and rivers went to work, carving valleys into the uplifted tableland, so that Ozark people say that their mountains may not be very high but their valleys sure are deep. Underground water hollowed out more than 5,000 caves in the limestone bedrock and created thousands of springs, including some of the world's largest. Big Spring in the eastern Ozarks each day discharges enough water into the Current River to fill 12 million swimming pools. The Ozarks also contain the world's most productive lead mines.

In the southeastern corner of the state, along the Mississippi, lies the "boot heel" region. A low-lying floodplain that was once swampy and heavily forested, the boot heel was drained and cleared to make fertile fields for growing cotton, soybeans, and rice. Meandering streams were straightened to improve drainage; levees were built to hold back floodwaters.

Over the years most of Missouri's wetlands were converted to farmlands. The great, soggy forests that once grew along river floodplains have become croplands. Birds and animals that depended on these wetlands are threatened or endangered. But now conservation groups are working to restore Missouri's river wetlands.

Area: *19th largest state, 69,697 sq mi (180,516 sq km)*
Population: *5,117,073; ranks 15th*
Major Cities: *Kansas City, 435,146; St. Louis, 396,685; Springfield, 140,494*
Manufacturing: *transportation equipment, chemicals, food products, metal products, electronics, machinery, paper products, rubber and plastics, stone, clay, and glass products, metals, scientific instruments, clothing*
Agriculture: *soybeans, cattle, hogs, milk, corn, wheat, turkeys*
Mining and Quarrying: *stone, lead*
Other Important Activities: *tourism, printing and publishing*
Statehood: *the 24th state; admitted August 10, 1821*

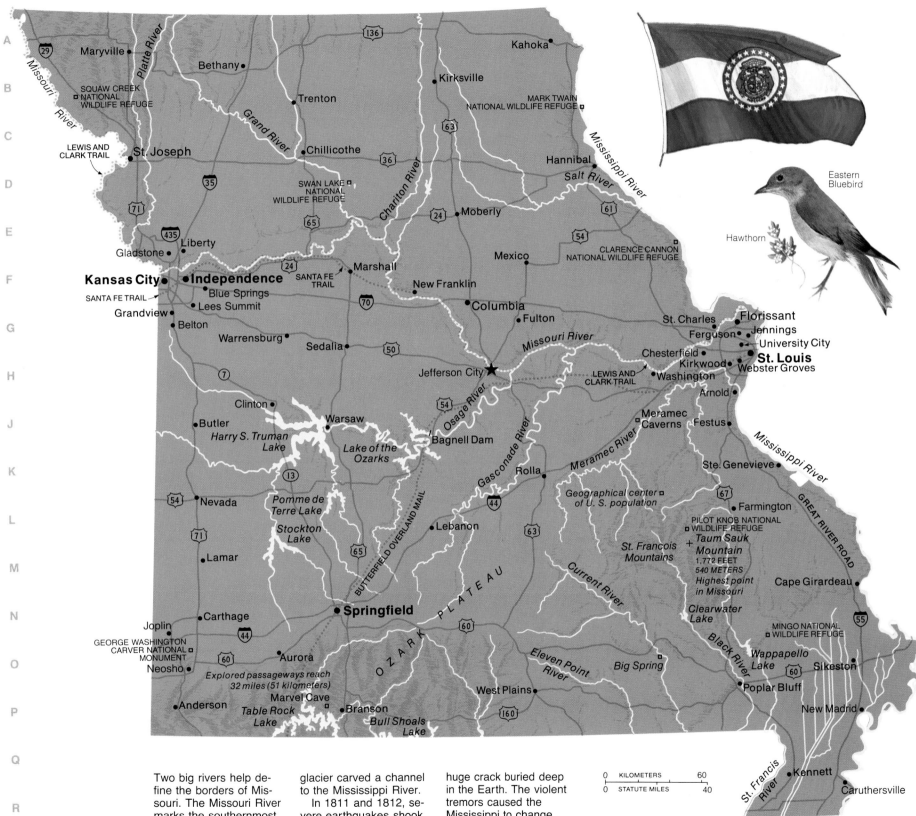

1 2 3 4 5 6 7 8 9 10 11 12 13 14 15 16 17 18 19

A

B

C

D

E

F

G

H

J

K

L

M

N

O

P

Q

R

Maryville

SQUAW CREEK NATIONAL WILDLIFE REFUGE

Missouri River

Platte River

LEWIS AND CLARK TRAIL

St. Joseph

Bethany

Trenton

Grand River

Chillicothe

Chariton River

Kahoka

Kirksville

MARK TWAIN NATIONAL WILDLIFE REFUGE

136

63

36

SWAN LAKE NATIONAL WILDLIFE REFUGE

Hannibal

Salt River

Mississippi River

35

71

65

24

Moberly

61

Liberty

435

Gladstone

Kansas City

Independence

SANTA FE TRAIL

Blue Springs

Grandview

Lees Summit

Belton

Marshall

SANTA FE TRAIL

New Franklin

24

70

Columbia

Fulton

Mexico

54

CLARENCE CANNON NATIONAL WILDLIFE REFUGE

St. Charles

Florissant

Jennings

Ferguson

University City

Warrensburg

Sedalia

50

Missouri River

Chesterfield

Kirkwood

St. Louis

Webster Groves

7

Clinton

Jefferson City

LEWIS AND CLARK TRAIL

Washington

Arnold

Butler

Warsaw

54

Osage River

Bagnell Dam

Meramec Caverns

Festus

Harry S. Truman Lake

Lake of the Ozarks

Gasconade River

Rolla

Meramec River

Ste. Genevieve

13

44

Geographical center of U.S. population

67

GREAT RIVER ROAD

Mississippi River

54

Nevada

Pomme de Terre Lake

Lebanon

63

PILOT KNOB NATIONAL WILDLIFE REFUGE

Farmington

71

Stockton Lake

BUTTERFIELD OVERLAND MAIL

65

St. Francois Mountains

Taum Sauk Mountain 1,772 FEET 540 METERS Highest point in Missouri

Lamar

Current River

Clearwater Lake

Cape Girardeau

55

Carthage

Springfield

60

MINGO NATIONAL WILDLIFE REFUGE

Joplin

44

Eleven Point River

Big Spring

Wappapello Lake

60

Sikeston

GEORGE WASHINGTON CARVER NATIONAL MONUMENT

Aurora

Black River

Neosho

60

Explored passageways reach 32 miles (51 kilometers)

West Plains

Poplar Bluff

OZARK PLATEAU

Marvel Cave

Branson

160

New Madrid

Anderson

Table Rock Lake

Bull Shoals Lake

St. Francis River

Kennett

Caruthersville

Eastern Bluebird

Hawthorn

KILOMETERS 0 60

STATUTE MILES 0 40

Two big rivers help define the borders of Missouri. The Missouri River marks the southernmost reach of the great glaciers. Meltwater running along the edge of the glacier carved a channel to the Mississippi River.

In 1811 and 1812, severe earthquakes shook the area around New Madrid, where the Mississippi flows above a huge crack buried deep in the Earth. The violent tremors caused the Mississippi to change course, and sinking land formed a new lake in neighboring Tennessee.

1

2

3

4

5

Missouri

1 *Canoeists wind past wooded Ozark bluffs in southern Missouri, exploring part of the mid-continent's only extensive highlands.*

2 *Soaring above riverboats on the Mississippi, St. Louis's Gateway Arch celebrates the city's early days as a key transportation link between East and West.*

3 *Quilters work in a Ste. Genevieve backyard, preserving skills that hark back to the town's founding by French traders and planters in the mid-1700s.*

4 *A St. Louis baseball fan keeps a vendor busy at a game in Busch Stadium. Service jobs in wholesale and retail trade employ more Missourians than any other work.*

5 *Patchwork fields form a tapestry of plenty along the fertile bottomlands of the Missouri River near the town of Washington.*

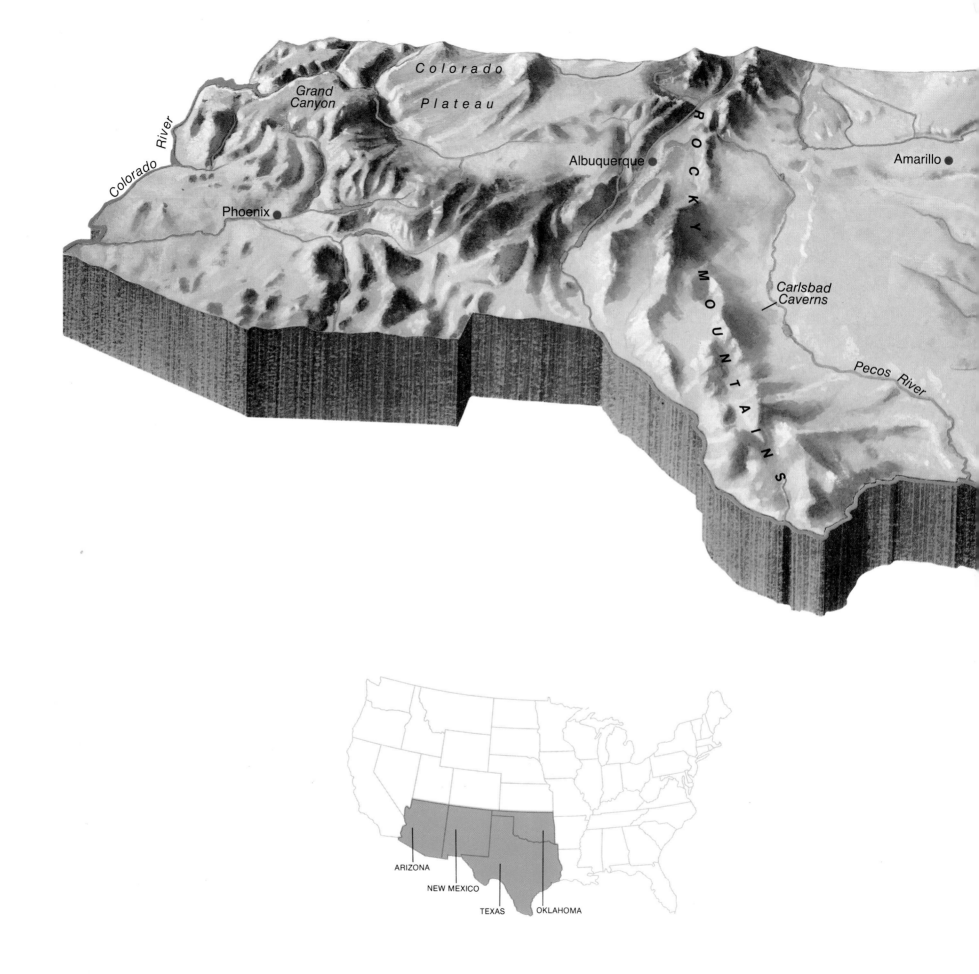

Colorado River

Colorado

Grand
Canyon

Colorado

Plateau

R
O
C
K
Y

M
O
U
N
T
A
I
N
S

Albuquerque

Amarillo

Phoenix

Carlsbad
Caverns

Pecos River

ARIZONA

NEW MEXICO

TEXAS   OKLAHOMA

Canadian River

● Oklahoma City

● Dallas

Brazos River

Houston ●

San Antonio ●

Rio Grande

The Southwest

Variety is the spice of life in the Southwest. This region sprawls across almost every kind of terrain imaginable. In the west, awesome chasms and canyons slice downward through multicolored layers of sedimentary and volcanic rock that form the uplifted tablelands of the Colorado Plateau. Here the Colorado River, fed by snowmelt from the mountains, slowly grinds its way through layers of shale, sandstone, and limestone to bedrock nearly two billion years old.

Here, too, bone-dry deserts dotted with flat-topped mesas and buttes, giant stone arches, and other spectacular rock formations spread across the land toward the western slopes of the Rocky Mountains and southern spurs, or branches, of the range. From time to time through geologic history much of the Southwest lay beneath shallow seas. Gradually, as continental plates nudged one another, the ancient seabeds got squeezed and bent and broken and lifted. Volcanoes helped shape the region, too, spewing immense layers of ash and lava across the countryside as part of the mountain-building process that gave rise to the Rockies.

In the Rocky Mountains, the Rio Grande—Spanish for "big river"—begins a journey that trails southeastward to form part of the boundary between the United States and Mexico. Winding through deep canyons and flat lowlands, the river provided life-giving water to Indian farmers who grew corn, beans, and squash here for hundreds of years before Spanish explorers arrived in the 16th century.

Broad and broken grasslands slope from the eastern foothills of the Rockies. In places the plains are so flat and featureless that early travelers drove stakes into the ground to help guide the way back home again. Along the Gulf coast, barrier islands shield small boats from the open water and offer shelter and food to millions of migrating ducks, geese, egrets, and to the rare and endangered whooping crane.

East of Oklahoma City, along the northeastern edge of this region, spread the Ozark hardwood forests. Farther south, piney woods blanket much of the coastal lowlands nearly all the way to an escarpment north of San Antonio. The escarpment, formed when Earth's crust broke and slipped, marks the boundary between the humid coastal lowlands and the drier plains.

Arizona

In 1858 a surveyor, Lt. Joseph Ives, visited Arizona and reported back to the U. S. Congress that the area was "altogether valueless." His opinion was not shared by the generations of Hopi Indians who have lived at Oraibi since the 12th century, making it perhaps the oldest continuously inhabited settlement in the country. And it's unlikely to be shared by the almost one million people who have moved to Arizona in the last ten years, making it, after Nevada, the fastest growing state in the United States.

Few people who have ever visited the Grand Canyon would agree with Lieutenant Ives. During a 1903 visit, the well-traveled President Theodore Roosevelt declared the Grand Canyon "the most impressive piece of scenery I have ever looked at." The Colorado River has been carving the Grand Canyon for some six million years, cutting into the layers of rock that form the Colorado Plateau. The river exposed rock almost two billion years old, some of the oldest on Earth. In places the canyon is a mile (1.6 km) deep and up to 18 miles (29 km) wide, and the action of wind and water continues to enlarge it.

The Grand Canyon is one of many ravines carved by rivers and streams in the tablelands of northern Arizona. Canyon de Chelly was fashioned by the Chinle Wash and its tributaries. Today the Chinle Wash is an intermittent stream. Ancient Native American groups settled among the area's red-rock canyons, caves, and mesas some 2,000 years ago. Later, the Anasazi, ancestors of the modern Hopi, built dwellings in thousand-foot (300-m) cliffs.

Canyon de Chelly is now part of the reservation that is the headquarters of the Navajo nation. The Navajo, along with the Apache, are relative newcomers to Arizona, having arrived just before the Spanish explored the region in the 1500s. The Navajo learned sheepherding from the Spanish and even today move their flocks from pasture to pasture. They have had a long and difficult relationship with the settled Hopi farmers who shared land where there were disputes over ownership and land use. In the 1980s, to help end the conflicts, the U. S. government divided the jointly used area.

Arizona's plateau region ends south of Flagstaff in a 200-mile-long (320-km) line of cliffs about 2,000 feet (610 m) high. To the south is the

The Cisco Kid, *filmed in 1913, used an adobe house in Tucson as a studio. The town and nearby mountains were a popular backdrop for silent movies and, later, talkies.*

Basin and Range region. Here a series of thickly forested mountain ranges runs northwest to southeast, providing vast stands of ponderosa pine for the state's lumber industry. Farther south and west are lower ranges that separate broad desert basins, such as the Sonoran Desert, a land of cactus and scrub where July temperatures average 103°F (39°C).

Though dry, this land can be very fertile, a fact discovered by the Hohokam, a people who built dams and ditches to irrigate their crops in the valleys of the Salt and Gila Rivers more than 1,500 years ago. They grew corn, beans, squash, and cotton, a crop that European settlers later reintroduced. Cotton, along with copper mining and cattle raising, was the basis of Arizona's economy until the mid-20th century.

When Spanish, Mexican, and Anglo settlers came to Arizona, beginning in the late 1700s, they found it hard to displace the Native Americans from their lands. Indian resistance continued until 1886, when Geronimo and his Apache raiders finally surrendered to the U.S. Army.

Early settlement concentrated in Tombstone, Bisbee, and other silver-mining and copper-mining towns. Tucson, in the mountains, retains much of the flavor of its early days as a walled Spanish city with strong ties to Mexico.

Like the Hohokam, farmers in Arizona today rely on irrigation. Billions of dollars have been spent to bring river water to thirsty crops. The Colorado has been dammed to provide water for farming and hydroelectricity. Agriculture around Phoenix, the capital, expanded rapidly after completion of the Theodore Roosevelt Dam and Lake on the Salt River in 1911. Arizonans also draw on underground water, at a rate faster than it can be replenished. As a result, the water table drops, land subsides, and deep cracks develop in the ground.

If dams and reservoirs met the need for water, air-conditioning conquered the extreme heat of southern Arizona. By the mid-20th century, the desert stood ready to receive hundreds of thousands of new inhabitants. Sunshine and clean air brought retirees and people with respiratory problems. Its wide-open spaces and clear blue skies made Arizona ideal for the location of air bases and other military sites. Manufacturers of computers, weapons, aircraft, and other high-tech products located their factories in Arizona. Today three-fourths of the population lives around Phoenix and Tuscon. Demand for homesites has developers bulldozing and negotiating for the federal lands (about 60 percent of the state) that sometimes come up for sale.

To meet the water needs of a growing population, the Central Arizona Project is being built. This 336-mile (540-km) series of pipes and canals will bring water from Lake Havasu on the Colorado River to Phoenix and Tucson. Scheduled to be completed in 1992, the project will draw Arizona's maximum allotment from the Colorado, a situation that worries Californians, who have long been using some of Arizona's share.

Area: *the sixth largest state, 114,000 sq mi (295,260 sq km)*
Population: *3,665,228; ranks 24th*
Major Cities: *Phoenix, 983,403; Tucson, 405,390; Mesa, 288,091*
Manufacturing: *transportation equipment, electronics, machinery, scientific instruments, food products, metals, stone, clay, and glass products, chemicals, metal products*
Mining and Quarrying: *copper, coal, sand and gravel, stone*
Agriculture: *cattle, cotton, lettuce, milk, hay*
Other Important Activities: *federal government, tourism, printing and publishing*
Statehood: *48th state; admitted February 14, 1912*

Badlands area of red rock formations where many western movies have been filmed

Monument Valley

Arizona is a dry state. Many of its rivers, including the Gila and the Little Colorado, have been drawn with dots and dashes. That's how mapmakers show an intermittent river, one that flows only part of the year, usually in the spring when rain or melting snow supplies water to fill the channel.

Arizona is so dry, notes one jokester, that even its forests have turned to stone. But logs do turn to stone when minerals dissolved in groundwater replace the cells and tissues of buried wood. You can see such trees in Petrified Forest National Park.

KILOMETERS 0 — 80
STATUTE MILES 0 — 40

15 KAIBAB INDIAN RESERVATION

PIPE SPRING NATIONAL MONUMENT

SPANISH TRAIL

Kanab Creek

GLEN CANYON NATIONAL RECREATION AREA

Lake Powell

Page

67

Marble Canyon

NAVAJO NATIONAL MONUMENT

89

Chinle Wash

Lake Mead

Hoover Dam

LAKE MEAD NATIONAL RECREATION AREA

Grand Canyon

HAVASUPAI INDIAN RESERVATION

GRAND CANYON NATIONAL PARK

160

P A I N T E D   D E S E R T

CANYON DE CHELLY NATIONAL MONUMENT

93

Colorado River

64

Oraibi

HOPI INDIAN RESERVATION

191

NAVAJO INDIAN RESERVATION

Window Rock

Lake Mojave

HUALAPAI INDIAN RESERVATION

WUPATKI NATIONAL MONUMENT

66

Humphreys Peak 12,633 FEET 3,851 METERS Highest point + in Arizona

SUNSET CRATER NATIONAL MONUMENT

NAVAJO INDIAN RESERVATION

Bullhead City

Kingman

40

Flagstaff

WALNUT CANYON NATIONAL MONUMENT

Puerco River

FORT MOJAVE INDIAN RESERVATION

Big Sandy River

Meteor Crater

87

Winslow

Little Colorado River

40

Holbrook

PETRIFIED FOREST NATIONAL PARK

666

HAVASU NATIONAL WILDLIFE REFUGE

TUZIGOOT NATIONAL MONUMENT

Sedona

ZUNI INDIAN RESERVATION

40

Lake Havasu City

HAVASU NATIONAL WILDLIFE REFUGE

Santa Maria River

YAVAPAI INDIAN RESERVATION

Cottonwood

MONTEZUMA CASTLE NATIONAL MONUMENT

Camp Verde

77

180

Lake Havasu

69

Prescott

CAMP VERDE INDIAN RESERVATION

Verde River

Show Low

60

95

89

17

PAYSON COMMUNITY INDIAN RESERVATION

Payson

Colorado River

COLORADO RIVER INDIAN RESERVATION

Wickenburg

FORT McDOWELL INDIAN RESERVATION

FORT APACHE INDIAN RESERVATION

Baldy Peak + 11,403 FEET 3,476 METERS

60

93

SALT RIVER INDIAN RESERVATION

Theodore Roosevelt Lake

Salt River

Black River

Cactus Wren

10

Sun City

Paradise Valley

Peoria

Glendale ★ **Scottsdale**

TONTO NATIONAL MONUMENT

666

CIBOLA NATIONAL WILDLIFE REFUGE

KOFA NATIONAL WILDLIFE REFUGE

95

Avondale

Phoenix

Mesa

Tempe

Chandler

Globe

SAN CARLOS INDIAN RESERVATION

S O N O R A N

Superior

60

Saguaro

IMPERIAL NATIONAL WILDLIFE REFUGE

GILA BEND INDIAN RESERVATION

80

GILA RIVER INDIAN RESERVATION

CASA GRANDE NATIONAL MONUMENT

San Carlos Reservoir

Clifton

Gila River

Yuma

Gila River

8

Gila Bend

MARICOPA INDIAN RESERVATION

Coolidge

TOHONO O'ODHAM INDIAN RESERVATION

70

Safford

COCOPAH INDIAN RESERVATION

D E S E R T

Casa Grande

San Pedro River

+ *Mount Graham* 10,713 FEET 3,265 METERS

BUTTERFIELD OVERLAND MAIL

85

Eloy

TOHONO O'ODHAM INDIAN RESERVATION

CABEZA PRIETA NATIONAL WILDLIFE REFUGE

Ajo

TOHONO O'ODHAM INDIAN RESERVATION

Santa Cruz River

SAGUARO NATIONAL MONUMENT

77

BUTTERFIELD OVERLAND MAIL

10

Arizona-Sonora Desert Museum

Refuge protects desert animals including pronghorns, tortoises, iguanas, bats, and cactus mice

ORGAN PIPE CACTUS NATIONAL MONUMENT

PASCUA YAQUI INDIAN RESERVATION

Tucson

86

South Tucson

CHIRICAHUA NATIONAL MONUMENT

Kitt Peak National Observatory

SAN XAVIER INDIAN RESERVATION

80

BUENOS AIRES NATIONAL WILDLIFE REFUGE

TUMACACORI NATIONAL MONUMENT

Sierra Vista

Tombstone

666

SAN BERNARDINO NATIONAL WILDLIFE REFUGE

19

Nogales

Bisbee

Douglas

Arizona

1 *Sprinkled with sacred cattail pollen, an Apache girl celebrates her coming-of-age among tribe members.*

2 *Sunset burnishes eroded slopes and towering buttes of the Grand Canyon. Rock revealed here is 1.7 billion years old.*

3

4

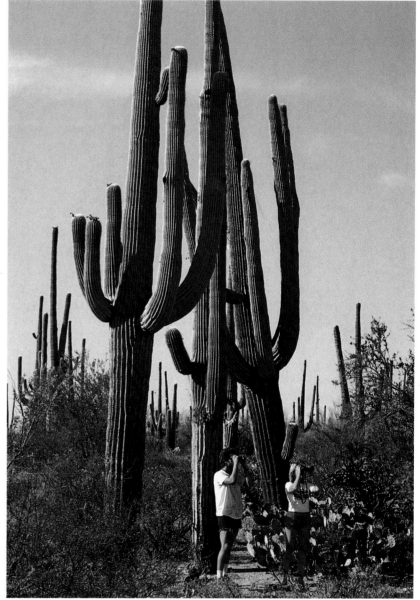

5

3 *Founded by the Spanish in 1700 to Christianize the Indians, San Xavier del Bac, near Tucson, is the Southwest's best preserved mission.*

4 *At dawn, the huge steel eyelids of the optical telescopes at Kitt Peak National Observatory shut tight for the day.*

5 *Giant saguaros dwarf bird-watchers at Saguaro National Monument. The armed cactuses are unique to this region.*

New Mexico

An elderly woman sat on the ground, coiling red clay with gnarled hands. Slowly and steadily the years of experience in her fingertips transformed the clay into a perfectly proportioned pot. Then she painted geometric designs on it and scratched her name on the bottom. She fired the pot in an open fire. There its color changed to black, the dull finish of the painted designs a subtle contrast to the pot's satiny smoothness.

The woman was Maria Martinez, a Native American who lived in the San Ildefonso Pueblo, north of Santa Fe. She died in 1980, but her pottery has become the trademark of her pueblo and is prized by museums and collectors. Maria Martinez's work is part of an artistic legacy that goes back some 2,000 years to the Anasazi, the ancestors of today's Pueblo Indians.

The landscape of New Mexico is varied and, in many places, rugged. The Great Plains extend into the eastern third of New Mexico. In the late 19th century, Texans began to settle there. Today, cattle ranches, oil fields, small towns and cities, and military bases give the region an appearance similar to its next-door neighbor, earning it the nickname Little Texas.

The southernmost spurs of the Rocky Mountains reach into central New Mexico, rising abruptly from the plains to the east. The Rio Grande, from its source in the Colorado Rockies, cuts down through the ranges of New Mexico. Snowmelt from mountain streams brings water to the fertile Rio Grande Valley. The river has also been dammed and diverted to irrigate crops and produce hydroelectricity.

The Spanish settled north-central New Mexico beginning in the late 16th century. They set up ranches, some on vast tracts of land granted by the king of Spain. Many intermarried with Indians. Far from the Spanish government in Mexico City, they existed in isolation. Until early in the 20th century, the language spoken in some villages was closer to that of 16th-century Spain than it was to that of neighboring Mexico, whose people have also come to settle, legally or illegally, in New Mexico. Mexicans and descendants of the original Spanish settlers give the state a population that is 37 percent Hispanic, the highest proportion in the country.

Santa Fe has been the seat of government in New Mexico since 1610. For some two centuries

New Mexico's first railroad line, the Atchison, Topeka, and Santa Fe, opened in 1878, connecting Albuquerque to small, isolated towns and permanently changing the lives of their inhabitants.

the Spanish discouraged outsiders from entering. Spanish soldiers, friars, colonists, and traders traveled between Mexico City and Santa Fe and Taos on El Camino Real, "the royal road." When Mexico gained independence from Spain in 1821 and New Mexico became a Mexican province, Santa Fe soon was bursting at the seams with merchants eager to do business there. They came in long wagon trains along the Santa Fe Trail until the Atchison, Topeka, and Santa Fe Railway neared Santa Fe in 1879.

For a hundred years, Taos and Santa Fe have drawn artists and writers from eastern states and from Europe. The clear blue sky, it is said, renders details more clearly. Multihued landscapes of rock and the changing tints of the desert also help explain the state's long tradition of creative inspiration. The writer John Gunther described a New Mexico night of "purple desert flowing endlessly under lonely stars."

In the 1940s, a group of men arrived in New Mexico. They were quickly spirited away to the site of a boarding school on a ranch near Santa Fe. Here, at Los Alamos, the federal government set up a laboratory to develop atomic

bombs. The scientists brought here for this purpose worked feverishly and in utmost secrecy to produce the bombs dropped on Hiroshima and Nagasaki to hasten the end of World War II. Los Alamos and Albuquerque are two of several centers in the state for research and development for weaponry, the space program, nuclear energy, and electronics. These industries receive a large part of their support from the federal government and attract a young and highly educated work force, often from outside the state. This helps make Albuquerque one of the fastest growing cities in the United States.

The Rio Grande courses south into the Basin and Range region, where rugged ranges separate low-lying desert basins. One basin, Jornada del Muerto ("journey of the dead man"), was the bane of the Spanish who had to flee across its burning sands and lava rock after a 1680 Indian revolt. The Jornada del Muerto also witnessed the ultimate challenge to human survival when the atomic bomb, developed at Los Alamos, was tested in 1945. So intense was the heat from the blast that it fused the basin's desert sand into glass. The area has remained a testing ground for rockets and missiles.

The northwestern corner of New Mexico is part of the Colorado Plateau, an immense upland cut into cliffs, canyons, valleys, and mesas. About a thousand years ago the Anasazi built large, complex settlements all over the area. Many Navajo now live there on a reservation that extends into Arizona and Utah. The Navajo, together with the Apache, fought Spanish and Anglo settlers in New Mexico until almost the end of the 19th century.

Area: *the fifth largest state, 121,593 sq mi (314,925 sq km)*
Population: *1,515,069; ranks 37th*
Major Cities: *Albuquerque, 384,736; Las Cruces, 62,126; Santa Fe, 55,859*
Mining: *oil and gas, coal, copper, uranium, potash, lead*
Manufacturing: *electronics, food products, stone, clay, and glass products, petroleum products, lumber and wood products*
Agriculture: *cattle, milk, hay, greenhouse and nursery products, chili peppers*
Other Important Activities: *federal government, tourism, printing and publishing*
Statehood: *the 47th state; admitted January 6, 1912*

Fire and water formed much of New Mexico. Shallow oceans covered the region several times, leaving sediments that became the parched plains in the southeast. Later, as the ancient seabeds folded and lifted into the Rocky Mountains, enormous volcanoes spewed lava and ash across the countryside for millions of years. Ship Rock, in the northwest corner, is the hardened lava throat of a worn-down volcano.

The town of Clovis, near the state's eastern boundary, gave its name to Ice Age hunters who roamed the West about 12,000 years ago, killing camels, mammoths, and bison with stone-tipped spears. The grooved spearheads, discovered near the town by archaeologists in the 1930s, are known as Clovis points.

Map labels

1 2 3 4 5 6 7 8 9 10 11 12 13 14 15 16

A B C D E F G H J K L M N O P Q R S

San Juan River
UTE MOUNTAIN I.R.
AZTEC RUINS N.M.
Navajo Reservoir
Brazos Peak 11,403 FEET 3,476 METERS
Wheeler Peak 13,161 FEET 4,011 METERS Highest point in New Mexico
Raton
CAPULIN VOLCANO NATIONAL MONUMENT
Aztec
Ship Rock 7,178 FEET 2,188 METERS
Farmington
JICARILLA APACHE INDIAN RESERVATION
El Vado Reservoir
Taos Mts.
MAXWELL NATIONAL WILDLIFE REFUGE
CIMARRON CUTOFF SANTA FE TRAIL
Chaco River
TAOS I.R.
Taos Pueblo
Clayton
HIGH PLAINS
Rio Chama
Abiquiu Dam Reservoir
Rio Grande
Sangre de Cristo Mts.
Taos
SPANISH TRAIL
PICURIS I.R.
SANTA FE TRAIL
NAVAJO INDIAN RESERVATION
Truchas Peak 13,102 FEET 3,993 METERS
SAN JUAN I.R.
Espanola
FORT UNION NATIONAL MONUMENT
SANTA CLARA I.R.
SAN ILDEFONSO I.R.
POJOAQUE I.R.
NAMBE I.R.
TESUQUE I.R.
Gallup
JEMEZ I.R.
Los Alamos
BANDELIER N.M.
COCHITI I.R.
Santa Fe
NAVAJO INDIAN RESERVATION
ZIA I.R.
PECOS NATIONAL MONUMENT
Las Vegas
LAS VEGAS NATIONAL WILDLIFE REFUGE
Conchas Lake
Mount Taylor 11,301 FEET 3,445 METERS
ZIA I.R.
SANTO DOMINGO I.R.
SAN FILIPE I.R.
Canadian River
Zuni
EL MORRO NATIONAL MONUMENT
LAGUNA I.R.
Rio Rancho
SANTA ANA I.R.
SANDIA I.R.
ROCKY
Tucumcari
EL MALPAIS NATIONAL MONUMENT
Grants
CANONCITO I.R.
Alameda
PETROGLYPH N.M.
ZUNI INDIAN RESERVATION
Inscription Rock
Albuquerque
RAMAH NAVAJO INDIAN RESERVATION
ACOMA INDIAN RESERVATION
Acoma Pueblo
LAGUNA INDIAN RESERVATION
Armijo
ISLETA INDIAN RESERVATION
Santa Rosa
LAGUNA I.R.
Belen
Lake Sumner
ALAMO NAVAJO INDIAN RESERVATION
Rio Puerco
Clovis
A series of giant bowl antennas make up a powerful radio telescope
SEVILLETA NATIONAL WILDLIFE REFUGE
SALINAS PUEBLO MISSIONS N.M.
Portales
Very Large Array
MOUNTAINS
GRULLA NATIONAL WILDLIFE REFUGE
San Francisco River
Socorro
Pecos River
BOSQUE DEL APACHE NATIONAL WILDLIFE REFUGE
BITTER LAKE NATIONAL WILDLIFE REFUGE
GILA CLIFF DWELLINGS NATIONAL MONUMENT
Elephant Butte Reservoir
Site of first atomic bomb test
Roswell
CONTINENTAL DIVIDE
Jornada del Muerto
Sierra Blanca Peak 12,003 FEET 3,659 METERS
Rio Hondo
Gila River
Truth or Consequences
MESCALERO INDIAN RESERVATION
Lovington
Silver City
Tularosa
Alamogordo
Artesia
Hobbs
WHITE SANDS NATIONAL MONUMENT High, shifting dunes of gleaming white sand, world's largest gypsum desert
Lake McMillan
SAN ANDRES NATIONAL WILDLIFE REFUGE
BUTTERFIELD OVERLAND MAIL
Rio Grande
Lordsburg
Carlsbad
CARLSBAD CAVERNS NATIONAL PARK
Limestone caves formed by earth upheaval and water seeping underground
Deming
Las Cruces
BUTTERFIELD OVERLAND MAIL

KILOMETERS 0 80
STATUTE MILES 0 40

Yucca

Roadrunner

1

2

3

New Mexico

1 *Electrical charges from a Particle Beam Fusion Accelerator at Albuquerque's Sandia National Laboratories hint at the hundred trillion watts of electricity the device can produce. Sandia is one of many New Mexico facilities that specialize in nuclear energy research.*

2 *Limestone-bearing drops of water create fantastic formations at Carlsbad Caverns, in southeastern New Mexico. Humorist Will Rogers called the vast cave system the "Grand Canyon with a roof on it."*

3 *Below peaks of the Taos Mountains sacred to Indians, winter snow covers desert vegetation of sagebrush, piñon, and juniper.*

4 *Mexican Americans harvest chili peppers on a farm north of Las Cruces. One in three New Mexico residents is Hispanic.*

5 *Young dancers enter the low door of a ceremonial room, or kiva, during the celebration of the corn harvest at their pueblo near Santa Fe. Although Indians were converted to Christianity under Spanish influence, today's Native Americans strive to preserve their ancient religious traditions.*

4

5

Oklahoma

Each summer, people of the town of Tahlequah in eastern Oklahoma reenact one of the most significant events in the state's history and one of the most tragic. Tahlequah is headquarters of the Cherokee nation. The Cherokee, along with the Choctaw, Chickasaw, Creek, and Seminole, lived originally in the southeastern states. There they had adopted many of the customs of the white settlers, who called them the Five Civilized Tribes. When white settlers demanded more farmland, these Indians were forcibly removed from their lands. Beginning in the 1820s, they were marched under guard of federal troops to the territory now known as Oklahoma. On one such march, in the winter of 1838-39, thousands of Indians died along the way. The journey to Oklahoma became known as the Trail of Tears, its memory kept alive by the yearly reenactment at Tahlequah.

In Oklahoma, the Five Civilized Tribes joined local Indians such as the Caddo, Wichita, Pawnee, and Osage, as well as Plains tribes such as the Comanche, Apache, and Cheyenne. For a time, most of Oklahoma became Indian territory. Today some 252,000 members of 67 different tribes give Oklahoma the country's largest Native American population.

The Five Civilized Tribes took the lead in the territory by establishing their own forms of government, courts, newspapers, and the first schools in Oklahoma. But the press for land by white settlers squeezed Oklahoma Indians into smaller areas. The federal government surveyed the land, marking precisely measured parcels of 160 acres (65 ha). On April 22, 1889, the first of several runs on Oklahoma land began. At the signal of gunshots, homesteaders rushed across the borders to stake their claims. Oklahoma City, just a spot on the plains, became a city of 10,000 tent-dwelling inhabitants in a matter of hours. By evening, Guthrie had a population of 15,000. Homesteaders came from all over the country, from Canada, Mexico, and Europe, and from as far away as China and Japan.

Oklahoma encompasses many different landforms. Highlands cover its eastern third, including part of the Ozark Plateau shared with Arkansas and Missouri. This area of steep bluffs and swiftly running streams contains deposits of lead, zinc, and coal. Miners from Europe came

here in the 1870s; their descendants still live among the descendants of the southeastern tribes. Many lakes, some created for flood control, irrigation, or hydroelectricity, make the plateau a major recreation area. To the south the sandstone ridges of the Ouachita Mountains form Oklahoma's roughest terrain. Forests make lumbering the area's chief industry.

West of the highlands stretch large areas of plains that alternate with bands of hills, all the way to the panhandle. In these areas farmers raise wheat and also cattle, which provide most of the state's agricultural income. Down along the southern border, in the humid valley of the Red River, farmers grow cotton, peanuts, and vegetables. This area has much in common with

A 1936 dust storm in Oklahoma's Panhandle sends a farmer and his sons running for cover. Severe droughts and wind erosion in the 1930s turned the plains into a wasteland called the Dust Bowl.

the southern states from which most of its settlers came in the 19th century.

Although oil and natural gas are found in nearly every county, the area around Tulsa saw the first oil strike in 1901 and remains the state's oil headquarters. Like the land rushes of the 1800s, oil created boom times in Oklahoma. Oil leases for Osage lands in the 1920s temporarily made tribe members the richest people in the state. Eighteen wells once pumped on the

grounds of the state capitol in Oklahoma City.

Today, about two-thirds of all Oklahomans live in urban areas, half of them in or around Tulsa and Oklahoma City. The two cities are major manufacturing centers. Tulsa also has large aircraft and aerospace industries. The city's data-processing centers handle the largest number of credit card slips in the world.

In the 1930s, another "Trail of Tears" carried hundreds of thousands of mostly white Oklahomans westward. Many were farmers hit by the Great Depression and years of drought that turned western Oklahoma into a Dust Bowl. "People sat in Oklahoma City . . . holding dust masks over their faces . . . while the farms blew by," wrote American journalist John Gunther.

Improved farming methods and tree planting have brought productive farmland back to the former Dust Bowl counties.

Area: *18th largest state, 69,956 sq mi (181,186 sq km)*
Population: *3,145,585; ranks 28th*
Major Cities: *Oklahoma City, 444,719; Tulsa, 367,302; Lawton, 80,561*
Mining: *oil and gas*
Manufacturing: *transportation equipment, machinery, electronics, rubber and plastics, food products, metal products, stone, clay, and glass products, chemicals, scientific instruments, paper products*
Agriculture: *cattle, wheat, greenhouse and nursery products, broilers, milk*
Other Important Activities: *printing and publishing*
Statehood: *the 46th state; admitted November 16, 1907*

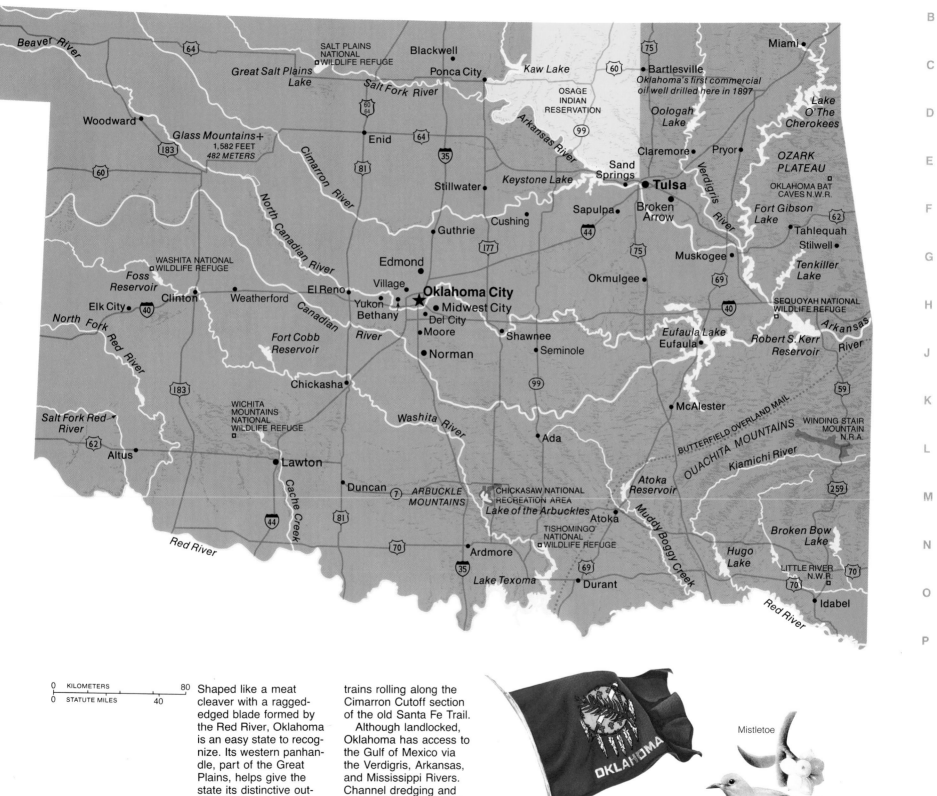

Beaver River

SALT PLAINS NATIONAL WILDLIFE REFUGE

Great Salt Plains Lake

Blackwell

Ponca City

Kaw Lake

Bartlesville
Oklahoma's first commercial oil well drilled here in 1897

Miami

Woodward

Salt Fork River

OSAGE INDIAN RESERVATION

Oologah Lake

Lake O' The Cherokees

Glass Mountains+ 1,582 FEET 482 METERS

Enid

Arkansas River

Claremore

Pryor

OZARK PLATEAU

Cimarron River

Sand Springs

OKLAHOMA BAT CAVES N.W.R.

North Canadian River

Stillwater

Keystone Lake

Tulsa

Fort Gibson Lake

Tahlequah

Stilwell

WASHITA NATIONAL WILDLIFE REFUGE

Guthrie

Cushing

Sapulpa

Broken Arrow

Verdigris River

Tenkiller Lake

Foss Reservoir

Edmond

Okmulgee

Muskogee

Elk City

Clinton

Weatherford

El Reno

Village

Oklahoma City

SEQUOYAH NATIONAL WILDLIFE REFUGE

Arkansas River

North Fork Red River

Canadian River

Yukon

Bethany

Midwest City

Del City

Moore

Shawnee

Eufaula Lake

Eufaula

Robert S. Kerr Reservoir

Fort Cobb Reservoir

Norman

Seminole

Salt Fork Red River

Chickasha

Washita River

Ada

McAlester

WINDING STAIR MOUNTAIN N.R.A.

WICHITA MOUNTAINS NATIONAL WILDLIFE REFUGE

BUTTERFIELD OVERLAND MAIL

OUACHITA MOUNTAINS

Kiamichi River

Altus

Lawton

ARBUCKLE MOUNTAINS

CHICKASAW NATIONAL RECREATION AREA

Atoka Reservoir

Duncan

Lake of the Arbuckles

Atoka

Muddy Boggy Creek

Broken Bow Lake

Cache Creek

Red River

TISHOMINGO NATIONAL WILDLIFE REFUGE

Hugo Lake

Ardmore

LITTLE RIVER N.W.R.

Lake Texoma

Durant

Red River

Idabel

KILOMETERS   80

STATUTE MILES   40

Shaped like a meat cleaver with a ragged-edged blade formed by the Red River, Oklahoma is an easy state to recognize. Its western panhandle, part of the Great Plains, helps give the state its distinctive outline. To this day the panhandle bears the wheel ruts made by wagon trains rolling along the Cimarron Cutoff section of the old Santa Fe Trail.

Although landlocked, Oklahoma has access to the Gulf of Mexico via the Verdigris, Arkansas, and Mississippi Rivers. Channel dredging and lock building completed in 1971 make Tulsa and Muskogee inland ports.

OKLAHOMA

Mistletoe

Scissor-tailed Flycatcher

1

2

Oklahoma

1   *The tanks of a Tulsa oil refinery sprawl along the bank of the Arkansas River.*

2   *Four generations of an Oklahoma Panhandle farm family stand in a field of milo, a kind of sorghum. This family survived the Dust Bowl years of the 1930s that drove a half million farmers out of Oklahoma and nearby states.*

3   *Oil wealth brought art to Tulsa, including these spirited bronzes by sculptor-painter Frederic Remington. They are displayed at the Thomas Gilcrease Institute of American History and Art.*

3

4

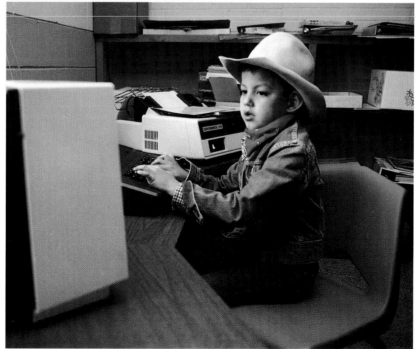

5

4 *An Oklahoma scientist uses computers to monitor the exchange of gases in a blade of grass. This research is part of a project to develop drought-resistant plants that could help avoid future Dust Bowl conditions.*

5 *Computing cowhand, a young Cherokee logs on at his school near Stilwell. Cherokee Indians opened Oklahoma's first schools in the mid-1800s, after completing a forced march that tore them from their homelands in the Southeast.*

Texas

The year 1901 saw North America's first gusher at Spindletop oil field near Beaumont. Within two years, hundreds of derricks owned by some 50,000 potential millionaires crowded the field.

For almost a decade during the mid-19th century, Texas was a country apart from the United States. From 1836 to 1845, after it fought off Mexican rule, the Republic of Texas existed as a sovereign nation that was recognized by Great Britain, France, the Netherlands, and the United States. It had its own army and navy, its own currency, and its own postal service. In 1839 Austin became its capital.

Spanish missionaries from Mexico were the first Europeans to successfully settle Texas, beginning in the 1690s. They established fortified missions, including one at San Antonio de Bexar, now San Antonio.

It was in the mission church, the Alamo, that some 188 Texans held off the army of the Mexican general Santa Anna for almost two weeks before losing in a bloody battle in 1836. All the Texans inside the Alamo died, including legendary heroes Davy Crockett and Jim Bowie. But

only six weeks later, with "Remember the Alamo!" as their war cry, the army of Texas under Sam Houston defeated Santa Anna and his men. This victory freed the territory from Mexican rule and eventually confirmed the independence of Texas.

Huge debts from its war with Mexico and the continued threat of Mexican invasion and Indian attacks led Texas to join the United States in 1845. The largest of the 48 contiguous states, Texas has the greatest amount of farmland and the largest reserves of oil and natural gas in the country, as well as a fast-growing population. One-third of its residents have arrived in the state since 1970.

Many early Texas settlers were southern farmers, drawn by the immense plots of land they could obtain. Europeans came too, including Belgians, French, English, Irish, Czechs, and large numbers of Germans escaping political turmoil in their homeland. The Germans created the communities of Fredericksburg and New Braunfels and also settled in San Antonio.

From Waco southward there is an escarpment, an east-facing rim of land, that curves southwestward to Del Rio. It separates the moist, green lowlands of the east from the higher, drier, and largely treeless plains of the west.

East of the escarpment the Gulf Coastal Plain contains the state's most fertile farmland, with cotton and rice as the major crops. In the valleys of the lower Rio Grande and the Nueces River, an 11-month growing season yields winter vegetables and citrus fruits. The Rio Grande has long witnessed Mexican immigration, both legal and illegal. Many border cities, such as El Paso, Laredo, and Brownsville, have economies that are closely tied to nearby cities in Mexico. One in five Texans today has Hispanic origins.

Along the Gulf coast are a number of major ports, including Corpus Christi, Port Arthur, and Brownsville. Houston, fueled by the oil industry and close to the rich East Texas fields, is the state's largest port. Although Houston is 50 miles (80 km) inland, a large ship channel, opened in 1914, connects it with Galveston Bay. Houston also leads the Texas space industry. Its Johnson Space Center guides the flights of all manned spacecraft, including the space shuttle. Fluctuation in oil prices has hit Houston hard,

but like other Texas cities, it seeks economic security through diversity of its industries.

Dallas and Fort Worth have expanded toward each other over the years. They now form a single large metropolitan area and share a huge international airport. Dallas, once a market center for cotton, has become a center for banking, insurance, rail freight, and, most recently, the computer and defense industries. The old cow town of Forth Worth shares Dallas's growth in high-tech and defense companies, especially in aviation.

West of the escarpment begin the upland plains, starting with rolling prairies where cattle raising is the major occupation. Among Texas cattle breeds are the original longhorns, brought in from Mexico and now making a comeback because of their leaner meat, and the Santa Gertrudis, a breed resistant to heat and insects and the first one developed in the United States.

Cattle ranches spill onto the high plains of the Texas Panhandle, where farmers also grow wheat, cotton, sugar beets, and other crops in irrigated fields. The 1920s strike in the oil fields of the southern panhandle made oil and finance centers of the cities of Midland and Odessa.

West Texas is a hot, dry, rugged land. With the help of underground water, wheat and feed crops grow in huge, target-shaped fields watered by pivoting sprinklers. There are huge ranches here and a frontier atmosphere. College students can take courses in rodeo riding, and bulldogging, saddle bronc riding, and calf roping are intercollegiate sports.

Area: *the second largest state, 266,807 sq mi (691,030 sq km)*
Population: *16,986,510; ranks third*
Major Cities: *Houston, 1,630,553; Dallas, 1,006,877; San Antonio, 935,933*
Manufacturing: *chemicals, food products, transportation equipment, electronics, petroleum products, machinery, scientific instruments, metal products, stone, clay, and glass products, rubber and plastics*
Mining: *oil and gas, coal*
Agriculture: *cattle, cotton, milk, greenhouse and nursery products, broilers, vegetables, corn, sorghum*
Other Important Activities: *finance and insurance, tourism, printing and publishing, shrimp fishing*
Statehood: *the 28th state; admitted December 29, 1845*

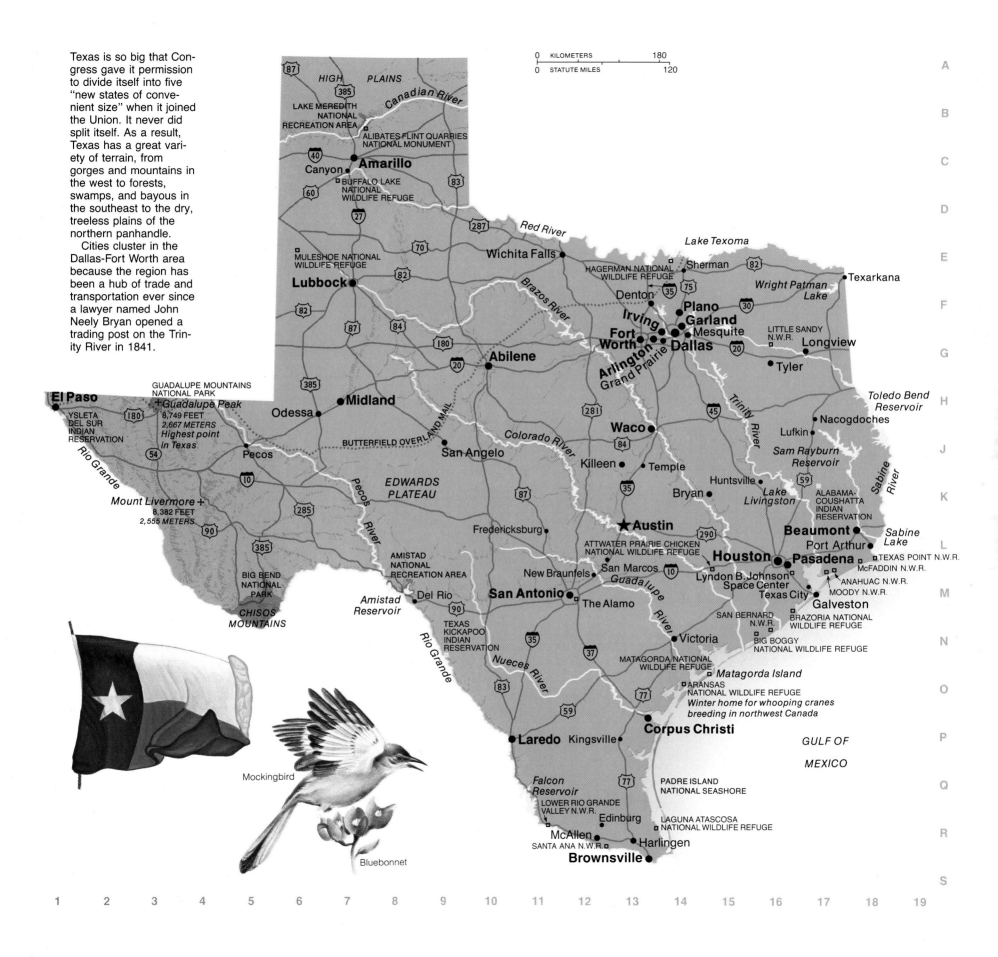

Texas is so big that Congress gave it permission to divide itself into five "new states of convenient size" when it joined the Union. It never did split itself. As a result, Texas has a great variety of terrain, from gorges and mountains in the west to forests, swamps, and bayous in the southeast to the dry, treeless plains of the northern panhandle.

Cities cluster in the Dallas-Fort Worth area because the region has been a hub of trade and transportation ever since a lawyer named John Neely Bryan opened a trading post on the Trinity River in 1841.

KILOMETERS 0 180
STATUTE MILES 0 120

A
B
C
D
E
F
G
H
J
K
L
M
N
O
P
Q
R
S

HIGH PLAINS
Canadian River
LAKE MEREDITH NATIONAL RECREATION AREA
ALIBATES FLINT QUARRIES NATIONAL MONUMENT
Canyon
Amarillo
BUFFALO LAKE NATIONAL WILDLIFE REFUGE
MULESHOE NATIONAL WILDLIFE REFUGE
Lubbock
Red River
Wichita Falls
Lake Texoma
Sherman
HAGERMAN NATIONAL WILDLIFE REFUGE
Denton
Brazos River
Wright Patman Lake
Texarkana
Plano
Irving
Garland
Mesquite
LITTLE SANDY N.W.R.
Longview
Fort Worth
Dallas
Arlington
Grand Prairie
Tyler
Toledo Bend Reservoir
Abilene
GUADALUPE MOUNTAINS NATIONAL PARK
El Paso
+Guadalupe Peak
8,749 FEET
2,667 METERS
Highest point in Texas
YSLETA DEL SUR INDIAN RESERVATION
Midland
Odessa
Waco
Nacogdoches
Lufkin
Sam Rayburn Reservoir
Rio Grande
Mount Livermore +
8,382 FEET
2,555 METERS
Pecos
BUTTERFIELD OVERLAND MAIL
San Angelo
Colorado River
Killeen
Temple
Huntsville
Lake Livingston
Sabine River
ALABAMA-COUSHATTA INDIAN RESERVATION
Bryan
EDWARDS PLATEAU
Fredericksburg
★ **Austin**
New Braunfels
San Marcos
ATTWATER PRAIRIE CHICKEN NATIONAL WILDLIFE REFUGE
Lyndon B. Johnson Space Center
Beaumont
Port Arthur
Sabine Lake
TEXAS POINT N.W.R.
McFADDIN N.W.R.
ANAHUAC N.W.R.
MOODY N.W.R.
Houston
Pasadena
Texas City
Galveston
AMISTAD NATIONAL RECREATION AREA
Del Rio
Amistad Reservoir
TEXAS KICKAPOO INDIAN RESERVATION
San Antonio
The Alamo
Guadalupe River
SAN BERNARD N.W.R.
BRAZORIA NATIONAL WILDLIFE REFUGE
BIG BEND NATIONAL PARK
CHISOS MOUNTAINS
Rio Grande
Nueces River
Victoria
BIG BOGGY NATIONAL WILDLIFE REFUGE
MATAGORDA NATIONAL WILDLIFE REFUGE
Matagorda Island
ARANSAS NATIONAL WILDLIFE REFUGE
Winter home for whooping cranes breeding in northwest Canada
Corpus Christi
GULF OF
MEXICO
Laredo
Kingsville
Falcon Reservoir
PADRE ISLAND NATIONAL SEASHORE
LOWER RIO GRANDE VALLEY N.W.R.
Edinburg
LAGUNA ATASCOSA NATIONAL WILDLIFE REFUGE
McAllen
Harlingen
SANTA ANA N.W.R.
Brownsville

Mockingbird
Bluebonnet

1 2 3 4 5 6 7 8 9 10 11 12 13 14 15 16 17 18 19

1

2

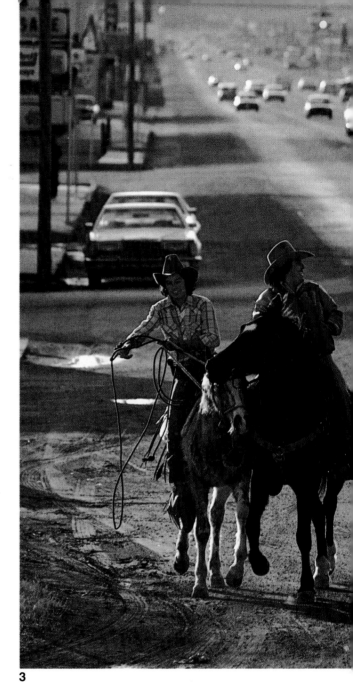

3

Texas

1 *Harvest of beauty: Giant claws gently vacuum coreopsis seeds for gardeners at a wildflower farm near Houston.*

2 *An agave symbolizes the desert that meets the Chisos Mountains as the Rio Grande makes its curve in Big Bend country.*

3 *Modern cowboys whoop it up in a town southwest of Pecos, proving that the spirit of the frontier lives on in West Texas.*

4 *Stone-still, a Texas horned lizard waits for insects. The species is threatened by loss of habitat and by collectors who prize its movie-monster looks.*

5 *Highways and high rises sprout from the northern plains in Dallas, the state's second largest city. Four of five Texans now reside in urban areas.*

5

4

Mountain States

High, wide, and rumpled describes these western states. Some parts are downright dry and desolate. The Rocky Mountains form the backbone of this region that makes up about a fifth of the land area of the 48 contiguous states. If you crossed the widest part, as some pioneers and gold seekers did, you would cover about a third of the distance between the Atlantic Ocean and the Pacific Ocean.

There's plenty of room here to get lonely, too. Fewer than 4 of every 100 Americans live in this region, mostly in the few big cities located on either side of the Rockies. The climate is dry, especially in the Great Basin area. That's because high mountains farther west wring out much of the moisture carried by winds from the Pacific Ocean. As the winds rise to clear these ridges, they cool. Their moisture condenses and falls as rain or snow. Only about 12 inches (30 cm) of precipitation dampens these mountain states most years, while the Great Basin receives much less. The Rockies themselves prevent moisture from reaching the plains farther east.

The Rockies are young mountains; only about 65 million years ago colliding continental plates thrust them thousands of feet above sea level. The Great Basin began forming 40 million years ago, cracking the crust into faults and folds. But here the pressure relaxed and some slices of crust slipped downward, forming parallel valleys and ridges.

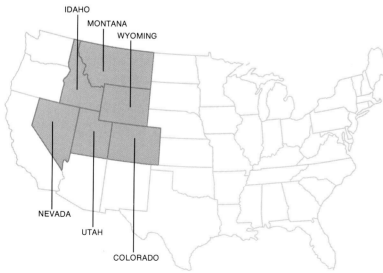

IDAHO
MONTANA
WYOMING
NEVADA
UTAH
COLORADO

R O C K Y

Black
Hills

North Platte River

M
O
U
N
T
A
I
N
S

Salt Lake
City

Cheyenne

Denver

Colorado River

Idaho

A Chinese immigrant peddles homegrown vegetables. The first Chinese came to Idaho in 1865 to work in gold mines, but many who followed opened shops, restaurants, and laundries.

Idaho leads the country in potato growing. Each year farmers harvest billions of pounds, mainly from the irrigated, fertile plain of the Snake River Valley. History credits a Presbyterian missionary with starting Idaho's potato industry. In the 1830s Henry Harmon Spalding showed Nez Perce Indians at his mission how to plant potatoes to supplement their diet when hunting was poor.

A generation ago most of Idaho's prized Russet Burbank spuds left the state whole. Today most potatoes exit after processing that includes transformation into potato chips and one-fourth of all the French fries served in fast-food restaurants. Not surprisingly, Idaho guards its precious tuber fiercely. It has sued those who use the name "Idaho" to market potatoes grown outside the state.

But many Idahoans feel that the Snake River Plain and its main cash crop get too much atten-

tion. Some argue that Idaho is really three states in one, three distinct regions that had little to do with one another until the development of modern communications and transportation. In fact, each year the people of the panhandle, the Snake River Plain, and the arid southeastern area flock to their own separate state fairs. Most other states have only one fair where people gather to celebrate their state's identity.

Made from leftover territory of some of its neighbors after they became states, Idaho lacks the rectangular regularity of nearby states. Its unusual shape and varied terrain create the three divisions. The panhandle region, which merges into the state's central wilderness, is made up of the Bitterroot, Clearwater, and other ranges of the Rocky Mountains. It contains large, deep lakes. The panhandle's dense forests of fir, pine, and spruce provide lumber and other wood products. Deposits of valuable minerals spurred a mining heyday there in the 19th century. Although many deposits played out, mining remains a major industry.

People of the panhandle have to be independent and self-reliant. They live in some of the most rugged and remote territory in the United States. Early travelers called the middle part of the Salmon the River of No Return because they could not navigate its volatile currents.

Rising in Yellowstone National Park, in Wyoming, the Snake River winds 500 miles (800 km) through southern Idaho. As the river turns north to form the border with Oregon, it carves deep down through the mountains, where it has helped create Hells Canyon.

But for most of its course the Snake River flows through a broad plain. Lava that erupted repeatedly from cracks in Earth's crust thousands of years ago contributes to the plain's rich soil. The lava also fashioned desolate landscapes where few plants can grow. The cinder buttes, spatter cones, and twisted lava flows of Craters of the Moon National Monument so resemble the moon's surface that Apollo astronauts traveled there in the 1960s.

Unlike many other parts of the West, Idaho does not often face a shortage of water. The state has many rivers and underground water sources. Waters of the Snake River, distributed by irrigation channels, nourish the plain's potato

crop and also sugar beets, wheat, alfalfa, and hops. Despite dams upstream, the Snake plunges 212 feet (65 m) at Shoshone Falls, higher than the Niagara's by about 30 feet (9 m).

Most Idahoans have settled on the Snake River Plain. Boise is one of the fastest growing cities in the West, strong in electronics, lumber, agribusiness, and other industries.

At the Basque Center in Boise, the haunting strains of a *txistu*, or flute, echo the homeland for Boise's 10,000 Basques. Work as sheepherders drew these natives of the French and Spanish Pyrenees to Idaho and nearby states. The life was a lonely one. For months at a time the herder, with his flock, would roam the high pastures. On visits to town he would seek out the company of other Basques to speak the ancient, unique Basque language. Though sheepherding is on the decline, and Basques have entered the ranks of ranchers, lawyers, and politicians, Basque culture proudly lives on in Boise.

Southeastern Idaho is part of the arid Great Basin region that extends into Nevada and other western states. Mountains interspersed with grass-covered valleys and plateaus support cattle and sheep and irrigated farming. Most people here are Mormons and have strong ties to Salt Lake City, Utah, the headquarters of the Mormon Church.

Some people think that Idaho's split personality makes a section of it ripe for secession. Proponents in the panhandle note the area's ties with nearby parts of Washington and Montana. One name proposed for this potential 51st state is Washtanaho—with a license plate that reads "No Small Potatoes."

Area: *the 13th largest state, 83,564 sq mi (216,432 sq km)*

Population: *1,066,749; ranks 42nd*

Major Cities: *Boise, 125,738; Pocatello, 46,080; Idaho Falls, 43,929*

Manufacturing: *food products, lumber and wood products, machinery, chemicals, electronics, rubber and plastics, metal products*

Agriculture: *cattle, potatoes, milk, wheat, sugar beets, barley, hay*

Mining and Quarrying: *silver, phosphate rock, lead, copper*

Other Important Activities: *tourism, printing and publishing*

Statehood: *the 43rd state; admitted July 3, 1890*

A B C D E F G H J K L M N O P Q R S T

1 2 3 4 5 6 7 8 9 10 11 12 13

KOOTENAI NATIONAL WILDLIFE REFUGE

KOOTENAI INDIAN RESERVATION

Priest Lake

Bonners Ferry

95

2 Sandpoint

200

Priest River

Pend Oreille Lake

Post Falls

Coeur d'Alene

90

Kellogg Osburn

Largest silver mine in the United States

Wallace

St. Maries

St. Joe River

COEUR D'ALENE INDIAN RESERVATION

95

Dworshak Reservoir

Moscow

Clearwater River

Orofino LEWIS & CLARK TRAIL

12

+ *Grave Peak* 8,281 FEET 2,524 METERS

Lewiston

NEZ PERCE INDIAN RESERVATION

Kamiah

CLEARWATER

Grangeville

13

MOUNTAINS

R O C K Y

HELLS CANYON N.R.A.

Salmon River

—This 100-mile-long chasm is the deepest gorge in North America, 8,000 feet (2,440 meters)

B I T T E R R O O T

LEWIS & CLARK TRAIL

Hells Canyon

SALMON RIVER

Salmon

M O U N T A I N S

Snake River

McCall

MOUNTAINS

Cascade Reservoir

Cascade

CONTINENTAL DIVIDE TRAIL

Leadore

CONTINENTAL DIVIDE

15

20 YELLOWSTONE NATIONAL PARK

Weiser

55

SAWTOOTH N.R.A.

SAWTOOTH RANGE

Salmon River

LOST RIVER RANGE

Payette

Payette River

52 Emmett

93

+ *Borah Peak* 12,662 FEET 3,859 METERS Highest point in Idaho

CAMAS NATIONAL WILDLIFE REFUGE

St. Anthony

Rexburg

Snake R.

Big Lost River

75

Lost River Sinks

Caldwell

Boise River

★ **Boise**

Nampa Meridian

Sun Valley Ketchum

Arco

Idaho Falls

Ammon

26

Mt. Baird 10,026 FEET 3,056 METERS

DEER FLAT NATIONAL WILDLIFE REFUGE

95

84

20

CRATERS OF THE MOON NATIONAL MONUMENT

91

GRAYS LAKE NATIONAL WILDLIFE REFUGE

Mountain Home

Blackfoot

S N A K E   R I V E R   P L A I N

American Falls Reservoir

FORT HALL INDIAN RESERVATION

+ *Cinnabar Mountain* 8,406 FEET 2,562 METERS

Snake R. Gooding

26

SNAKE

Chubbuck

Blackfoot Reservoir

HAGERMAN FOSSIL BEDS N.M.

Shoshone

Pocatello

30

Soda Springs

Jerome

Shoshone Falls

American Falls

OREGON TRAIL

Thousand Springs

86

Lava Hot Springs

Believed to be the reappearance of lost rivers that sink into the ground near Arco

Buhl

Twin Falls

Hansen

Burley

30

MINIDOKA NATIONAL WILDLIFE REFUGE

15

91

Montpelier

BEAR LAKE NATIONAL WILDLIFE REFUGE

51

93

84

89

CITY OF ROCKS NATIONAL RESERVE

CALIFORNIA TRAIL

Malad City

Preston

DUCK VALLEY INDIAN RESERVATION

Bear Lake

0 KILOMETERS 100
0 STATUTE MILES 60

Jumbled peaks slashed by steep-sided canyons and roaring rivers make up much of central Idaho. This wild region owes its origins in part to a huge blister-like dome—the Idaho batholith—that formed millions of years ago.

Erosion soon wore away the crust, exposing the jagged peaks of the Bitterroot, Sawtooth, and other ranges. Rivers carved two of the continent's deepest chasms, Hells Canyon and the gorge of the Salmon River as it cuts west across the mountains.

Syringa (Mock Orange)

Mountain Bluebird

1

2

Idaho

1 *Boise, Idaho's capital, lies in a valley protected from winter's worst storms by mountains to the north of the city.*

2 *Powder snow flies around a skier above the Sun Valley resort, in the Sawtooth Range of the Rocky Mountains.*

3 *A Basque sheepherder pursues his lonely work in the hills of southwestern Idaho.*

4 *French fries for your Big Mac undergo inspection for proper size and texture. Most are made from Idaho's long, oval Russet Burbank, a potato variety that finds ideal growing conditions along the Snake River.*

5 *A sprinkler rig brings water from the Snake River to irrigate crops.*

3

4

5

Montana

As a young boy in the 1940s, writer Ivan Doig lived on a small sheep ranch in a valley of Montana's Rocky Mountain foothills. The world he knew was one of mountains sliced by slanting rivers and covered with timber and high pastures. Ivan was a teenager before he glimpsed the state's other, larger landscape, "a land of steady expanse, of crisp-margined distances set long and straight on the earth."

Montana is two-fifths mountains and three-fifths rolling, shortgrass prairie. Range after range of the Rockies rises in western Montana. The Continental Divide rides the crests of these ranges. It also gives Montana two climates. West of the divide, the climate is moderate and relatively humid year-round. East of it, extremes are the norm: very cold winters and very hot summers with less rainfall than the west. Sometimes, though, winter's grip on the eastern plains will be broken by chinooks. These warm winds blow down the eastern slopes of the Rockies, raising temperatures and melting snow so that pasture for livestock is exposed.

Eighty million years of mountain building put broad streaks of gold, silver, and copper into many Montana ranges. Water, wind, and glaciers carried minerals to rivers and streams, forming deposits called placers. Beginning in 1862, Montana's gold rush made places like Butte and Virginia City wild and wealthy towns. As the gold rush waned, miners sought silver and the copper that long drove the economy. Mining interests held great power. Until the mid-1960s the Anaconda Copper Mining Company owned many Montana newspapers and controlled many of the politicians.

Anaconda closed its main smelter in 1980. Today metal mining continues on a smaller scale, and Montana leads the country in the extraction of talc and vermiculite, used chiefly in insulation. Butte supplements its reduced mining income with light industry and livestock sales.

Miners have long shared Montana's mountains with loggers. The fir, pine, cedar, and spruce they cut are turned into lumber and other wood products before leaving the state. How much lumbering is in Montana's future has rekindled a dispute between conservationists who worry about Montana's federal forestlands and loggers and sawmill workers who worry about jobs. For one section a landmark compromise was reached in 1990 that would set aside almost equal areas of wilderness and land for logging, mining, and other development.

Montana's eastern prairie supports most of the state's agriculture. Only Texas has more acreage devoted to farming. Furrowed stripes

In 1887 immigrants from Europe and Asia built the Great Northern Railroad across 640 miles of plains and mountains in Montana and North Dakota in just one season.

of wheat cover much of the plains, along with barley, hay, and other crops. Where cattle once ranged freely, grazing on prairie grasses under the watch of cowboys, fences now mark the boundaries of Montana's vast ranches.

Today both ranchers and environmentalists eye with apprehension the further development of eastern Montana's energy resources. Oil brings in about half of Montana's mineral income. Worldwide concern about oil puts a premium on the state's enormous reserves as well as its reserves of coal.

Lewis and Clark were the first white Americans to view the Great Falls of the Missouri River, which drains most of the state and is its principal waterway. "The grandest sight I ever beheld," wrote Meriwether Lewis in his 1805 journal. But would he recognize the Missouri today? At Fort Peck, one of the world's largest earthen dams impounds the river's water, creating a lake bigger than the city of Chicago.

And what would the explorers say about the Blackfeet, Flathead, Crow, Sioux, Cheyenne, and other tribes that in their time commanded the mountain passes and the plains teeming with bison? About 6 percent of Montanans today are Native Americans whose reservation councils often face controversy over whether or not to exploit their land's natural resources, particularly coal and oil. More than a century ago, their ancestors gave an answer to the federal troops moving onto their lands. On a lonely hill near the Little Bighorn River, on a June Sunday in 1876, Lt. Col. George A. Custer and 215 men of his Seventh Cavalry fell at the hands of some 2,000 Indian warriors.

Area: *the fourth largest state, 147,046 sq mi (380,848 sq km)*

Population: *799,065; ranks 44th*

Major Cities: *Billings, 81,151; Great Falls, 55,097; Missoula, 42,918*

Manufacturing: *lumber and wood products, food products, petroleum products*

Mining and Quarrying: *oil and gas, coal, gold, silver, sand and gravel*

Agriculture: *cattle, wheat, barley, hay, sugar beets, milk*

Other Important Activities: *tourism, printing and publishing*

Statehood: *the 41st state; admitted November 8, 1889*

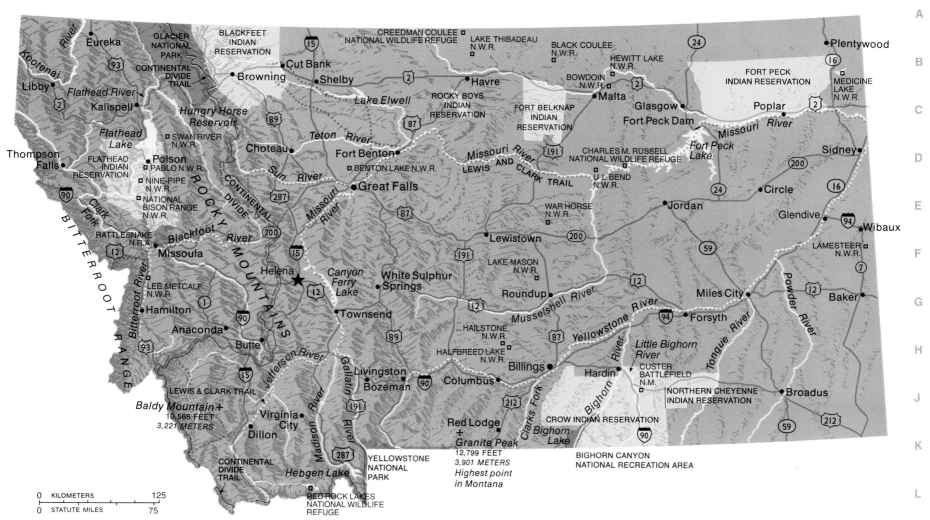

| | 1 | 2 | 3 | 4 | 5 | 6 | 7 | 8 | 9 | 10 | 11 | 12 | 13 | 14 | 15 | 16 | 17 | 18 | 19 |

A

B

C

D

E

F

G

H

J

K

L

River Kootenai

Eureka

GLACIER NATIONAL PARK

CONTINENTAL DIVIDE TRAIL

BLACKFEET INDIAN RESERVATION

CREEDMAN COULEE NATIONAL WILDLIFE REFUGE

LAKE THIBADEAU N.W.R.

BLACK COULEE N.W.R.

HEWITT LAKE N.W.R.

FORT PECK INDIAN RESERVATION

• Plentywood

93

Libby •

Flathead River

Kalispell •

• Cut Bank

• Browning

• Shelby

• Havre

ROCKY BOYS INDIAN RESERVATION

FORT BELKNAP INDIAN RESERVATION

BOWDOIN N.W.R.

• Malta

Glasgow •

Fort Peck Dam •

MEDICINE LAKE N.W.R.

2

Lake Elwell

24

16

Poplar •

Hungry Horse Reservoir

Flathead Lake

89

Teton River

87

Missouri River

191

CHARLES M. RUSSELL NATIONAL WILDLIFE REFUGE

Fort Peck Lake

Missouri River

Sidney •

2

Thompson Falls •

FLATHEAD INDIAN RESERVATION

SWAN RIVER N.W.R.

Polson •

PABLO N.W.R.

Choteau •

Fort Benton •

BENTON LAKE N.W.R.

LEWIS AND CLARK TRAIL

U L BEND N.W.R.

24

Circle •

16

90

NINE-PIPE N.W.R.

NATIONAL BISON RANGE N.W.R.

Sun River

• Great Falls

200

Glendive •

94

• Wibaux

Clark Fork

RATTLESNAKE N.R.A.

ROCKY MOUNTAINS

CONTINENTAL DIVIDE

Blackfoot River

200

Missouri River

87

Lewistown •

LAKE MASON N.W.R.

Jordan •

59

LAMESTEER N.W.R.

7

12

Missoula •

15

Helena ★

12

Canyon Ferry Lake

White Sulphur Springs

191

WAR HORSE N.W.R.

12

Roundup •

Musselshell River

12

Miles City •

Baker •

12

BITTERROOT RANGE

Bitterroot River

LEE METCALF N.W.R.

1

Hamilton •

Townsend •

89

87

Yellowstone River

94

Forsyth •

Powder River

Tongue River

Anaconda •

90

Jefferson River

Gallatin River

HAILSTONE N.W.R.

Bighorn River

Billings •

Little Bighorn River

CUSTER BATTLEFIELD N.M.

Butte •

HALFBREED LAKE N.W.R.

Livingston •

Bozeman •

90

Columbus •

Hardin •

NORTHERN CHEYENNE INDIAN RESERVATION

Broadus •

LEWIS & CLARK TRAIL

Baldy Mountain +
10,568 FEET
3,221 METERS

Virginia City •

Dillon •

Madison River

19

212

Clarks Fork

Bighorn Lake

CROW INDIAN RESERVATION

59

212

287

YELLOWSTONE NATIONAL PARK

Red Lodge •
+ Granite Peak
12,799 FEET
3,901 METERS
Highest point
in Montana

90

BIGHORN CANYON NATIONAL RECREATION AREA

CONTINENTAL DIVIDE TRAIL

Hebgen Lake

RED ROCK LAKES NATIONAL WILDLIFE REFUGE

| 0 | KILOMETERS | 125 |
| 0 | STATUTE MILES | 75 |

Angling westward from Yellowstone National Park, the Continental Divide follows Rocky Mountain ridges, forming part of the border with Idaho before turning eastward. A hiking trail traces the watershed through Montana to Glacier National Park.

Journeying to the Pacific Ocean, Meriwether Lewis and William Clark followed the Missouri River in 1804 and returned along the Yellowstone in 1806.

Many other trails also led west (map at right), including those traveled by pioneer families during the great migrations of the 1840s and 1850s.

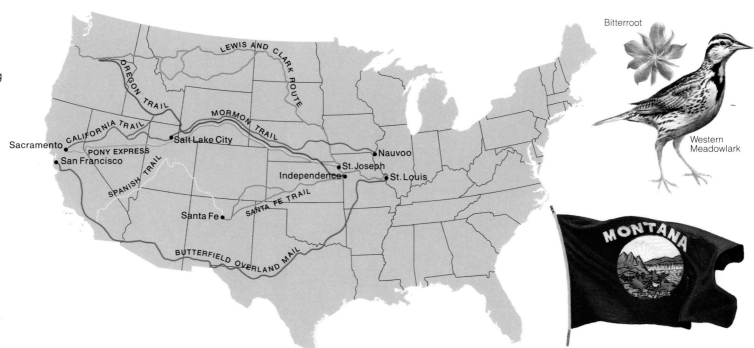

LEWIS AND CLARK ROUTE

OREGON TRAIL

MORMON TRAIL

CALIFORNIA TRAIL

Sacramento •

Salt Lake City •

PONY EXPRESS

San Francisco •

SPANISH TRAIL

Independence •

St. Joseph •

Nauvoo •

St. Louis •

Santa Fe •

SANTA FE TRAIL

BUTTERFIELD OVERLAND MAIL

Bitterroot

Western Meadowlark

MONTANA

1

2

3

4

Montana

1 *In the mountains of south-central Montana, cowboys herd their cattle on a fall drive from high summer pastures to a lower, warmer winter range.*

2 *A bighorn sheep, safe in the mountain meadows of Glacier National Park, nibbles on favorite blossoms.*

3 *On the Continental Divide, a gigantic limestone wall is honeycombed with fossils of creatures that lived here 500 million years ago, when shallow seas covered the land.*

4 *Harvested wheat, Montana's most valuable crop, pours from a combine as the farmer levels his load.*

5 *A mile-wide (1.6-km) pit, once mined for copper, edges Butte. Now the pit is being filled with groundwater drained from nearby underground metal mines.*

5

Wyoming

Endless lines of covered wagons, creaking and groaning under the weight of precious possessions. Zealous Latter-day Saints, or Mormons, searching for a peaceful promised land. Hopeful prospectors rushing to stake their claims in California's goldfields. Wiry youths spurring on their lightning-fast mounts to the next relay point. All of these pioneers, forty-niners, and Pony Express riders passed through Wyoming on essentially the same trail: a route that followed the North Platte and Sweetwater Rivers, up a gradual slope and across the Continental Divide at South Pass, the best natural gap in the Rocky Mountains. So well chosen was this route that rail and road traffic still follow it today.

In the 19th century, hundreds of thousands of people passed through Wyoming, but few stayed. Most early settlements rose around army forts and along the route of the Union Pacific Railroad in southern Wyoming. Mining, cattle ranching, and the discovery of oil near Casper in 1888 added other settlements. Some places, like Cheyenne, bear the names of Indian groups driven off their land by the newcomers.

In Wyoming, the Great Plains meet the Rocky Mountains. From the Absaroka Range and Bighorn Mountains in the north to the Wind River Range to the Laramie Mountains in the southeast, most Wyoming ranges stretch north to south. Between them lie high, dry, cold basins covered with the sagebrush and shortgrasses that are natural forage for the widespread herds of pronghorns. In places, flat-topped towers of weathered rock called buttes punctuate the desolate basins. Most of Wyoming is high; its average elevation of 6,100 feet (1,860 m) is second only to Colorado's.

Driving the high roads of the mountain West, writer and California native Gretl Ehrlich can always sense when she approaches her adopted state. "When the wind starts blowing, I know I'm near Wyoming," she wrote. Wyoming is so windy that winter often brings "ground blizzards." Though no snow is falling and the day may be sunny and bright, westerly winds whip up dry snow from the ground into blinding swirls, easy to get lost in.

The railroad spread across southern Wyoming in the late 1860s. As it did, cattlemen came from Texas, eager to graze their longhorns on

the nutritious grasses before moving them to market by rail. As ranchers they would take the 160 acres (65 ha) that the federal government allotted to homesteaders and then graze their animals on the open range. To combat cattle rustlers, the ranchers banded together in a Stock Growers' Association that registered the brands used by each ranch. Other homesteaders, who were farmers, resented the ranchers' grazing practices and began to fence in their spreads to protect their crops. Sheep ranchers

A rancher shows off Buster, a fine-wooled Rambouillet sheep, in 1945. Buster's thick coat provides good protection in subfreezing winters. His ancestors came to the U. S. from Spain and Germany.

competed for pasture with the cattle ranchers. All these rivalries developed into a series of ferocious range wars among sheepherders, cattlemen, and farmers.

Essential to each ranch's operations was the cowboy. Willing to perform ceaseless chores and endure long, lonesome hours in the saddle, braving the wind and weather, cowboys have kept

Wyoming's vast cattle ranches running. Today cowboying in Wyoming has taken on an international flavor. While some Americans still want the job, some ranches have *vaqueros* from Mexico, Chile, and Peru, and one Wyoming sheep rancher has looked even farther—all the way to Mongolia—for herders to look after his flocks.

Wyoming's people live mostly in small towns. Although the state has the smallest population in the nation, what it lacks in year-round residents it makes up for in visitors. Each year some five million tourists flock to the natural wonders of Yellowstone National Park, to the wildlife and scenery of the Teton Range, to vacation ranches, and to the rodeos and other celebrations of Wyoming's frontier heritage. The money they spend every year rivals the income earned from agriculture and creates many jobs for Wyoming citizens.

Most of Wyoming's economic resources lie with the mineral riches under the land. The area around Green River contains the world's largest source of trona, the ore that yields soda ash, a chemical used in making glass, detergent, and baking soda. Wyoming also holds the second largest reserve of uranium in the country (after New Mexico), most of it in the state's central basins. Enormous deposits of oil, natural gas, and coal have been mined in fits and starts, depending on the nation's energy needs—thus producing ups and downs in Wyoming's economy. Knowing that its future most likely lies with increased mining, Wyoming is acting to prevent permanent damage to the environment. At all strip-mining projects in eastern Wyoming, earthmovers continually backfill the cut as the excavation proceeds, and the fill is then replanted under the supervision of ecologists.

Area: *the ninth largest state, 97,809 sq mi (253,326 sq km)*
Population: *453,588; ranks 50th*
Major Cities: *Cheyenne, 50,008; Casper, 46,742; Laramie, 26,687*
Mining: *oil and gas, coal, trona, clay*
Manufacturing: *chemicals, petroleum products, food products, lumber and wood products*
Agriculture: *cattle, hay, sugar beets, sheep and wool, wheat, barley*
Other Important Activities: *tourism, printing and publishing*
Statehood: *the 44th state; admitted July 10, 1890*

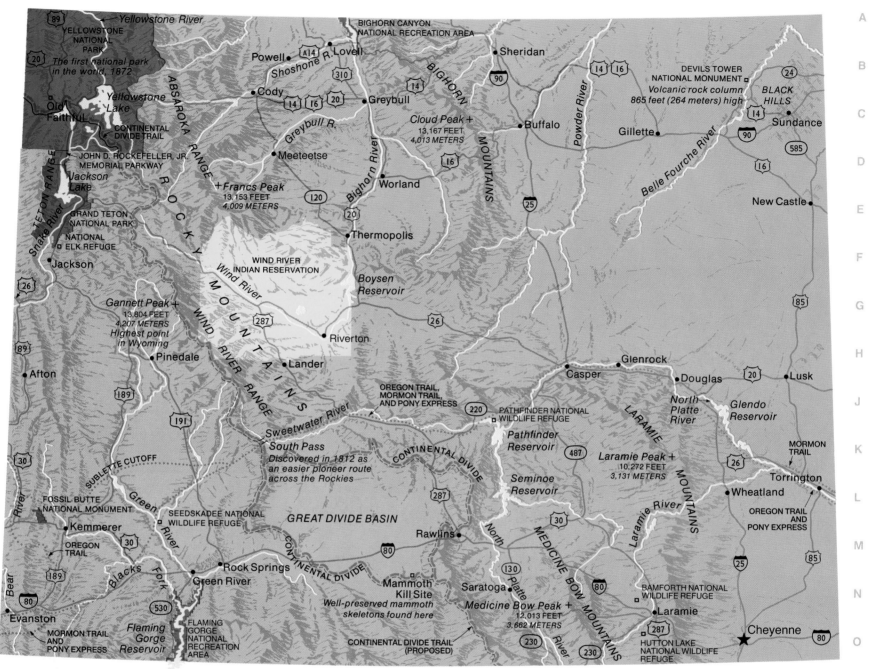

1 2 3 4 5 6 7 8 9 10 11 12 13 14 15 16 17 18

A B C D E F G H J K L M N O

Yellowstone River

YELLOWSTONE NATIONAL PARK
The first national park in the world, 1872

Old Faithful
Yellowstone Lake

ABSAROKA RANGE

CONTINENTAL DIVIDE TRAIL

TETON RANGE

JOHN D. ROCKEFELLER, JR. MEMORIAL PARKWAY

Jackson Lake

GRAND TETON NATIONAL PARK

NATIONAL ELK REFUGE

Snake River

Jackson

ROCKY

Powell
Lovell
Shoshone R.
BIGHORN CANYON NATIONAL RECREATION AREA

Sheridan

Cody
Greybull
BIGHORN MOUNTAINS

Meeteetse
Greybull R.

+Francs Peak
13,153 FEET
4,009 METERS

Cloud Peak +
13,167 FEET
4,013 METERS

Buffalo

Powder River

DEVILS TOWER NATIONAL MONUMENT
Volcanic rock column 865 feet (264 meters) high

BLACK HILLS

Gillette

Sundance

Worland

Bighorn River

Thermopolis

WIND RIVER INDIAN RESERVATION

Wind River

Boysen Reservoir

Belle Fourche River

New Castle

MOUNTAINS

Gannett Peak +
13,804 FEET
4,207 METERS
Highest point in Wyoming

WIND RIVER RANGE

Pinedale

Afton

Lander

Riverton

Glenrock

Casper

North Platte River

Douglas

Lusk

Glendo Reservoir

OREGON TRAIL, MORMON TRAIL, AND PONY EXPRESS

PATHFINDER NATIONAL WILDLIFE REFUGE

Pathfinder Reservoir

LARAMIE MOUNTAINS

MORMON TRAIL

Sweetwater River

South Pass
Discovered in 1812 as an easier pioneer route across the Rockies

CONTINENTAL DIVIDE

Seminoe Reservoir

Laramie Peak +
10,272 FEET
3,131 METERS

SUBLETTE CUTOFF

Green River

FOSSIL BUTTE NATIONAL MONUMENT

SEEDSKADEE NATIONAL WILDLIFE REFUGE

GREAT DIVIDE BASIN

CONTINENTAL DIVIDE

Rawlins

Laramie River

Torrington

Wheatland

OREGON TRAIL AND PONY EXPRESS

Kemmerer

Bear River

OREGON TRAIL

Blacks Fork

Rock Springs

Green River

Saratoga

North Platte River

MEDICINE BOW MOUNTAINS

Mammoth Kill Site
Well-preserved mammoth skeletons found here

Medicine Bow Peak +
12,013 FEET
3,662 METERS

BAMFORTH NATIONAL WILDLIFE REFUGE

Laramie

Cheyenne

Evanston

MORMON TRAIL AND PONY EXPRESS

Flaming Gorge Reservoir

FLAMING GORGE NATIONAL RECREATION AREA

CONTINENTAL DIVIDE TRAIL (PROPOSED)

HUTTON LAKE NATIONAL WILDLIFE REFUGE

Western Meadowlark

Indian Paintbrush

Just south of Wyoming's Wind River Range the Continental Divide splits in two and circles the rim of Great Divide Basin. In an otherwise forbidding wall of mountains, South Pass provided such an easy route that many travelers never realized they had crested the Rocky Mountains.

In the northwest, the Teton Range began to rise about ten million years ago, making these mountains the youngest in the Rockies. And still they grow, about a foot (0.3 m) every 400 years.

0 KILOMETERS 75
0 STATUTE MILES 50

1

Wyoming

1 *A froth of white water drenches a kayaker riding the rapids of the Snake River.*

2 *A herd winters at the National Elk Refuge below the Teton Range. To supplement grazing, the refuge distributes hay pellets to the animals. The elk help pay the food bill when Boy Scouts gather antlers shed by the bulls and auction the antlers to contribute to the costs.*

2

3

4

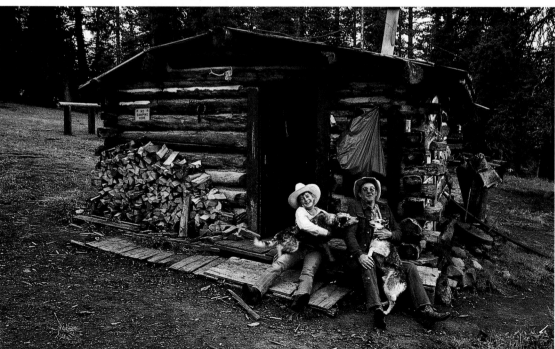

5

3 *Old Faithful, Yellowstone National Park's most reliable geyser, blasts off about every 50 to 100 minutes. Molten rock beneath Earth's crust heats groundwater, which turns into steam that forces water above it to explode from the hot spring.*

4 *In southwestern Wyoming a helicopter and a cowboy round up wild mustangs. Every year, under the federal government's Adopt-a-Horse program, several thousand find new homes all across the country.*

5 *A ranch foreman and his young apprentice take a break at their cabin on the ranch's summer range near Meeteetse. With their two dogs, they herd 2,500 head of cattle.*

Nevada

In 1864 Mark Twain, working in Virginia City, wrote of Nevada: "The country looks something like a singed cat, owing to the scarcity of shrubbery, and also resembles that animal in the respect that it has more merits than its personal appearance would seem to indicate."

More than 125 years later Twain's description still fits pretty well. Most of the state is windy and barren, and most of it lies within the Great Basin, which is not one basin but at least 90. These valleys are separated by some 160 mountain ranges that on a map, said a geographer, look like an army of caterpillars crawling toward Mexico. In the west the Sierra Nevada range blocks moisture borne on westerly winds from the Pacific Ocean, making Nevada the driest state in the country. It receives, on average, only nine inches (23 cm) of precipitation a year, resulting in scant desert vegetation of shrubby shad scale and sagebrush and, higher up, scattered piñon and juniper trees.

The Great Basin sends no rivers to the sea. The rivers dead-end into lakes or into wide, shallow depressions called sinks. These sinks dry up in the summer, leaving cracked, salty or alkaline mud flats. Most of Nevada's rivers appear only seasonally and dry up in the long, hot summers. Even permanent rivers such as the snow-fed Humboldt are not large.

In contrast to Nevada's wide, parched basins are its forest-rimmed mountain lakes. One of the merits of the state that Mark Twain praised was beautiful, deep, crystal-clear Lake Tahoe, on the California border. Human hands, not natural forces, created Lake Mead, Nevada's largest lake, the reservoir of one of the world's largest dams. Built of enough concrete to make a two-lane highway from New York City to San Francisco, Hoover Dam holds back the water of the Colorado River for hydroelectricity and irrigation. Lake Mead, with Lake Mohave, forms one of the nation's largest recreation areas.

For millennia, bands of Northern and Southern Paiute, Shoshone, and Washoe Indians and their ancestors roamed Nevada, living by hunting and gathering. A staple food was the nutritious nut of the piñon pine.

In the 1770s, Spanish monks blazed parts of a trail from New Mexico to California to promote communication between Spanish settlements

In 1905 Las Vegas, less than a year old, had grown from a temporary settlement for railroad workers into a thriving town with stores, hotels, restaurants, tent homes, and this men's clothing store.

and to find Indians to convert to Christianity. The Spanish Trail, as it became known, was used later by traders and pioneers. It passed through a mountain-ringed valley that the Spanish called Las Vegas, "the meadows." In the 1850s, Mormons settled at Las Vegas and other Nevada sites, where they raised livestock and, by irrigation, coaxed crops out of the arid land. The discovery of the multimillion-dollar Comstock Lode of silver and gold ore in 1859 brought hordes of miners to western Nevada to settle Virginia City and other mining camps. One of them was Carson City, which became the capital in 1861, while Nevada was still a territory.

Early in the 20th century, Nevada found its mining fortunes waning and its population greatly outnumbered by sheep and cattle. In 1931 the state legislature decided to legalize gambling. Reno and Las Vegas became the centers of the gaming industry. Hotels patterned after Roman palaces or medieval castles provide nonstop opportunities for 30 million people a year to gamble, eat, and be entertained.

Gambling, along with the hotels, restaurants, and other services that support it, employs about 57 percent of Nevada's population and brings in more revenue than agriculture, mining, and manufacturing combined. Slot machines and other gambling equipment are important manufactured goods.

Between 1980 and 1990, Nevada's population increased by almost 50 percent, making it the fastest growing state in the country. Nearly all newcomers settle in existing urban areas. In Las Vegas, houses rise at an astonishing rate of a thousand a month, straining water and power supplies. The reach of gambling and population has spread even to Lake Tahoe, where casinos and condominiums crowd the shores and pollute the once pristine waters.

Nevadans often refer to the parts of the state beyond Las Vegas and Reno as the "cow counties." Raising cattle and sheep and growing alfalfa for hay are the main agricultural activities. Many of Nevada's sheepherders and cowboys are Basques from the French and Spanish Pyrenees. The Basques migrated to the mountain West because their tradition ties them to mountain villages and farms where they followed this often lonely kind of work.

Mining is also important in several of the cow counties. Nevada leads the nation in the production of gold and silver. Copper, sand, and gravel are used by the construction industry that houses Nevada's booming population.

More than 85 percent of Nevada's land is federally owned. Many Nevadans want control over it to avoid hazards such as the nuclear weapons testing that went on in the 1950s, '60s, and '70s. More than 20,000 years must pass before radiation will disappear from the test site in the Nevada desert.

Much of the land of Nevada resembles an old-fashioned washboard. Most of the mountains run parallel to one another and are separated by broad, flat valleys.

Geologists explain that, beginning some 150 million years ago, Nevada was squeezed together and then, 17 million years ago, stretched apart like a giant accordion as the continent's crust shifted. These movements created long, parallel cracks, or faults, in the crust. As the crust continued to move, some strips slipped downward, forming valleys. The upthrust strips became fault-block mountains.

Area: *the seventh largest state, 110,561 sq mi (286,352 sq km)*
Population: *1,201,833; ranks 39th*
Major Cities: *Las Vegas, 258,295; Reno, 133,850; Henderson, 64,942*
Manufacturing: *food products, machinery, stone, clay, and glass products, chemicals, metal products, electronics, metals, rubber and plastics, scientific instruments*
Mining: *gold, diatomite, oil and gas, silver*
Agriculture: *cattle, hay, milk, potatoes, barley*
Other Important Activities: *legalized gambling, tourism, entertainment, printing and publishing*
Statehood: *the 36th state; admitted October 31, 1864*

KILOMETERS 0 — 100
STATUTE MILES 0 — 60

SHELDON NATIONAL WILDLIFE REFUGE
DUCK VALLEY INDIAN RESERVATION
FORT McDERMITT INDIAN RESERVATION
SUMMIT LAKE INDIAN RESERVATION
CALIFORNIA TRAIL
Wells
Winnemucca
Humboldt River
Carlin
Elko
Ruby Dome
+ 11,387 FEET
3,471 METERS
Wendover
PYRAMID LAKE INDIAN RESERVATION
Lovelock
Battle Mountain
TE-MOAK INDIAN RESERVATION
Pyramid Lake
ANAHO ISLAND N.W.R.
Humboldt Lake
RUBY LAKE NATIONAL WILDLIFE REFUGE
GREAT BASIN
GOSHUTE INDIAN RESERVATION
CARSON ROUTE
Reese River
FALLON NATIONAL WILDLIFE REFUGE
PONY EXPRESS
Truckee River
FALLON INDIAN RESERVATION
STILLWATER NATIONAL WILDLIFE REFUGE
Reno Sparks
Fallon
Austin
Eureka
One of several old mining towns
McGill
Virginia City
Carson River
Ely
Lake Tahoe
Carson City
WALKER RIVER INDIAN RESERVATION
Wheeler Peak
13,063 FEET
3,982 METERS +
Minden
Yerington
DUCKWATER INDIAN RESERVATION
GREAT BASIN NATIONAL PARK
Walker Lake
Babbitt
Hawthorne
Lunar Crater
Volcanic action 1.8 million years ago formed a pit 430 feet (131 meters) deep
Tonopah
Pioche
+ *Boundary Peak*
13,143 FEET
4,006 METERS
Highest point in Nevada
Goldfield
PAHRANAGAT NATIONAL WILDLIFE REFUGE
DEATH VALLEY NATIONAL MONUMENT
Nuclear warheads tested underground
DEPARTMENT OF ENERGY NEVADA TEST SITE
DESERT NATIONAL WILDLIFE REFUGE
Meadow Valley Wash
AMARGOSA DESERT
SPANISH TRAIL
Virgin River
Mountain Bluebird
ASH MEADOWS N.W.R.
North Las Vegas
LAKE MEAD NATIONAL RECREATION AREA
Las Vegas
Paradise
Lake Mead
Henderson
Hoover Dam
Boulder City
Sagebrush
Lake Mohave
Colorado River

1

2

Nevada

1 *Defying centuries of harsh weather, a bristlecone pine clings to a peak in Great Basin National Park. Some bristlecones are 4,600 years old, and stood on western mountains when pharaohs ruled Egypt.*

2 *A three-minute haircut at the hands of a skilled shearer crops a year's growth of wool from sheep on their way to spring lambing grounds in eastern Nevada.*

3 *Neon glitter spells out the attractions of Las Vegas, where nightclubs and gambling casinos yearly lure millions of tourists.*

3

4

5

4 *Virginia City, a boomtown in the 1860s and 1870s, stands over the remains of the Comstock Lode, one of the richest veins of gold and silver ever discovered.*

5 *Paiute Indians pull trout from a spawning channel at Pyramid Lake. Sometimes nomadic, Paiute fished and hunted in this region centuries ago.*

Utah

The weary party had reached journey's end but did not yet know it. Their 1,350-mile (2,172-km) trek across the Great Plains and through the Rocky Mountains would take many lives from among the 1,900 refugees who would follow them, seeking freedom from religious persecution in the East. Now, in July 1847, a small advance band stood on the western slope of the Wasatch Range, gazing out over the Great Salt Lake and the valley below. Their ailing leader, Brigham Young, peered from his wagon to share the view. "This is the right place," he announced, and so the immigrants made their way to the valley floor.

Brigham Young and his followers are known as Mormons, or members of the Church of Jesus Christ of Latter-day Saints. Mormon doctrine contains many precepts for everyday life. It forbids the consumption of alcohol, tobacco, coffee, and tea. Marriages in a Mormon temple can last beyond death, since families may be united for all eternity. Also, young Mormon men, and sometimes young women and retired couples, work for a time without pay as missionaries.

But above all, it was the Mormon values of discipline, hard work, and of putting the community before the needs of the individual that enabled them to quickly settle their land. Within a month of their arrival, the Mormons had plowed, irrigated, and planted more than a hundred acres (40 ha). Within a year, they laid out a plan for Salt Lake City that included a site for their temple. They soon established hundreds of other settlements in places far less hospitable than the Salt Lake Valley.

The eastern edge of the Salt Lake Valley is green and lush because of irrigation. It lies at the foot of the Wasatch Range, part of the Rockies. Sediments wash down from the mountains to create a narrow strip of productive soil. Most of Utah's population today clusters along this front: 80 percent in the 80-mile (129-km) stretch from Ogden to Provo.

Forming an "L" with the Wasatch, the Uinta Mountains are the only range of the Rockies with an east-west orientation. While numerous ski resorts cover the slopes of the Wasatch, the Uinta's heavily forested slopes provide a primitive recreation area.

The Great Salt Lake grows and shrinks with

The Saltair resort and amusement palace was an attraction for visitors, invited to "try to sink" in the Great Salt Lake in the early 1900s. This area now lies beneath the lake's surface.

changes in inflow and evaporation. In recent years, heavy rains and strong spring snowmelt sent it over its beaches to high levels. Giving its name to the fertile valley, the Great Salt Lake actually lies in an arid area of small mountain ranges separated by broad basins. Minerals in the runoff from rivers to the east give it a high salt content. The lake is the remnant of an ancient inland freshwater sea called Lake Bonneville. During the Ice Age, Bonneville covered an area almost the size of Lake Michigan. Lake Bonneville has also left its legacy on the slopes of the Wasatch: wide shorelines, or terraces, with the caves of hunter-gatherers who inhabited the area 12,000 years ago.

The Colorado Plateau forms the largest part of Utah. This is an area of rugged uplands cut by deep canyons and valleys. National monuments, state parks, and national parks, including Bryce Canyon, Zion, and Canyonlands, preserve the fantastic landforms shaped by the action of wind, water, snow, and ice on the plateau's multihued layers of rock. The parks, together with

the large recreational Lake Powell created on the Colorado River by the Glen Canyon Dam, bring millions of tourists to southern Utah each year—one of the largest sources of revenue.

Today seven of every ten Utahns are Mormons. The mining of copper and other minerals and the opening of the railroad in the late 1800s brought in large numbers of gentiles, as non-Mormons are called. But the Mormon Church continues to extend its influence to many aspects of life in Utah. The church holds tracts of land throughout the state. It also owns a newspaper, a radio station, a television station, an insurance company, and half-interest in a department store. The Mormon preference for large families keeps Utah's birthrate at about twice the national average. A high regard for learning places the population among the nation's best educated.

The federal government is another major influence in Utah. Owning almost two-thirds of the land, the government is also the state's largest employer. Since World War II, federally sponsored manufacturing of rocket engines and weapons parts by private companies has played a large role in the economy. Food processing and, more recently, the electronics and computer industries also employ many residents.

The growth of urban areas brings the usual problems of traffic, pollution, and industrial waste to the Salt Lake Valley. Potential growth and development threaten the southern plateau region. The nation's energy demands are likely to press the exploration of this area's large reserves of coal, natural gas, oil shale, and uranium, much to the dismay of those who seek to preserve the fragile and unique terrain.

Area: *the 11th largest state, 84,899 sq mi (219,889 sq km)*
Population: *1,722,850; ranks 35th*
Major Cities: *Salt Lake City, 159,936; West Valley City, 86,976; Provo, 86,835*
Manufacturing: *transportation equipment, food products, scientific instruments, machinery, metal products, electronics, metals, stone, clay, and glass products, chemicals, clothing*
Mining: *oil and gas, coal, copper, gold*
Agriculture: *cattle, milk, hay, turkeys, wheat*
Other Important Activities: *tourism, federal government, printing and publishing*
Statehood: *the 45th state; admitted January 4, 1896*

CALIFORNIA TRAIL

Bear Lake

Logan

Promontory

Bear River

WASATCH RANGE

Brigham City

BEAR RIVER
NATIONAL WILDLIFE
REFUGE

Ogden
Roy
Clearfield
Layton

Great Salt Lake
Evaporation makes this
inland sea as much as
7.5 times saltier than
the oceans

MORMON
TRAIL

*Flaming Gorge
Reservoir*

FLAMING GORGE
NATIONAL RECREATION AREA

UINTA MOUNTAINS

Sego Lily

California
Gull

GREAT SALT LAKE DESERT

*Bonneville
Salt Flats*

Bear River

Bountiful

W. Valley City   ★ **Salt Lake City**
Kearns   Holladay
                Murray   Park City
                Sandy
Tooele   Heber City

SKULL VALLEY
INDIAN RESERVATION

American Fork

Jordan River

TIMPANOGOS CAVE
NAT. MONUMENT

Orem
Provo
Springville
Spanish Fork

Utah Lake

PONY EXPRESS

Payson

DEEP CREEK RANGE

GOSHUTE
INDIAN
RESERVATION

FISH SPRINGS
NATIONAL WILDLIFE
REFUGE

Nephi

Kings Peak +
13,528 FEET
4,123 METERS
Highest point
in Utah

One of the world's largest
collections of dinosaur bones

DINOSAUR
NATIONAL
MONUMENT

Vernal

Uinta River

UINTAH AND OURAY
INDIAN RESERVATION

*Strawberry
Reservoir*

Strawberry River

Roosevelt

OURAY
NATIONAL
WILDLIFE
REFUGE

Green River

*White
River*

WASATCH RANGE

S E V I E R

D E S E R T

Yuba Lake

Price

Price River

San Rafael River

SPANISH TRAIL

Green River

ARCHES
NATIONAL
PARK

Sevier Lake
Dry air and no outlet
streams create this
shrinking salt lake

Fillmore

Salina

Richfield

Muddy Creek

Moab

Beaver

Fremont River

Sevier River

CAPITOL REEF
NATIONAL PARK
Layered cliffs are capped
with white, reef-like
sandstone formations

PAIUTE
INDIAN RESERVATION

Dirty Devil River

CANYONLANDS
NATIONAL
PARK

Colorado River

Monticello

NATURAL BRIDGES
NATIONAL
MONUMENT

Escalante River

Panguitch

CEDAR BREAKS
NATIONAL
MONUMENT

Cedar City

Blanding

HOVENWEEP
NATIONAL MONUMENT

ZION
NATIONAL
PARK

BRYCE CANYON
NATIONAL PARK

GLEN CANYON
NATIONAL
RECREATION AREA

Kanab Creek

PAIUTE
INDIAN
RESERVATION

Virgin River

St. George

Kanab

Lake Powell

RAINBOW BRIDGE
NATIONAL MONUMENT

San Juan River

NAVAJO INDIAN RESERVATION

Monument Valley   Four Corners

Only point in the
United States where
four states meet

The Sevier and Great
Salt Lake Deserts of
western Utah—vast, flat
basins with wave-cut ter-
races etched into moun-
tains—resemble an
ancient ocean floor.
That's because much of
Utah *was* underwater.
Thousands of years ago,
when the climate was
cooler and wetter, these
deserts formed the bot-
tom of an inland sea,
Lake Bonneville.

Then a natural dam
broke, draining much of
the lake into the Snake
River to the north. A hot-
ter, drier climate left only
today's Great Salt Lake,
a remnant a little more
than a tenth the size of
the ancient lake.

0   KILOMETERS   75
0   STATUTE MILES   50

1

2

3

5

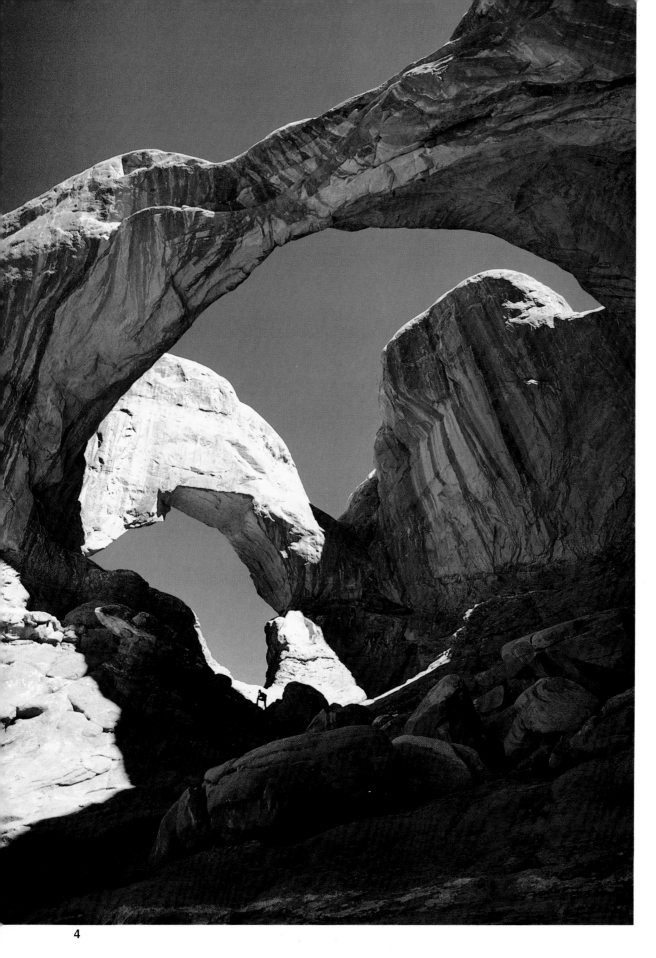

4

Utah

1 *Before their 11,000-pipe organ, the Mormon Tabernacle Choir raise their voices.*

2 *On the Bonneville Salt Flats, drivers have tried to set land speed records since 1914.*

3 *Now a metropolis, Salt Lake City gleams below the Wasatch Range, where, in 1847, Brigham Young and his followers saw the valley of the Great Salt Lake.*

4 *Weathered red sandstone "windows" in Arches National Park tower over the tiny silhouette of a visitor.*

5 *On the wall of a remote canyon in southeastern Utah, ancient Indians, using red earth for pigment, painted figures of humans and animals.*

Colorado

The state of Colorado is named for the Colorado River but, in a way, it is also named for the land itself. Spanish explorers called the river *colorado*, meaning "ruddy," for the reddish silt it carried, eroded from red-rock canyon walls. The river originates in a lake in the Rocky Mountains. Some people think that if you wanted to choose a natural feature to name the state, the Rockies would be a better choice.

Colorado's share of the Rocky Mountain system is certainly the loftiest. Of the Rockies' 80 or so "fourteeners," peaks over 14,000 feet (4,270 m) above sea level, Colorado boasts more than 50 of them. And with an average elevation of 6,800 feet (2,100 m), Colorado stands head and shoulders above all other states. Even the

state's plains start high and get higher. Forming two-fifths of the state, the sunny, semiarid plains slope gradually upward from the eastern border to the foothills of the mountains.

Along the high peaks of Colorado's Rockies runs the natural watershed of the Continental Divide. The Rockies also divide Colorado's water resources. The western slopes receive two-thirds of the runoff from rain and snow, while the eastern slopes, with two-thirds of the land, receive only one-third. To compensate, dams and tunnels carry water from the west through the mountains to the east for homes and industry and irrigation of crops on the plains.

West of the Rockies lies the Colorado Plateau, a region of hills, valleys, plateaus, and flat-topped hills called mesas, from the Spanish for "tables." Farmers plant crops in the valleys and graze sheep and cattle on the high pastures.

In Colorado's southwestern corner lived ancient Indian farmers known as the Anasazi. They planted corn, beans, and squash, and carved elaborate buildings in the sandstone cliffs of the Colorado Plateau. The Anasazi lived in settlements such as Mesa Verde for a few generations, then they departed. Much mystery surrounds the lives of these Indians, but archaeologists have recently come to believe that they followed a pattern of repeated settling, then moved on to create new communities.

Deep snow halts a steam locomotive in the 1920s along a high stretch of the old Santa Fe Trail. Trains that were unable to plow through the drifts often needed a team of shovelers to help out.

The source of Denver's population is no mystery. Soon after an 1858 gold strike was made in the region, people flocked there. Successful "fifty-niners" poured money into the town. Many failed prospectors stayed on, too, finding work or opening up businesses. By 1870, railroads linked Denver to the rest of the country. More people came, and more cattle left, fattened on surrounding grasslands before making their journey to eastern markets.

Denver became first the territorial, then the state capital. Today it is the trade, transportation, and financial center for the mountain West and the focus of an ever broadening string of cities along the eastern front of the Rocky Mountains. Eighty percent of Colorado's people live here, many of them drawn to the area in the 1970s and early '80s by the boom in Colorado's energy resources such as coal, petroleum, natural gas, and oil shale, a type of rock that can yield oil with expensive processing.

Denver has one of the two working federal mints that produce circulating coins. Defense-related employers—ranging from the Air Force Academy at Colorado Springs, to manufacturers of rockets and nuclear weapons, to the North American Aerospace Defense Command Center, an underground fortress near Colorado Springs—bring millions of dollars to the state.

There was a time when victims of lung diseases made trips to Colorado to breathe the pure air. Those days are clearly over, for Denver at least. The change can be blamed mostly on automobile pollution. Cars burn fuel inefficiently at the high altitude, and brown smog sits over the city in its bowl-shaped location. In winter the smog shows up on the ground, quickly turning new-fallen snow to brown slush.

Fortunately, fresh, white snow is abundant elsewhere. People come from all over the world to ski the famous dry powder at places such as Aspen, Vail, and Telluride. Skiers and other tourists spend billions of dollars a year.

Area: *the eighth largest state, 104,091 sq mi (269,596 sq km)*
Population: *3,294,394; ranks 26th*
Major Cities: *Denver, 467,610; Colorado Springs, 281,140; Aurora, 222,103*
Manufacturing: *scientific instruments, food products, machinery, electronics, transportation equipment, metal products, stone, clay, and glass products, rubber and plastics, chemicals, metals*
Mining and Quarrying: *oil and gas, coal, gold, sand and gravel, stone*
Agriculture: *cattle, wheat, corn, vegetables, milk, hay, poultry, eggs*
Other Important Activities: *tourism, finance, printing and publishing*
Statehood: *the 38th state; admitted August 1, 1876*

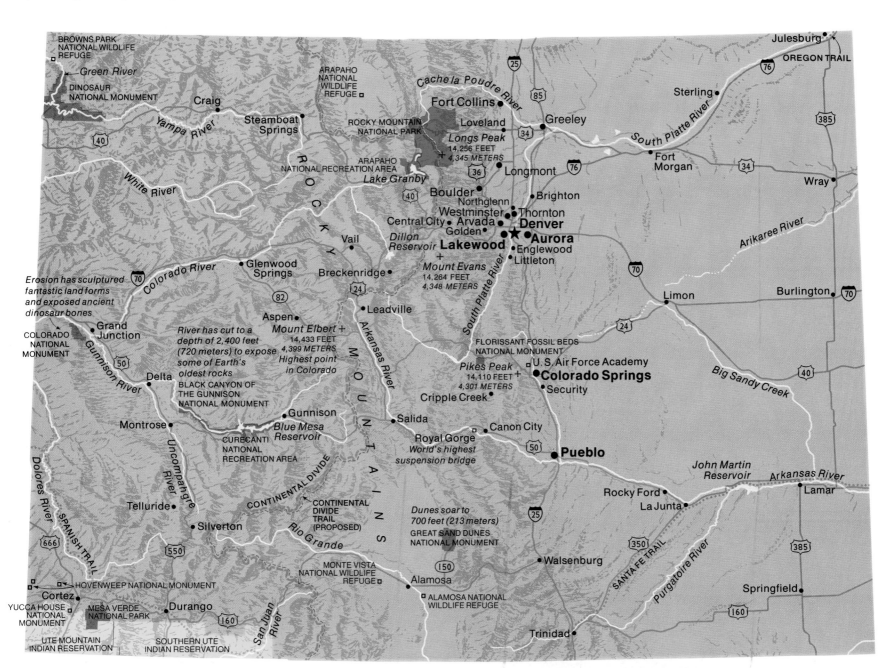

BROWNS PARK NATIONAL WILDLIFE REFUGE

Green River

DINOSAUR NATIONAL MONUMENT

Craig

Yampa River

Steamboat Springs

ARAPAHO NATIONAL WILDLIFE REFUGE

Cache la Poudre River

Fort Collins

ROCKY MOUNTAIN NATIONAL PARK

Loveland

Greeley

Sterling

Julesburg

OREGON TRAIL

South Platte River

Longs Peak
14,256 FEET
4,345 METERS

Longmont

Fort Morgan

Wray

White River

ARAPAHO NATIONAL RECREATION AREA

Lake Granby

Boulder

Northglenn

Brighton

Westminster

Thornton

Central City

Arvada

Denver

Vail

Golden

Lakewood

Aurora

Dillon Reservoir

Englewood

Littleton

Erosion has sculptured fantastic land forms and exposed ancient dinosaur bones

Glenwood Springs

Breckenridge

Mount Evans
14,264 FEET
4,348 METERS

Colorado River

South Platte River

Limon

Burlington

Leadville

Arkansas River

FLORISSANT FOSSIL BEDS NATIONAL MONUMENT

Big Sandy Creek

Grand Junction

River has cut to a depth of 2,400 feet (720 meters) to expose some of Earth's oldest rocks

Mount Elbert +
14,433 FEET
4,399 METERS
Highest point in Colorado

U.S. Air Force Academy

Colorado Springs

COLORADO NATIONAL MONUMENT

Pikes Peak
14,110 FEET +
4,301 METERS

Security

BLACK CANYON OF THE GUNNISON NATIONAL MONUMENT

Delta

Gunnison River

Cripple Creek

Montrose

Gunnison

Blue Mesa Reservoir

Salida

Canon City

CURECANTI NATIONAL RECREATION AREA

Royal Gorge
World's highest suspension bridge

Pueblo

John Martin Reservoir

Arkansas River

Lamar

Uncompahgre River

CONTINENTAL DIVIDE

CONTINENTAL DIVIDE TRAIL (PROPOSED)

Rocky Ford

La Junta

Telluride

Rio Grande

Dunes soar to 700 feet (213 meters)
GREAT SAND DUNES NATIONAL MONUMENT

SANTA FE TRAIL

Silverton

SPANISH TRAIL

MONTE VISTA NATIONAL WILDLIFE REFUGE

Walsenburg

Purgatoire River

Springfield

Cortez

HOVENWEEP NATIONAL MONUMENT

Alamosa

ALAMOSA NATIONAL WILDLIFE REFUGE

YUCCA HOUSE NATIONAL MONUMENT

MESA VERDE NATIONAL PARK

Durango

San Juan River

Trinidad

UTE MOUNTAIN INDIAN RESERVATION

SOUTHERN UTE INDIAN RESERVATION

0 KILOMETERS 75
0 STATUTE MILES 50

Four out of five Coloradans live on the high plains near the foot of the Rocky Mountains. That's where the biggest cities are, in a strip reaching from Fort Collins to Pueblo.

To the east stretch the plains, high, dry, and populated mostly where streams provide water.

To the west rise a thousand or so peaks reaching almost two miles (3 km) or more above sea level—beautiful country, but, again, not heavily populated.

Job opportunities, scenery, and water have helped make the foot of the mountains an attractive place to live.

Columbine

Lark Bunting

1

2

3

4

5

Colorado

1 *The U. S. Space Command in Colorado Springs monitors the paths of orbiting satellites and Soviet space vehicles.*

2 *At the U. S. Air Force Academy in Colorado Springs a female cadet challenges classmates at push-ups.*

3 *Quaking aspens, named for their trembling leaves that shimmer in sunlight, stand in a Colorado autumn woodland.*

4 *In the early 13th century, Anasazi Indians built multistoried dwellings in the cliffs at Mesa Verde.*

5 *Looking to the eastern slopes of the Rocky Mountains, Denver stands a mile (1.6 km) above sea level.*

Pacific Coast States

Plate tectonics has created plenty of spectacular scenery along this span of states edged by the Pacific Ocean. Rugged, snowcapped mountains, some of them volcanoes, thrust into the sky. Great evergreen forests cloak the lower slopes—soggy, mossy forests along the Cascade Range; drier ones along the Sierra Nevada. Streams fed by rain or melting snow spill from the heights, channeling water to thirsty crops and cities in the fertile valleys below.

Beyond the Cascades and the Sierra Nevada, the forests give way to arid highlands and to hot deserts. Mountains between the deserts and the ocean block rain clouds drifting inland, depriv-ing the deserts of nearly all airborne moisture.

Along the coast rise lesser mountains known as the Coast Ranges. Like others, they are the result of a geological process called plate tecton-ics. "Tectonic" comes from a Greek word mean-ing "builder." In part it describes what happens when large, seemingly rigid slabs of Earth's crust, called plates, slowly drift and bump to-gether. As the plates collide, they crumple and fold, thrusting up mountain ranges where one plate remains on top and creating deep valleys, called trenches, when one plate slides under-neath. When a continental plate encounters an oceanic plate, the heavier ocean floor slides be-neath the more buoyant rocks of the continent.

Eventually the oceanic plate melts far be-neath the continent, and parts of it rise toward the surface as molten rock, blistering the land with volcanoes and lava flows. This is what hap-pened in the Cascades region. The volcanic mountains here formed within the last million years or so. They may seem quiet now, but they aren't always. The most recent eruption was in 1980, when Mount St. Helens, near Portland, suddenly blew up, killing 57 people. East of the Cascades, enormous cracks in the Earth's crust opened up some 20 million years ago. What was then a deep basin filled with molten rock, creat-ing the highlands south of the Columbia River.

In contrast, the Sierras are fault-block moun-tains, enormous chunks of crust that crunched together and tilted as the North American plate rode up over the Pacific plate. Even today the two plates continue to grind slowly past each other, cracking along fracture zones, called faults. From time to time, as tension builds be-tween the plates, they snap apart, touching off a round of earthquakes and aftershocks.

Some of the Channel Islands are mountain peaks that emerge from the ocean. Today they are a refuge for seals, whales, dolphins, and sea-birds. About a million years ago, when sea levels were lower, the Channel Islands were the home of pygmy elephants. Scientists think that the elephants swam there from the mainland.

Washington

On Sunday morning, May 18, 1980, Mount St. Helens erupted. A towering cloud of burning gases, pulverized rock, and gray ash spread destruction that toppled 230 square miles (600 sq km) of forest. Tons of melted snow and ice created floods and mud slides. Dozens of people died. The eruption, the first in the contiguous 48 states since California's Lassen Peak exploded in 1915 and 1921, was a violent reminder that Mount St. Helens is part of a chain of volcanoes, the snowcapped Cascade Range.

The Cascades divide the state of Washington into two very different worlds: the soggy, rainy west and the much drier east. The mountains themselves are largely responsible for these different climates. As moist ocean winds sweep eastward, they drop their moisture on the windward slopes. Leeward slopes, on the opposite side, get very little rain or snow. A journey of only a few miles, from one side of a mountain to the other, can spell the difference between forest and semidesert.

On the Olympic Peninsula in Washington's northwest corner, more than 200 inches (500 cm) of precipitation a year nourishes a lush rain forest shadowed by towering pines and hemlocks and thickly carpeted with ferns and mosses. A Quileute Indian myth tells of Thunderbird, a huge winged creature that lived in a cave in the Olympic Mountains and dined on whales he snatched from the sea. Thunderbird had "feathers as long as a canoe paddle." The flapping of his wings created wind and thunder, and lightning flashed from his eyes. Today much of Thunderbird's domain has been preserved as wilderness in Olympic National Park.

Generous rainfall also sustains vast forests on the western slopes of the Cascades. Here Douglas fir and other conifers provide raw materials for Washington's lumber, plywood, and paper industry. As much as 20 percent of the harvested timber is trucked as logs to dockside terminals in Tacoma and shipped to ports in Japan, China, and South Korea.

Puget Sound, a flooded valley carved by glaciers, is the site of several islands and many good harbors as it curves inland near the foot of Mount Olympus. The state capital, Olympia, rises at the head of the sound. The San Juan Islands dot the waters north of the sound. Island

The Tacoma Narrows Bridge collapsed in 1940 under winds of 42 miles an hour (68 kmph). Nicknamed Galloping Gertie, the suspension bridge rippled and bounced with every breeze.

dwellers rely on ferries to commute to work in Seattle and other mainland cities. Sometimes the boats are also used for picnic cruises, weddings, and school outings.

Seattle, which grew up as a center for the logging industry, was named for Chief Sealth, a Duwamish Indian who befriended the settlers. On a clear day, Seattle residents can see the snowy summits of Mount Rainier to the southeast, Mount Baker to the north, and the Olympic Mountains to the west.

More than half of Washington's people live within 50 miles (80 km) of Seattle. The city and neighboring communities are headquarters for a host of companies that make products ranging from giant airliners to computer software programs. One reason so many firms locate here is that the region offers a variety of outdoor recreational activities. On weekends, area residents can sail and swim in Puget Sound or the Pacific

Ocean, or go hiking, fishing, mountain climbing, hunting, or skiing.

Although about two-thirds of the state of Washington lies east of the Cascade Range, only about one-third of the people live there. Spokane, the region's only large city, rises along the Spokane River. Two waterfalls add sparkle to the downtown business district, and provide hydroelectric power as well. Factories in Spokane produce aluminum, computer hardware, and communications equipment.

North of the city, the Columbia River flows into Franklin Delano Roosevelt Lake, formed by Grand Coulee Dam, the largest concrete dam in the United States. Many tributaries feed into the Columbia and irrigate fields that produce apples, asparagus, cherries, and red raspberries. Grapes ripen in vineyards of the Columbia River basin, where warm summer days, cool nights, and sandy loam soil create growing conditions much like those found in the great vineyards of France.

Curving westward through the mountains, the Columbia forms much of the boundary between Washington and Oregon. Several dams along this stretch of the river make Washington the number one state in the country for hydroelectric power production. Major customers for this electricity are the aluminum smelting plants at Tacoma, Vancouver, and Longview.

Another producer of electricity is the Hanford nuclear power plant. Once a secret facility that produced plutonium for atomic weapons, Hanford today faces an urgent need to safely clean up its stock of dangerous radioactive wastes.

Area: *20th largest state, 68,138 sq mi (176,477 sq km)*
Population: *4,866,692; ranks 18th*
Major Cities: *Seattle, 516,259; Spokane, 177,196; Tacoma, 176,664*
Manufacturing: *food products, lumber and wood products, paper products, chemicals, machinery, scientific instruments, metals, metal products, petroleum and coal products*
Agriculture: *cattle, milk, apples, wheat, potatoes, greenhouse and nursery products, hay, pears, barley, cherries, eggs*
Mining and Quarrying: *gold, stone, sand and gravel, coal*
Other Important Activities: *federal government, tourism, printing and publishing, salmon fishing*
Statehood: *42nd state; admitted November 11, 1889*

Point Roberts •

1 2 3 4 5 6 7 8 9 10 11 12 13 14 15 16 17 18 19

A

NOOKSACK
I.R.
Ferndale •
LUMMI
I.R.
Bellingham •
MOUNT BAKER
N.R.A.

NORTH CASCADES
NATIONAL PARK

ROSS LAKE
NATIONAL
RECREATION AREA

+ Mount Baker
10,778 FEET
3,285 METERS

NORTH CASCADES
NATIONAL PARK

B

Cape
Flattery

SAN JUAN ISLANDS
NATIONAL WILDLIFE REFUGE

San Juan Islands

Anacortes •

SWINOMISH
INDIAN RESERVATION

UPPER
SKAGIT I.R.

Skagit River

Mount Vernon •

Mount Logan
8,966 FEET
2,733 METERS

Okanogan River

(20)

(21)

Columbia
River

Pend Oreille River

Colville •

LITTLE
PEND OREILLE
NATIONAL
WILDLIFE
REFUGE

C

FLATTERY
ROCKS
N.W.R.

MAKAH
INDIAN
RESERVATION

DUNGENESS
N.W.R.

Oak Harbor •

PROTECTION ISLAND
N.W.R.

SAUK
SUIATTLE I.R.

Glacier Peak
10,541 FEET
3,213 METERS

LAKE CHELAN
NATIONAL
RECREATION
AREA

(97)

Rufus Woods
Lake

COLVILLE
INDIAN RESERVATION

KALISPEL I.R.

COULEE-DAM
NATIONAL
RECREATION
AREA

Franklin
Delano
Roosevelt
Lake

Newport •

(395)

(2)

D

OZETTE I.R.

LOWER ELWHA I.R.

OLYMPIC
NATIONAL
PARK

Port Angeles •

QUILEUTE I.R.

Townsend

JAMESTOWN
KLALLAM I.R.

STILLAGUAMISH I.R.

TULALIP
INDIAN RESERVATION

Lake
Chelan

Grand Coulee Dam •

SPOKANE
INDIAN RESERVATION

E

QUILLAYUTE
NEEDLES
N.W.R.

Hoh River

HOH I.R.

+ Mount Olympus
7,965 FEET
2,428 METERS

OLYMPIC
MOUNTAINS

Port •

PORT
TOWNSEND
GAMBLE I.R.
PORT
MADISON I.R.

(101)

Everett •

Snohomish •

Lynnwood
Edmonds
Mountlake Terrace
Kirkland

Puget Sound

(2)

PACIFIC CREST TRAIL

CASCADE RANGE

Wenatchee River

Banks
Lake

Davenport •

Spokane River

Spokane •

Dishman •

F

QUINAULT
INDIAN
RESERVATION

COPALIS
N.W.R.

SKOKOMISH
INDIAN
RESERVATION

Bremerton •

Seattle •

White Center
Burien
Des Moines

Redmond
Bellevue
Mercer Island
Renton
Kent

(2)

(97)

(21)

(28)

Cheney •

TURNBULL
NATIONAL
WILDLIFE
REFUGE

G

PACIFIC
OCEAN

GRAYS HARBOR
N.W.R.

COAST RANGES

Shelton •

SQUAXIN ISLAND I.R.

Tacoma •

PUYALLUP I.R.

Auburn
Parkland

MUCKLESHOOT I.R.

Puyallup

Columbia River

Ephrata •

Moses
Lake

Potholes
Reservoir

Moses Lake •

COLUMBIA
NATIONAL
WILDLIFE
REFUGE

Ritzville •

(195)

(90)

H

Hoquiam •
Aberdeen •
Westport •

Olympia ★
Tumwater
Lacey

NISQUALLY NATIONAL
WILDLIFE REFUGE

NISQUALLY I.R.

Ellensburg •

(82)

SADDLE MOUNTAIN
NATIONAL WILDLIFE REFUGE

Colfax •

J

SHOALWATER BAY
INDIAN RESERVATION

Raymond •

Chehalis River

(12)

CHEHALIS I.R.

Centralia •
Chehalis •

MOUNT RAINIER
NATIONAL PARK

+ Mount Rainier
14,410 FEET
4,392 METERS
Highest point
in Washington

(12)

(395)

Yakima •

Snake River

Pullman •

Clarkston •

K

WILLAPA NATIONAL
WILDLIFE REFUGE

(101)

(5)

JULIA
BUTLER
HANSEN
NATIONAL
WILDLIFE
REFUGE

Riffe
Lake

Cowlitz River

HANFORD
SITE

(12)

L

Columbia River

Kelso •
Longview •

Mount St. Helens
8,366 FEET
2,550 METERS

Mount Adams
12,307 FEET
3,751 METERS

Yakima River

TOPPENISH
NATIONAL
WILDLIFE
REFUGE

Toppenish •

YAKIMA INDIAN RESERVATION

Sunnyside •

Richland •
Kennewick •
Pasco •

McNARY NATIONAL
WILDLIFE REFUGE

Walla Walla •

M

RIDGEFIELD
NATIONAL
WILDLIFE
REFUGE

FRANZ LAKE
N.W.R.
PIERCE N.W.R.

PACIFIC
CREST
TRAIL

(97)

CONBOY LAKE
NATIONAL
WILDLIFE
REFUGE

UMATILLA NATIONAL
WILDLIFE REFUGE

N

Vancouver •
Camas •

Bonneville Dam

STEIGERWALD LAKE N.W.R.

(14)

The Dalles Dam •

LEWIS AND CLARK TRAIL

0   KILOMETERS   60
0   STATUTE MILES   40

Floods of lava and floods of water formed the plateau region of southeastern Washington, an area outlined by mountains and the Spokane and Columbia Rivers.

The region is a basin with gently rounded ridges. Beginning about 20 million years ago, giant cracks opened along what is now the state's eastern border. Soupy lava gushed forth, flooding the basin. Much later,

during the Ice Age, ice dams east of Spokane collapsed, unleashing glacial lakes that flooded the region and deepened the Columbia River's channel through the Cascade and Coast Ranges.

Coast
Rhododendron

American
Goldfinch

1

2

3

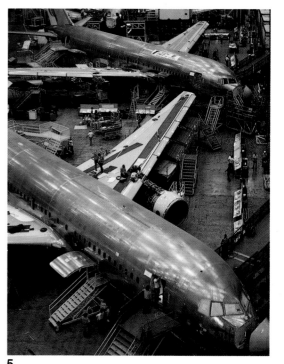

5

Washington

1 *Slickers keep field hands dry on this tulip farm near Mount Vernon. Abundant rain nurtures the area's prizewinning flowers.*

2 *Wielding a traditional dip net, a Yakima Indian snags his prey near the Columbia River, where his tribe has fishing rights.*

3 *A logger shoulders the chain saw that took 15 minutes to topple this 600-year-old Douglas fir in Olympic National Forest.*

4 *Seattle's landmark Space Needle holds a revolving restaurant that offers vistas of Puget Sound and the Cascade Range.*

5 *Aircraft workers assemble Boeing 747s in an Everett plant that encloses more indoor space than any other building in the world.*

Oregon

Oregon is a tangle of topography, a land of wild and rugged coasts, snowcapped mountains, high deserts, awesome chasms, and fertile valleys. Along much of the Pacific coast, great cliffs rise sheer from the sea, creating a massive wall of indented bays and jutting promontories known as headlands. In places, rocky pinnacles called sea stacks stand like ponderous sentinels in the surf. Wind and waves eroded these megaliths, leaving only the hardest rock, basalt, as a reminder of a long-vanished headland.

A few towns and fishing villages and many state parks line the coast. Mostly this is the foggy, forested realm of shorebirds, sea lions, and occasional flotillas of humpback whales. When the wild gales of winter lash the headlands and beaches, dedicated "storm watchers" hurry to seaside parks or cozy, cliff-top inns to witness the ocean slamming against the continent in a howling symphony of wind and spray.

Parallel to the shore rise the Coast Ranges, low mountains clad mostly with misty, rain-drenched forests of Douglas firs, hemlocks, and spruce. This part of the region was created 200 to 50 million years ago, when the Pacific plate collided with the North American plate and thrust up enormous sandstone and basalt blocks. At least one mystery still shrouds the mountains of the Pacific Northwest. Here, according to local lore, roams Sasquatch, the shadowy, ape-like monster also known as Bigfoot. Most people doubt the reality of Sasquatch. But scores of people claim to have seen the creature, just as people have believed in the existence of monsters throughout human history.

Between the Coast Ranges and the Cascade Range lies the Willamette Valley. By the 1840s, word of the valley's fertility had spread back East. It became the destination for most pioneer families following the Oregon Trail. Willamette Valley farmers boasted that you could poke a broomstick into the ground and it would grow. Settlers cleared forests and built the covered bridges and trim, white-clapboard houses that reflected their New England origins. Many of these houses and bridges still stand. Salem, the state capital, was founded by a New Englander as a missionary settlement. Its name comes from *shalom*, a Hebrew word meaning "peace."

Today the mineral-rich soil supports abundant crops of vegetables and fruits, including peas, onions, snap beans, berries, and plums, as well as nearly all the nation's hazelnuts.

Portland, a major port, ranks as the state's leading commercial and industrial center. Here dockworkers unload most of the Japanese cars sold in the United States. Views of snowcapped Mount Hood to the east and the Coast Ranges to the west, and more than 160 parks and gardens help make the city a pleasant place to live.

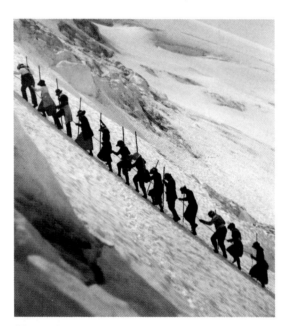

Men and women of the Mazama mountaineering club, founded on the summit of Mount Hood, participate in a 1913 expedition up the mountain. Mazama means "mountain goat."

Eugene, a riverside city threaded by hiking paths and bike trails, is also a processing hub for the valley's agricultural products.

Traditionally, Oregon's most important product has been the logs and lumber hauled from forests that cover half the state, mostly in the mountains of the west and northeast. Oregon's evergreen forests supply more than a fourth of the nation's softwood boards, more than half of its plywood, and much of its particleboard, paper, and pulp. The lumber industry got its start in 1883, when the Northern Pacific Railroad reached Oregon. By 1939 it was the state's leading industry, a position it still holds.

But today controversy swirls over the cutting down of old-growth forests, moss-grown stands of giant firs, cedars, spruce, and hemlocks untouched by saw or ax. Some of these trees grew here when Columbus reached the New World. Modern clear-cutting techniques strip away trees from entire mountainsides, scarring the land, choking streams with mud and debris, and destroying the habitats of scores of forest creatures, including the endangered northern spotted owl that nests in old-growth forests. Loggers prefer the old-growth forests because their giant trees yield great quantities of straight-grain, knot-free lumber. But once downed, such a forest may take a thousand years to renew itself, if it can be replaced at all.

East of the Cascade Range, the Harney Basin is wide open and semiarid. Here cowboys ride the range, and wheat and hay grow under irrigation. To the north rise the Blue Mountains, uplifted fragments of ancient continental plates eroded into peaks and valleys. The Snake River traces part of the state boundary here. Nearby, vast marshes serve as winter homes for migrant ducks and Canada geese.

In 1805, nearing the end of their long westward journey, the explorers Meriwether Lewis and William Clark followed the Snake River to the Columbia. At the mouth of the Columbia, they climbed a high cape above the shoreline of the Pacific Ocean. Clark recorded in his journal their joyous astonishment at "the high waves dashing against the rocks & this emence Ocian."

Area: *10th largest state, 97,073 sq mi (251,419 sq km)*
Population: *2,842,321; ranks 29th*
Major Cities: *Portland, 437,319; Eugene, 112,669; Salem, 107,786*
Manufacturing: *lumber and wood products, food products, paper products, machinery, scientific instruments, electronics, metals, metal products, transportation equipment*
Agriculture: *cattle, greenhouse and nursery products, milk, wheat, onions, ryegrass, potatoes, fescue, pears, mint*
Mining and Quarrying: *stone, sand and gravel*
Other Important Activities: *tourism, printing and publishing, crab and salmon fishing*
Statehood: *33rd state; admitted February 14, 1859*

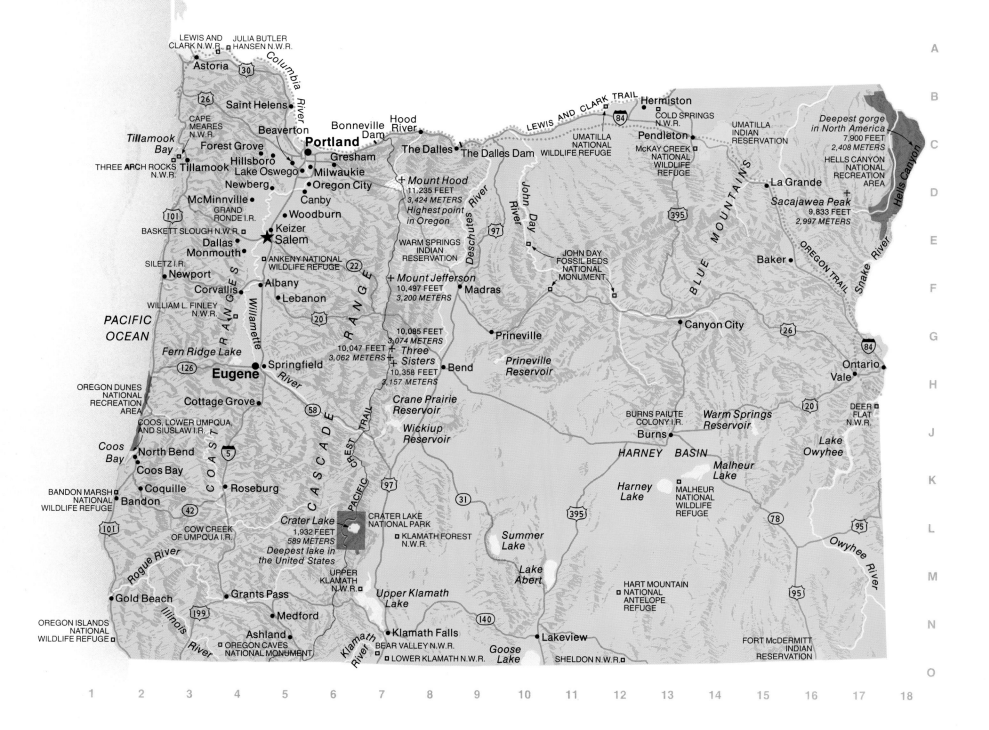

LEWIS AND CLARK N.W.R.   JULIA BUTLER HANSEN N.W.R.

Astoria
30

Columbia River

26
Saint Helens

CAPE MEARES N.W.R.

Tillamook Bay

Beaverton
Forest Grove

Bonneville Dam

Hood River

LEWIS AND CLARK TRAIL

Hermiston
84
COLD SPRINGS N.W.R.

Pendleton

UMATILLA INDIAN RESERVATION

Deepest gorge in North America
7,900 FEET
2,408 METERS

HELLS CANYON NATIONAL RECREATION AREA

THREE ARCH ROCKS N.W.R.
Tillamook
Hillsboro
Lake Oswego

Portland
Gresham
Milwaukie

The Dalles
The Dalles Dam

UMATILLA NATIONAL WILDLIFE REFUGE

McKAY CREEK NATIONAL WILDLIFE REFUGE

La Grande

Hells Canyon

Newberg
McMinnville
Oregon City
Canby
Woodburn

GRAND RONDE I.R.

BASKETT SLOUGH N.W.R.
Keizer
Salem
Dallas
Monmouth

+ Mount Hood
11,235 FEET
3,424 METERS
Highest point in Oregon

Deschutes River

John Day River

395

Sacajawea Peak
9,833 FEET
2,997 METERS

Baker

OREGON TRAIL

Snake River

WARM SPRINGS INDIAN RESERVATION

97

ANKENY NATIONAL WILDLIFE REFUGE
22

SILETZ I.R.
Newport

Albany
Lebanon

+ Mount Jefferson
10,497 FEET
3,200 METERS

Madras

JOHN DAY FOSSIL BEDS NATIONAL MONUMENT

BLUE MOUNTAINS

Corvallis

WILLIAM L. FINLEY N.W.R.

20

PACIFIC OCEAN

COAST RANGES

Willamette River

10,085 FEET
3,074 METERS
10,047 FEET
3,062 METERS
+ Three Sisters
10,358 FEET
3,157 METERS

Bend

Prineville

Prineville Reservoir

Canyon City

26

Ontario
84

Fern Ridge Lake

Eugene
Springfield

Bend

58

CASCADE RANGE

PACIFIC CREST TRAIL

Crane Prairie Reservoir

Wickiup Reservoir

Warm Springs Reservoir

Vale

20

DEER FLAT N.W.R.

OREGON DUNES NATIONAL RECREATION AREA

Cottage Grove

BURNS PAIUTE COLONY I.R.

Lake Owyhee

COOS, LOWER UMPQUA, AND SIUSLAW I.R.
5

Coos Bay
North Bend
Coos Bay

97

HARNEY BASIN

Burns

Malheur Lake

Harney Lake

MALHEUR NATIONAL WILDLIFE REFUGE

78

95

BANDON MARSH NATIONAL WILDLIFE REFUGE
Coquille
Roseburg

31

395

Owyhee River

Bandon
42

COW CREEK OF UMPQUA I.R.

Crater Lake
1,932 FEET
589 METERS
Deepest lake in the United States

CRATER LAKE NATIONAL PARK

KLAMATH FOREST N.W.R.

Summer Lake

Lake Abert

HART MOUNTAIN NATIONAL ANTELOPE REFUGE

95

101

Rogue River

199

Gold Beach

Grants Pass

Illinois River

Medford

UPPER KLAMATH N.W.R.

Upper Klamath Lake

Lake

140

Goose Lake

Lakeview

FORT McDERMITT INDIAN RESERVATION

OREGON ISLANDS NATIONAL WILDLIFE REFUGE

Ashland

OREGON CAVES NATIONAL MONUMENT

Klamath River

Klamath Falls
BEAR VALLEY N.W.R.
LOWER KLAMATH N.W.R.

SHELDON N.W.R.

A B C D E F G H J K L M N O

1 2 3 4 5 6 7 8 9 10 11 12 13 14 15 16 17 18

0 KILOMETERS 80
0 STATUTE MILES 40

Like a pot of gold at the end of the Oregon Trail, the fertile soils of the Willamette River Valley attracted thousands of settlers in the 1800s. Today more than half the people in the state live along the 60-mile-wide (97-km) valley.

The Oregon Trail joins the Lewis and Clark Trail, then crosses a modern-day footpath, the ridge-running Pacific Crest Trail that winds between Canada and Mexico. This trail skirts Crater Lake, born when a volcano known as Mount Mazama blew its top some 7,000 years ago. A volcanic cone forms an island in the lake.

Western Meadowlark

Oregon Grape

STATE OF OREGON
1859

1

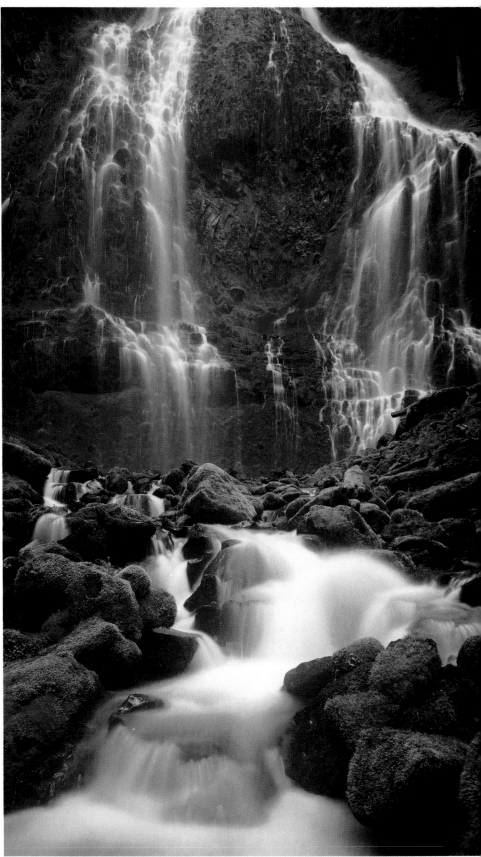

2

Oregon

1 *A lariat loops toward a calf at a roundup in southeast Oregon's Great Basin country.*

2 *A waterfall tumbles into a jumble of boulders near the Three Sisters peaks in the Cascades. Mist and rain nourish a lush carpet of mosses.*

3 *Beyond the twilight sparkle of Portland, alpenglow rouges Mount Hood's snowy cone. The city stands near the confluence of the Willamette and Columbia Rivers.*

4 *At a Willamette Valley vineyard near the foot of the Coast Ranges, workers harvest Chardonnay grapes for white wine.*

5 *A seabird roosts on a sea stack, a remnant of a coastal headland crumbling under the pounding of Pacific Ocean waves.*

3

4

5

California

California is almost a country unto itself. The value of goods and services the state produces would, if California were a separate country, rank it sixth among the world's richest nations.

No other state turns out more manufactured goods, whether airplanes, computers, or missiles. No other state ships as many canned or frozen or dried fruits and vegetables to all parts of the United States. Or wine. Or television and movie films. California's fields and orchards grow more than 200 kinds of fruits, nuts, and vegetables. California's fields also produce great amounts of illegal marijuana.

Mountains, valleys, and deserts mark California's geography. In the northwest, the Klamath Mountains are high and steep. In the northeast stands an active volcano, Lassen Peak. The Sierra Nevada form a great wall of rock with many high peaks. Naturalist John Muir said that here, in Yosemite Valley, "Nature had gathered her choicest treasures." Some of the mountains in the Coast Ranges rise abruptly from the sea. In southern California, deserts such as the Mohave are part of the Basin and Range region that extends into Nevada and other states. Near Los Angeles are mountains that, unlike the others, trend east-west.

The chief agricultural region is the great Central Valley, between the Coast Ranges and the Sierra Nevada. Two major rivers bring water to the valley, the south-flowing Sacramento and the north-flowing San Joaquin. Both meet about halfway through the valley and turn west, flowing out to sea at San Francisco Bay. The valley's mild climate gives it a long growing season, and so its produce can be shipped to market while farmlands elsewhere lie covered in snow.

California has almost every kind of climate you can think of—damp and cool, with more than a hundred inches (254 cm) of rain along parts of the northern coast; sunny and mild most of the year in the south. Inland, snow drapes the Sierra Nevada, while Death Valley, in July 1913, had a temperature of 134°F (57°C), the highest ever recorded in the United States.

California also has the biggest, the oldest, and some of the tallest trees in the world. The biggest trees, the giant sequoias of the southern Sierra Nevada, can reach a girth of 80 feet (24 m). The oldest trees, bristlecone pines high in the

A family dines outdoors the day after the 1906 San Francisco earthquake. Unstable buildings and widespread fires made cooking, eating, and sleeping indoors unsafe.

eastern Sierra, were seedlings when Stonehenge and the Egyptian Pyramids were being built 4,600 years ago. The redwoods that grow along the northern coast reach higher than 300 feet (90 m). No other state has a bigger, rarer, or more endangered bird—the California condor, with a wingspan of nine feet (2.7 m) or more. Ancestors of this bird soared widely over Ice Age North America. Its last stronghold was the rugged mountains of southern California, but by 1987 there were none left in the wild. Breeding programs with captive birds have been successful enough that officials now hope that the release of a pair of young condors into a bird sanctuary will begin the recovery of the species.

California's people are almost as diverse as the land. Spanish explorers first entered the territory in the mid-1500s. Priests set up missions in the 1770s, using Indian converts as laborers. Spanish and Mexican settlers, called Californios, soon followed, carving out huge ranches worked by Indian slaves. Today California has nearly 250,000 Native Americans, more than any other state except Oklahoma.

The 1848 discovery of gold near Sacramento brought a stampede of gold prospectors from all over the world, the forty-niners. In 12 years

California's population soared from about 26,000 to 380,000. Thousands of Chinese arrived during this period to take part in the Gold Rush and to build the transcontinental railroads.

World War II brought in thousands of military personnel and defense workers, including blacks from the rural South. Many stayed. More recent arrivals have included large numbers of Asians and Hispanics.

Most of California's growth has taken place along the coast south of San Francisco. But much of the region is arid. To bring in water, the state and federal governments have built canals and aqueducts, some from as far away as the Colorado River and northern California. As more and more people move to southern California, they need more and more water. Northern Californians have begun to protest, and some southern Californians must ration water.

Within California are more than a dozen major faults, fractures in Earth's crust. The best known of these is the San Andreas Fault, which reaches from near the Mexican border through San Francisco to the coast and into the sea near Clear Lake. Severe earthquakes have taken place along the San Andreas, such as those that hit San Francisco in 1906 and 1989. Others will come. Many Californians appreciate the need to prepare for the next big one. Laws require the strengthening of old buildings. Engineers develop earthquake-resistant construction for new ones. Youngsters are encouraged to help in "hazard hunts" at home, finding and securing heavy shelves and other objects that could cause injury if shaken loose during an earthquake.

Area: *the third largest state, 158,706 sq mi (411,049 sq km)*
Population: *29,760,021; ranks first*
Major Cities: *Los Angeles, 3,485,398; San Diego, 1,110,549; San Jose, 782,248*
Manufacturing: *transportation equipment, electronics, machinery, food products, scientific instruments, metal products, chemicals, rubber and plastics, clothing*
Agriculture: *milk, cattle, greenhouse and nursery products, grapes, cotton, tomatoes, lettuce, almonds, hay, strawberries*
Mining: *oil and gas*
Other Important Activities: *tourism, printing and publishing, tuna and crab fishing*
Statehood: *31st state; admitted September 9, 1850*

Shoved, pulled, bent, lifted, fractured. All this and more has happened to California. A glance at the map shows the results: inland, a rugged landscape of mountains traced by the Pacific Crest Trail; along the coast, range upon range of accordion-pleated mountains where continental plates slowly crunch past one another.

West of the San Andreas Fault, the Pacific plate creeps northwestward past the rest of the state at a rate of about two inches (5.5 cm) a year. The result: earthquakes, as tension between the two plates suddenly snaps.

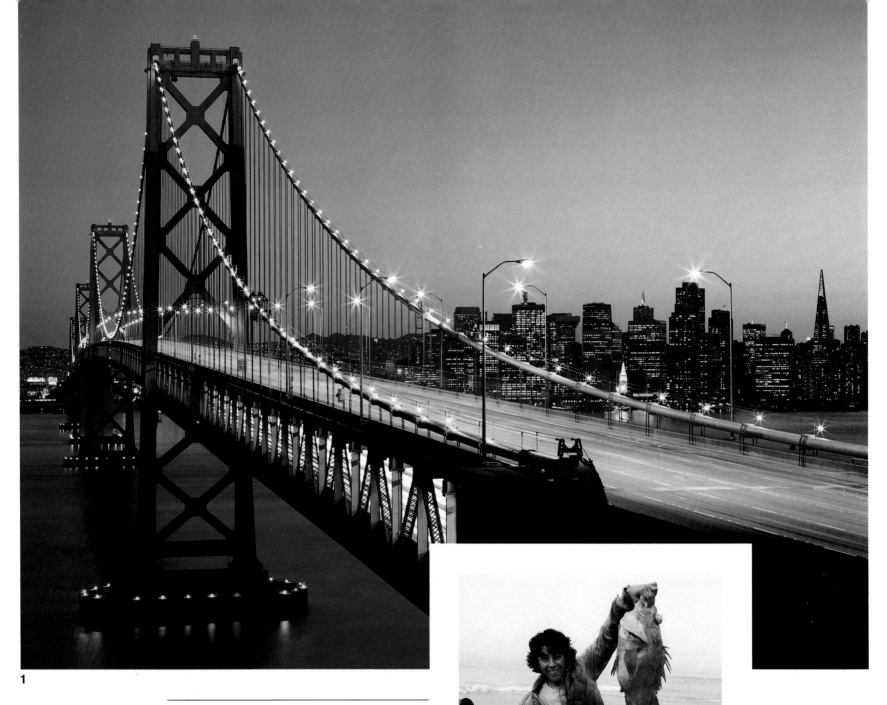

California

1 *The double-deck, earthquake-resistant Bay Bridge crosses San Francisco Bay to link San Francisco (background) with Oakland and Berkeley.*

2 *A young Newport Beach fisherman shows off a rockfish from his morning catch. For a hundred years, fishermen of his fleet have set out from Newport Beach, each man working alone in his flat-bottomed, sharp-bowed dory.*

3

5

4

---

3 *In a Stanford University sleep laboratory at Palo Alto, pulsing red lights glow as sensors detect the eye movements that accompany vivid dreams.*

4 *Lettuce ready for harvest greens an irrigated field in the valley of the Salinas River. Other vegetables grown here include artichokes, broccoli, and cauliflower.*

5 *Shadows of storm clouds over Death Valley darken dunes and a silhouetted figure.*

Alaska, Hawaii, and Distant Shores

A L E U T I A N   I S L A N D S

NIIHAU

KAUAI

OAHU

Honolulu

MOLOKAI

MAUI

Mauna Kea

HAWAII

Volcanoes are at work in the nation's two newest states, Alaska and Hawaii. Alaska's Aleutian Islands have 80 volcanoes, more than half of them active. This island arc marks the edge of an oceanic plate as it dives beneath North America. (For more on plate tectonics, see page 221.) Earthquakes often shake Alaska. In 1964 a massive quake jolted Anchorage five feet (1.5 m) toward the southeast. In 1912 a volcanic blast created the Valley of Ten Thousand Smokes just west of the Alaska Range.

Hawaii's volcanoes, on the other hand, rise from the ocean floor far from the edge of any colliding plate. A stationary hot spot deep beneath Earth's crust builds these islands as the ocean plate slowly slides across it. The Big Island, Hawaii, is also the newest, about 750,000 years old. As each island moves away from the hot spot, its volcanoes die out. Erosion eventually sends it back into the sea. Hawaii's oldest islands, mere specks of rock, are about 25 million years old.

Volcanoes also built most of the United States' far-flung overseas territories (map opposite). Puerto Rico's islands are not volcanoes, but they are mountaintops pushed up from the ocean floor.

BROOKS RANGE

Yukon River

Porcupine River

ALASKA RANGE

Anchorage

Juneau

Alaska

Pacific Ocean

UNITED STATES

Atlantic Ocean

Northern
Mariana
Islands

Wake I.

Midway
Islands

Hawaii

Puerto Rico

Guam

Johnston Atoll

U. S. Virgin Islands

Palau

Kingman Reef

Panama Canal
Zone

Howland I.

Jarvis I.

Baker I.

American Samoa

Pacific Ocean

Atlantic Ocean

Alaska

In 1867 two cents bought an acre of the Russian territory known as Alaska. The whole region cost 7.2 million dollars. What did Americans get for their money? A land so big that if placed on top of the contiguous 48 states it would stretch from Florida to Los Angeles and reach north to Lake Superior. A land where the grizzly bear roams free and caribou in the tens of thousands migrate across the tundra.

Alaska is an immense peninsula. The name Alaska is a Russian word, adapted from a native Aleut term that means "great land." Smaller peninsulas extend from the mainland. The 200-island Aleutian chain reaches far into the Pacific Ocean and Bering Sea. With the Arctic Ocean, these waters wash a coastline that is more than 6,000 miles (9,700 km) long.

Mountain systems arc through the state. Among the southernmost are the Saint Elias and the actively volcanic Wrangell Ranges. The

---

Warmly dressed young Alaskans in a Yukon fishing camp study a mail-order catalog to keep up on 1929 fashions from the United States. The book also helped them practice reading English.

Aleutian Range is a caldron of volcanic activity. In the interior, Mount McKinley rises out of the Alaska Range; the Brooks Range is the northernmost reach of the Rocky Mountains.

The native groups of Alaska today form almost 15 percent of the population. Traditionally, Eskimos lived mainly in the north and west along the coasts, hunting whales and other marine mammals. The Aleuts inhabited the rugged, fogbound islands named for them. Of the Indian groups, the Tlingit, Haida, and Tsimshian lived in the coastal areas of southeastern Alaska, sharing a culture based on fishing and the carving of tall cedar totem poles depicting animals and supernatural spirits. Central Alaska was the domain of Athapaskans. Old customs persist in some places, but the years have brought changes in ways of life and work.

When the United States acquired Alaska, many resources spurred settlement. Salmon fishing prompted the building of canneries and turned many towns into commercial fishing ports. The discovery of gold in the Canadian Yukon in 1896 brought people through southeastern Alaska and later to the goldfields of Nome and Fairbanks. Logging brought settlers and led to the construction of pulp and plywood mills near Juneau. During the Depression, farmers from Dust Bowl states came to the Matanuska River Valley, Alaska's main farming region. The 1968 discovery of immense fields of oil and gas at Prudhoe Bay on the North Slope started an oil boom. Thousands of people came from the lower 48 states to work on a pipeline that would carry the oil from the Arctic Ocean to the ice-free port of Valdez on Prince William Sound, where a disastrous oil spill occurred in 1989.

In the summer, Matanuska Valley farmers benefit from Alaska's far northern location. Then the North Pole tilts toward the rays of the sun, giving the valley mild weather and sunny, 19-hour days. The farther north you go, the longer summer days become. At Point Barrow the midsummer sun never sets. In the winter, parts of northern Alaska seldom see the sun. Even in the south, winter sunlight is scarce, and children attend school in the dark.

Alaska's climate challenges and limits human activity. Mountains, ice fields, and other barriers make travel difficult. The state has fewer

miles of road than Vermont, although it is 60 times larger. Military needs during World War II pushed the building of the Alaska Highway.

While ferries ply coastal and inland waterways, many villages and towns can be reached only by air. Alaska has the country's highest proportion of pilots; about one in 50 Alaskans is licensed to fly. Planes bring food, supplies, and medical care to isolated residents.

A 1971 law gave Alaskan Native Americans 44 million acres (18 million ha) and 962 million dollars to be managed by native corporations. Profits from oil, gas, and timber have brought some groups wealth, but others want to sell land back to the government. The proposed exploitation of natural resources that lie on both native lands and federal lands pits conservationists against developers in a controversy likely to rage for decades.

Area: *largest state, 591,004 sq mi (1,530,700 sq km)*
Population: *550,043; ranks 49th*
Major Cities: *Anchorage, 226,338; Fairbanks, 30,843; Juneau, 26,751*
Mining and Quarrying: *oil and gas, gold, sand and gravel, stone*
Manufacturing: *food products, petroleum products, lumber and wood products*
Other Important Activities: *federal government, salmon and crab fishing, printing and publishing, greenhouse and nursery products, milk, fur*
Statehood: *the 49th state; admitted January 3, 1959*

Attu
Island

A L E U T I A N   I S L A N D S

Alaska, twice as big as the next largest state, Texas, is 488 times bigger than the smallest state, Rhode Island.

In the southern panhandle, fingers of the Pacific Ocean reach far inland, making a watery maze of fjords. The Inside Passage provides a sheltered water route between Skagway and Seattle, Washington.

White patches rimming the Gulf of Alaska show ice fields and glaciers. The mountains here capture as much moisture as a tropical forest, while farther north the air is desert dry. Hence, northern mountains have only a few small glaciers.

KILOMETERS 300
STATUTE MILES 200

Point Barrow
Northernmost point of the United States • Barrow

BEAUFORT SEA

Vast oil deposit discovered in 1968
• Prudhoe Bay

NORTH SLOPE

ARCTIC OCEAN

CHUKCHI SEA

CAPE KRUSENSTERN N.M.

Colville River

BROOKS RANGE

ARCTIC NATIONAL WILDLIFE REFUGE

BERING LAND BRIDGE NATIONAL PRESERVE

Little Diomede Island

Noatak River

KOBUK VALLEY N.P.

GATES OF THE ARCTIC NATIONAL PARK AND PRESERVE

CONTINENTAL

DIVIDE

Kotzebue

Bering Strait

SEWARD PENINSULA

Kotzebue Sound

Kobuk River

ARCTIC CIRCLE

SELAWIK NATIONAL WILDLIFE REFUGE

Koyukuk River

YUKON FLATS NATIONAL WILDLIFE REFUGE

Nome

IDITAROD (GOLDRUSH) TRAIL

Norton Sound

KOYUKUK NATIONAL WILDLIFE REFUGE

Yukon River

KANUTI N.W.R.

Yukon River

St. Lawrence Island

BERING SEA

Yukon Delta

INNOKO N.W.R.

Manley Hot Springs • Eureka

Livengood • Circle

WHITE MOUNTAINS N.R.A.

Eagle

NOWITNA N.W.R.

College • Fairbanks

St. Matthew Island

ALASKA MARITIME NATIONAL WILDLIFE REFUGE

INNOKO N.W.R.

Highest point in United States
Mount McKinley
20,320 FEET; 6,194 METERS

Delta Junction

DENALI NATIONAL PARK AND PRESERVE

ALASKA HIGHWAY

Tanana River

Nunivak Island

YUKON DELTA NATIONAL WILDLIFE REFUGE

KUSKOKWIM MOUNTAINS

Mount Foraker
17,400 FEET
5,304 METERS

RANGE

TETLIN NATIONAL WILDLIFE REFUGE

Bethel

Kuskokwim River

ALASKA

IDITAROD (GOLDRUSH) TRAIL

Susitna River

WRANGELL MOUNTAINS

WRANGELL-ST. ELIAS NATIONAL PARK AND PRESERVE

Matanuska River

Copper River

Mount Bona
16,421 FEET
5,005 METERS

Pribilof Islands

TOGIAK NATIONAL WILDLIFE REFUGE

Iliamna Lake

RANGE

Anchorage

Palmer
Chugach Mts.

McCarthy

Spenard

Valdez

LAKE CLARK NATIONAL PARK AND PRESERVE

Kenai

Whittier

KENAI N.W.R.

Soldotna

Cordova

ST. ELIAS MOUNTAINS

Homer

Kenai Mts.

Seward

Kayak Island

Mount St. Elias
18,008 FEET
5,489 METERS

Cook Inlet

KENAI FJORDS N.P.

Prince William Sound

Malaspina Glacier
Largest glacier in North America

Skagway

Haines

Bristol Bay

BECHAROF N.W.R.

Becharof Lake

KATMAI NATIONAL PARK AND PRESERVE

ALASKA MARINE HIGHWAY SYSTEM

GULF OF ALASKA

Juneau Icefield

GLACIER BAY NATIONAL PARK AND PRESERVE

Juneau

ALASKA PENINSULA

ALASKA PENINSULA N.W.R.

Kodiak

ANIAKCHAK NATIONAL MONUMENT AND PRESERVE

Kodiak Island

KODIAK NATIONAL WILDLIFE REFUGE

ADMIRALTY ISLAND NATIONAL MONUMENT

COAST MOUNTAINS

ALASKA MARITIME NATIONAL WILDLIFE REFUGE

ALEUTIAN

IZEMBEK N.W.R.

ALASKA PENINSULA N.W.R.

Sitka

Petersburg

Wrangell

MISTY FIORDS N.M.

Unimak Island

Unalaska Island

ALEXANDER

INSIDE PASSAGE

ARCHIPELAGO

PACIFIC OCEAN

Ketchikan

ANNETTE I. INDIAN RESERVATION

Forget-Me-Not

Willow Ptarmigan

9 10 11 12 13 14 15 16 17 18 19 20 21 22 23 24 25 26 27 28

1

2

Alaska

1 *A brown bear snags a chum salmon meal in southern Alaska. The coastal brown bear and its interior kin, the grizzly, feed at rivers during the salmon's spawning voyage, which begins in late summer.*

2 *Buried where possible, the 800-mile (1,290-km) trans-Alaska pipeline rises on supports in areas where its heat would thaw underground permafrost. Its height provides clearance for migrating caribou.*

3 *Sorting quickly, fishermen look for "keepers" in a haul of Alaska king crab. Females and small males go back into the water. Per pound, king crab is the state's most valuable shellfish.*

4 *An Eskimo youth displays skill in the traditional sport of the high kick at a school gym in Kotzebue.*

5 *Glaciers from the Juneau Icefield merge in the mountains north of Alaska's capital. The long dark stripes are moraines formed by debris shed at the glaciers' edges.*

3

4

Hawaii

Hawaii is a young landform. The islands that make up the state grew as volcanic mountains from the seafloor of the Pacific Ocean. The tops of these volcanoes are now the mostly lush, tropical islands of Hawaii.

The chain's northern islands are the oldest. The island of Hawaii, called the Big Island, is the youngest, and there is another island on the way. About 20 miles (32 km) southeast of the Big Island, the underwater Loihi Seamount must grow about half a mile (0.8 km) more before it reaches daylight. This could take from 2,000 to 20,000 years, depending on volcanic activity.

As Hawaii's volcanic slopes began to erode into soil, settlement by plant and animal life began. The early seeds of Hawaii's native vegetation arrived on the waves or the wind, or were carried by birds. Insects, too, rode the wind or pieces of driftwood. Only two mammals made the trip to land on their own, the monk seal and the hoary bat. Brought by people in canoes and on ships, introduced mammals such as rats, pigs, and goats now flourish on the islands.

The first settlers were Polynesians from islands 2,400 miles (3,860 km) to the southeast. About 1,500 years ago they sailed to Hawaii in double-hulled canoes with only the stars and migratory birds to guide them. Some 500 years later other Polynesian people arrived from Tahiti. The Polynesians settled the larger islands, living in tribal groups ruled by chiefs.

Capt. James Cook was the first known European to land here, in 1778, changing Hawaiian life forever. Diseases unknown in Hawaii, carried on Cook's and later ships, included cholera and measles. Such diseases eventually brought death to almost 250,000 vulnerable islanders.

In 1795 a Hawaiian chief unified the islands, naming himself King Kamehameha I. When missionaries landed in 1820, Kamehameha II and the islanders were interested in the new beliefs and most converted to Christianity.

European and American planters established sugarcane and pineapple plantations on the islands, importing workers from Japan, Korea, China, and the Philippines. The newcomers and the Polynesians, joined by settlers from Europe and the United States, endowed Hawaii with its unique ethnic diversity. People descended from the original Polynesian settlers now form

Japanese women work in a sugarcane field on Maui. By the early 1900s, people had come to Hawaii from Europe, Asia, and other Pacific islands to work on sugar and pineapple plantations.

less than one percent of the population.

Hawaii's major islands have mountainous interiors that slope shoreward. Hawaiians distinguish two main directions: *mauka*, toward the mountains, and *makai*, toward the sea. Most islands also have a windy, wet windward side and a calmer, drier leeward side. The difference can be great. On Kauai, winds bring 55 *feet* (17 m) of rain each year to the heights of Waialeale, while sheltered parts of some islands receive less than 20 inches (51 cm). The islands see many typhoons and tsunamis, destructive ocean waves

caused by earthquakes and volcanic eruptions.

Of the eight major islands, one, Kahoolawe, is uninhabited. Barren and windy, it has served as a target for military bombing practice. The island of Niihau is owned by a family that discourages visitors. Niihau is home to the state's only group of pure-blooded Hawaiians, who raise sheep and cattle and keep their language alive.

Visitors to Hawaii are greeted with flower leis and a warm aloha, meaning both "hello" and "good-bye" as well as "love." Tourists come to Hawaii at a rate of five million a year, and the money they spend is now the state's major source of income. Four of every five Hawaiians live on Oahu. U. S. military personnel and their families form about 12 percent of the state's population. The Japanese bombing of the strategic military base at Pearl Harbor near Honolulu brought the United States into World War II.

The island of Molokai, to which victims of leprosy once were banished, has a large ethnic Hawaiian population. Residents ranch and farm and tend to visitors. Lanai has the largest pineapple plantation in the world. Tourism may take hold there, too, if the island's owner follows through with plans to end pineapple cultivation. Maui's beaches attract droves of tourists. The slopes of Haleakala, a dormant volcano, are home to honeycreepers, possibly descendants of the first land birds to reach Hawaii.

The Big Island comprises 60 percent of the

Hibiscus

Nene
(Hawaiian Goose)

JAMES C. CAMPBELL
NATIONAL
WILDLIFE REFUGE

83

Wahiawa   *OAHU*

Pearl   Kaneohe
City   • Kailua
Waipahu •
          HI
PEARL HARBOR
N.W.R.   ★ **Honolulu**

Pearl Harbor   *Diamond Head*

Waikiki Beach

MOLOKAI
Kalaupapa   *Kamakou*
              4,970 FEET
Kaunakakai   + *1,515 METERS*
        KAKAHAIA
        N.W.R.   450

PACIFIC OCEAN

              Wailuku • Kahului   *MAUI*
Lahaina   •   • Pukalani   HALEAKALA
          30   NATIONAL PARK
• Lanai City   *Haleakala Crater* +
                  10,023 FEET
LANAI   *3,055 METERS*
                  31

KAHOOLAWE

state's land. It is diverse with fields of sugarcane, groves of macadamia trees, and the only
coffee plantations in the United States.

The volcano Kilauea erupts regularly, drawing scientists and tourists to its slopes. When
Mark Twain visited Hawaii in 1866, working as a
newspaper correspondent, he watched molten
lava flowing in streams of fire across the black,
cooled lava of the crater's floor. He described
how "masses of the dark crust broke away and
floated slowly down these streams like rafts
down a river . . . [then] plunged downward and
were swallowed in the crimson cauldron."

Area: *47th largest state, 6,471 sq mi (16,759 sq km)*
Population: *1,108,229; ranks 41st*
Major Cities: *Honolulu, 365,272; Hilo, 37,808; Kai-
lua, 36,818*
Manufacturing: *food products, clothing, stone, clay,
and glass products, metal products, chemicals*
Agriculture: *sugarcane, pineapples, greenhouse and
nursery products, macadamia nuts, milk, cattle*
Mining and Quarrying: *stone*
Other Important Activities: *tourism, federal gov-
ernment, tuna fishing*
Statehood: *the 50th state; admitted August 21, 1959*

The state of Hawaii is an
archipelago, a closely
scattered chain of is-
lands. There are eight
big islands and more
than a hundred smaller
ones (see map, page 6).
The major islands are
cone shaped, with peaks
and ridges near their
centers. That's because
the islands are volcanic.
They rise from the ocean
floor as some of Earth's
tallest mountains, mea-
sured from base to sum-
mit. If you could stand
Mount Everest next to all
of Hawaii's Big Island,
the island would reach
more than 20,000 feet
(6,100 m) higher than
Mount Everest.

• Honokaa

19   *HAWAII*
        Big Island
HAKALAU FOREST
N.W.R.
Mauna Kea Observatory   Papaikou
Kiholo Bay   *Mauna Kea*   • Hilo
                13,796 FEET   *Wailuku River*
                4,205 METERS
                Highest point
                in Hawaii
19 190

Kailua Kona •

                              HAWAII VOLCANOES
                              NATIONAL PARK
Captain Cook •   *Mauna Loa* +
                  13,677 FEET   + *Kilauea Crater*
                  4,169 METERS   *4,077 FEET*
                  Active volcano   *1,243 METERS*
                  11   *One of the world's*
                                    most active volcanoes
              11
        • Pahala

  0   KILOMETERS   60
  0   STATUTE MILES   40

    • Naalehu

South Cape (Ka Lae)   *Southernmost point*
                          of the 50 states

Hawaii

1 *A fountain of lava spews from Kilauea on Hawaii's Big Island. Among the world's most active volcanoes, Kilauea's eruptions create lava flows that may damage property but rarely cause loss of life.*

2 *Where fields of taro once stood, high rises crowd Honolulu's reef-protected Waikiki Beach. Diamond Head, an extinct volcano (background), got its name from glittery crystals that 19th-century sailors mistook for diamonds.*

3 *In traditional costume, chanting hula dancers interpret island stories with their hands and faces.*

4 *Colored-sand beaches are a legacy of Hawaii's volcanoes. Pounding surf breaks up obsidian, or volcanic glass, creating this black sand on the Big Island's southeastern coast. Green sand occurs, too, from pulverized olivine, a volcanic mineral.*

5 *A conveyor belt moves pineapples harvested on Lanai. Laborers wear protective clothing to guard against the prickly fruit.*

1

2

3

4

5

Distant Shores

At a 1950s festival on St. Thomas, a Mockoo Jumby balances on stilts. Dressed in women's clothing for the starring carnival role, he dances the bamboula, *brought from Africa by slaves.*

A number of island territories scattered throughout the Pacific Ocean and the Caribbean Sea are associated with the United States under different kinds of relationships. These include commonwealth status, with U. S. citizenship and other rights and obligations, and self-government with special help from the U. S.

Most of these islands grew from volcanic activity. In some places erosion wore away a central volcanic island, leaving behind only a fringe of built-up coral reefs called an atoll. Some of the islands have mountainous interiors, while many rise only a few feet above surrounding seas.

Altogether there are more than 2,300 islands and islets under U. S. jurisdiction. Together they form less land area than Connecticut. The Commonwealth of Puerto Rico alone accounts for half of that area and also for 90 percent of the

total population. Jarvis, Baker, and Howland Islands in the central Pacific (see map, page 235) are uninhabited and are wildlife refuges.

Except for the Midway Islands, all the U. S. territories lie in the tropics. Ocean breezes keep temperatures from climbing too high, and varying amounts of rainfall produce lush vegetation in some places, near-desert conditions in others. Hurricanes in the Atlantic and typhoons in the Pacific often buffet the islands. Another threat in the Pacific comes from tsunamis, powerful waves that are caused by earthquakes and volcanic eruptions. Tsunamis can wipe out settlements and cause great loss of life.

Puerto Rico lies 1,000 miles (1,600 km) southeast of Florida in a group of islands that separates the Caribbean waters from the rest of the Atlantic Ocean. Puerto Rico was claimed for Spain by Christopher Columbus and named "rich port" by Ponce de León. Arawak Indians were the original inhabitants, but Spanish contact brought death, disease, and intermarriage, and the Arawak no longer exist as a separate group. Many residents of the coastal lowlands descend from Africans brought in to work on sugarcane plantations in the 16th century, but most Puerto Ricans today are largely of Spanish descent. Puerto Ricans are mainly urban dwellers, with one in eight living in San Juan.

Sugar, coffee, and tobacco long formed the basis of Puerto Rico's economy. They remain important, but manufacturing is the largest source of income. The chief industries include chemicals, especially medicines, electronics, and food processing. In addition, the tourists who flock to Puerto Rico's beaches and historic districts spend about a billion dollars a year.

Puerto Rico may soon be asked to decide officially whether it wants to remain a commonwealth, become an independent country, or become the 51st state. Although statehood and independence have some support among Puerto Ricans, many favor remaining a commonwealth because their U. S. citizenship gives them freedom to emigrate to the mainland but does not require them to pay federal income tax.

In 1917 the Danish sold to the United States a group of islands and islets in the Caribbean east of Puerto Rico. The main islands, St. Thomas, St. Croix, and St. John, held sugarcane planta-

tions that were abandoned when slavery was abolished there in 1848. Today vacationers arrive by plane or cruise ship to swim and snorkel in sparkling blue waters and to absorb the Danish atmosphere of the island towns. Tourism brings in 70 percent of the Virgin Islands' income and employs 70 percent of the people. Other islanders work in the large oil refinery on St. Croix or raise fruits, vegetables, and cattle.

In 1988 the country's newest national park was established in American Samoa, a territory made up of five volcanic islands and two uninhabited atolls in the Pacific. The park preserves a unique rain forest that includes five different forest zones: lowland, mountainous, coastal, ridge, and cloud forest. The Samoan rain forest is the only one of its kind on U. S. soil and is similar to forests in Africa and Asia.

Populated by descendants of ancient Polynesians, American Samoa is perhaps the least changed of the territories in the Pacific. Islanders still live in remote village settlements in family groups headed by chiefs and raise subsistence crops. Most Samoans have converted to Christianity, and their large churches of coral cement blend into the traditional rural landscape. Pago Pago, the capital and chief port on Tutuila, has a more modern flavor, with shopping malls and tourist hotels. Tuna canning has long been the islands' chief industry.

Some volcanoes on the Northern Mariana Islands are likely to erupt at any time. This arc of 14 islands in the western Pacific Ocean is a commonwealth. Most of the people live on Saipan, Tinian, and Rota at the southern end of the chain. The original inhabitants came from Indonesia and the Philippines. Spanish rule from the 17th through the 19th century produced a people of mixed ancestry called Chamorros. Culturally they are Spanish but speak the Chamorro language, related to Indonesian. Islanders raise crops for their own use and also work for the government or in the growing tourist trade.

The U. S. military owns about one-third of the land on Guam. The people, most of Chamorro ancestry, are a varied ethnic mix with cultures from Europe, Asia, and Pacific islands. Military bases employ many residents, as do hotels and other facilities that serve nearly a million, mostly Japanese, tourists who visit Guam each year.

ATLANTIC OCEAN

Crown
Mountain
1,556 FEET
474 METERS
*ST.
THOMAS*
ST. JOHN
Charlotte
Amalie
VIRGIN ISLANDS
NATIONAL PARK
BUCK ISLAND
NATIONAL WILDLIFE REFUGE
*Highest point in the
U. S. Virgin Islands*

CARIBBEAN SEA

U.S. VIRGIN ISLANDS

0 KILOMETERS 30
0 STATUTE MILES 20

BUCK ISLAND REEF
NATIONAL MONUMENT
Christiansted
GREEN CAY
N.W.R.
Frederiksted
ST. CROIX
SANDY
POINT
NATIONAL
WILDLIFE
REFUGE

OFU
Ofu
OLOSEGA
Olosega
NATIONAL PARK
OF AMERICAN SAMOA

Manua Islands

PACIFIC OCEAN

TAU
Maia
Faleasao
Leusoalii
Tau
Siufaga
Lata Mountain
3,170 FEET
966 METERS
NATIONAL PARK
OF AMERICAN SAMOA
*Highest point in
American Samoa*

AMERICAN SAMOA

0 KILOMETERS 8
0 STATUTE MILES 4

NATIONAL PARK
OF AMERICAN SAMOA
Tula
Pago Pago
Aua
Fagaitua
Alao
Fagatogo
TUTUILA
Matafao Peak
2,142 METERS
653 METERS
*Pago Pago
Harbor*
Nuuuli
AUNUU
Amanave
Leone
Iliili

PACIFIC OCEAN

ATLANTIC OCEAN

Arecibo
Vega Baja
Toa Baja
San Juan
Aguadilla
2
Manatí
Cataño
Carolina
Arecibo Observatory
*The world's largest radio
telescope collects electro-
magnetic waves from space*
10
Bayamón
Guaynabo
Trujillo Alto
Cerro de Punta
4,390 FEET
1,338 METERS
*Highest point
in Puerto Rico*
El Yunque
3,494 FEET
1,065 METERS
Mayagüez
Utuado
Caguas
30
CORDILLERA
CENTRAL
52
Humacao
14
San Germán
2
Cayey
10
Coamo
3
Ponce
Guayama
LAGUNA CARTAGENA
N.W.R.
52
1
CABO ROJO
NATIONAL
WILDLIFE
REFUGE
*Phosphorescent Bay
Microscopic organisms luminesce
to turn water into a sea of fire
at night*
PUERTO RICO

CARIBBEAN SEA

CULEBRA NATIONAL
WILDLIFE REFUGE
Fajardo
CULEBRA
Isabel Segunda
VIEQUES

PUERTO RICO

0 KILOMETERS 30
0 STATUTE MILES 20

Lands associated with
the United States lie far
and wide (see map,
page 235). Residents of
the islands here elect
their governors, legisla-
tures, and—for some—
nonvoting delegates to
Congress. All except
American Samoans are
U. S. citizens. Samoans
are U. S. nationals, a
status that confers some
benefits of citizenship.

ROTA
Shinapaaru
Songsong
1,611 FEET
491 METERS

Tanapag
Kalabera
SAIPAN
*Entire island is the
administrative center of
the Northern Mariana Islands*
Capital Hill
1,526 FEET
465 METERS
Susupe
Chalan Kanoa

TINIAN
San Jose

PACIFIC OCEAN

NORTHERN
MARIANA ISLANDS

0 KILOMETERS 15
0 STATUTE MILES 10

AGUIJAN

GUAM

0 KILOMETERS 15
0 STATUTE MILES 10

Ritidian Point

PHILIPPINE SEA

Tumon Bay
Yigo
Dededo
Agana
Tamuning
Barrigada
Apra Harbor
Sinajana
Mongmong
GUAM
Yona
Agat
Mount Lamlam
1,332 FEET
406 METERS
*Highest point
in Guam*
Umatac
Inarajan
Merizo

PACIFIC OCEAN

1 *Guam*

2 *American Samoa*

3 *Puerto Rico*

4 *U. S. Virgin Islands*

5 *Puerto Rico*

Guam

1 *Tourists cruise Tumon Bay in a double-hulled sight-seeing boat. Tourism, the island's fastest growing industry, helps give Guam a low unemployment rate.*

American Samoa

2 *Dinner by the bunch comes home at the end of the day with a Samoan villager. Rural Samoans live in large family groups, in which all resources are shared.*

Puerto Rico

3 *The guns of El Morro, the stout, 16th-century Spanish fortress, defended San Juan from attack by sea, including a 1595 attempt by an English pirate, Sir Francis Drake, to loot its treasure. Inside the walls are tunnels, barracks, and dungeons.*

U. S. Virgin Islands

4 *Closeup views of yellow tube sponges, sea fans, and yellow and orange reef sponges bring many divers to the Virgin Islands. Coral, sponge, and fish species abound in the warm, shallow waters.*

Puerto Rico

5 *Workers tend bins full of capsules at a pharmaceutical factory in Manatí. Industrialization brought to Puerto Rico dozens of companies that manufacture medicines.*

Facts at Your Fingertips

Populations of U.S. Cities

These pages list the largest legally incorporated cities in each state. Populations here and those given for cities in the state stories are from the 1990 census.

Alabama
Birmingham 265,968
Huntsville 159,789
Mobile 196,278
Montgomery 187,106
Tuscaloosa 77,759

Alaska
Anchorage 226,338

Arizona
Chandler 90,533
Glendale 148,134
Mesa 288,091
Phoenix 983,403
Scottsdale 130,069
Tempe 141,865
Tucson 405,390
Yuma 54,923

Arkansas
Fort Smith 72,798
Jonesboro 46,535
Little Rock 175,795
North Little Rock 61,741
Pine Bluff 57,140

California
Alameda 76,459
Alhambra 82,106
Anaheim 266,406
Antioch 62,195
Bakersfield 174,820
Baldwin Park 69,330
Bellflower 61,815
Berkeley 102,724
Buena Park 68,784
Burbank 93,643
Carlsbad 63,126
Carson 83,995
Chino 59,682
Chula Vista 135,163
Compton 90,454
Concord 111,348
Corona 76,095
Costa Mesa 96,357
Daly City 92,311
Downey 91,444
El Cajon 88,693
El Monte 106,209

Encinitas 55,386
Escondido 108,635
Fairfield 77,211
Fontana 87,535
Fremont 173,339
Fresno 354,202
Fullerton 114,144
Garden Grove 143,050
Glendale 180,038
Hawthorne 71,349
Hayward 111,498
Huntington Beach 181,519
Huntington Park 56,065
Inglewood 109,602
Irvine 110,330
Lakewood 73,557
Lancaster 97,291
Livermore 56,741
Long Beach 429,433
Los Angeles 3,485,398
Lynwood 61,945
Mission 72,820
Modesto 164,730
Montebello 59,564
Monterey 60,738
Moreno Valley 118,779
Mountain View 67,460
Napa 61,842
National City 54,249
Newport Beach 66,643
Norwalk 94,279
Oakland 372,242
Oceanside 128,398
Ontario 133,179
Orange 110,658
Oxnard 142,216
Palmdale 68,842
Palo Alto 55,900
Pasadena 131,591
Pico Rivera 59,177
Pomona 131,723
Rancho Cucamonga 101,409
Redding 66,462
Redlands 60,394
Redondo Beach 60,167
Redwood City 66,072
Rialto 72,388
Richmond 87,425
Riverside 226,505
Sacramento 369,365
Salinas 108,777
San Bernardino 164,164
San Diego 1,110,549
San Francisco 723,959
San Jose 782,248
San Leandro 68,223
San Mateo 85,486

Santa Ana 293,742
Santa Barbara 85,571
Santa Clara 93,613
Santa Clarita 110,642
Santa Maria 61,284
Santa Monica 86,905
Santa Rosa 113,313
Simi Valley 100,217
South Gate 86,284
South San Francisco 54,312
Stockton 210,943
Sunnyvale 117,229
Thousand Oaks 104,352
Torrance 133,107
Upland 63,374
Vacaville 71,479
Vallejo 109,199
Ventura 92,575
Visalia 75,636
Vista 71,872
Walnut Creek 60,569
West Covina 96,086
Westminster 78,118
Whittier 77,671

Colorado
Arvada 89,235
Aurora 222,103
Boulder 83,312
Colorado Springs 281,140
Denver 467,610
Fort Collins 87,758
Greeley 60,536
Lakewood 126,481
Pueblo 98,640
Thornton 55,031
Westminster 74,625

Connecticut
Bridgeport 141,686
Bristol 60,640
Danbury 65,585
Hartford 139,739
Meriden 59,479
New Britain 75,491
New Haven 130,474
Norwalk 78,331
Stamford 108,056
Waterbury 108,961
West Haven 54,021

Delaware
Wilmington 71,529

Florida
Boca Raton 61,492
Cape Coral 74,991

Clearwater 98,784
Coral Springs 79,443
Daytona Beach 61,921
Fort Lauderdale 149,377
Gainesville 84,770
Hialeah 188,004
Hollywood 121,697
Jacksonville 672,971
Lakeland 70,576
Largo 65,674
Melbourne 59,646
Miami 358,548
Miami Beach 92,639
Orlando 164,693
Palm Bay 62,632
Pembroke Pines 65,452
Pensacola 58,165
Plantation 66,692
Pompano Beach 72,411
Port St. Lucie 55,866
St. Petersburg 238,629
Sunrise 64,407
Tallahassee 124,773
Tampa 280,015
West Palm Beach 67,643

Georgia
Albany 78,122
Atlanta 394,017
Columbus 179,278
Macon 106,612
Savannah 137,560

Hawaii
Honolulu 365,272

Idaho
Boise City 125,738
Idaho Falls 43,929
Pocatello 46,080

Illinois
Arlington Heights Village 75,460
Aurora 99,581
Champaign 63,502
Chicago 2,783,726
Cicero 67,436
Decatur 83,885
Elgin 77,010
Evanston 73,233
Joliet 76,836
Naperville 85,351
Oak Lawn 56,182
Oak Park 53,648
Peoria 113,504
Rockford 139,426
Schaumburg 68,586

Skokie 59,432
Springfield 105,227
Waukegan 69,392

Indiana
Anderson 59,459
Bloomington 60,633
Evansville 126,272
Fort Wayne 173,072
Gary 116,646
Hammond 84,236
Indianapolis 731,327
Muncie 71,035
South Bend 105,511
Terre Haute 57,483

Iowa
Cedar Rapids 108,751
Council Bluffs 54,315
Davenport 95,333
Des Moines 193,187
Dubuque 57,546
Iowa City 59,738
Sioux City 80,505
Waterloo 66,467

Kansas
Kansas City 149,767
Lawrence 65,608
Olathe 63,352
Overland Park 111,790
Topeka 119,883
Wichita 304,011

Kentucky
Bowling Green 40,641
Covington 43,264
Lexington-Fayette 225,366
Louisville 269,063
Owensboro 53,549

Louisiana
Baton Rouge 219,531
Kenner 72,033
Lafayette 94,440
Lake Charles 70,580
Monroe 54,909
New Orleans 496,938
Shreveport 198,525

Maine
Lewiston 39,757
Portland 64,358

Maryland
Baltimore 736,014
Frederick 40,148

Gaithersburg 39,542
Rockville 44,835

Massachusetts
Boston 574,283
Brockton 92,788
Cambridge 95,802
Chicopee 56,632
Fall River 92,703
Lawrence 70,207
Lowell 103,439
Lynn 81,245
Malden 53,884
Medford 57,407
New Bedford 99,922
Newton 82,585
Quincy 84,985
Somerville 76,210
Springfield 156,983
Waltham 57,878
Worcester 169,759

Michigan
Ann Arbor 109,592
Dearborn 89,286
Dearborn Heights 60,838
Detroit 1,027,974
Farmington Hills 74,652
Flint 140,761
Grand Rapids 189,126
Kalamazoo 80,277
Lansing 127,321
Livonia 100,850
Pontiac 71,166
Rochester Hills 61,766
Royal Oak 65,410
Saginaw 69,512
St. Clair Shores 68,107
Southfield 75,728
Sterling Heights 117,810
Taylor 70,811
Troy 72,884
Warren 144,864
Westland 84,724
Wyoming 63,891

Minnesota
Bloomington 86,335
Brooklyn Park 56,381
Duluth 85,493
Minneapolis 368,383
Rochester 70,745
St. Paul 272,235

Mississippi
Biloxi 46,319
Greenville 45,226
Hattiesburg 41,882

Jackson 196,637
Meridian 41,036

Missouri
Columbia 69,101
Independence 112,301
Kansas City 435,146
St. Charles 54.555
St. Joseph 71,852
St. Louis 396,685
Springfield 140,494

Montana
Billings 81,151
Great Falls 55,097
Missoula 42,918

Nebraska
Grand Island 39,386
Lincoln 191,972
Omaha 335,795

Nevada
Henderson 64,942
Las Vegas 258,295
North Las Vegas 47,707
Reno 133,850
Sparks 53,367

New Hampshire
Manchester 99,567
Nashua 79,662

New Jersey
Bayonne 61,444
Camden 87,492
Clifton 71,742
East Orange 73,552
Elizabeth 110,002
Jersey City 228,537
Newark 275,221
Passaic 58,041
Paterson 140,891
Trenton 88,675
Union City 58,012
Vineland 54,780

New Mexico
Albuquerque 384,736
Las Cruces 62,126
Roswell 44,654
Santa Fe 55,859

New York
Albany 101,082
Binghamton 53,008
Buffalo 328,123
Mount Vernon 67,153

New Rochelle 67,265
New York 7,322,564
Niagara Falls 61,840
Rochester 231,636
Schenectady 65,566
Syracuse 163,860
Troy 54,269
Utica 68,637
Yonkers 188,082

North Carolina
Asheville 61,607
Charlotte 395,934
Durham 136,611
Fayetteville 75,695
Gastonia 54,732
Greensboro 183,521
High Point 69,496
Raleigh 207,951
Wilmington 55,530
Winston-Salem 143,485

North Dakota
Bismarck 49,256
Fargo 74,111
Grand Forks 49,425

Ohio
Akron 223,019
Canton 84,161
Cincinnati 364,040
Cleveland 505,616
Columbus 632,910
Dayton 182,044
Elyria 56,746
Euclid 54,875
Hamilton 61,368
Kettering 60,569
Lakewood 59,718
Lorain 71,245
Parma 87,876
Springfield 70,487
Toledo 332,943
Youngstown 95,732

Oklahoma
Broken Arrow 58,043
Lawton 80,561
Norman 80,071
Oklahoma City 444,719
Tulsa 367,302

Oregon
Beaverton 53,310
Eugene 112,669
Gresham 68,235
Portland 437,319
Salem 107,786

Pennsylvania
Allentown 105,090
Bethlehem 71,428
Erie 108,718
Lancaster 55,551
Philadelphia 1,585,577
Pittsburgh 369,879
Reading 78,380
Scranton 81,805

Rhode Island
Cranston 76,060
East Providence 50,380
Pawtucket 72,644
Providence 160,728
Warwick 85,427

South Carolina
Charleston 80,414
Columbia 98,052
Greenville 58,282
North Charleston 70,218
Spartanburg 43,467

South Dakota
Rapid City 54,523
Sioux Falls 100,814

Tennessee
Chattanooga 152,466
Clarksville 75,494

Knoxville 165,121
Memphis 610,337
Nashville-Davidson
   510,784

Texas
Abilene 106,654
Amarillo 157,615
Arlington 261,721
Austin 465,622
Baytown 63,850
Beaumont 114,323
Brownsville 98,962
Carrollton 82,169
Corpus Christi 257,453
Dallas 1,006,877
Denton 66,270
El Paso 515,342
Fort Worth 447,619
Galveston 59,070
Garland 180,650
Grand Prairie 99,616
Houston 1,630,553
Irving 155,037
Killeen 63,535
Laredo 122,899
Longview 70,311
Lubbock 186,206
McAllen 84,021
Mesquite 101,484
Midland 89,443

Odessa 89,699
Pasadena 119,363
Plano 128,713
Port Arthur 58,724
Richardson 74,840
San Angelo 84,474
San Antonio 935,933
Tyler 75,450
Victoria 55,076
Waco 103,590
Wichita Falls 96,259

Utah
Ogden 63,909
Orem 67,561
Provo 86,835
Salt Lake City 159,936
Sandy 75,058
West Valley City 86,976

Vermont
Burlington 39,127

Virginia
Alexandria 111,183
Chesapeake 151,976
Hampton 133,793
Lynchburg 66,049
Newport News 170,045
Norfolk 261,229
Portsmouth 103,907

Richmond 203,056
Roanoke 96,397
Virginia Beach 393,069

Washington
Bellevue 86,874
Everett 69,961
Seattle 516,259
Spokane 177,196
Tacoma 176,664
Yakima 54,827

West Virginia
Charleston 57,287
Huntington 54,844

Wisconsin
Appleton 65,695
Eau Claire 56,856
Green Bay 96,466
Kenosha 80,352
Madison 191,262
Milwaukee 628,088
Oshkosh 55,006
Racine 84,298
Waukesha 56,958
West Allis 63,221

Wyoming
Casper 46,742
Cheyenne 50,008

Largest U.S. Metropolitan Areas

What is a metropolitan area? It is a region that results when a city spreads beyond its limits, engulfing nearby communities and suburbs. The people in a metropolitan area become linked by jobs, schools, stores, and transportation systems such as subways. According to the 1990 census, 77.5% of the U. S. population lives in metropolitan areas of 56,000 or more people. And more than half of the nation lives in 39 metropolitan areas that have populations of over one million. Here are the ten largest.

Metropolitan Area	Location	Population
1. New York City	New York, New Jersey, Connecticut	18,087,251
2. Los Angeles	California	14,531,529
3. Chicago	Illinois, Indiana, Wisconsin	8,065,633
4. San Francisco	California	6,253,311
5. Philadelphia	Pennsylvania, New Jersey, Delaware, Maryland	5,899,345
6. Detroit	Michigan	4,665,236
7. Boston	Massachusetts, New Hampshire	4,171,643
8. Washington, D.C.	D.C., Maryland, Virginia	3,923,574
9. Dallas	Texas	3,885,415
10. Houston	Texas	3,711,043

More Facts at Your Fingertips

Top Products/Top States

Here, in order of their dollar value, are major farm products, fish, and minerals and the states that led in their production from 1987 through 1990. Nationwide leaders in each category are listed at right. Rank may change from year to year.

Farm Products

	Leaders
1. *Cattle and calves*—Texas, Nebraska, Kansas, Colorado	1. California
2. *Dairy products*—Wisconsin, California, New York, Pennsylvania	2. Texas
3. *Soybeans*—Iowa, Illinois, Minnesota, Indiana	3. Iowa
4. *Corn*—Illinois, Iowa, Nebraska, Indiana	4. Nebraska
5. *Hogs*—Iowa, Illinois, Minnesota, Indiana	5. Kansas
6. *Broiler chickens*—Arkansas, Georgia, Alabama, North Carolina	6. Illinois
7. *Greenhouse and nursery*—California, Florida, Ohio, New York	7. Minnesota
8. *Wheat*—Kansas, North Dakota, Oklahoma, Washington	8. Florida
9. *Cotton*—Texas, California, Mississippi, Arizona	9. Wisconsin
10. *Eggs*—California, Georgia, Arkansas, Indiana	10. North Carolina
11. *Hay*—California, Arizona, Washington, Idaho	
12. *Tobacco*—North Carolina, Kentucky, Virginia, South Carolina	
13. *Turkeys*—Minnesota, North Carolina, California, Arkansas	
14. *Oranges*—Florida, California, Texas, Arizona	
15. *Potatoes*—Idaho, Maine, Washington, California	
16. *Grapes*—California, Washington, New York, Arizona	
17. *Tomatoes*—California, Florida, Ohio, New Jersey	
18. *Rice*—Arkansas, California, Texas, Louisiana	

Fish

	Leaders
1. *Salmon*—Alaska, Washington, Oregon, California	1. Alaska
2. *Shrimp*—Texas, Louisiana, Florida, Alabama	2. Massachusetts
3. *Crabs*—Alaska, Florida, Maryland, Washington	3. Louisiana
4. *Cod*—Alaska, Massachusetts, Maine, New Hampshire	4. Texas
5. *Flounder*—Alaska, Massachusetts, Rhode Island, California	5. Florida

Minerals

	Leaders
1. *Crude petroleum and natural gas*—Texas, Louisiana, Alaska, California	1. Texas
2. *Natural gas liquids*—Texas, Louisiana, Oklahoma, Kansas	2. Louisiana
3. *Coal and lignite surface mining*—Kentucky, West Virginia, Pennsylvania, Wyoming	3. California
4. *Coal underground mining*—West Virginia, Kentucky, Virginia, Pennsylvania	4. Alaska
5. *Crushed stone*—Pennsylvania, Florida, Texas, Virginia	5. Oklahoma
6. *Copper*—Arizona, New Mexico, Utah, Montana	6. Kentucky
7. *Cement*—California, Texas, Pennsylvania, Mississippi	7. West Virginia
8. *Construction sand and gravel*—Illinois, Michigan, California, New Jersey	8. Wyoming
9. *Gold*—Nevada, California, South Dakota, Utah	9. New Mexico
10. *Iron ore*—Minnesota, Michigan, Missouri, Utah	10. Pennsylvania
11. *Clay*—Georgia, Ohio, North Carolina, Texas	
12. *Phosphate rock*—Florida, North Carolina, Idaho, Utah	
13. *Lime*—Ohio, Missouri, Pennsylvania, Alabama	
14. *Salt*—Louisiana, Texas, New York, Ohio	
15. *Sodium carbonate*—Wyoming, California	
16. *Magnesium*—Mississippi, California, Utah, Florida	
17. *Sulfur*—Texas, Louisiana	
18. *Boron*—California	

Superfacts

World's Rainiest Spot
Waialeale (mountain), Hawaii; annual average rainfall 661 inches (1,680 cm); rain falls 350 days a year

World's Strongest Surface Wind
231 mph (372 kmph), Mount Washington, New Hampshire; recorded April 12, 1934

World's Oldest Living Tree
Methuselah bristlecone pine, California; about 4,700 years old

World's Tallest Living Tree
Harry Cole redwood, California; 371 feet (113 m) tall

World's Largest Living Tree
General Sherman sequoia, California; 275 feet (84 m) tall, 82 feet (25 m) in circumference

World's Longest Cave System
Mammoth-Flint Ridge cave system, Kentucky; total mapped passageway length of more than 330 miles (531 km)

World's Largest Gorge
Grand Canyon, Colorado River, Arizona; 290 miles (466 km) long, 600 feet to 18 miles (183 m to 29 km) wide, 1 mile (1.6 km) deep

Driest Spot in U.S.
Death Valley, California; annual average rainfall 1.8 inches (4.6 cm)

Highest Temperature in U.S.
134°F (56.6°C), Death Valley, California; recorded July 10, 1913

Lowest Temperature in U.S.
Minus 80°F (−62.2°C) at Prospect Creek, Alaska; recorded January 23, 1971

Highest Point in U.S.
Mount McKinley, Alaska; 20,323 feet (6,194 m)

Lowest Point in U.S.
Death Valley, California; 282 feet (86 m) below sea level

Longest River System in U.S.
Mississippi-Missouri; 3,708 miles (5,971 km) long

Highest Town in U.S.
Climax, Colorado; 11,560 feet (3,526 m)

Lowest Town in U.S.
Calipatria, California; 185 feet (56 m) below sea level

Most Crowded State in U.S.
New Jersey; 992.7 people per sq mi (383.27 per sq km)

Least Crowded State in U.S.
Alaska; 0.93 people per sq mi (0.36 per sq km)

Illustrations Credits

Abbreviations for terms appearing below: (t)-top; (b)-bottom; (l)-left; (r)-right; (c)-center; NGP-National Geographic Photographer; NGS-National Geographic Staff; TIB-The Image Bank; LC-The Library of Congress; PA-Photographers/Aspen; WC-Woodfin Camp.

Cover and 2-3, Michel Tcherevkoff; eagle photograph, Tom and Pat Leeson.

America's Many Faces
9, Tom Bean. 10-11, Barry Lewis, Network. 12-13, Francisco Hidalgo, TIB. 14-15, Hank Morgan. 16-17, James A. Sugar.
The Maps in Your Atlas
18, William H. Bond, NGS.
The District of Columbia
20, LC. 22, (t) Larry Chapman; (b) Seny Norasingh. 23, (tl) Mark Avino, National Air & Space Museum; (tr) Olivier Martel, Black Star; (b) Adam Woolfitt, Susan Griggs Agency.
New England
24-25, William H. Bond, NGS. 26, Wills T. White, Images from the Past, Bennington, Vermont. 28, (t) Mike Clemmer; (b) Cynthia B. Foster. 29, (tl) (r) Michael Melford; (b) Nathan Benn, WC. 30, New Hampshire Hist. Soc. 32, (l) David Brownell, TIB; (t) Sandy Felsenthal. 32-33, Sandy Felsenthal. 33, (t) Sandy Felsenthal; (r) Sam Abell, NGP. 34, Joseph Coburn Smith. 36, (t) Michael Melford; (b) Kunio Owaki, The Stock Market. 37, (l) Phil Schermeister, PA; (t) Michael S. Yamashita; (b) Phil Schermeister. 38, Worthington Cornell, LC; Martin Sandler Productions. 40, (t) David Muench; (b) Peter Southwick, Stock Boston. 41, (t) Seth Resnick; (bl) Michael Carroll, New England Stock Photo; (br) Stephen J. Krasemann, Photo Researchers Inc. 42, Luis Marden. 44, (l) Gabe Palmer, The Stock Market; (r) Sarah Leen; (b) Robert Benson. 44-45, Tor Eigeland. 45, Randa Bishop. 46, Adler Art Associates. 48, (t) Robert D. Hagan; (b) Steve Dunwell, TIB; (r) Ira Block. 49, Steve Dunwell, TIB.
Mid-Atlantic States
50-51, William H. Bond, NGS. 52, LC. 54, (l) Bob Clemenz; (b) Lacrosse USA, Inc. 54-55, Jodi Cobb, NGP. 55, (b) Kenneth Garrett; (r) Ted Spiegel. 56, Lewis W. Hine, LC. 58-59, William T. Douthitt, NGS. 59, (tl) William T. Douthitt, NGS; (bl) J. Nettis, H. Armstrong Roberts; (tr) Russ Kennedy; (br) James L. Stanfield, NGP. 60, John E. Fletcher. 62, (t) David Muench; (b) Martha Cooper. 63, Bob Krist. 64, Hagerstown Chamber of Commerce. 66, (l) David Alan Harvey; (t) Lowell Georgia; (b) Greg Pease. 67, (l) Kevin Fleming; (r) Dan Dry. 68, E. I. du Pont de Nemours & Co. 70, Kevin Fleming. 70-71, Kevin Fleming. 71, (t) Kevin Fleming; (b) Stephen R. Brown.
Appalachian Highlands
72-73, William H. Bond, NGS. 74, B. Anthony Stewart. 76, (t) Bill Luster; (b) William Strode. 76-77, Bill Luster. 77, (b) Michael O'Brien; (r) Chip Clark. 78, Ben Shahn, LC. 80, (l) Michael O'Brien; (t) James P. Blair, NGP. 80-81, Sam Abell, NGP. 81, (t) Joseph H. Bailey, NGP; (r) James P. Blair, NGP. 82, Frances B. Johnston, The Mu-

seum of Modern Art, New York. 84, (l) D. Cary Jackson; (t) Nathan Benn. 84-85, Karen Kasmauski. 85, (t) Karen Kasmauski; (r) David Alan Harvey. 86, J. Baylor Roberts. 88, (l) David Muench; (b) Karen Kasmauski. 88-89, Joe Viesti. 89, (b) Karen Kasmauski; (r) Nathan Benn. 90, Lewis W. Hine, George Eastman House. 92, (tl) John Dominis; (bl) Joseph H. Bailey, NGP; (r) David Alan Harvey. 93, Bill Weems.
The Southeast
94-95, William H. Bond, NGS. 96, B. Anthony Stewart. 98, (t)(bl) Matt Bradley; (br) Charles O'Rear. 99, Garry McMichael, Root Resources. 100, Smithsonian Institution, National Museum of the American Indian. 102, Gail Mooney. 103, (tl) Gail Mooney; (tr) J. D. Schwalm, Stock South; (b) Nathan Benn, WC. 104, LC. 106, Ed Malles, Photo Options. 107, (t)(bc) Ed Malles, Photo Options; (bl) Charles O'Rear; (br) Randa Bishop. 108, Georgia Dept. of Archives and History. 110, (t) David Muench; (b) Jim Richardson. 111, (l) Jim Richardson, West Light; (tr) Bill Weems, WC; (br) Al Stepheson, WC. 112, LC. 114, (t) Tom Blagden Jr.; (b) David Dobbs, Photo Options. 114-115, Annie Griffiths Belt. 115, (t) Bill Curtsinger; (b) Annie Griffiths Belt. 116, Louisiana State Museum: Jan White Brantley. 118, (tl) C. C. Lockwood; (tr)(b) Nathan Benn. 119, (l) C. C. Lockwood; (r) Philip Gould. 120, Detroit Publishing Co., LC. 122, (t) Comstock; (bl) Nathan Benn; (br) James P. Blair, NGP. 123, (l) Roger Ressmeyer, Starlight; (r) Bill Curtsinger.
Great Lakes States
124-125, William H. Bond, NGS. 126, H. H. Bennett Studio Foundation. 128, (tl) Paul Damien; (tr) Jim Brandenburg; (b) Paul Damien. 128-129, Seny Norasingh. 129, Kenneth Garrett. 130, Michigan Dept. of State. 132, Michael S. Yamashita. 132-133, Robert M. Lightfoot III. 133, (tl) Phil Schermeister; (tr) Lowell Georgia; (b) Fred Ward, Black Star. 134, UPI, Bettmann Archive. 136, (t) Lynn Johnson; (bl) James L. Stanfield, NGP; (br) Ira Block. 137, (t) Louie Psihoyos; (b) Kevin Fleming. 138, J. C. Allen & Son. 140, (t) The Selmer Co., L.P.; (b) Sandy Felsenthal. 140-141, Karen Keeney. 141, (bl) Sandy Felsenthal; (r) Frank Cezus, Tony Stone Worldwide. 142, William H. Jenkins, Martin Sandler Productions. 144, (t) Jack Van Antwerp; (b) Dennis Barnes. 144-145, Richard Alexander Cooke III. 145, (t) Louie Psihoyos, Contact Stock Images, WC; (b) Joseph H. Bailey, NGP.
The Heartland
146-147, William H. Bond, NGS. 148, State Hist. Soc. of North Dakota. 150, (t) Richard Alexander Cooke III; (b) Annie Griffiths Belt. 151, Annie Griffiths Belt. 152, The Minnesota Hist. Soc. 154, (l) Raymond Gehman; (r) Richard Hamilton Smith. 155, (tl) Randall Hyman; (b) Annie Griffiths Belt; (r) Jim Brandenburg. 156, South Dakota State Hist. Soc. 158, (t) Jim Brandenburg; (b) Tom Nebbia. 158-159, Jim Brandenburg. 159, (t) Tom Nebbia; (b) Jim Brandenburg. 160, Nebraska State Hist. Soc. 162, (l) Terry Eiler; (t) Charles O'Rear. 162-163, Grant Heilman, Grant Heilman Photography Inc. 163, (t) David Muench; (r) James L. Amos. 164, Harold H. Jorgensen. 166, (l) Craig Aurness; (b) Tom Bean. 166-167, David Muench. 167, (t) Craig Aurness; (b) Scott Rutherford. 168, Grant Heilman Photography Inc. 170, Cotton Coulson. 171, (tl)(tr) Cotton Coulson, WC; (b) David Hornback. 172, Missouri Hist. Soc. 174, José Azel, Contact Press Images. 174-175, Annie Griffiths Belt. 175, (tl) Randy Olson; (tr) Nathan Benn; (b) Randall Hyman.
The Southwest
176-177, William H. Bond, NGS. 178, Bud DeWald. 180, Martha Cooper, Peter Arnold Inc. 180-181, Gordon Anderson. 181, (tl) Kerrick James; (bl) James A. Sugar; (r) Mike Clemmer. 182, Ben Wittick, Museum of New Mexi-

co. 184, (tl) Danny Lehman; (tr) Adam Woolfitt, WC; (b) Dan Budnik, WC. 185, (t) Danny Lehman; (b) Terry Eiler. 186, Arthur Rothstein, LC. 188, (tl) Annie Griffiths Belt; (b) Martin Rogers. 188-189, Chris Johns. 189, (t) Chris Johns; (b) Matt Bradley. 190, Fred A. Schell, American Petroleum Institute. 192, (l) Charles O'Rear; (c) Matt Bradley. 192-193, Dan Dry. 193, (bl) Steven C. Wilson, Entheos; (r) David Alan Harvey.
Mountain States
194-195, William H. Bond, NGS. 196, Idaho State Hist. Soc. 198, Chris Huskinson, F-Stock Photo Inc. 198-199, David R. Stoecklein. 199, (t) Dave Shippee; (bl) J. R. Simplot Co.; (br) Scott Rutherford. 200, Burlington Northern Railroad. 202, (tl) Scott Rutherford; (bl) Jeff Foott; (r) Dewitt Jones. 203, (t) Nicholas DeVore III, PA; (b) Paul Chesley. 204, B. Anthony Stewart. 206, (l) Raymond Gehman; (r) David Alan Harvey. 207, (tl) Jeremy Schmidt; (tr) Phil Schofield; (b) Tomasz Tomaszewski. 208, Maureen H. Wilson: Stanley Paher. 210, (tl) Tom Bean; (bl) Kerby Smith; (r) Jack Gucia, TIB. 211, (t) Phil Schermeister; (b) Phil Schofield. 212, Utah State Hist. Soc. 214, (t) Dennis Chamberlin; (bl) Jim Richardson; (br) Dennis Chamberlin. 215, (l) George F. Mobley, NGP; (r) Floyd Holdman. 216, O. E. Aultman. 218, (t) Steve Raymer, NGS; (bl) Craig Aurness; (br) Paul Chesley. 218-219, David Muench. 219, Amy Deputy.
Pacific Coast States
220-221, William H. Bond, NGS. 222, News Tribune, Tacoma, Washington. 224, (t) Gary Braasch; (bl)(br) Sandy Felsenthal. 225, (l) Randy Wells, Allstock; (r) Robert W. Madden, NGS. 226, George M. Weister, Knight Library, University of Oregon. 228, (l) Annie Griffiths Belt; (r) David Muench. 229, (t) Ray Atkeson; (bl) Robert W. Madden, NGS; (br) Harald Sund. 230, The Bancroft Library, University of California at Berkeley. 232, (t) Richard Alexander Cooke III; (b) Vince Streano. 233, (tl) Louie Psihoyos; (bl) Brent Bear, West Light; (r) Craig Aurness.
Alaska, Hawaii, and Distant Shores
234-235, William H. Bond, NGS. 236, Amos Burg. 238, (tl) John L. Hinderman; (tr) Cradoc Bagshaw, West Light; (bl) Jim Rearden; (br) David Alan Harvey. 239, Tom Bean. 240, Ray Jerome Baker, Bishop Museum. 242, Richard Alexander Cooke III. 243, (t) Paul Chesley; (bl) Steve Raymer, NGS; (bc) Paul Chesley, PA; (r) Paul Chesley. 244, Charles Allmon. 246, (tl) Ken Straiton, The Stock Market; (bl) Frederic Koehler Sutter, ASG. 246-247, Ira Block. 247, (t) Stephen Frink, The Waterhouse; (b) Stephanie Maze.

Acknowledgments

We wish to express our appreciation to the many individuals and organizations who helped in the preparation of the *National Geographic Picture Atlas of OUR FIFTY STATES:* Jim G. Rigby, Nevada Bureau of Mines and Geology; Whitney Smith, Flag Research Center; the Bureau of the Census; the Bureau of Indian Affairs; the National Marine Fishery Service; the National Park Service; Native American tribal associations; the United States Department of Agriculture; and the state divisions of forestry, geology, and tourism.

We are grateful to several divisions of the National Geographic Society: Valerie Mattingley and Jennifer Moseley of the United Kingdom Office; Administrative Services; Illustrations Library; the National Geographic Library, including its Map and News Collections; Messenger Center; Photographic Services; Production Services, Pre-Press Division; Records Library.

Index

Map pages are in **boldface
type (133)**. Letters and
numbers following in
lightface (M8) will locate the
place named. *See* page 18 for
help in using them.
Illustrations are in *italic
(250)*. Text references are in
lightface type (178).

Abbeville, La. **117** N7
Aberdeen, Wash. **223** H2
Abert, Lake, Oreg. **227** M11
Abilene, Kans. **169** D13
Abilene, Tex. **191** G10
Abiquiu Dam Reservoir,
 N. Mex. **183** D8
Absaroka Range, Wyo. **205** C4
Acadia NP, Me. **35** P10, Q9
Ace Basin NWR, S. C. **113** M11
Acoma IR, N. Mex. **183** H4
Acoma Pueblo, N. Mex. **183** H5
Adams, Mount, Wash. **223** L8
Adirondack Mountains, N. Y.
 53, **53** E15
Admiralty Island NM, Alas. **237**
 O25
Adrian, Mich. **131** T14
Agana, Guam **245** R17
Agassiz NWR, Minn. **153** D3
Agat, Guam **245** S16
Agate Fossil Beds NM, Nebr.
 161, **161** B1
Agriculture *see* Crops; Dairy
 farming; Farm machinery;
 Fruit growing; Irrigation;
 Livestock; Poultry; Ranches
Agua Caliente IR, Calif. **231** S13
Aguijan, Northern Mariana
 Islands **245** N16
Aiken, S. C. **113** H7
Akron, Ohio **143** E12; soap box
 derby *145*
Alabama 104-107
Alabama-Coushatta IR, Tex.
 191 K17
Alabama River, Ala. **105** P4
The Alamo, Tex. 190, **191** M12
Alamo Navajo IR, N. Mex. **183**
 J5
Alamogordo, N. Mex. **183** O9
Alamosa, Colo. **217** N9
Alamosa NWR, Colo. **217** N9
Alao, American Samoa 235, **245**
 Q11
Alaska 8, 13, 16, 234, **234-235**,
 236-239

Alaska, Gulf of **237** O20
Alaska Highway 236, **237** H20
Alaska Maritime NWR, Alas.
 237 P11, J10
Alaska Range, Alas. 235, 236,
 237 K18
Albany, Ga. **109** O6
Albany, N. Y. 52, **53** L17
Albany, Oreg. **227** F4
Albemarle, N. C. **91** F12
Albert Lea, Minn. **153** T9
Albion, Mich. **131** S12
Albuquerque, N. Mex. 176, 182,
 183 G7; laboratory *184*
Alcoa, Tenn. 86, **87** D20
Aleutian Islands, Alas. 8, 234,
 234, 236, 236-237
Aleutian Range, Alas. 236, **237**
 N15
Alexander Archipelago, Alas.
 237 P25
Alexandria, La. **117** G6
Alexandria, Va. **83** C21
Alibates Flint Quarries NM,
 Tex. **191** B8
All American Canal, Calif. **231**
 T17-U15
Allagash, Me. **35** B8
Allagash River, Me. **35** D7
Allatoona Lake, Ga. **109** D4
Allegany IR, N. Y. **52** N3
Allegheny Mountains 57, 79, 83;
 hiking trail 81
Allegheny NRA, Pa. **57** B6, C5
Allegheny River, N. Y.-Pa. 50,
 52 N3, **57** C8
Allentown, Pa. **57** G17
Alliance, Ohio **143** F13
Alligator River NWR, N. C. **91**
 D26
Altamaha River, Ga. **109** N14
Alton, Ill. **135** N4
Altoona, Pa. **57** H8
Alum Creek Lake, Ohio **143** J7
Amana, Iowa **165** G14
Amargosa Desert, Nev. **209** P8
Amarillo, Tex. 176, **191** C7
American Falls, Idaho **197** R9
American Falls Reservoir,
 Idaho **197** Q10
American Fork, Utah **213** G8
American Samoa 235, 244, 245,
 245; villager *246*
Americus, Ga. **109** M5
Ames, Iowa **165** F9
Amherst, Mass. **38** F7
Amidon, N. Dak. **149** K2
Amistad Reservoir, Tex. **191** M8
Ammonoosuc River, N. H. **31**
 J5
Amory, Miss. **101** E11
Amsterdam, N. Y. **53** K16
Anaconda, Mont. **201** H5
Anaheim, Calif. **231** Q11
Anaho Island NWR, Nev. **209**
 F2
Anahuac NWR, Tex. **191** M17
Anchorage, Alas. 234, 235, **237**
 L19
Anderson, Ind. **139** J9
Anderson, S. C. **113** D3

Andersonville, Ga. **109** L5
Androscoggin River,
 Me.-N. H. **31** F8, **35** P4
Ankeny NWR, Oreg. **227** F4
Ann Arbor, Mich. 130, **131** S14
Anna, Lake, Va. **83** F19
Annandale, Va. **83** C21
Annapolis, Md. 64, **65** G18, *67*
Annette Island IR, Alas. **237**
 Q27
Anniston, Ala. **105** F10
Antietam NB, Md. **65** C10
Apalachicola River, Fla. **121** B6
Apopka, Lake, Fla. **121** G14
Apostle Islands, Wis. **127** B6
Apostle Islands NL, Wis. **127** B6
Appalachian Mountains,
 Canada-U.S. 8, 50, 72, 79, 94,
 104, 105; balds **109**; gap *88*;
 maps 24-25, 50-51, 72-73, 95
Appalachian Trail 27, 31, 35, 38,
 43, 53, 57, 61, 65, 83, 83, 109
Appleton, Wis. **127** M12
Appomattox, Va. 82, **83** J16
Appomattox River, Va. **83** J18
Apra Harbor, Guam **245** R15
Aquifers 60, 160, 163, 168
Aransas NWR, Tex. **191** O14
Arapaho NWR, Colo. **217** B8
Arbuckle Mountains, Okla. **187**
 M18
Arches NP, Utah **213** M14, *215*
Arctic NWR, Alas. **237** D21
Arecibo Observatory, Puerto
 Rico **245** B10
Ardmore, Okla. **187** N19
Arecibo, Puerto Rico **245** B10
Arikaree River, Colo. **217** E16
Arizona 16, 178-181
Arizona-Sonora Desert
 Museum, Ariz. 179 Q10
Arkabutla Lake, Miss. **101** B6
Arkansas 96-99
Arkansas City, Kans. **169** K13
Arkansas River 96, **97**, 146,
 169, 187, 187, *188*, **217**
Arlington, Tex. **191** G14
Arlington, Va. **83** C21
Arlington Heights, Ill. **135** C10
Aroostook River, Me. **35** D11
Arrowwood NWR, N. Dak. **149**
 G14
Artesia, N. Mex. **183** O13
Arthur R. Marshall
 Loxahatchee NWR, Fla. **121**
 M18
Arvada, Colo. **217** E11
Asbury Park, N. J. 60, **61** K10,
 63
Asheville, N. C. 90 E6, *92*
Ashland, Ky. **75** C24
Ashtabula, Ohio **143** B14
Aspen, Colo. **217** G7
Assateague Island, Md.-Va. 64,
 65 O26
Assateague Island NS, Md.-Va.
 65 N26, **83** F27
Assawompset Pond, Mass. **39**
 L20
Astoria, Oreg. **227** A3
Atchafalaya Bay, La. **117** P10

Atchafalaya NWR, La. **117** L9
Atchison, Kans. **169** B18
Athens, Ga. **109** D8
Athens, Ohio **143** N10
Atlanta, Ga. 95, 108, **109** E5,
 110, 111
Atlantic City, N. J. *60*, **61** R8
Atlantic Coastal Plain 50, 68,
 72, 82, 91, 94, 112
Atoka, Okla. **187** M22
Atoka Reservoir, Okla. **187** M22
Attleboro, Mass. **39** K17
Attu Island, Alas. **236** K1
Attwater Prairie Chicken
 NWR, Tex. **191** M15
Atwood Lake, Ohio **143** H13
Au Sable River, Mich. **131** L14
Aua, American Samoa **245** R7
Auburn, Mass. **39** G13
Auburn, N. Y. **53** K9
Aucilla River, Fla. **121** C9
Audubon NWR, N. Dak. **149** F8
Augusta, Ga. **109** F12
Augusta, Kans. **169** H13
Augusta, Me. **35** P5
Aunuu, American Samoa **245**
 R11
Aurora, Colo. **217** F11
Aurora, Ill. **135** D9
Austin, Tex. 16, 190, **191** L13
Avery Island, La. 117, **117** N8,
 119
Aztec Ruins NM, N. Mex. **183** B4

Babylon, N. Y. **53** T19
Back Bay NWR, Va. **83** M25
Backbone Mountain, Md. **64** D1
Bad River, S. Dak. **157** G8
Bad River IR, Wis. **127** C6
Badlands, N. Dak. 148, **149** G2
Badlands, S. Dak. **157** H4, *158-
 159*
Badlands NP, S. Dak. **157** H4
Bagnell Dam, Mo. **173** J9
Baker, Oreg. **227** E15
Baker, Mount, Wash. **223** B7
Baker Island, Pacific Ocean 235
 244
Bakersfield, Calif. **231** O9
Bald Knob, W. Va. **79** L11;
 mine *80*
Baldy Mountain, Mont. **201** J5
Baldy Peak, Ariz. **179** L14
Baltimore, Md. 50, 51, 64, **65**
 D17
Bamberg, S. C. **113** K10
Bamforth NWR, Wyo. **205** N14
Bandelier NM, N. Mex. **183** E8
Bandon Marsh NWR, Oreg. **227**
 K1
Bangor, Me. **35** N9
Banks Lake, Wash. **223** E14
Banks Lake NWR, Ga. **109** Q9
Bantam Lake, Conn. **43** E5
Bar Harbor, Me. **35** P11
Baraboo, Wis. **127** P9
Barataria Bay, La. **117** P15
Bardstown, Ky. **75** G14
Barkhamsted Reservoir, Conn.
 43 B7

Barkley, Lake, Ky.-Tenn 74
 M7, **87** A8
Barnegat Bay, N. J. **61** N9, *63*
Barnstable, Mass. **39** M24
Barre, Vt. 26, **27** H7, *29*
Barren River, Ky. **75** L11
Barrigada, Guam **245** R18
Barrington, R. I. **47** G10
Barrow, Alas. **237** B18
Bartlesville, Okla. **187** C23
Baskett Slough NWR, Oreg.
 227 E4
Bastrop, La. **117** B8
Bath, Me. **35** R5
Baton Rouge, La. **117** L11
Batten Kill River, Vt. **27** R3
Battle Creek, Mich. **131** S11
Battle Mountain, Nev. **209** E7
Baxter SP, Me. 24
Bay City, Mich. **131** O14
Bay Head, N. J. 60, **61** L10
Bay Mills IR, Mich. **131** F13
Bayamón, Puerto Rico **245** B14
Bayonne, N. J. **61** G9
Bayou Bartholomew , Ark. **97**
 N11
Bayou D'Arbonne, La. **117** B5
Bayou Dorcheat, La. **117** B3
Bayou La Batre, Ala. **105** T2, *106*
Bayou Macon, La. **117** C9
Bayou Sauvage NWR, La. **117**
 M15
Beanblossom, Ind. **139** N7
Bear Butte NWR, S. Dak. **157**
 F2
Bear Lake NWR, Idaho **197** T12
Bear River, Idaho-Utah **205**
 N1, **213** E10
Bear River NWR, Utah **213** C6
Bear Valley NWR, Oreg. **227** O7
Beaufort, S. C. **113** O11
Beaumont, Tex. **191** L18
Beaver Island, Mich. **131** H10
Beaver Lake, Ark. **97** B3
Beaver River, Okla. **187** C10
Beaver River, Pa. **57** G2
Beaverton, Oreg. **227** D5
Becharof Lake, Alas. **237** N16
Beckley, W. Va. **79** O6
Bed Rock Lakes NWR, Mont.
 201 L7
Belle Fourche River, S. Dak.-
 Wyo. 157, **157** F3, **205** D15
Belleville, Ill. **135** O5
Bellevue, Nebr. **161** F18
Bellevue, Wash. **223** F6
Bellingham, Wash. **223** B6
Beloit, Wis. **127** S11
Bemidji, Minn. **153** F5
Bennington, Vt. **27** T3; clothing
 factory *26*
Benton Lake NWR, Mont. **201** D8
Berea, Ky. **75** H18
Bering Land Bridge National
 Preserve, Alas. **237** F14
Beringia 13
Berkeley, Calif. **231** J5
Berkeley Springs, W. Va. **79** E17
Berkshire Hills, Mass. **38** F4,
 39, *40*
Berlin, N. H. 30, **31** G8

Bessemer, Ala. **105** G7; welder *107*
Bethany Beach, Del. **69** S8
Bethel, Conn. **43** K3
Bethel Park, Pa. **57** J3
Bethesda, Md. **65** G14
Bethlehem, Pa. **57** G17
Bettendorf, Iowa **165** H17
Beverly, Mass. **38, 39** D20
Big Bay de Noc, Mich. **131** H7
Big Bend Dam, S. Dak.-Iowa **157** G11, **165** C1
Big Bend NP, Tex. **191** M5
Big Black River, Miss. **101** J6
Big Blue River, Nebr. **161** G15
Big Boggy NWR, Tex. **191** N16
Big Bone Lick SP, Ky. **75** B16
Big Cypress IR, Fla. **121** N16
Big Cypress NP, Fla. **121** P16
Big Eau Pleine Reservoir, Wis. **127** K8
Big Lake NWR, Ark. **97** D16
Big Lost River, Idaho **197** N7
Big Muddy River, Ill. **135** Q7
Big Sandy Creek, Colo. **217** H16
Big Sandy River, Ariz. **179** J4
Big Sandy River, Ky.-W. Va. **75** D24, 76, **79** M1
Big Sioux River, Iowa-S. Dak. **157** F17
Big South Fork National River and Recreation Area, Ky.-Tenn. **75** M17, **87** A18
Big Spring, Mo. *172*, **173** O14
Big Stone NWR, Minn. **153** O2
Big Sur, Calif. **231** M5
Bighorn Canyon NRA, Mont.-Wyo. **201** K12, **205** A8
Bighorn Lake, Mont. **201** K12
Bighorn Mountains, Wyo. **205** C10
Bighorn River, Mont.-Wyo. **201** J13, **205** D8
Billings, Mont. **201** H12
Biloxi, Miss. *100*, **101** S10
Binghamton, N. Y. *52*, **53** N11
Birds *64*, *82*, *87*, *108*, *109*; California condor *230*; ibises *122*; pelicans *114*, *151*; sandhill cranes *163*
Birmingham, Ala. *104*, **105** G7
Bisbee, Ariz. *178*, **179** T14
Biscayne NP, Fla. **121** P19
Bismarck, N. Dak. *146*, *148*, **149** J9
Bistineau, Lake, La. **117** C3
Bitter Creek NWR, Calif. **231** P9
Bitter Lake NWR, N. Mex. **183** M13
Bitterroot Range, Idaho-Mont. *197*, **197** K7, **201** G2
Bitterroot River, Mont. **201** G3
Black Canyon of the Gunnison NM, Colo. **217** J5
Black Coulee NWR, Mont. **201** B12
Black Hills, S. Dak.-Wyo. *146*, *156*, *157*, **157** G2, *195*, **205** C17
Black Lake, Mich. **131** J13
Black Mesa, Okla. **186** B1

Black Mountain, Ky. **75** L23
Black River, Ariz. **179** M13
Black River, Ark.-Mo. **97** D13, **173** O15
Black River, La. **117** G8
Black River, S. C. **113** H15
Black River, Wis. **127** M6
Black Warrior River, Ala. **105** K4
Blackbeard Island NWR, Ga. **109** O15
Blackfeet IR, Mont. **201** B5
Blackfoot, Idaho **197** Q10
Blackfoot Reservoir, Idaho **197** Q12
Blackstone River, R. I. *46*, **47** B7
Blackwater NWR, Md. **65** L20
Blanchard, N. Dak. **149** G18
Blanchard River, Ohio **143** F3
Block Island, R. I. **47**, **47** S5, *48*
Block Island NWR, R. I. **47** S5
Bloomfield, Conn. **43** D10
Bloomfield, N. J. **61** F9
Bloomington, Ill. **135** H7
Bloomington, Ind. **139** N6
Bloomington, Minn. **153** P9
Blowing Wind Cave NWR, Ala. **105** C9
Blue Mesa Reservoir, Colo. **217** K6
Blue Mountain, Ark. **97** J2
Blue Mountain, N. H. **31** E7
Blue Mountains, Oreg. *226*, **227** E14
Blue Ridge Mountains *72*, *80*, *82*, *83*, **83** F16, *91*, **91** B10, **109** B9, *108*, *112*
Blue Springs, Mo. **173** F4
Bluegrass region, Ky. *74*
Bluestone River, W. Va. **79** Q7
Boats and ships: dory *232*; paddle wheeler *103*; sailboats *48*; shrimp boats *106*; sightseeing boat *246*; steamboat (circa 1900) *108*
Boca Raton, Fla. **121** N18
Bogalusa, La. **117** J15
Bogue Chitto NWR, La.-Miss. **101** R7, **117** K15
Bois Blanc Island, Mich. **131** H12
Bois Brule River, Wis. **127** C4
Bois Forte IR, Minn. **153** D9
Boise, Idaho *196*, **197** O3, *198*
Boise River, Idaho **197** O2
Bombay Hook NWR, Del. **69** H5
Bomoseen, Lake, Vt. **27** N2
Bon Secour NWR, Ala. **105** T4
Bond Swamp NWR, Ga. **109** J7
Bonneville Dam, Oreg.-Wash. **223** N7, **227** C7
Bonneville Salt Flats, Utah *18*, **213** E2, *214*
Booneville, Miss. **101** B10
Boothbay Harbor, Me. **35** R6
Borah Peak, Idaho **197** N8
Borgne, Lake, La. **117** M16
Bosque del Apache NWR, N. Mex. **183** L6
Bossier City, La. **117** C2
Boston, Mass. *25*, *38*, **39** F19, *41*; office workers (1902) *38*
Boston Mountains, Ark. **97** E5

Boulder, Colo. **217** E10
Boundary Peak, Nev. **209** M4
Boundary Waters Canoe Area, Minn. *152*, **153** B3
Bow Lake, N. H. **31** Q8
Bowdoin NWR, Mont. **201** C13
Bowie, Md. **65** G16
Bowling Green, Ky. **75** L11
Bowling Green, Ohio **143** D5
Boyer River, Iowa **165** F4
Boysen Reservoir, Wyo. **205** G8
Bozeman, Mont. **201** J8
Bradford Mountain, Conn. **43** B4
Brandon, Miss. **101** L6
Brandywine Creek, Del.-Pa. *57* L16, *68*, **69** A4
Branson, Mo. **173** P7
Brasstown Bald, Ga. *109*, **109** A7
Brattleboro, Vt. **27** T6
Brazoria NWR, Tex. **191** M16
Brazos Peak, N. Mex. **183** B8
Brazos River, Tex. *177*, **191** F11
Breaks Interstate Park, Ky.-Va. **75** J25, **82** K5
Bremerton, Wash. **223** F5
Breton NWR, La. **117** O18
Breton Sound, La. **117** O17
Bridgeport, Conn. *42*, **43** M5
Bridges *66*, *133*, *134*, *222*, *232*
Bridgeville, Pa. **57** J2
Brigham City, Utah **213** C7
Brighton IR, Fla. **121** L16
Bristol, Conn. **43** F8
Bristol, R. I. **47** H10
Bristol, Tenn.-Va. **82** N5, **87** A25
Broad River, S. C. **113** D8
Brockton, Mass. **39** H19
Broken Bow Lake, Okla. **187** N27
Bromley Mountain, Vt. **27** Q4
Brookhaven, Miss. **101** O5
Brookline, Mass. **39** F18
Brooks Range, Alas. *8*, *235*, *236*, **237** D18
Brookville Lake, Ind. **139** M11
Browns Park NWR, Colo. **217** A2
Brownsville, Tex. **191** S13
Brule River, Wis. **127** E12, **131** G4
Bryan, Tex. **191** K15
Bryce Canyon NP, Utah **213** Q7
Buck Island Reef NM, U. S. Virgin Islands **245** G5
Buenos Aires NWR, Ariz. **179** S9
Buffalo, N. Y. *50*, *52*, **52** K2
Buffalo Lake NWR, Tex. **191** C7
Buffalo River, Tenn. **87** E8
Buggs Island Lake, Va. **83** N17
Bull Shoals Lake, Mo. **173** Q9
Bulls Bay, S. C. **113** L16
Burley, Idaho **197** R8
Burlington, Iowa **165** L16
Burlington, N. C. **91** C15
Burlington, Vt. **27** F3
Burns Paiute Colony IR, Oreg. **227** J13
Burt Lake, Mich. **131** J12
Butte, Mont. *200*, **201** H6, *203*
Butterfield Overland Mail **173,**

179, *183*, *187*, *191*, *231*
Buzzards Bay, Mass. **39** O21

Cabeza Prieta NWR, Ariz. **179** Q5
Cabin Creek, W. Va. **79** M5
Cabo Rojo NWR, Puerto Rico **245** E7
Cabot, Mount, N. H. **31** G7
Cabrillo NM, Calif. **231** U13
Cache Creek, Okla. **187** M15
Cache la Poudre River, Colo. **217** B10
Cache River NWR, Ark. **97** G12
Caddo Lake, La. **117** B1
Cadillac, Mich. **131** M10
Cadillac Mountain, Me. **35** P11
Caguas, Puerto Rico **245** C15
Cahaba River, Ala. **105** J6
Caillou Bay, La. **117** Q11
Cairo, Ill. *134*, **135** T7, *136*
Calamus River, Nebr. **161** C10
Calcasieu Lake, La. **117** N3
Calcasieu River, La. **117** L4
Calhoun, Ga. **109** B3
California *16*, *16-17*, *230-233*
California Aqueduct, Calif. **231** O8
California Trail **197**, **209**, **213**, **231**
Caloosahatchee NWR, Fla. **121** M14
Calumet City, Ill. **135** D11
Camas NWR, Idaho **197** N10
Cambridge, Md. **65** K20
Cambridge, Mass. *38*, **39** F18
Camden, Me. **35** P8
Cameron, La. **117** N3
Cameron Prairie NWR, La. **117** N4
Camp David, Md. **65** B12
Camp Verde IR, Ariz. **179** J9
Canaan, Conn. **43** A4
Canaan Valley, W. Va. **79** H12
Canadian River *176-177*, **183** F13, **187** H16, **191** B9
Canaveral NS, Fla. **121** F17
Candlewood Lake, Conn. **43** J3
Cannonball River, N. Dak. **149** K4
Canoncito IR, N. Mex. **183** G6
Canterbury, N. H. *30*, **31** P6; Shaker dwelling *33*
Canton, Ohio **143** G12
Canyon, Tex. **191** C7
Canyon de Chelly NM, Ariz. *178*, **179** D15
Canyon Ferry Lake, Mont. **201** G7
Canyonlands NP, Utah **213** O13
Cape Ann, Mass. **39** B22
Cape Canaveral, Fla. *120*, **121** G17
Cape Cod, Mass. *24*, *25*, *38*, *39*, **39** M26, *41*
Cape Elizabeth, Me. **35** S4
Cape Fear, N. C. *90*, **91** L20
Cape Fear River, N. C. **91** H17
Cape Flattery, Wash. **223** C1
Cape Girardeau, Mo. **173** N18
Cape Hatteras, N. C. *90*, **91** F27; lighthouse *92*
Cape Henlopen, Del. **69** O8

Cape Henry, Va. **83** L25
Cape Lookout, N. C. *90*, **91** J24
Cape Lookout NS, N. C. **91** H25
Cape May, N. J. *60*, **61** U5
Cape Meares NWR, Oreg. **227** C3
Cape Romain NWR, S. C. **113** L16
Cape Romano, Fla. **121** O15
Cape Sable, Fla. **121** Q16
Cape San Blas, Fla. **121** D6
Capital Hill, Northern Mariana Islands **245** H19
Capitol Reef NP, Utah **213** P9
Captain Cook, Hawaii **241** N21
Capulin Volcano NM, N. Mex. **183** B13
Caribou, Me. **35** C11
Carlin, Nev. **209** E9
Carlisle, Pa. **57** J11
Carlsbad, N. Mex. **183** P13
Carlsbad Caverns NP, N. Mex. *176*, **183** Q12, *184*
Carneiro, Kans. **169** E11
Carolina, Puerto Rico **245** B15
Carolina Sandhills NWR, S. C. **113** C13
Carson City, Nev. *194*, *208*, **209** H1
Carson River, Nev. **209** H3
Carters Lake, Ga. **109** B4
Carthage, Miss. **101** J7
Carthage, Mo. **173** N4
Casa Grande NM, Ariz. **179** O9
Cascade, Idaho **197** M3
Cascade Range, Oreg.-Wash. *8*, *220*, *221*, *222*, *223* F9, *227* G6; waterfall *228*
Cascade Reservoir, Idaho **197** M4
Casper, Wyo. **205** H12
Cass Lake, Minn. **153** F6
Cass River, Mich. **131** O16
Castillo De San Marcos NM, Fla. **121** C15
Castle Rock Lake, Wis. **127** N8
Cataholua NWR, La. **117** F8
Cataño, Puerto Rico **245** B14
Cataract Lake, Ind. **139** M5
Catawba River, S. C. **113** B10
Catoctin Mountain Park, Md. **65** B12
Catskill Mountains, N. Y. **53** O14
Cattaraugus IR, N. Y. **52** L2
Cave Run Lake, Ky. **75** F21
Caves *74*, *77*, *184*
Cayey, Puerto Rico **245** D14
Cecil M. Harden Lake, Ind. **139** L4
Cedar Bluff Reservoir, Kans. **169** E6
Cedar Breaks NM, Utah **213** Q5
Cedar Creek, N. Dak. **149** M5
Cedar Falls, Iowa **165** D12
Cedar Island NWR, N. C. **91** G24
Cedar Keys NWR, Fla. **121** F11
Cedar Point NWR, Ohio **143** C6
Cedar Rapids, Iowa *164*, **165** F14; motorcyclist (early 1900s) *164*
Cedar River, Iowa **165** G15
Cedartown, Ga. **109** D2

Celina, Ohio **143** H2
Center Hill Lake, Tenn. **87** C14
Central City, Colo. **217** E10
Central Falls, R. I. **47** C8
Central Valley, Calif. 230
Centralia, Ill. **135** O7
Centralia, Wash. **223** J4
Cerro de Punta, Puerto Rico
 245 D11
Chaco River, N. Mex. **183** D3
Chalan Kanoa, Northern
 Mariana Islands **245** J18
Chalmette, La. **117** N15
Chamberlain Lake, Me. **35** F7
Chambersburg, Pa. **57** K10
Champaign, Ill. **135** J9
Champlain, Lake, Canada-
 U. S. 24, **24**, 26, 27 E2, **53** B18
Chandeleur Sound, La. **117** N18
Chandler, Ariz. **179** N9
Channel Islands, Calif. 221,
 221, **231** T10
Channel Islands NP, Calif. **231**
 R8
Chapel Hill, N. C. **91** D16
Chappaquiddick Island, Mass.
 39 Q23
Chargoggagoggmanchauga-
 goggchaubunagungamaug,
 Lake (Lake Webster), Mass.
 39 J13
Chariton River, Mo. **173** D9
Charles M. Russell NWR,
 Mont. **201** D13
Charles Mound, Ill. **135** A4
Charles River, Mass. **39** H16
Charles Town, W. Va. **79** G19
Charleston, S. C. *112*, **113** M14,
 114-115
Charleston, W. Va. 78, **79** M5
Charlestown, R. I. **47** O4
Charlotte, N. C. **91** F11
Charlotte Amalie, U. S. Virgin
 Islands **245** B2
Charlotte Harbor, Fla. **121** M13
Charlottesville, Va. **83** G17
Chase Lake NWR, N. Dak. **149**
 H12
Chassahowitzka NWR, Fla. **121**
 G12
Chatsworth, N. J. **61** N7
Chattahoochee River, Ala.-Ga.
 105 Q13, **109** D6-R3
Chattahoochee River NRA, Ga.
 109 D5
Chattanooga, Tenn. 86, **87** G16;
 hosiery mill (1940s) *86*
Chattooga River, Ga.-N. C.-S.
 C. **113** C1
Chautauqua Lake, N. Y. **52** N1
Chautauqua NWR, Ill. **135** H5
Cheaha Mountain, Ala. **105** G10
Cheat River, W. Va. **79** F12
Chehalis IR, Wash. **223** J4
Chelan, Lake, Wash. **223** D11
Chelsea, Mass. **39** E19
Chemehuevi IR, Calif. **231** P17
Cheney Reservoir, Kans. **169** H11
Cherokee IR, N. C. **90** E3
Cherokee Lake, Tenn. **87** B22
Chesapeake, Va. **83** L24

Chesapeake and Delaware
 Canal, Del.-Md. **65** C22, **69** D3
Chesapeake and Ohio Canal
 NHP, Md. **65** E12
Chesapeake Bay, Md.-Va. **51**,
 56, 64, 65, **65** J19, 73, **83** H24;
 bridge *66*; fishermen *84*
Chester, Conn. **43** J12
Chester, Pa. **57** L17
Chester River, Md. **65** E22
Chesterfield, S. C. **113** C13
Chestertown, Md. **65** E21
Chesuncook Lake, Me. **35** G7
Cheyenne, Wyo. **195**, **204**, **205**
 O16
Cheyenne River, S. Dak. 157,
 157 E6
Cheyenne River IR, S. Dak.
 157 D7
Chicago, Ill. **124**, 125, 126, 134,
 135 C11, *136*; bridges (1933)
 134; factory *137*
Chicago Heights, Ill. **135** E11
Chickamauga, Ga. **109** A2
Chickamauga Lake, Tenn. **87**
 F17
Chickasaw NRA, Okla. **187** M19
Chickasaw NWR, Tenn. **86** D2
Chickasawhay River, Miss. **101**
 P11
Chicopee, Mass. **38** H7
Chicot, Lake, Ark. **97** P12
Chillicothe, Ohio **143** N7
Chimney Rock, Nebr. **161** D2,
 163
Chincoteague NWR, Md.-Va.
 65 P26, **83** F27
Chinle Wash, Ariz. 178, **179** B14
Chippewa, Lake, Wis. **127** E5
Chippewa Falls, Wis. **127** J4
Chiricahua NM, Ariz. **179** R15
Chisos Mountains, Tex. **191** M5,
 192
Chitimacha IR, La. **117** N10
Chocorua, Mount, N. H. **31** L8
Choctaw NWR, Ala. **105** N2
Choctawhatchee River, Fla.
 121 B5
Choptank River, Md. **65** G22
Christiansted, U. S. Virgin
 Islands **245** H4
Chugach Mountains, Alas. **237**
 L20
Chula Vista, Calif. **231** U13
Churchill Lake, Me. **35** E6
Cibola NWR, Ariz. **179** N1
Cicero, Ill. **135** D10
Cimarron Cutoff, Kans. **169** H3
Cimarron Cutoff, Santa Fe
 Trail, N. Mex.-Okla. **183** C14,
 186 B2, 187
Cimarron River, Kans.-Okla.
 169 K4, **187** E16
Cincinnati, Ohio **124**, 142, **143**
 O2, *145*
Cinnabar Mountain, Idaho **197**
 Q2
Circle, Alas. **237** G21
City of Rocks NR, Idaho **197** T8
Clarence Cannon NWR, Mo.
 173 E14

Clark Fork, Mont. **201** E3
Clarksburg, W. Va. **79** G9
Clarksdale, Miss. **101** D4
Clarksville, Tenn. **87** A9
Clear Lake, Calif. **231** G4
Clear Lake, Iowa **165** B9
Clear Lake NWR, Calif. **231** A6
Clearwater, Fla. **121** J12
Clearwater Lake, Mo. **173** N15
Clearwater Mountains, Idaho
 197 H4
Clearwater River, Idaho **197** G2
Clemson, S. C. **113** C3
Clermont, Fla. **121** G14, *122*
Cleveland, Ohio 125, **125**, **143**
 D11, *144*
Cleveland, Tenn. **87** G17
Cleveland Heights, Ohio **143** D12
Clifton, N. J. **61** E9
Clinch River, Tenn.-Va. **82** M4,
 87 A22
Clingmans Dome, Tenn. **87** E21
Clinton, Iowa **165** G18
Clinton, Miss. **101** L5
Cloud Peak, Wyo. **205** C10
Clovis, N. Mex. 183, **183** J15
Cocoa Beach, Fla. **121** H17
Cochiti IR, N. Mex. **183** E8
Cocopah IR, Ariz. **179** P1
Cody, Wyo. **205** C6
Coeur d'Alene, Idaho **197** D2
Coeur d'Alene IR, Idaho **197** E2
Coffeyville, Kans. **169** K17
Cohansey Aquifer, N. J. 60
Cold Springs NWR, Oreg. **227**
 B13
Coldwater River, Miss. **101** A6
Colfax, Wash. **223** J18
College Park, Md. **65** G15
Colorado 9, 216-219
Colorado NM, Colo. **217** H2
Colorado Plateau **176**, 182, 212,
 216
Colorado River 8, 10, **79**, **176**,
 178, **179**, **191**, **195**, **209**, **213**,
 216, **217**, **221**, **231**; dams 178,
 208, 212
Colorado River Aqueduct,
 Calif. **231** R16
Colorado River IR, Ariz.-Calif.
 179 L2, **231** R17
Colorado Springs, Colo. 216,
 217 H12, *218*
Columbia, Md. **65** E16
Columbia, Miss. **101** P7
Columbia, Mo. **173** G10
Columbia, S. C. 112, **113** F10
Columbia NWR, Wash. **223** J13
Columbia River, Canada-
 U. S. **220**, 222, **223** B17-L2,
 223, *224*, 226, **227** A2-B13
Columbus, Ga. **109** K3
Columbus, Ind. **139** N8
Columbus, Miss. **101** F11
Columbus, Nebr. **161** E15
Columbus, Ohio **143** L7
Colville IR, Wash. **223** D14
Colville River, Alas. **237** D18

Combahee River, S. C. **113** N11
Conanicut Island, R. I. **47** L8
Conboy Lake NWR, Wash. **223**
 M8
Concord, Mass. **39** E16
Concord, N. H. **31** Q7; bicycle
 parade (1896) *30*
Concord, N. C. **91** E11
Conecuh River, Ala. **105** O9
Conemaugh River, Pa. **57** H5
Congaree Swamp NM, S. C.
 113 G11
Connecticut 42-45
Connecticut River 24, **24-25**, 26,
 27, 30, 31, 38, **38**, 39, 42, 43,
 43; oystering *44*
Connersville, Ind. **139** L11
Continental Divide 200, 201,
 183, **201**, *202-203*, 204, 205,
 205, **216**, **217**, **237**
Continental Divide Trail 201,
 201, **205**, **217**
Conway, Lake, Ark. **97** H9
Cook Inlet, Alas. **237** M17
Cooper River, S. C. **113** K14
Cooperstown, N. Y. **53** L14
Coos, Lower Umpqua, and
 Suislaw IR, Oreg. **227** K2
Coosa River, Ala.-Ga. **105** H8,
 109 C2
Copalis NWR, Wash. **223** G1
Copper Harbor, Mich. **131** C5
Copper River, Alas. **237** L21
Coralville Lake, Iowa **165** G14
Cordillera Central, Puerto Rico
 245 D11
Corinth, Miss. **101** A11
Corning, N. Y. **53** N7
Corpus Christi, Tex. **191** P13
Corvallis, Oreg. **227** F4
Coshocton, Ohio **143** J11
Coulee Dam NRA, Wash. **223**
 D16
Council Bluffs, Iowa **165** J3
Coventry, Conn. **43** D13; herb
 farm *45*
Covington, Ky. **75** A17
Cow Creek of Umpqua IR,
 Oreg. **227** L4
Cowboys *192-193*, *204*, *207*;
 cattle drive *202*
Cowlitz River, Wash. **223** K7
Crab Orchard NWR, Ill. **135** R7
Cranberry Isles, Me. **35** Q10
Crane Prairie Reservoir, Oreg.
 227 J7
Cranston, R. I. **47** F7
Crater Lake, Oreg. 227, **227** L6
Crater Lake NP, Oreg. **227** L6
Crater of Diamonds SP, Ark. **97**
 M4
Craters of the Moon NM, Idaho
 196, **197** P8
Crawfordsville, Ind. **139** J5
Creedman Coulee NWR, Mont.
 201 A10
Crescent Lake NWR, Nebr.
 161 D4
Cripple Creek, Colo. **217** J11
Crisfield, Md. **65** P22
Crocodile Lake NWR, Fla. **121**

Q18
Crops: corn 125, 134, *136*, 146,
 160, *166-167*; cotton 86, *89*,
 96, 104, 112, lettuce *233*;
 marijuana 74, 86, 230; milo
 188-189; peanuts 104, 108,
 111; peppers *119*, *185*;
 pineapples *243*; potatoes 34,
 36, 196, *199*; rice 96, *99*, 116;
 soybeans 125; sugarcane *240*,
 241; sunflowers 148, *151*;
 tobacco 64, 90, 112, *115*,
 auction *93*; tulips *224*;
 vegetables *62*, 120, 230, 233;
 wheat 146, 148, 162, 168, 200,
 harvest *203*; wildflowers *192*;
 see also Fruit growing
Cross Creeks NWR, Tenn. **87** B8
Cross Island NWR, Me. **35** O13
Crow Creek IR, S. Dak. **157**
 G11
Crow IR, Mont. **201** K13
Crow Wing River, Minn. **153** J6
Crown Mountain, U. S. Virgin
 Islands **245** B2
Crystal Springs, Miss. **101** M5
Culebra, Puerto Rico **245** C19
Culebra NWR, Puerto Rico **245**
 B20
Cumberland, Md. **64** A5
Cumberland, Lake, Ky. **75** L16
Cumberland Falls, Ky. **75**
Cumberland Gap, Ky.-Tenn.-
 Va. 74, **75** M21, **82** M1, **87**
 A21, *88*
Cumberland Island NS, Ga. **109**
 Q15
Cumberland Mountain, Ky. **75**
 M21
Cumberland Plateau, Ky.-
 Tenn. 74, **75** J21, **87** E16
Cumberland River, Ky.-Tenn.
 74 K5, **75** M14-K24, **87** B14
Curecanti NRA, Colo. **271** K6
Current River, Mo. *172*, **173** M2
Currituck NWR, N. C. **91** A26
Custer, S. Dak. **157** H2
Custer Battlefield NM, Mont.
 201 J14
Cut Bank, Mont. **201** B6
Cuyahoga Falls, Ohio **143** E12
Cuyahoga River, Ohio **143** E12
Cuyahoga Valley NRA, Ohio
 143 E12
Cypress Creek NWR, Ill. **135** S7
Cypress Swamp, Del. 68, **69** S6

Dahlonega, Ga. **109** B6
Dairy farming 125, 126, *128*
Dale Hollow Lake, Ky.-Tenn.
 75 M15, **87** A16
Dallas, Tex. *10-11*, **177**, 190, **191**
 G14, *193*
The Dalles Dam, Oreg.-Wash.
 223 N9, **227** C9
Dalton, Ga. **109** A3
Dalton, Mass. **38** E3
Dams 72, 87, 148, 200, 208, 222;
 hydroelectricity 178, 182, 222
Danbury, Conn. **43** J3

Danby, Vt. 27 P4
Danville, Ill. 135 J11
Danville, Kans. 169 K11, *170*
Danville, Ky. 75 H17, *76*
Danville, Va. 83 N14
D'Arbonne NWR, La. 117 B7
Dardanelle, Lake, Ark. 97 F5
Darien, Conn. 43 N3
Dauphin Island, Ala. 105 U2
Davenport, Iowa 165 H17
Davenport, Wash. 223 F16
Davis, Mount, Pa. 57 L5
Dawson, Ga. 109 N5
Dayton, Ohio 143 M3
Daytona Beach, Fla. 121 E16
De Gray Lake, Ark. 97 L6
De Kalb, Ill. 135 C8
Deadwood, S. Dak. 157 F1;
   saloon *159*
Dearborn, Mich. 131 S15;
   automobile museum *132*
Dearborn Heights, Mich. 131 S15
Death Valley NM, Calif.-Nev.
   209 O7, 230, 231 M12, *233*
Decatur, Ga. 109 E5
Decatur, Ill. 135 K7
Dedham, Mass. 39 G18
Deep Creek Lake, Md. 64 B2
Deep Creek Range, Utah 213 J2
Deer Creek IR, Minn. 153 E9
Deer Flat NWR, Idaho-Oreg.
   197 P2, 227 H17
Deer Isle, Me. 35 Q9
Deer Park, N. Y. 53 T19
Deerfield, Mass. 38 D7
Defiance, Ohio 143 E2
Delaware 68-71
Delaware, Ohio 143 J7
Delaware and Raritan Canal,
   N. J. 61 J6
Delaware Bay, Del.-N. J. 61
   T4, 69 J6
Delaware Lake, Ohio 143 J7
Delaware River 50, 51, 53, 56,
   57, 60, 61, 68, 69
Delaware Water Gap NRA,
   N. J.-Pa. 57 E18, 60, 61 C5
Delevan NWR, Calif. 231 G4
Delmarva Peninsula, Del.-Md.-
   Va. 64, 65 N24, 68, 69 M4, 73,
   82, 83, 83 G26
Delray Beach, Fla. 121 N19
Delta NWR, La. 117 P18
Demopolis, Ala. 105 L4
Denali NP and Preserve, Alas.
   237 J19
Denison, Iowa 165 F4
Denton, Tex. 191 F13
Denver, Colo. 195, 216, 217
   F11, *219*
Derby, Conn. 43 K6
Des Lacs NWR, N. Dak. 149 B6
Des Moines, Iowa 164, 165 H9,
   166; state fair *167*
Des Moines River, Iowa 165
   L13
Des Plaines, Ill. 135 C10
Deschutes River, Oreg. 227 E9
Desert NWR, Nev. 209 P10
Deserts 178, 230
Desoto NWR, Iowa-Nebr. 161

E17, 165 H2
Detroit, Mich. 125, 125, 130,
   131 S16, *132*
Detroit Lakes, Minn. 153 J3
Detroit River, Mich. 131 T16
Devils Lake IR, N. Dak. 149
   E14
Devils Postpile NM, Calif. 231
   K9
Devils Tower NW, Wyo. 205 B16
Dewey Beach, Del. 69 Q8
Diamond Head, Hawaii 241
   F11, *243*
D'Iberville, Miss. 101 S10
Dickson Mounds, Ill. 135 H5
Dillon, Mont. 201 K6
Dillon Lake, Ohio 143 K10
Dillon Reservoir, Colo. 217 F9
Dinosaur NM, Colo.-Utah 213
   F15, 217 B2
Dinosaur SP, Conn. 43 F10
Dirty Devil River, Utah 213 O11
District of Columbia *see*
   Washington, D. C.
Dixville Notch, N. H. 31 D8
Dodge City, Kans. 169 H6
Dolores River, Colo. 217 L1
Donner Pass, Calif. 231 F7
Door Peninsula, Wis. 127 J15;
   fish boil *128-129*
Dothan, Ala. 105 Q12; factory
   107
Douglas Lake, Tenn. 87, 87 C22
Dover, Del. 69 J4
Dover, N. H. 31 Q10
Downers Grove, Ill. 135 D10
Drift Prairie, N. Dak. 148
Driftless Area NWR, Iowa 165
   C15
Driskill Mountain, La. 117 C4
Dry Tortugas, Fla. 121 S12
Du Bay, Lake, Wis. 127 K9
Du Quoin, Ill. 135 Q7
Dubuque, Iowa 165 D17
Duck River, Tenn. 87 D9
Duck Valley IR, Idaho-Nev.
   197 T3, 209 A8
Duckwater IR, Nev. 209 J9
Duluth, Minn. 147, 152, 153 J12
Dummerston Center, Vt. 27 S6;
   apple pies *29*
Dungeness NWR, Wash. 223 D4
Durango, Colo. 217 O4
Durham, N. C. 91 C16; hospital
   technician *92*
Dust Bowl era 186, *186*, 188
Dworshak Reservoir, Idaho 197
   F3

E
Eagle, Alas. 237 H22
Eagle Mountain, Minn. 153 E15
Earthquakes 220, 230, 231, 234
East Chicago, Ind. 139 B3
East Cleveland, Ohio 143 C12
East Cote Blanche Bay, La. 117
   O9
East Detroit, Mich. 131 S16
East Fork White River, Ind.
   139 P7
East Hartford, Conn. 43 E10

East Lansing, Mich. 131 R13
East Lyme, Conn. 43 J14
East Orange, N. J. 61 F9
East Point, Ga. 109 E5
East Ridge, Tenn. 87 G16
East St. Louis, Ill. 135 O4
Eastern Neck NWR, Md. 65 G22
Eastern Shore, Md.-Va. 64, 65
   H21, 66, 82
Eastern Shore of Virginia
   NWR, Va. 83 K25
Easton, Md. 65 J22
Easton, Pa. 57 G18
Eastport, Me. 35 M15
Eau Claire, Wis. 127 K4
Eau Claire River, Wis. 127 J10
Edgartown, Mass. 39 P23
Edisto River, S. C. 113 K11
Edmonds, Wash. 223 E6
Edwards Plateau, Tex. 191 K8
Edwin B. Forsythe NWR
   (Barnegat), N. J. 60, 61 O9
Edwin B. Forsythe NWR
   (Brigantine), N. J. 60, 61 Q8
Eel River, Calif. 231 D2
Eel River, Ind. 139 L4
Effigy Mounds NM, Iowa 165
   B15
Egmont Key NWR, Fla. 121 K12
El Cajon, Calif. 231 T13
El Centro, Calif. 231 T15
El Dorado, Ark. 97 Q7
El Morro (fortress), San Juan,
   Puerto Rico *246-247*
El Morro NM, N. Mex. 183 G3
El Paso, Tex. 191 H1
El Vado Reservoir, N. Mex.
   183 B7
Elbert, Mount, Colo. 217 H8
Elberton, Ga. 109 D10, *111*
Elephant Butte Reservoir, N.
   Mex. 183 M6
Eleven Point River, Mo. 173 O12
Elgin, Ill. 135 C9
Elizabeth, N. J. 61 G9, *63*
Elizabeth City, N. C. 91 B25
Elizabeth Islands, Mass. 39 P21
Elizabethton, Tenn. 87 B25
Elk River, Kans. 169 J16
Elk River, Tenn. 87 G11
Elk River, W. Va. 79 K7
Elkhart, Ind. 139 B8; factory *140*
Elkhorn River, Nebr. 161 C13
Elko, Nev. 209 D9
Ellis Island, N. Y. 52, 53
Elmhurst, Ill. 135 C10
Elmira, N. Y. 53 N8
Elwell, Lake, Mont. 201 C8
Ely, Minn. 153 E12
Elyria, Ohio 143 D10
Emporia, Kans. 169 F15
Enfield, Conn. 43 B11
Enid, Okla. 187 E17
Enka, N. C. 90 E5
Enterprise, Ala. 104, 105 P10
Equinox Mountain, Vt. 27 Q3
Erie, Pa. 56, 57 A3
Erie, Lake, Canada-U. S. 50,
   52, 56, 57, 125, 131, 142, 143
Erie Canal, N. Y. 53, 53 J7, 134
Erie NWR, Pa. 57 C3

Erling, Lake, Ark. 97 Q4
Escalante River, Utah 213 Q9
Escanaba, Mich. 131 H7
Escanaba River, Mich. 131 G6
Essex, Md. 65 D18
Eskimos 236, *238*
Euclid, Ohio 143 C12
Eufaula, Okla. 187 J24
Eufaula NWR, Ala.-Ga. 105
   N13, 109 M3
Eugene, Oreg. 226, 227 H4
Eureka, Calif. 231 C1
Eureka, Mont. 201 B2
Eureka Springs, Ark. 97 B4
Evans, Mount, Colo. 217 F10
Evanston, Ill. 135 C11
Evansville, Ind. 139 T2
Everett, Wash. 223 E6; aircraft
   assembly *225*
Everett, Mount, Mass. 38 J1
Everglades (region), Fla. 94,
   95, 120, *122*
Everglades NP, Fla. 120, 121
   P16

F
Fairbanks, Alas. 236, 237 H20
Fairfax, Va. 83 C20
Fairfield, Conn. 43 N5
Falcon Reservoir, Tex. 191 Q11
Fall River, Kans. 169 J16
Fall River, Mass. 39 M18
Fallon IR, Nev. 209 H4
Falmouth, Me. 35 R4
Falmouth, Mass. 39 O22
Fargo, N. Dak. 149 J19
Faribault, Minn. 153 R9
Farm machinery 134, 146;
   combines *103*, *203*; steam
   thresher (1930s) *168*
Farmington, Conn. 43 E9
Farmington, N. Mex. 183 B3
Fayetteville, Ark. 97 C2;
   superconductor experiment *98*
Fayetteville, N. C. 91 G17
Feather River, Calif. 231 F5
Featherstone NWR, Va. 83 D20
Felsenthal NWR, Ark. 97 Q9
Fergus Falls, Minn. 153 K3
Ferguson, Mo. 173 G16
Fern Cave NWR, Ala. 105 B9
Fern Ridge Lake, Oreg. 227 H4
Ferndale, Wash. 223 B6
Findlay, Ohio 143 F5
Finger Lakes, N. Y. 52, 53 L8
Fire Island NS, N. Y. 53 T20
First Connecticut Lake, N. H.
   31 B8
Fish Creek, Wis. 127 H16, *128-
   129*
Fish Springs NWR, Utah 213 J4
Fisherman Island NWR, Va. 83
   K25
Fishing industry *41*, *84*; catfish
   100; crawfish 116; rockfish
   232; salmon 236; seafood 64,
   65, 116, Alaska king crab *238*,
   clams *66*, *71*, lobsters 34, *36*,
   oysters *44*, shrimp *115*
Fitchburg, Mass. 39 C13
Flagstaff, Ariz. 179 G9

Flagstaff Lake, Me. 35 L4;
   logging camp *34*
Flambeau River, Wis. 127 G5
Flaming Gorge NRA, Utah-
   Wyo. 205 O4, 213 E13
Flaming Gorge Reservoir,
   Utah-Wyo. 205 O4, 213 E14
Flandreau IR, S. Dak. 157 G18
Flathead IR, Mont. 201 E3
Flathead Lake, Mont. 201 D3
Flathead River, Mont. 201 C3
Flint, Mich. 131 Q14
Flint Hills, Kans. 168, 169 H15
Flint Hills NWR, Kans. 169 F16
Flint River, Ga. 109 P5
Flint River, Mich. 131 P15
Florence, Ala. 105 B4
Florence, Ky. 75 A17
Florence, S. C. 113 E14
Florida 16, 94, 120-123
Florida, Straits of, Fla. 121 S18
Florida Bay, Fla. 121 R17
Florida Keys, Fla. 95, 120, 121,
   121 R17
Florida Panther NWR, Fla. 121
   N15
Florissant, Mo. 173 G16
Florissant Fossil Beds NM,
   Colo. 217 H11
Fond du Lac, Wis. 127 O12
Fond du Lac IR, Minn. 153 J10
Fontana Lake, N. C. 90 E2
Foraker, Mount, Alas. 237 J18
Forest products 26, 30, 34, 96,
   104, 226; furniture 90, *93*
Fort Apache IR, Ariz. 179 L13
Fort Belknap IR, Mont. 201 C12
Fort Benton, Mont. 201 D9
Fort Berthold IR, N. Dak. 149
   F5
Fort Bidwell IR, Calif. 231 A8
Fort Cobb Reservoir, Okla. 187
   J15
Fort Collins, Colo. 217 C11
Fort Dodge, Iowa 165 E7
Fort Frederica NM, Ga. 109 P15
Fort Gibson Lake, Okla. 187 F25
Fort Hall IR, Idaho 197 Q11
Fort Jefferson NM, Fla. 121 S12
Fort Knox, Ky. 75 G12
Fort Lauderdale, Fla. 121 N18
Fort McDermitt IR, Nev.-
   Oreg. 209 A6, 227 O16
Fort McDowell IR, Ariz. 179 M9
Fort Madison, Iowa 165 L15
Fort Matanzas NM, Fla. 121 D15
Fort Mojave IR, Ariz.-Calif.
   179 H2, 231 P16
Fort Morgan, Colo. 217 D14
Fort Peck Dam, Mont. 200, 201
   C15
Fort Peck IR, Mont. 201 C16
Fort Pierce, Fla. 121 K18
Fort Pulaski NM, Ga. 109 L16
Fort Randall Dam, S. Dak. 157
   K13
Fort Scott, Kans. 169 H19
Fort Smith, Ark. 97 F1
Fort Sumter NM, S. C. 113 M14
Fort Union NM, N. Mex. 183
   E11

Fort Wayne, Ind. **139** E11
Fort Worth, Tex. 190, **191** G13
Fort Yates, N. Dak. **149** M9
Fort Yuma IR, Calif. **231** U17
Foss Reservoir, Okla. **187** H12
Fossils *158*, 161, 169, *202, 203*
Four Corners, Utah **213** T15
Fox River, Ill.-Wis. **135** E8
Fox River NWR, Wis. **127** O10
Framingham, Mass. **39** G16
Francis, Lake, N. H. **31** C8
Francis Case, Lake, S. Dak. **157** J12
Francs Peak, Wyo. **205** E5
Frankfort, Ind. **139** H6
Frankfort, Ky. **75** E16
Franklin, Ind. **139** M7
Franklin, Ky. **75** M10
Franklin, Tenn. **87** D11
Franklin Delano Roosevelt Lake, Wash. 222, **223** D16
Franklin Island NWR, Me. **35** R7
Franz Lake NWR, Wash. **223** N6
Frederick, Md. **65** C12
Fredericksburg, Tex. 190, **191** L11
Fredericksburg, Va. **83** E20
Frederiksted, American Samoa **245** H3
Freeman, Lake, Ind. **139** F5
Freeport, Ill. **135** B6
Freeport, Me. **35** R4
Fremont, Mich. **131** P9
Fremont, Nebr. 160, **161** E16
Fremont, Ohio **143** D7
Fremont River, Utah **213** O9
French Broad River, N. C. **90** F5
Frenchman Bay, Me. **35** O11
Fresno, Calif. **231** M8
Frissell, Mount, Conn. **43** A3
Front Royal, Va. **83** C17
Fruit growing 52, *55*, 125, 230; blueberries 34; cranberries 38, *40*; grapes 222, *229*; oranges 120, *122*; peaches 114, *114*
Fulton, Mo. **173** G11

Gadsden, Ala. **105** E10
Gaffney, S. C. **113** A7
Gaillard, Lake, Conn. **43** K9
Gainesville, Fla. **121** D13
Gainesville, Ga. **109** C7
Galesburg, Ill. **135** F4
Galilee, R. I. **47** O6
Gallatin, Tenn. **87** B12
Gallup, N. Mex. **183** F2
Galveston, Tex. **191** M17
Galveston Bay, Tex. 190
Gannett Peak, Wyo. **205** G4
Garden City, Iowa **165** F10, *167*
Garden Grove, Calif. **231** S11
Gardner, Mass. **39** D12
Garfield Heights, Ohio **143** D12
Garland, Tex. **191** F14
Garrison Dam, N. Dak. **149** G7
Gary, Ind. 124, 125, 138, **139** B3
Gary, W. Va. **79** Q5

Gasconade River, Mo. **173** L11
Gaston, Lake, N. C.-Va. **83** N18, **91** A20
Gastonia, N. C. **91** F10
Gates of the Arctic NP and Preserve, Alas. **237** E18
Gateway NRA, N. J.-N. Y. **53** T17, **61** H10
Gatlinburg, Tenn. **87** D21
Gauley River NRA, W. Va. **79** M7
Gavins Point Dam, S. Dak. **157** L16
Geist Reservoir, Ind. **139** K8
Genesee River, N. Y.-Pa. **53** J5
Geneva, N. Y. **53** K7
George, Lake, Fla. **121** E15
George, Lake, N. Y. **53** G18
George Washington Carver NM, Mo. **173** O4
Georgetown, S. C. **113** J16
Georgia 10, 108-111
Gettysburg, Pa. **57** L11
Gila Bend IR, Ariz. **179** O6
Gila Cliff Dwellings NM, N. Mex. **179** N24
Gila River, Ariz.-N. Mex. 179, **179** P1-P16, **183** O2
Gila River IR, Ariz. 18, **179** N8
Gilbert, Minn. 152, **153** F11
Glacier Bay NP and Preserve, Alas. **237** N24
Glacier NP, Mont. **201** B4; bighorn sheep *202*
Glacier Peak, Wash. **223** D9
Glaciers 237, *239;* Ice Age 24, 34, 52, 56, 57, 61, 126, 127, 134, 138, 149, 156, 164, 165
Glass Mountains, Okla. **187** E15
Glastonbury, Conn. **43** E11
Glen Canyon NRA, Ariz.-Utah **179** B9, **213** R10
Glen Cove, N. Y. **53** S18
Glendale, Ariz. **179** M8
Glendale, Calif. **231** R11
Glendo Reservoir, Wyo. **205** J16
Glens Falls, N. Y. **53** H18
Gloucester, Mass. **39** C21
Gnaw Bone, Ind. **139** N7
Gogebic, Lake, Mich. **131** F2
Gogebic Range, Mich. **131** E1
Golden, Colo. **217** F11
Golden Gate NRA, Calif. **231** J4
Goldsboro, N. C. **91** F19
Goose Creek, S. C. **113** L14
Goose Lake, Calif.-Oreg. **227** O10, **231** A7
Gore Mountain, Vt. **27** B11
Goshen, Ind. **139** C8
Goshute IR, Nev.-Utah **209** G13, **213** J2
Grafton, Vt. **27** Q6, *28*
Graham, Mount, Ariz. **179** P14
Granby, Vt. **27** E11; one-room schoolhouse *29*
Granby, Lake, Colo. **217** D9
Grand Bay NWR, Ala.-Miss. **101** S11, **105** T2
Grand Canyon, Ariz. 10, **176**, 178, **179** C7, *180*
Grand Canyon NP, Ariz. **179** D7

Grand Cote NWR, La. **117** H9
Grand Coulee Dam, Wash. 222, **223** E14
Grand Forks, N. Dak. **149** E18; missile *151*
Grand Isle, La. **117** P15
Grand Junction, Colo. **217** G2
Grand Lake, La. **117** N5
Grand Lake, Ohio **143** H2
Grand Portage IR, Minn. **153** E17
Grand Portage NM, Minn. **153** E17
Grand Prairie, Tex. **191**.G14
Grand Rapids, Mich. **124**, **131** Q10
Grand River, Mich. **131** Q11
Grand River, Mo. **173** C6
Grand River, S. Dak. **157** B6
Grand Ronde IR, Oreg. **227** D3
Grand Teton NP, Wyo. **205** E2
Grand Traverse Bay, Mich. **131** K11
Grand Traverse IR, Mich. **131** K10
Grandview, Mo. **173** G4
Granite Peak, Mont. **201** K10
Granogue (estates), Del. *70*
Grants, N. Mex. **183** G4
Grants Pass, Oreg. **227** N4
Grasslands 10, 146, 156, 160, 168; bluegrass 74
Grave Peak, Idaho **197** G6
Gravel Island NWR, Wis. **127** H16
Grays Harbor NWR, Wash. **223** H2
Grays Lake NWR, Idaho **197** Q12
Great Basin **194**, 196, 208, **209** F9; cattle roundup *228*; formation 194
Great Basin NP, Nev. **209** J12, *210*
Great Bay, N. H. **31** R10
Great Bay, N. J. **61** Q8
Great Bend, Kans. **169** F9
Great Dismal Swamp, N. C.- Va. 82, 90, **91** A25
Great Dismal Swamp NWR, Va. 82, **83** M23, **91** A24
Great Divide Basin, Wyo. 205, **205** M8
Great Falls, Mont. **201** E8
Great Lakes, Canada-U. S. 52, **124-125**, 125, 126, 130
Great Meadows NWR, Mass. **39** F16
Great Miami River, Ohio **143** K3
Great Plains 146, 148, 160, 182, 204; farm *162-163*
Great Quittacas Pond, Mass. **39** L20
Great River Road **127**, **135**, **153**, **165**, **173**
Great Sacandaga Lake, N. Y. **53** J16
Great Salt Lake, Utah 212, **213** D5; resort *212*
Great Salt Lake Desert, Utah 213, **213** E3

Great Salt Plains Lake, Okla. **187** C16
Great Sand Dunes NM, Colo. **217** M10
Great Serpent Mound, Ohio **143** P6
Great Smoky Mountains, N. C.-Tenn. 86, 90
Great Smoky Mountains NP, N. C.-Tenn. 86, **87** E21, **90** E3
Great Swamp NWR, N. J. 61, **61** F6
Great White Heron NWR, Fla. **121** R15
Greeley, Colo. **217** C12
Green Bank, W. Va. **79** L11; radio telescopes *80*
Green Bay, Mich. **131** J6
Green Bay (city), Wis. 126, **127** L13
Green Bay (inlet), Wis. 126, **127** J14
Green Bay NWR, Wis. **127** H16
Green Cay NWR, U. S. Virgin Islands **245** G4
Green Mountains, Vt. 24, 26, 27, **27** F7-P5, 39; sugar maple *28*
Green River, Colo.-Utah-Wyo. **205** L4, **213** J13, **217** B2
Green River, Ky. **75** J9
Green River (town), Utah **213** M12
Green River (town), Wyo. 204, **205** N5
Green River Lake, Ky. **75** J15
Green Swamp, N. C. **91** L18
Greenbrier River, W. Va. **79** P8
Greeneville, Tenn. **87** B23
Greenfield, Mass. **38** D7
Greensboro, N. C. 90, **91** C14
Greenville, Miss. **101** G3
Greenville, N. C. **91** E21
Greenville, S. C. **113** B4
Greenwich, Conn. **43** K162
Greenwood, Miss. **101** F5
Greenwood, S. C. **113** F5
Greenwood, Lake, S. C. **113** E5
Greers Ferry Lake, Ark. **97** E10
Greeson, Lake, Ark. **97** L4
Grenada Lake, Miss. **101** E7
Gretna, La. **117** N15
Greylock, Mount, Mass. **38** C3, *40*
Griffin, Ga. **109** G5
Groton, Conn. **43** K16
Grulla NWR, N. Mex. **183** K16
Guadalupe Mountains NP, Tex. **191** H3
Guadalupe Peak, Tex. **191** H3
Guadalupe River, Tex. **191** M13
Guam 235, 244, 245, *246*, 247
Guayama, Puerto Rico **245** E14
Guaynabo, Puerto Rico **245** B14
Gulf Coastal Plain 96, 100, 134, 190
Gulf Islands NS, Fla.-Miss. **101** T11, **121** C2
Gulfport, Miss. 100, **101** S9
Gunnison River, Colo. **217** J3
Gunpowder River, Md. **65** C18

Guthrie, Okla. 186, **187** G18
Guyandotte River, W. Va. **79** N3

Hackensack, N. J. **61** E10
Haddonfield, N. J. **61** N4
Hagerman NWR, Tex. **191** E14
Hagerman Fossil Beds NM, Idaho **197** Q5
Hagerstown, Md. **65** B11; book wagon (circa 1920) *64*
Hailstone NWR, Mont. **201** H11
Hakalau Forest NWR, Hawaii **241** L24
Haleakala Crater, Hawaii 240, **241** G19
Haleakala NP, Hawaii **241** G19
Halfbreed Lake NWR, Mont. **201** H11
Halsey, Nebr. **161** D8
Hamden, Conn. **43** J8
Hamden Slough NWR, Minn. **153** H3
Hamilton, Ohio **143** N2
Hammonasset Point, Conn. **43** L11
Hammond, Ind. **139** B3
Hampton, Va. **83** K24; Hampton Institute *82*
Hampton NHS, Md. **65** C18
Hampton Harbor Inlet, N. H. **31** T10
Hampton Roads, Va. 82, **83** L24
Hanalei NWR, Hawaii **240** B4
Hancock, Md. **65** A8
Hanford Site, Wash. 222, **223** K13
Hannahville IR, Mich. **131** H6
Hannibal, Mo. **173** D13
Hanover, Pa. **57** L12
Harbor Island NWR, Mich. **131** G14
Harlingen, Tex. **191** R13
Harmonie, Ind. 138
Harney Basin, Oreg. 226, **227** J13
Harney Lake, Oreg. **227** K13
Harney Peak, S. Dak. **157** H2
Harpers Ferry, W. Va. **79** G19, *80*
Harpers Ferry NHP, Md.-W. Va. **65** D10
Harris Neck NWR, Ga. **109** N15
Harrisburg, Pa. **57** J12
Harrisonburg, Va. **83** E15
Harrodsburg, Ky. **75** G16
Harry S. Truman Lake, Mo. **173** J7
Hart Mountain National Antelope Refuge, Oreg. **227** M12
Hartford, Conn. 24, 42, 43, **43** E10; assembly plant *44*
Hartwell Lake, Ga.-S. C. **109** C10, **113** C3
Harvey, Ill. **135** D11
Hatchie NWR, Tenn. **86** F4
Hatchie River, Tenn. **86** E3
Hattiesburg, Miss. **101** P8
Havasu, Lake, Ariz. 178, **179** J2
Havasu NWR, Ariz. **179** H2,

K3; **231** P17
Havasupai IR, Ariz. **179** D7
Haverhill, Mass. **39** A18
Hawaii 8, 234, **234**, **235**, 240-243
Hawaii (island), Hawaii 234, **234**, **235**, 240-241, **241** N23, *242;* beach *243;* volcano 241, *242*
Hawaii Volcanoes NP, Hawaii **241** O24
Hawkinsville, Ga. **109** L8; steamboat (circa 1900) *108*
Hays, Kans. **169** D8
Haystack Mountain, Vt. **27** T4
Hazard, Ky. **75** J22
Hazleton, Pa. **57** F15
Heart River, N. Dak. **149** J5
Hebgen Lake, Mont. **201** L7
Helena, Mont. **201** G6
Hells Canyon, Idaho 196, 197, **197** K2
Hells Canyon NRA, Oreg. **227** C18
Hempstead, N. Y. **53** T18
Henderson, Ky. **74** G7
Henderson, Nev. **209** R11
Henderson, N. C. **91** B18
Hershey, Pa. **57** J13
Hewitt Lake NWR, Mont. **201** B13
Hialeah, Fla. **121** O18
Hibbing, Minn. 152, **153** G10
Hickory, N. C. **91** D9
Higgins Lake, Mich. **131** M12
High Plains **169** E3, **183** C15, **186** C4, **191** A7
High Point, N. J. **61** A6
High Point, N. C. **91** D13
High Rock Lake, N. C. **91** E12
Highland, Ind. **139** C3
Highland Park, Ill. **135** B10
Hilo, Hawaii **241** M25
Hilton Head Island, S. C. 112, **113** P11
Hingham, Mass. **39** G20
Hiwassee Lake, N. C. **90** G1
Hiwassee River, Tenn. **87** F18
Hobe Sound NWR, Fla. **121** L18
Hobbs, N. Mex. **183** O16
Hoboken, N. J. **61** F10
Hocking River, Ohio **143** N10
Hoh IR, Wash. **223** E1
Holla Bend NWR, Ark. **97** G6
Holland, Mich. 130, **131** R9
Hollywood, Calif. **231** R11
Hollywood IR, Fla. **121** O18
Holyoke, Mass. **38** H7
Homestead NM of America, Nebr. **161** H16
Homochitto River, Miss. **101** O2
Honokaa, Hawaii **241** K23
Honolulu, Hawaii 234, **241** E11; beach *243*
Hood, Mount, Oreg. 220, 226, **227** D7, *229;* expedition (1913) *226*
Hoopa Valley IR, Calif. **231** C4
Hoover Dam, Ariz.-Nev. **179** D2, 208, **209** R12
Hoover Reservoir, Ohio **143** K7
Hopatcong, N. J. **61** E6

Hopewell, Va. **83** J21
Hopi IR, Ariz. **179** E12
Hoquiam, Wash. **223** H2
Horicon NWR, Wis. **127** O12
Horsehead Lake, N. Dak. **149** H11
Horses: diving horse (1958) *60;* horse farms *58, 74, 76-77;* plow team *66;* racehorses *55, 76;* wild mustangs *207*
Horseshoe Point, Fla. **121** E11
Hot Springs, Ark. **97** K6
Hot Springs, Va. **83** G12
Hot springs *see* Thermal springs
Hot Springs NP, Ark. 96, **97** K6
Houghton Lake, Mich. **131** M12
Houma, La. **117** O12
Housatonic River, Conn.-Mass. **38** H1, 39, **43** J5
Houston, Tex. **177**, 190, **191** L16, *192*
Hovenweep NM, Colo.-Utah **213** R15, **217** N2
Howland Island, Pacific Ocean **235**, 244
Hualapai IR, Ariz. **179** E5
Hubbard Lake, Mich. **131** L14
Hudson River, N. Y. **51**, 52, **53** N17, *54-55*, **61** E10
Huleia NWR, Hawaii **240** C5
Humboldt Lake, Nev. **209** F4
Humboldt River, Nev. 208, **209** E7
Humphreys Peak, Ariz. **179** G9
Hungry Horse Reservoir, Mont. **201** C4
Huntington, Ind. **139** F9
Huntington, W. Va. **79** L2
Huntington Lake, Ind. **139** F10
Huntsville, Ala. **105** B8; space camp *107*
Huron, Lake, Canada-U. S. **125, 131**
Huron NWR, Mich. **131** D5
Hutchinson, Kans. **169** G11
Hutton Lake NWR, Wyo. **205** O14
Hyannis, Mass. **39** N24
Hyde Park, N. Y. **53** O17

Ice Age Trail, Wis. 126, **127**
Idaho 196-199
Idaho Falls, Idaho **197** P11
Iditarod (Goldrush) Trail, Alas. **237** G14, K18
Iliamna Lake, Alas. **237** M16
Illinois 134-137
Illinois River, Ill. **124**, 134, **135** J4
Illinois River, Oreg. **227** N3
Imperial NWR, Ariz.-Calif. **179** O2, **231** T17
Imperial Valley, Calif. **221**, **231** T15
Independence, Kans. **169** K17
Independence, Mo. **173** F4
Indian Lake, Ohio **143** H4
Indian River Bay, Del. **69** R8
Indian tribes: Algonquian 20, 34, 42; Apache 178, *180*, 182;

Arawak 244; Cherokee 90, 186, *189;* Chickasaw 186; Choctaw 100, *100*, 186; Creek 186; Hopi 178; Iroquois *54-55;* Lumbee 90; Navajo 178, 182; Nez Perce 196; Paiute *211;* Passamaquoddy 34; Penobscot 34; Pueblo 182; Seminole 120, 186; Sioux 156; Wampanoag *44;* Winnebago 126; Yakima *224*
Indiana 138-141
Indiana Dunes NL, Ind. 138, **139** B4
Indianapolis, Ind. 138, **139** L7; hospital *140;* stadium *141*
Indians: 16, 182, 200, 208, 236; chief *160;* dancers *150, 185;* fishing *211, 224;* population growth 16; transportation of students (1890s) *156*
Indians, ancient 13, 83, 104, 117, 121, 142, 164, 178, 182, 216, 219; cliff dwellings *218-219;* earthen mounds *144-145;* rock paintings *215*
Innuko NWR, Alas. **237** H16
Inside Passage, Alas. 237, **237** P26
International Falls, Minn. **153** C9
Intracoastal Waterway 94, 117
Iowa 164-167
Iowa City, Iowa **165** H15
Iowa IR, Kans.-Nebr. **161** J19, **169** A17
Iowa River, Iowa **165** G13
Ipswich, Mass. **39** B20
Iron Mountain, Mich. **131** H5
Iroquois NWR, N. Y. **52** J4
Irrigation 160, 178, 230; sprinkler rig *199*
Irving, Tex. **191** G14
Irvington, N. J. **61** F8
Isabella IR, Mich. **131** N14, O12
Island Bay NWR, Fla. **121** M13
Isle Au Haut, Me. **35** Q9
Isle La Motte, Vt. **27** B2
Isle of Palms, S. C. **113** M15
Isle Royale, Mich. 131, **131** B3
Isle Royale NP, Mich. **131** B3
Isles of Shoals, N. H. **31** S12
Isleta IR, N. Mex. **183** H7
Istokpoga, Lake, Fla. **121** K15
Itasca, Lake, Minn. 152, 153, **153** G5
Ithaca, N. Y. **53** M9; farmer's market *55*
Izembeck NWR, Alas. **237** O12

J. Clark Salyer NWR, N. Dak. **149** C9
J. N. "Ding" Darling NWR, Fla. **121** N14
J. Percy Priest Lake, Tenn. **87** C12
Jackson, Mich. **131** S13
Jackson, Miss. 100, **101** L5
Jackson, Tenn. **86** E5
Jackson, Wyo. **205** F2
Jackson Lake, Wyo. **205** E2

Jacksonville, Ark. **97** H9
Jacksonville, Fla. **121** B14
Jacksonville, Ill. **135** K4
Jacksonville, N. C. **91** H21
James C. Campbell NWR, Hawaii **241** C10
James River, N. Dak.-S. Dak. 149, **149** K15, **157** D13
James River, Va. 82, **83** H16
Jamestown, N. Y. **52** N1
Jamestown, N. Dak. **149** J14
Jamestown, Va. **83** K22
Jamestown Klallam IR, Wash. **223** E4
Janesville, Wis. **127** S11
Jarvis Island, Pacific Ocean **235**, 244
Jay Peak, Vt. **27** B7
Jefferson, Mount, Oreg. **227** F7
Jefferson City, Mo. **173** H10
Jefferson River, Mont. **201** J6
Jeffersonville, Ind. **139** R9
Jekyll Island, Ga. **109** P15
Jemez IR, N. Mex. **183** E7
Jennings, Mo. **173** G16
Jerimoth Hill, R. I. **47** D2
Jersey City, N. J. **61** F10
Jewel Cave NM, S. Dak. **157** H1
Jicarilla Apache IR, N. Mex. **183** C6
John Day Fossil Beds NM, Oreg. **227** E11
John F. Kennedy Space Center, Fla. **121** G17
John H. Kerr Reservoir, N. C. **91** A18
John Martin Reservoir, Colo. **217** L16
John Redmond Reservoir, Kans. **169** F16
Johnson City, Tenn. **87** B25
Johnston, R. I. **47** E7
Johnstown, Pa. **57** J6
Joliet, Ill. **135** E10
Jonesboro, Ark. **97** D14
Joplin, Mo. **173** N4
Jordan River, Utah **213** F7
Jornada del Muerto, N. Mex. 182, **183** M6
Joshua Tree NM, Calif. **231** R15
Juan de Fuca, Strait of, Wash. **223** D2
Julesburg, Colo. **217** A18
Julia Butler Hansen NWR, Oreg.-Wash. **223** L3, **227** A4
Junction City, Kans. **169** D14
Juneau, Alas. **235**, **237** N25
Juneau Icefield, Alas. **237** N25, *239*
Juniata River, Pa. **57** H10

Kahoolawe, Hawaii 240, **241** J17
Kaibab IR, Ariz. **179** B7
Kailua, Hawaii **241** E11
Kailua Kona, Hawaii **241** N20
Kakahaia NWR, Hawaii **241** F15
Kalamazoo, Mich. **131** S10
Kalamazoo River, Mich. **131** S10
Kalispell, Mont. **201** C3
Kalispell IR, Wash. **223** C18

Kamakou, Hawaii **241** F15
Kanab, Utah **213** T6
Kanab Creek, Ariz.-Utah **179** B7, **213** S6
Kanawha River, W. Va. 78, **79** K4
Kaneohe, Hawaii **241** E11
Kankakee River, Ind.-Ill. **135** F10, **139** D3
Kannapolis, N. C. **91** E11
Kansas 168-171
Kansas City, Kans. **169** D19, *171*
Kansas City, Mo. 147, 172, **173** F4
Kansas River, Kans. **169** D15
Kanuta NWR, Alas. **237** F19
Karl E. Mundt NWR, Nebr.-S. Dak. **157** K13, **161** A12
Kaskaskia, Ill. 135, **135** Q5
Kaskaskia River, Ill. **135** N7
Katahdin, Mount, Me. 24, **25**, 35, **35** H8
Katmai NP and Preserve, Alas. **237** N17
Kauai, Hawaii **234**, 240, **240** C4
Kaukauna, Wis. **127** M12
Kaw Lake, Okla. **187** C20
Kearney, Nebr. **161** G11
Kearns, Utah **213** F7
Keene, N. H. **31** S3
Kelleys Island, Ohio **143** C8
Kellogg, Idaho **197** D3
Kenai, Alas. **237** L18
Kenai Fjords NP, Alas. **237** M18
Kennebec River, Me. 34, **35** K5
Kenner, La. **117** M14
Kennett Square, Pa. **57** L16
Kenosha, Wis. **127** S14
Kent, Ohio **143** E12
Kent Island, Md. **65** G19
Kenton, Okla. **186** B1
Kentucky 74-77
Kentucky Lake, Ky.-Tenn. **74** M6, **86** B7
Kentucky River, Ky. **75** G20
Kentwood, Mich. **131** Q10
Keokuk, Iowa 164, **165** M15
Keowee, Lake, S. C. **113** C2
Kern NWR, Calif. **231** O8
Keshena, Wis. **127** J12
Kesterson NWR, Calif. **231** L6
Ketchikan, Alas. **237** Q27
Ketchum, Idaho **197** O6
Kettering, Ohio **143** M3
Keweenaw Bay, Mich. **131** E4
Keweenaw Peninsula, Mich. 131, **131** C5
Key Largo, Fla. **121** Q18
Key West, Fla. **121** S15
Key West NWR, Fla. **121** S14
Keystone Lake, Okla. **187** F21
Kiamichi River, Okla. **187** L25
Kiawah Island, S. C. **113** M14
Kickapoo IR, Kans. **169** B17
Kiholo Bay, Hawaii **241** M20
Kilauea (volcano), Hawaii 241, **241** O24, *242*
Killeen, Tex. **191** J13
Killington Peak, Vt. **27** N5
Kings Canyon NP, Calif. **231** M10
Kings Peak, Utah **213** E11
Kings River, Calif. **231** M8
Kingsley Dam, Nebr. **161**F5

Kingsport, Tenn. 87 A24
Kingston, N. Y. 53 O17
Kingsville, Tex. 191 P13
Kinston, N. C. 91 F21
Kirkland, Wash. 223 F6
Kirksville, Mo. 173 B9
Kirkwood, Mo. 173 H16
Kirwin NWR, Kans. 169 B8
Kissimee, Lake, Fla. 121 J15
Kissimee River, Fla. 120, 121 K16
Kitt Peak National Observatory, Ariz. 179 R9, 181
Kittatinny Mountain, N. Y.-N. J.-Pa. 60, 61 C5
Kitts Hammock, Del. 69 K5
Kitty Hawk, N. C. 91 C26
Klamath Falls, Oreg. 227 N7
Klamath Mountains, Calif. 230, 231 C4
Klamath River, Calif.-Oreg. 227 O7, 231 A4
Knoxville, Iowa 165 J10
Knoxville, Tenn. 87 C20, 88
Kobuk River, Alas. 237 F17
Kodiak Island, Alas. 237 O17
Kodiak NWR, Alas. 237 O17
Kofa NWR, Ariz. 179 N3
Kokomo, Ind. 139 G7
Kootenai IR, Idaho 197 A3
Kootenai NWR, Idaho 197 A3
Kootenai River, Canada-U. S. 201 B1
Koshkonong, Lake, Wis. 127 R11
Kotzebue, Alas. 237 E15; Eskimo youth 238
Kotzebue Sound, Alas. 237 E15
Koyukuk NWR, Alas. 237 G17
Koyukuk River, Alas. 237 F18
Kuskokwim Mountains, Alas. 237 K15
Kuskokwim River, Alas. 237 K15
Kutztown, Pa. 57 H16

La Crosse, Wis. 127 N5
La Grange, Ga. 109 H3
La Porte, Ind. 139 B5
Lac Courte Oreilles IR, Wis. 127 F5
Lac des Allemands, La. 117 N13
Lac du Flambeau IR, Wis. 127 E8
Lac Vieux Desert IR, Mich. 131 G2
Lacassine NWR, La. 117 N5
Lackawanna, N. Y. 52 K2
Laconia, N. H. 31 O7
Lacreek NWR, S. Dak. 157 K6
Lafayette, Ind. 139 H5
Lafayette, La. 116, 117 M8
Lafitte, La. 117 O14
Laguna Atascosa NWR, Tex. 191 R14
Laguna Cartagena NWR, Puerto Rico 245 E8
Laguna IR, N. Mex. 183 F6, G5, H5
Lake Alice NWR, N. Dak. 149 D13
Lake Andes NWR, S. Dak. 157

K13
Lake Charles, La. 116, 117 M4
Lake Chelan NRA, Wash. 223 C10
Lake Clark NP and Preserve, Alas. 237 L17
Lake George NWR, N. Dak. 149 J12
Lake Havasu City, Ariz. 179 J2
Lake Ilo NWR, N. Dak. 149 G4
Lake Isom NWR, Tenn. 86 B3
Lake Mason NWR, Mont. 201 G11
Lake Mead NRA, Ariz.-Nev. 179 D2, 208, 209 Q12
Lake Meredith NRA, Tex. 191 B7
Lake Nettie NWR, N. Dak. 149 F8
Lake O' The Cherokees, Okla. 187 D26
Lake of the Ozarks, Mo. 173 K9
Lake of the Woods, Minn. 153, 153 A7
Lake Ophelia NWR, La. 117 H8
Lake Providence, La. 117 A10
Lake Thibadeau NWR, Mont. 201 B10
Lake Traverse IR, N. Dak.-S. Dak. 149 M17, 157 B16
Lake Woodruff NWR, Fla. 121 F15
Lake Worth, Fla. 121 M19
Lake Zahle NWR, N. Dak. 149 C2
Lakeland, Fla. 121 J14
Lakewood, Colo. 217 F11
Lakewood, N. J. 61 L9
Lakewood, Ohio 143 D11
Lamesteer NWR, Mont. 201 F18
Lamlam, Mount, Guam 245 T16
Lamoille River, Vt. 26, 27 D4
Lanai, Hawaii 240, 241 G15; pineapples 243
Lancaster, Ohio 143 M8
Lancaster, Pa. 57 K14
Land Between the Lakes, Ky. 74 L6
Land O' Lakes, Wis. 127 E10
L'Anse IR, Mich. 131 E4
Lansing, Mich. 131 R12
Laramie, Wyo. 205 N14
Laramie Mountains, Wyo. 205 K14
Laramie Peak, Wyo. 205 K15
Laramie River, Wyo. 205 L14
Laredo, Tex. 191 P10
Largo, Fla. 121 J12
Larned, Kans. 169 G8
Las Cruces, N. Mex. 183 P7, 185
Las Vegas, Nev. 16, 194, 208, 208, 209 Q11, 210
Las Vegas, N. Mex. 183 F11
Las Vegas NWR, N. Mex. 183 F11
Lassen Peak, Calif. 222, 230, 231 D6
Lassen Volcanic NP, Calif. 231 D6
Lata Mountain, American Samoa 245 N9

Laurel, Miss. 101 N9
Lava Beds NM, Calif. 231 B6
Lava Hot Springs, Idaho 197 R11
Lawrence, Kans. 169 D18
Lawrence, Mass. 39 B18
Lawton, Okla. 187 L15
Lead, S. Dak. 157 F1
Lead Mountain, Me. 35 M11
Leadore, Idaho 197 M8
Leadville, Colo. 217 G8
Leavenworth, Kans. 169 C18
Lebanon, Kans. 169 A9
Lebanon, Pa. 57 J14
Leech Lake, Minn. 153 G7
Leech Lake IR, Minn. 153 G7
Leesburg, Va. 83 B19
Leesville Lake, Ohio 143 H13
Lehigh River, Pa. 57 G16
Leipsic River, Del. 69 H4
Lenoir, N. C. 91 D8
Levittown, N. Y. 53 T18
Lewes, Del. 69 P8
Lewis and Clark NWR, Oreg. 227 A3
Lewis and Clark Trail 149, 157, 161, 165, 169, 173, 197, 201, 201, 223, 227, 227
Lewis Smith Lake, Ala. 105 E6
Lewiston, Idaho 197 G2
Lewiston, Me. 34, 35 Q4
Lexington, Ky. 74, 75 F17, 76
Lexington, Mass. 39 E17
Lexington, Nebr. 161 G10
Lexington, N. C. 91 D12
Liberal, Kans. 169 K3
Liberty, Mo. 173 E4
Liberty Reservoir, Md. 65 C16
Licking River, Ky. 75 D19
Lima, Ohio 143 G3
Lincoln, Nebr. 160, 161 G16
Litchfield, Conn. 43 E5
Lititz, Pa. 57 J14, 59
Little Bay, N. H. 31 R11
Little Bighorn River, Mont. 201 J13
Little Blue River, Nebr. 161 H13
Little Colorado River, Ariz. 179, 179 H13
Little Diomede Island, Alas. 237 E13
Little Kanawha River, W. Va. 79 H6
Little Miami River, Ohio 143 N3
Little Missouri River, N. Dak. 149 K1
Little Pee Dee River, S. C. 113 F16, 115
Little Pend Oreille NWR, Wash. 223 C17
Little Red River, Ark. 97 G11
Little River NWR, Okla. 187 O26
Little Rock, Ark. 96, 97 J9
Little Sandy NWR, Tex. 191 G16
Little Sioux River, Iowa 165
Little Tallahatchie River, Miss. 101 C7
Little Traverse Bay, Mich. 131 J10
Little Wabash River, Ill. 135 O9
Littleton, Colo. 217 F11
Livengood, Alas. 237 G20

Livermore, Mount, Tex. 191 K4
Livestock: cattle 123, 146, 160, 168, 190, 202, 204, 208, roundup 228; hogs 138, 160; sheep 178, 196, 199, 204, 204, 208, shearing 210; see also Horses; Poultry
Livingston, Mont. 201 J9
Livingston, Lake, Tex. 191 K16
Livonia, Mich. 131 S15
Lockport, N. Y. 52 J3
Logan, Utah 213 B8
Logan, Mount, Wash. 223 C9
Logan Cave NWR, Ark. 97 B2
Logansport, Ind. 139 F6
Lompoc, Calif. 231 Q7
Long Beach, Calif. 231 S11
Long Beach, Miss. 101 T9
Long Branch, N. J. 61 J10
Long Island, N. Y. 52, 53 T21
Long Island Sound, Conn.-N. Y. 42, 43 M9, 53 R20
Long Lake, N. Dak. 149 J11
Long Lake NWR, N. Dak. 149 J11
Long Pond, Mass. 39 L19
Long Trail, Vt. 27, 27
Longfellow Mountains, Me. 35 K7
Longmont, Colo. 217 D11
Longs Peak, Colo. 217 D10
Longview, Tex. 191 G17
Longview, Wash. 222, 223 L4
Lookout Mountain, Tenn. 87 G16
Lorain, Ohio 143 D10
Los Alamos, N. Mex. 182, 183 E8
Los Angeles, Calif. 221, 231 R11
Los Angeles Aqueduct, Calif. 231 O11
Lost River Range, Idaho 197 M7
Lost River Sinks, Idaho 197 O9
Lostwood NWR, N. Dak. 149 B5
Louisiana 94, 116-119
Louisville, Ky. 72, 74, 75 E13
Loup River, Nebr. 161 F14
Loveland, Colo. 217 C11
Lowell, Mass. 38, 39 C17
Lower Brule IR, S. Dak. 157 G10
Lower Elwha IR, Wash. 223 D3
Lower Hatchie NWR, Tenn. 86 E2
Lower Klamath NWR, Calif.-Oreg. 227 O7, 231 A5
Lower Red Lake, Minn. 153 E5
Lower Rio Grande Valley NWR, Tex. 191 R11
Lower Sioux IR, Minn. 153 Q5
Lower Suwannee NWR, Fla. 121 E11
Lubbock, Tex. 191 F7
Lumber industry 26, 34, 178, 200, 222, 226; logging 34, 37, 130, 133, 224, 236
Lummi IR, Wash. 223 B5
Lums Pond, Del. 69 D2
Lunar Crater, Nev. 209 L9
Lutherville-Timonium, Md. 65 C17
Lynchburg, Va. 83 J15
Lyndon B. Johnson Space Center, Tex. 191 M16

Lynn, Mass. 39 E19

McAlester, Okla. 187 K23
McAllen, Tex. 191 R12
McClellanville, S. C. 113 K16, 115
McConaughy, Lake, Nebr. 161 F5
Machias Bay, Me. 35 O13
Mackay Island NWR, N. C. 83 M25, 91 A25
McKeesport, Pa. 57 J3
Mackinac Island, Mich. 131 H12
McKinley, Mount, Alas. 236, 237 J19
McMillan, Lake, N. Mex. 183 O13
Macomb, Ill. 135 H3
Macon, Ga. 109 J7
Madeline Island, Wis. 127 B6
Madison, Wis. 127 Q9
Madison River, Mont. 201 J7
Magazine Mountain, Ark. 97 G4
Maia, American Samoa 245 M10
Maine 34-37
Makah IR, Wash. 223 C1
Malaspina Glacier, Alas. 237 M23
Malden, Mass. 39 E18
Malheur Lake, Oreg. 227 K14
Malheur NWR, Oreg. 227 K13
Mammoth Cave, Ky. 74, 77
Mammoth Cave NP, Ky. 75 K12
Mammoth Kill Site, Wyo. 205 N9
Mammoth Spring, Ark. 97 A12
Manassas, Va. 83 C20
Manati, Puerto Rico 245 B12; pharmaceutical factory 247
Manchester, N. H. 30, 31 S7
Manchester Center, Vt. 27 Q4
Mandan, N. Dak. 149 J9
Manhattan, Kans. 169 C14
Manhattan Island, N. Y. 54
Manistee, Mich. 131 N8
Manistee River, Mich. 131 M10
Manistique, Mich. 131 G8
Manitou Islands, Mich. 131 K9
Manitowoc, Wis. 127 M14
Mankato, Minn. 153 R7
Manley Hot Springs, Alas. 237 H19
Mansfield, Ohio 143 G9
Mansfield, Mount, Vt. 27 E5
Mansfield Hollow Lake, Conn. 43 E15
Manufacturing: aircraft 44, 108, 110, 168, 225; automobiles 86, 89, 125, 130, 138; chemicals 133; glass products 78, 81; musical instruments 74, 140; shipbuilding 30, 42; see also Forest products; Textiles
Maquoketa River, Iowa 165 E16
Marble Canyon, Ariz. 179 C9
Marblehead, Mass. 39 D20
Marcy, Mount, N. Y. 53 E17
Mariana Islands see Northern Mariana Islands
Marietta, Ga. 109 D4
Marietta, Ohio 142, 143 N12
Marion, Ind. 139 G9
Marion, Iowa 165 F14
Marion, Lake, S. C. 113 J13
Mark Twain NWR, Ill.-Iowa-

Mo. **135** N3; **165** J16, **173** C12
Marlborough, Mass. **39** F15
Marquesas Keys, Fla. **121** S14
Marquette, Mich. **131** F6
Marshall, Mo. **173** F7
Marshalltown, Iowa **165** F11
Marshfield, Wis. **127** K7
Martha's Vineyard, Mass. 38, **39** Q22
Martin, Lake, Ala. **105** K10
Martin NWR, Md. **65** P21
Martinsburg, W. Va. **79** F18
Martinsville, Va. **83** M12
Marvel Cave, Mo. **173** P7
Mary, Lake, Miss. **101** P1
Maryland 64-67
Maryville, Tenn. **87** D20
Mason-Dixon Line 69
Mason City, Iowa **165** B10
Massabesic Lake, N. H. **31** S8
Massachusetts 38-41
Massachusetts Bay, Mass. **39** E21
Massena, N. Y. **53** A14
Matafao Peak, American Samoa **245** S6
Matagorda Island, Tex. **191** O15
Matanuska River Valley, Alas. 236, **237** K20
Mattamuskeet NWR, N. C. **91** E25
Mattaponi River, Va. **83** G21
Mattoon, Ill. **135** L9
Maui, Hawaii **234**, 240, **241** G18; sugarcane workers *240*
Maumee, Ohio **143** C5
Maumee River, Ind.-Ohio **139** E11, **143** E2
Maumelle, Lake, Ark. **97** H8
Mauna Kea, Hawaii **234**, **241** L23
Mauna Kea Observatory, Hawaii **241** L23
Mauna Loa, Hawaii **241** N22
Maurepas, Lake, La. **117** L13
Maurice River, N. J. **61** R3
Mayagüez, Puerto Rico **245** C7
Mead, Lake, Ariz.-Nev. **179** D2, 208, **209** Q12
Meadowcroft Rockshelter, Pa. 13, 57, **57** J1
Medford, Mass. **39** E18
Medford, Oreg. **227** N5
Medford, Wis. **127** J7
Medicine Bow Mountains, Wyo. **205** N13
Medicine Bow Peak, Wyo. **205** N12
Medicine Lake NWR, Mont. **201** B18
Medicine Lodge, Kans. **169** K9
Meeteetse, Wyo. **205** D6, *207*
Melbourne, Fla. **121** H17
Melrose, Mass. **39** E18
Memphis, Tenn. 72, 86, **86** G1; cotton workers *89*
Memphremagog, Lake, Vt. **27** A8
Menasha, Wis. **127** M12
Menominee IR, Wis. **127** J11
Menominee River, Wis. **127** H14, **131** J5

Menomonee Falls, Wis. **127** Q13
Mentor, Ohio **143** C12
Meramec Caverns, Mo. **173** J14
Meramec River, Mo. **173** K13
Merced, Calif. **231** L7
Mercer Island, Wash. **223** F6
Meriden, Conn. **43** G9
Meridian, Miss. **101** L10
Merrimack River, Mass.-N. H. **31** P6, **39** B17
Merritt Island NWR, Fla. **121** G17
Mesa, Ariz. **179** N9
Mesa Verde NP, Colo. **217** O2, *218-219*
Mesabi Range, Minn. 152, **153** F10
Mescalero IR, N. Mex. **183** N10
Mesquite, Tex. **191** G14
Meteor Crater, Ariz. **179** H11
Methuen, Mass. **39** B17
Mexico, Mo. **173** F11
Miami, Fla. 95, **121** O18
Miami Beach, Fla. **121** O18, *122*
Michigan 130-133
Michigan, Lake **124**, 126, **127**, **131**, 135
Michigan City, Ind. **139** B5
Michigan Islands NWR, Mich. **131** H10, K15
Middle Loup River, Nebr. **161** D9
Middlebury, Vt. **27** J3
Middletown, Conn. **43** G10
Middletown, Ohio **143** N2
Middletown, R. I. **47** L10
Midland, Mich. **131** O13; scientist *133*
Midland, Tex. 190, **191** H7
Midway Islands, Pacific Ocean **235**, 244
Midwest City, Okla. **187** H18
Milford, Conn. **43** M7
Milford, Mass. **39** H15
Milford Lake, Kans. **169** D13
Mille Lacs Lake, Minn. **153** K8
Millington, Tenn. **86** F2
Millinocket, Me. **35** J9
Millville, N. J. **61** Q4
Millwood Lake, Ark. **97** N3
Milwaukee, Wis. **124**, 126, **127** Q14
Milwaukee River, Wis. **127** O13
Mineral Point, Wis. **127** R7
Mines and mining 200, 204, 208; coal *56*, 74, 78, *80*, 134, 138; copper 178, 200, pit *203*; gold 90, 156, 200, 208, 211, 236; iron 152; lead 172; salt 78; silver 200, 208, 211
Minneapolis, Minn. 147, *152*, **153** O9; grain market *154*; winter pageant (1925) *152*
Minnesota 152-155
Minnesota River, Minn. **153** Q5
Minnetonka, Minn. **153** P8
Minot, N. Dak. **149** D8
Mishawaka, Ind. **139** B7
Missisquoi NWR, Vt. **27** B3
Missisinewa Lake, Ind. **139** G8

Mississippi 100-103
Mississippi Choctaw IR, Miss. **101** J8
Mississippi Petrified Forest, Miss. **101** K5
Mississippi River 72, 74, 86, 94, **94**, 96, **97**, 101, 117, *118*, 124, 126, **127**, 135, *136*, 147, 153, 156, 164, **165**, 173, **173**, 187; alluvial plain 100, 116; avulsions 101; earthquakes (1811-1812) 87; flood (1881) 135; levees *103*, 116; riverboats *103*, *174-175*; source 152
Mississippi River Delta, La. 94, **94**, 116, **117** Q17
Mississippi Sandhill Crane NWR, Miss. **101** S10
Mississippi Sound, Ala. **105** T1
Missoula, Mont. **201** F4
Missouri 172-175
Missouri River 146-147, 148, 149, 157, 160, 164, **161**, **165**, 169, 173, **173**, 201, **201**; dams 157, 200
Mitchell, S. Dak. **157** H14
Mitchell, Mount, N. C. **90** D6
Moab, Utah **213** N14
Mobile, Ala. 104, **105** S3
Mobile Bay, Ala. 104, **105** T3
Mobile River, Ala. **105** R3
Modesto, Calif. **231** K6
Mohave, Lake, Nev. 208, **209** S11
Mohawk River and Valley, N. Y. 52, 53, **53** J15
Mohican River, Ohio **143** J10
Mojave, Lake, Ariz. **179** F2
Mojave Desert, Calif. **221**, 230, **231** P14
Moline, Ill. 134, **135** E4
Molokai, Hawaii **234**, 240, **241** F15
Monadnock Mountain, N. H. 31, **31** T3
Monhegan Island, Me. **35** R7
Mono Lake, Calif. **231** J9
Monocacy River, Md. **65** B13
Monomoy NWR, Mass. **39** N27
Monona, Wis. **127** Q10
Monongahela River, Pa.-W. Va. **57** K3, **79** F10
Monroe, Ga. **109** E7
Monroe, Mich. **131** T15
Monroe Lake, Ind. **139** O6
Monroeville, Pa. **57** H3
Montana 200-203
Montauk Point, N. Y. **53** R23
Montclair, N. J. **61** E9
Monte Vista NWR, Colo. **217** N8
Monterey, Calif. **231** M5
Monterey Bay, Calif. **231** L5
Montevideo, Minn. **153** P4
Montezuma Castle NM, Ariz. **179** J9
Montgomery, Ala. 95, **105** L9
Montpelier, Vt. 26, **27** G6
Monument Valley, Ariz.-Utah **179** B14, **213** T12
Moon Lake, Miss. 101, **101** C4

Moore, Okla. **187** J18
Moosehead Lake, Me. **35** J6
Moosehorn NWR, Me. **35** L14
Mooselookmeguntic Lake, Me. **35** M2
Moreau River, S. Dak. **157** C5
Morgan Horse Farm, Vt. **27** J3
Morgan Point, Conn. **43** L8
Morgantown, W. Va. **79** E11
Mormon Trail **161**, *163*, **165**, **205**, 213
Morristown, N. J. **53** F7
Morristown, Tenn. **87** B22
Morse Reservoir, Ind. **139** J7
Moscow, Idaho **197** F2
Moses Lake, Wash. **223** H13
Mosquito Creek Lake, Ohio **143** D14
Moss Point, Miss. **101** S11
Mott, N. Dak. **149** L5; citizens (1905) *148*
Moultrie, Ga. **109** P7
Moultrie, Lake, S. C. **113** J14
Mound City Group NM, Ohio **143** N7
Mound State Monument, Ala. **105** J4
Moundsville, W. Va. **79** D8
Mount Desert Island, Me. 25, 34, **35** P11; lobster traps *36*
Mount Hope Bay, R. I. **47** H11
Mount Pleasant, S. C. **113** M14
Mount Rainier NP, Wash. **223** J7
Mount Rushmore NM, S. Dak. 156, **157** H2, *158*
Mount Sterling, Ky. **75** F19
Mount Vernon, Ill. **135** P8
Mount Vernon, N. Y. **53** S17
Mount Vernon, Ohio **143** J9
Mount Vernon, Wash. **223** C6, *224*
Mount Washington, N. H.: observatory *32*
Mountain Brook, Ala. **105** G7
Mountain View, Ark. **97** C9; woodcarvers *98*
Mountlake Terrace, Wash. **223** F6
Muddy Boggy Creek, Okla. **187** N23
Muir Woods NM, Calif. **231** J4
Mullett Lake, Mich. **131** J12
Mullica River, N. J. **61** O6
Muncie, Ind. **139** J10
Murfreesboro, Ark. **97** M4
Murfreesboro, Tenn. **87** D12
Murray, Lake, S. C. **113** F8
Muscatatuck NWR, Ind. **139** O8
Muscatatuck River, Ind. **139** O9
Muscatine, Iowa **165** H16
Music and musicians 86; bluegrass band *88*; brass band *118*; instrument makers *74*, *140*; jazz orchestra (circa 1920) *116*
Muskegon, Mich. **131** Q9
Muskegon Lake, Mich. **131** Q9
Muskegon River, Mich. **131** P10
Muskingum River, Ohio **143** M11
Muskogee, Okla. 187, **187** G24
Musselshell River, Mont. **201** G12
Myrtle Beach, S. C. **113** G18

Mystic, Conn. 42, **43** J17
Mystic Seaport, Conn. **43** J17

Nacogdoches, Tex. **191** H17
Namekagon River, Wis. **127** E4
Nampa, Idaho **197** O2
Nanticoke River, Del.-Md. **65** M21, **69** R3
Nantucket, Mass. 38, **39** Q26
Nantucket Island, Mass. **39** R26
Nantucket Sound, Mass. **39** O25
Napa, Calif. **231** J4
Naples, Fla. **121** O14
Narragansett Bay, R. I. 46, 47, **47** J9
Narragansett IR, R. I. **47** O4
Nashua, N. H. **31** U7; microelectronics technician *33*
Nashville, Tenn. 72, 86, **87** C11
Natchez, Miss. **101** O1, *102*
Natchez Trace Parkway, Ala.-Miss.-Tenn. **87** G8, **101** N3, **105** B3
Natchitoches, La. **117** F4
National Bison Range, Mont. **201** E3
National Elk Refuge, Wyo. **205** F2, *206*
National Key Deer Refuge, Fla. **121** R15
National Park of American Samoa, American Samoa 244, **245** L3, N9, Q7
Natural Bridges NM, Utah **213** Q13
Naugatuck, Conn. **43** H7
Naugatuck River, Conn. **43** J6
Nauvoo, Ill. **135** H1
Navajo IR, Ariz.-N. Mex.-Utah **179** E13, **183** D2, **213** S12
Navajo NM, Ariz. **179** B11
Navajo Reservoir, N. Mex. **183** B5
Nebraska 160-163
Necedah NWR, Wis. **127** M7
Needham, Mass. **39** F17
Needles, Calif. **231** P16
Neenah, Wis. **127** M12
Neosho River, Kans. **169** F15
Nepaug Reservoir, Conn. **43** D8
Neptune, N. J. **61** K10
Neuse River, N. C. **91** F19
Nevada 16, 208-211
New Albany, Ind. **139** R8
New Bedford, Mass. 38, **39** N20
New Berlin, Wis. **127** Q13
New Bern, N. C. **91** G22
New Braunfels, Tex. 190, **191** M12
New Britain, Conn. **43** F9
New Brunswick, N. J. **61** H7
New Canaan, Conn. **43** M3
New Castle, Del. 69, **69** C4
New Castle, Ind. **139** K10
New Castle, Pa. **57** F2
New City, N. Y. **53** R17
New Concord, Ohio **143** K11
New Fairfield, Conn. **43** J3
New Hampshire 30-33

260

New Harmony, Ind. 138, **139**
S1, *140*
New Haven, Conn. 42, **43** K8
New Hope, Pa. **57** H18
New Iberia, La. **117** N8
New Jersey 60-63
New Jersey Turnpike, N. J. 60,
61
New London, Conn. 42, **43** K15;
diving bell (1938) *42;* U.S.
Coast Guard Academy *44-45*
New Madrid, Mo. **173, 173** P18
New Mexico 182-185
New Orleans, La. 94, **94,** *116,*
117 N14, *118*
New Philadelphia, Ohio **143** H12
New River, N. C. **91** H21
New River, Va.-W. Va. **79** N7,
83 L9
New Rochelle, N. Y. **53** S17
New Ulm, Minn. **153** R6
New York 52-55
New York City, N. Y. *12,* **51,**
52, 53 T17, *54-55*
Newark, Del. **69** C2
Newark, N. J. **61** F9, *63*
Newark, Ohio **143** K9
Newburgh, N. Y. **53** Q17
Newburyport, Mass. **39** A20
Newfound Lake, N. H. **31** N5
Newington, Conn. **43** E10
Newport, Ky. **75** A17
Newport, R. I. 46, **47** M9, 49, *49*
Newport, Vt. **27** B8
Newport Beach, Calif. **231** S11,
232
Newport News, Va. 82, **83** L24;
submarine *84-85*
Newton, Mass. **39** F17
Nez Perce IR, Idaho **197** G3
Niagara Falls, N. Y. 52, **52** J2,
52, 54
Niagara River, N. Y. 52, **52** H2
Niantic Bay, Conn. **43** K15
Niihau, Hawaii **234, 240, 240** D2
Niles, Ill. **143** E14
Niobrara River, Nebr. **161** A9
Noatak River, Alas. **237** E17
Nogales, Ariz. **179** T11
Nolin Lake, Ky. **75** J12
Nomans Land Island NWR,
Mass. **39** R21
Nome, Alas. 236, **237** G14
Nonquit Pond, R. I. **47** J11
Norfork Lake, Ark. **97** B9
Normal, Ill. **135** H7
Norman, Okla. **187** J18
Norman, Lake, N. C. **91** E10
Norris Lake, Tenn. **87** B20
Norristown, Pa. **57** K17
North Adams, Mass. **38** C3
North Branch Potomac River,
Md.-W. Va. 64 C2, **79** G13
North Canadian River, Okla.
187 F15
North Carolina 90-93
North Cascades NP, Wash. **223**
B9
North Charleston, S. C. **113** L14
North Chicago, Ill. **135** B10
North Dakota 148-151

North Fork Red River, Okla.
187 J11
North Haven, Conn. **43** J8
North Las Vegas, Nev. **209** Q11
North Little Rock, Ark. 96, **97**
J9
North Olmsted, Ohio **143** D10
North Platte River, Nebr.-
Wyo. **161** E4, **195, 204, 205**
J15, N11
North Providence, R. I. **47** D8
North Slope, Alas. 236, **237** C18
Northampton, Mass. **38** F7
Northern Cheyenne IR, Mont.
201 J15
Northern Mariana Islands **235,**
244, **245**
Northwest Angle, Minn. 153,
153 A5
Norton Sound, Alas. **237** G14
Norwalk, Conn. **43** N3
Norwalk Islands, Conn. **43** O4
Norwich, Conn. **43** G16
Norwood, Mass. **39** G17
Norwood, Ohio **143** O2
Nottoway River, Va. **83** L18
Noxontown Pond, Del. **69** F2
Noxubee NWR, Miss. **101** G10
Nueces River, Tex. **191** O11
Nunivak Island, Alas. **237** K12
Nuuuli, American Samoa **245** S6

Oahe, Lake, N. Dak.-
S. Dak.**149** L9, **157** D9
Oahe Dam, S. Dak. **157** F9
Oahu, Hawaii **234, 240, 241** E10
Oak Park, Ill. **135** C10
Oak Ridge, Tenn. 86, **87** C19
Oakland, Calif. **231** K4
Ocala, Fla. **121** F13
Ocean City, Md. 64, **65** M27
Ocheyedan Mound, Iowa **165** A4
Ochlockonee River, Fla. **121** B8
Ocmulgee NM, Ga. **109** J8
Ocmulgee River, Ga. **109** M9;
steamboat (circa 1900) *108*
Oconee River, Ga. **109** J10
Ocracoke, N. C. **91** F26
Odessa, Tex. 190, **191** H6
Oelwein, Iowa **165** D14
Ofu, American Samoa **245** L2
Ogallala, Nebr. **161** G5
Ogallala Aquifer 160, 162, 168
Ogden, Utah **213** D7
Ogdensburg, N. Y. **53** B12
Ohio 142-145
Ohio River 56, **57** G2, **72-73, 74,**
75, 79, 124-125, 135, *136,* **139,**
142, 153
Oil City, Pa. **57** D4
Oil industry 116, 118, 186, *190,*
236; derricks *190;* first well
56; pipeline 238; refinery *188;*
rig *118*
Okanogan River, Wash. **223** B13
Okatibbee Lake, Miss. **101** K10
Okeechobee, Lake, Fla. 120,
121 L17
Okefenokee NWR, Fla.-Ga. **109**
Q12, **121** B13

Okefenokee Swamp, Ga. 10, 13,
108, 109, **109** R12, *110*
Oklahoma 186-189
Oklahoma Bat Caves NWR,
Okla. **187** E26
Oklahoma City, Okla. **177, 186,**
187 H18
Okmulgee, Okla. **187** H23
Olathe, Kans. **169** D19
Old Faithful, Wyo. **205** C2, *207*
Old Saybrook, Conn. **43** K13
Old Speck Mountain, Me. **35** O2
Old Sturbridge Village, Mass.
39 H11
Olentangy River, Ohio **143** H7
Olosega, American Samoa **245** L3
Olympia, Wash. **222, 223** H5
Olympic Mountains, Wash. **223**
F3
Olympic NF, Wash. *224*
Olympic NP, Wash. **222, 223** F3
Olympus, Mount, Wash. **223** E3
Omaha, Nebr. **147, 160, 161** E18
Omaha IR, Nebr. **161** C16
Oneida, N. Y. **53** J12
Oneida IR, Wis. **127** L13
Oneida Lake, N. Y. **53** H11
Onondaga IR, N. Y. **53** K10
Onslow Bay, N. C. **91** J22
Ontario, Lake, Canada-U. S.
50, 53
Ontonagon IR, Mich. **131** D2
Oologah Lake, Okla. **187** D24
Opelika, Ala. **105** K12
Opelousas, La. **117** K7
Optima NWR, Okla. **186** C7
Oraibi, Ariz. 178, **179** E12
Oregon 226-229
Oregon Caves NM, Oreg. **227** O4
Oregon Dunes NRA, Oreg. **227**
J2
Oregon Trail **161,** *163,* **169,** 172,
197, 205, 217, 227, 227
Orem, Utah **213** G8
Organ Pipe Cactus NM, Ariz.
179 R6
Orlando, Fla. 120, **121** G15
Osage IR, Okla. **187** D21
Osage River, Mo. **173** J10
Oshkosh, Wis. **127** N12;
aviation convention *129*
Ossabaw Island, Ga. **109** N16
Ossipee Lake, N. H. **31** M9
Oswego, N. Y. **53** H9
Ottawa, Ill. **135** E8
Ottawa NWR, Ohio **143** C6
Ottawa NWR, Ohio **143** G4
Otter Creek, Vt. **27** M3
Ottumwa, Iowa **165** K12
Ouachita, Lake, Ark. **97** J5
Ouachita Mountains, Ark.-
Okla. 96, 97, **97** H3, 186, **187**
L24
Ouachita River, Ark.-La. **97**
O7, **117** D7
Ouray NWR, Utah **213** G14
Outer Banks, N. C. 72, 73, 90,
91 G26
Overland Park, Kans. **169** D19
Owatonna, Minn. **153** R9
Owens River, Calif. **231** L11

Owensboro, Ky. **75** G8
Owosso, Mich. **131** Q13
Owyhee River, Oreg. **227** M17
Oxford, Md. **65** J20; cook *66*
Oxford, Miss. **101** C8
Oxnard, Calif. **231** R9
Ozark Plateau, Ark.-Mo.-Okla.
94, 96, 97, **97** E5, *98,* 134,
147, 172, **173** O9, 177, 186,
187 E26; canoeists *174;* crafts
96, 98

Pablo NWR, Mont. **201** D3
Pachaug Pond, Conn. **43** G17
Pacific Crest Trail **223, 227,**
227, 231, 231
Pacific Ocean territories 234
Paden City, W. Va. **79** F8;
marble factory *81*
Padre Island NS, Tex. **191** Q13
Paducah, Ky. **74** L4
Page, Ariz. **179** B10
Pago Pago, American Samoa
244, **245** R6
Pahala, Hawaii **241** P23
Painted Desert, Ariz. **179** E10
Palm Beach, Fla. **121** M19;
cyclists (1895) *120*
Palm Springs, Calif. **231** R13
Palo Alto, Calif. **231** K4; sleep
laboratory *233*
Palomar Mountain, Calif. **231** S13
Pamlico River, N. C. **91** F24
Pamunkey River, Va. **83** H21
Panama City, Fla. **121** C5
Paradise Valley, Ariz. **179** M8
Paramus, N. J. **61** E9
Park Forest, Ill. **135** E11
Parkersburg, W. Va. **79** G5
Parkland, Wash. **223** H6
Parkville, Md. **65** D18
Parma, Ohio **143** D11
Parris Island, S. C. **113** O11
Parsons, Kans. **169** J18
Pasadena, Calif. **231** R11
Pasadena, Tex. **191** L16
Pascagoula, Miss. **101** S11
Pascagoula River, Miss. **101** R11
Pasco, Wash. **223** L14
Passaic, N. J. **61** E9
Passamaquoddy IR, Me. **35**
L12, M14
Patapsco River, Md. **65** E18
Paterson, N. J. **61** E9
Pathfinder NWR, Wyo. **205** K11
Patoka River, Ind. **139** R3
Patuxent NWR, Md. **65** F16
Patuxent River, Md. **65** K16
Pawcatuck River, R. I. **47** O2
Pawleys Island, S. C. **113** J17
Pawtucket, R. I. 46, **47** D8
Pawtuxet River, R. I. **47** G7
Payette, Idaho **197** N2
Payette River, Idaho **197** O2
Pea Island NWR, N. C. **91** D27
Peabody, Mass. **39** D19
Peace River, Fla. **121** K14
Pearl City, Hawaii **241** E10
Pearl Harbor, Hawaii 240, **241**
E10

Pearl Harbor NWR, Hawaii **241**
E10
Pearl River, La.-Miss. **101** H9-
T7, **117** J15, *119*
Pecos, Tex. **191** J5, *192*
Pecos NM, N. Mex. **183** F9
Pecos River, N. Mex.-Tex. **176,**
183 L13, **191** K7
Pee Dee NWR, N. C. **91** G13
Pee Dee River, N. C.-S. C. **91**
G13, **113** F16
Peekskill, N. Y. **53** R17
Pekin, Ill. **135** H6
Pelican Island NWR, Fla. **121**
J17
Pembina Mountains, N. Dak.
149 B15
Pemigewasset River, N. H. **31**
K6
Pend Oreille Lake, Idaho **197** B3
Pend Oreille River, Wash. **223**
B18
Pendleton, Oreg. **227** C13
Pennsauken, N. J. **61** M3
Pennsylvania 13, 56-59
Penobscot Bay, Me. **35** P9
Penobscot IR, Me. **35** M9
Penobscot River, Me. 34, **35** K10
Pensacola, Fla. 120, **121** B2
Peoria, Ill. **135** G6
Pepin, Lake, Minn.-Wis. **127**
L2, **153** Q12
Perdido River, Fla. **121** B1
Pere Marquette River, Mich.
131 Q9
Perth Amboy, N. J. **61** H8
Peru, Ind. **139** F7
Peshtigo River, Wis. 126, **127**
H13
Petenwell Lake, Wis. **127** M8
Peterborough, N. H. **31** T4
Petersburg, Va. **83** K20
Petrified Forest NP, Ariz. 179,
179 H14
Petroglyph NM, N. Mex. **183** G7
Philadelphia, Miss. **101** J9
Philadelphia, Pa. 50, **51,** 56, 57,
57 K18, *59*
Phillipsburg, N. J. **53** F3
Phoenix, Ariz. **176,** 178, **179** M8
Phosphorescent Bay, Puerto
Rico **245** E8
Pickwick Lake, Miss.-Tenn. 86
H7, **101** A12
Pictured Rocks NL, Mich. **131**
F8
Piedmont NWR, Ga. **109** H7
Piedmont Plateau 50, 64, 68, 72,
82, 90, 91, 112
Pierre, S. Dak. **157** F9
Pikes Peak, Colo. **217** H11
Pikesville, Md. **65** D17
Pikeville, Ky. **75** H24, *77*
Pine Barrens, N. J. 60, **61** R5, *62*
Pine Bluff, Ark. **97** L10
Pine Creek Gorge, Pa. **57** C11
Pine Hill, Ala. **105** N4
Pine Island NWR, Fla. **121** M14
Pine Mountain, Ky. **75** K22
Pine Ridge IR, S. Dak. 156, **157**
J4

Pine Ridge NRA, Nebr. **161** B13
Pinellas Bay NWR, Fla. **121** K12
Pinnacles NM, Calif. **231** M6
Pioneers 146, 160, 201, 204; trails 201
Pipe Spring NM, Ariz. **179** B7
Pipestone NM, Minn. **153** R2
Piscataqua River, N. H. **31** Q11
Pittsburg, Kans. **169** J19
Pittsburgh, Pa. 50, 56, **57** H3
Pittsfield, Me. **35** N7
Pittsfield, Mass. **38** E2, 39
Placid, Lake, N. Y. **53** D16
Plainfield, N. J. **61** G7
Plains, Ga. **109** M5
Plantation, Fla. **121** N18
Plants: agave *192;* flame azaleas *81;* saguaro cactuses *181; see also* Crops; Grasslands; Trees
Plaquemine, La. **117** L10
Plate tectonics 26, 221, 234
Platte City, Iowa-Mo. **173** A3
Platte River, Nebr. 160, **161** F14; sandhill cranes *163*
Plattsburgh, N. Y. **53** B18
Pleasure Ridge Park, Ky. **75** F13
Plimoth Plantation, Mass. **39** K22
Plum Island, Mass. **39** B20
Plum Tree Island NWR, Va. **83** K24
Plymouth, Mass. **39** K21
Plymouth Bay, Mass. **39** J22
Pocatello, Idaho **0197** Q10
Pocomoke River, Md. **65** O24
Pocono Mountains, Pa. 56, **57** E17
Poinsett, Lake, S. Dak. **157** F16
Point Barrow, Alas. 236, **237** B18
Point Judith, R. I. **47** P7
Point Reyes NS, Calif. **231** J3
Point Roberts, Wash. **223** A4
Pomme de Terre Lake, Mo. **173** L7
Pompano Beach, Fla. **121** N18
Ponca City, Okla. **187** C19
Ponce, Puerto Rico **245** E11
Ponce de Leon Bay, Fla. **121** Q16
Pontchartrain, Lake, La. 116, **117** M14
Pontiac, Ill. **135** G8
Pontiac, Mich. **131** R15
Pony Express Trail 160, **161**, **169**, 172, 205, 209, 213, 231
Population 13, 15, 16; density 60, 250; geographical center 15, 172, 173
Port Angeles, Wash. **223** D3
Port Arthur, Tex. **191** L18
Port Chester, N. Y. **53** S18
Port Huron, Mich. **131** Q17
Port Royal, S. C. **113** O11
Portage Lake, Mich. **131** D4
Portland, Conn. **43** G10; Wampanoag Indians *44*
Portland, Me. 25, **35** S4
Portland, Oreg. **220**, 226, **227** C5, *229*
Portsmouth, N. H. 30, **31** R11, *32-33*

Portsmouth, Ohio **143** Q7
Portsmouth, Va. **83** L24
Potawatomi IR, Kans. **169** C16
Potawatomi IR, Wis. **127** G12
Potholes Reservoir, Wash. **223** H13
Potomac River, Md.-Va.-W. Va. 20, **21**, 50, **50-51**, 65 E12, **73**, 79 E18, *80*, 82, **83** F22
Potsdam, N. Y. **53** B14
Pottstown, Pa. **57** J16
Poughkeepsie, N. Y. **53** P17
Poultry 96, 108; chicks *99;* rooster *103*
Poverty Point NM, La. **117**, **117** B10
Powder River, Mont.-Wyo. **201** G17, **205** C13
Powell, Wyo. **205** B6
Powell, Lake, Ariz.-Utah **179** A10, 212, **213** S9
Poygan, Lake, Wis. **127** M11
Prairie *see* Grasslands
Prairie du Chien, Wis. **127** Q5
Prairie Island IR, Minn. **153** Q10
Pratt, Kans. **169** H9
Prattville, Ala. **105** L8
Prehistoric animals 13, 159, 169; skeleton *158*
Prescott, Ariz. **179** J7
Presidential Range, N. H. 30, 31, **31** H7
Presque Isle, Me. **35** D11, *36*
Presquile NWR, Va. **83** J21
Prettyboy Reservoir, Md. **65** B17
Pribilof Islands, Alas. **237** M10
Price River, Utah **213** K11
Prichard, Ala. **105** S3
Priest Lake, Idaho **197** A2
Priest River, Idaho **197** B2
Prime Hook NWR, Del. **69** O6
Prince William Sound, Alas. 236, **237** L20
Princeton, N. J. **61** J6
Prineville Reservoir, Oreg. **227** H9
Promontory, Utah **213** B6
Protection Island NWR, Wash. **223** D5
Providence, R. I. 24, 46, **47** E8; flood (1938) *46;* silversmith *48*
Providence River, R. I. **47** F8
Provincetown, Mass. **39** H25
Provo, Utah **213** G8
Prudence Island, R. I. **47** J9
Prudhoe Bay, Alas. 236, **237** C20
Pueblo, Colo. **217** K12
Puerco River, Ariz. **179** G15
Puerto Rico 234, **235**, 244, **245**, *246-247*
Puget Sound, Wash. 222, **223** E5
Pullman, Wash. **223** J18
Pumpkin Center, Ind. **139** Q6
Purgatoire River, Colo. **217** N14
Puyallup IR, Wash. **223** G6
Pymatuning Reservoir, Pa. **57** C1

Pyramid Lake IR, Nev. **209** F2, *211*

Quabbin Reservoir, Mass. **39** F9
Quarrying 26, *29;* granite 108, *111;* limestone 138, 139; marble 26
Queen River, R. I. **47** L5
Quinault IR, Wash. **223** G2
Quincy, Ill. **135** K1
Quincy, Mass. **39** G19
Quinebaug River, Conn. **43** E17
Quivira NWR, Kans. **169** G9

Rabun Gap, Ga. **109** A8
Raccoon River, Iowa **165** F7
Racine, Wis. **127** R14
Radford, Va. **83** L10
Railroads 178, 182, *182*, 204; antique train *70-71;* construction (1887) *200;* steam locomotive *216;* westward expansion 204
Rainbow Bridge NM, Utah **213** S10
Rainier, Mount, Wash. **223** J7
Rainy River, Minn. **153** C7
Raisin River, Mich. **131** T14
Raleigh, N. C. **73**, **91** D17
Raleigh Bay, N. C. **91** G26
Ramah Navajo IR, N. Mex. **183** H3
Ranches *123*, 156, *204, 207*
Randolph, Mass. **39** G19
Rangeley Lake, Me. **35** M2
Rantoul, Ill. **135** J9
Rapid City, S. Dak. **157** G2; museum *158*
Rapidan River, Va. **83** E19
Rappahannock River, Va. 82, **83** F22
Raritan River, N. J. **61** H7
Rathbun Lake, Iowa **165** L11
Raystown Lake, Pa. **57** J9
Reading, Ohio **143** O2
Reading, Pa. **57** J15
Red Bank, N. J. **61** J10
Red Cliff IR, Wis. **127** B6
Red Hills, Kans. 168, **169** J7
Red Lake IR, Minn. **153** A5, E5
Red River 97, 117, 187, 191
Red River of the North 149, **149**, **153**; valley *150, 151*
Red Rock Reservoir, Iowa **165** J10
Red Wing, Minn. **153** Q11
Redding, Calif. **231** D4
Redwood NP, Calif. **231** B2
Reelfoot Lake, Tenn. 87
Reelfoot NWR, Tenn. **74** N2, **86** B4
Reese River, Nev. **209** F7
Rehoboth Bay, Del. **69** Q8; oyster catch *71*
Rehoboth Beach, Del. **69** P8
Reidsville, N. C. **91** B14
Rend Lake, Ill. **135** Q7
Reno, Nev. 208, **209** G1

Renton, Wash. **223** G6
Republican River, Kans.-Nebr. **161** J12, **169** C13
Reston, Va. **83** B20
Reynoldsburg, Ohio **143** L8
Rhinelander, Wis. **127** G10
Rhode Island 46-49
Rhode Island (island), R. I. **47** L10
Rhode Island Sound **39** P19, **47** O11
Rib Mountain, Wis. **127** J9
Richland, Wash. **223** L13
Richmond, Ind. **139** K11
Richmond, Ky. **75** G18
Richmond, Va. **73**, 82, **83** H20
Ridgefield, Conn. **43** L3
Ridgewood, N. J. **61** D9
Riffe Lake, Wash. **223** K6
Rio Chama, N. Mex. **183** C7
Rio Grande, Colo.-N. Mex.-Tex. 177, **177**, 182, **183**, 190, **191**, *192*, 217
Rio Hondo, N. Mex. **183** M11
Rio Puerco, N. Mex. **183** J6
Ripon, Wis. **127** N11
Ritidian Point, Guam **245** O18
Riverhead, N. Y. **53** S21
Riverside, Calif. **231** R12
Riviera Beach, Fla. **121** M19
Roanoke, Va. **83** K12
Roanoke Island, N. C. 90, **91** C26
Roanoke Rapids, N. C. **91** B20
Roanoke River, N. C.-Va. **83** L15, **91** B21
Roanoke River NWR, N. C. **91** C22
Robert S. Kerr Reservoir, Okla. **187** J26
Rochester, Minn. **153** R11, *154*
Rochester, N. Y. 52, **53** J6
Rock Hill, S. C. **113** B10
Rock Island, Ill. **135** E4
Rock River, Ill.-Wis. **127** Q11, **135** C6
Rockford, Ill. **135** B7
Rockland, Me. **35** Q8
Rockville, Md. **65** F14
Rocky Boys IR, Mont. **201** C10
Rocky Fork Lake, Ohio **143** O5
Rocky Hill, Conn. **43** F10
Rocky Mountain NP, Colo. **217** D9
Rocky Mountains, Canada-U. S. *9*, 10, **176**, **183**, 194, **195**, **197**, 200, 201, 204, **205**, 216, **217**, 236; formation 177, 183, 194
Rogers, Mount, Va. 82, M7
Rogue River, Oreg. **227** M2
Rolla, Mo. **173** K12
Rome, Ga. **109** C2
Rome, N. Y. **53** H12
Rosebud IR, S. Dak. **157** K8
Roseburg, Oreg. **227** K4
Roseville, Mich. **131** R16
Ross Lake NRA, Wash. **223** B9
Ross R. Barnett Reservoir, Miss. **101** K6
Roswell, N. Mex. **183** M12
Rota, Northern Mariana

Islands 244, **245** J14
Rotterdam, N. Y. **53** K16
Rough River, Ky. **75** H9
Round Valley IR, Calif. **231** E2
Roundup, Mont. **201** G12
Royal Gorge, Colo. **217** K10
Royal Oak, Mich. **131** S16
Ruby Dome, Nev. **209** E10
Rufus Woods Lake, Wash. **223** D13
Rugby, N. Dak. **149** C11
Rum River, Minn. **153** N9
Rumford, Me. **35** O3
Russell, Kans. **169** D9
Russell Cave NM, Ala. 104, **105** A10
Ruston, La. **117** C5
Rutland, Vt. **27** N4

Sabine Lake, La.-Tex. **117** N2, **191** L18
Sabine NWR, La. **117** N3
Sabine River, La.-Tex. **94**, **117** K2, **191** K18
Sac and Fox IR, Iowa-Kans.-Nebr. **165** G11, **161** J19, **169** A17
Sacajawea Peak, Oreg. **227** D17
Sacramento, Calif. **231** H6
Sacramento NWR, Calif. **231** F4
Sacramento River, Calif. 230, **231** E5
Sag Harbor, N. Y. **53** S22
Saginaw, Mich. 130, **131** P14
Saginaw Bay, Mich. **131** N14
Saginaw River, Mich. **131** P14
Saguaro NM, Ariz. **179** Q10-12, 182
St. Albans, Vt. **27** C3
St. Andrew Sound, Ga. **109** Q15
St. Augustine, Fla. 120, **121** D15
St. Charles, Mo. **173** G15
St. Clair River, Mich. **131** R17
St. Clair Shores, Mich. **131** S16
St. Cloud, Minn. **153** N7
St. Croix, U. S. Virgin Islands 244, **245** G4
St. Croix IR, Wis. **127** F2
St. Croix River, Me. **35** K13
St. Croix River, Minn.-Wis. **127** H1, **153** M10
St. Elias Mountains, Alas. 236, **237** M23
St. Francis, Ark. **97** A16
St. Francis River, Ark.-Mo. **97** F15, **173** R16
St. Helens, Mount, Wash. 221, 222, **223** L6
St. Joe River, Idaho **197** E4
St. John, U. S. Virgin Islands 244, **245** B4
St. Johns River, Fla. **121** D15
St. John River, Me. 34, **35** B8
St. Joseph, Mo. **173** D3
St. Joseph River, Ind.-Mich. **131** T10, **139** D11
St. Lawrence Island, Alas. **237** G12
St. Lawrence River, Canada 52, **53** C11
St. Lawrence Seaway, Canada-U. S. 134

St. Louis, Mo. **147, 173** H16, *174-175;* World's Fair (1904) *172*
St. Louis Park, Minn. **153** P9
St. Louis River, Minn. **153** H11
St. Marks NWR, Fla. **121** C8
St. Marys City, Md. **65** N18
St. Marys River, Fla.-Ga. 13, **109** Q13, **121** A14
St. Marys River, Ind.-Ohio **139** F11
St. Marys River, Mich. **131** F13
St. Matthew Island, Alas. **237** J10
St. Michaels, Md. **65** J20
St. Paul, Minn. **147, 152, 153** P10; winter carnival *155*
St. Petersburg, Fla. **95, 120, 121** J12
St. Regis IR, N. Y. **53** A14
St. Simons Island, Ga. 109, **109** P15
St. Thomas, U. S. Virgin Islands 244, **245** B2; festival (1950s) *244*
St. Vincent NWR, Fla. **121** D6
Ste. Genevieve, Mo. **173** K17; quilters *175*
Saipan, Northern Mariana Islands 244, **245** H18
Sakakawea, Lake, N. Dak. 148, **149** F5, *150*
Sakonnet River, R. I. **47** K11
Salamonie Lake, Ind. **139** F9
Salamonie River, Ind. **139** G10
Salem, Mass. **39** D20
Salem, N. H. **31** T8
Salem, Oreg. 226, **227** E5
Salem, Va. **83** K12
Salina, Kans. **169** E12
Salinas, Calif. **231** M5
Salinas Pueblo Missions NM, N. Mex. **183** K8
Salinas River and valley, Calif. **231** N6, *233*
Saline River, Ark. **97** M9
Saline River, Kans. **169** D11
Salisbury, Md. **65** M23
Salisbury, N. C. **91** E12
Salkehatchie River, S. C. **113** K9
Salmon River, Idaho 196, 197, **197** K4-M7
Salmon River Mountains, Idaho **197** L4
Salt Fork Red River, Okla. **187** K11
Salt Fork River, Okla. **187** C17
Salt Lake City, Utah **195,** 212, **213** E7, *214*
Salt Lake Valley, Utah *212, 215*
Salt Plains NWR, Okla. **187** C16
Salt River, Ariz. 178, **179** M11
Salt River, Mo. **173** D13
Salt River IR, Ariz. **179** M9
Salton Sea NWR, Calif. **231** S15
Saluda River, S. C. **113** F7
Salvador, Lake, La. **117** N14
Sam Rayburn Reservoir, Tex. **191** J17
San Andreas Fault, Calif. 230, **231** F1-P9

San Andres NWR, N. Mex. **183** O7
San Angelo, Tex. **191** J9
San Antonio, Tex. **177, 190, 191** M12
San Bernardino, Calif. **231** R12
San Bernardino NWR, Ariz. **179** T15
San Carlos IR, Ariz. **179** N13
San Carlos Reservoir, Ariz. **179** N12
San Diego, Calif. **221, 231** U13
San Francisco, Calif. **220, 230,** *230,* **231** K4, *232*
San Francisco River, N. Mex. **183** L2
San Ildefonso IR, N. Mex. **183** E8
San Joaquin River, Calif. 230, **231** L7
San Joaquin Valley, Calif. **220-221, 231** N8
San Jose, Calif. **231** K4
San Jose, Northern Mariana Islands **245** L17
San Juan, Puerto Rico 244, **245** B14, *246-247*
San Juan Islands, Wash. 222, **223** C5
San Juan River, Colo.-N. Mex.-Utah **183** B2, **213** S12, **217** O6
San Luis NWR, Calif. **231** L6
San Luis Obispo, Calif. **231** O7
San Pedro River, Ariz. **179** P12
San Rafael River, Utah **213** M11
San Xavier IR, Ariz. **179** R11
Sand Hills, Nebr. 160, **161** C7
Sand Lake NWR, S. Dak. **157** B14
Sand Springs, Okla. **187** F22
Sandusky, Ohio **143** D8
Sandusky River, Ohio **143** F6
Sandwich, Mass. **39** L23
Sandy Hook, N. J. **61** H10
Sanford, Me. **35** T2
Sangamon River, Ill. **135** K7
Sangre de Cristo Mountains, N. Mex. **183** D9
Sanibel Island, Fla. **121** N14
Santa Ana IR, N. Mex. **183** F7
Santa Ana NWR, Tex. **191** R12
Santa Barbara, Calif. **231** Q8
Santa Catalina, Gulf of, Calif. **231** T11
Santa Clara IR, N. Mex. **183** D8
Santa Claus, Ind. **139** S4
Santa Cruz River, Ariz. **179** P10
Santa Fe, N. Mex. 182, **183** E9
Santa Fe Trail **169,** 172, **173, 183,** *216,* **217**
Santa Maria, Calif. **231** P7
Santa Maria River, Ariz. **179** J5
Santa Rosa, Calif. **231** H4
Santa Rosa Island, Fla. **121** C3
Santee NWR, S. C. **113** J13
Santee Point, S. C. **113** K17
Santee River, S. C. **113** H15
Santee Sioux IR, Nebr. **161** A13
Santo Domingo IR, N. Mex. **183** F8

Saranac Lake, N. Y. **53** D16
Sarasota, Fla. **121** K13
Saratoga Springs, N. Y. **53** J17; racehorse *55*
Sardis Lake, Miss. **101** C7
Sassafras Mountain, S. C. **113** A3
Satilla River, Ga. **109** O10
Saugatuck Reservoir, Conn. **43** L4
Saugus, Mass. **39** E19
Sault Ste. Marie, Mich. **131** F12
Sault Ste. Marie IR, Mich. **131** F12
Saunderstown, R. I. **47** M7
Savannah, Ga. **95, 108, 109** L16
Savannah, Tenn. **86** G7
Savannah NWR, Ga.-S. C. **109** L15, **113** P10
Savannah River, Ga.-S. C. **109** H14, **113** N9
Sawtooth Range, Idaho 197, **197** N5; ski resort *198-199*
Sayreville, N. J. **61** H8
Scarborough, Me. **35** S3
Schenectady, N. Y. 52, **53** K17
Schuylkill River, Pa. **57** H15
Scioto River, Ohio **143** H4-Q7
Scituate, Mass. **39** G21
Scituate Reservoir, R. I. **47** F5
Scotlandville, La. **117** K11
Scotts Bluff NM, Nebr. **161** D1
Scottsdale, Ariz. **179** M8
Scranton, Pa. **57** D16
Sea Island, Ga. **109** P15
Seaford, Del. **69** Q3; Du Pont plant (1950) *68*
Seal Island NWR, Me. **35** R9
Seattle, Wash. **220, 222, 223** F6, *225*
Sebago Lake, Me. **35** R3
Sebring, Fla. **121** K15
Second Lake, N. H. **31** B9
Sedalia, Mo. **173** H7
Sedona, Ariz. **179** H9
Seedskadee NWR, Wyo. **205** M4
Seekonk River, R. I. **47** D8
Selma, Ala. **105** L6
Seminoe Reservoir, Wyo. **205** L11
Seminole, Lake, Ga. **109** R3
Seney NWR, Mich. **131** F9
Sequoia NP, Calif. **231** M10
Sequoyah NWR, Okla. **187** H25
Severna Park, Md. **65** F18
Sevier Desert, Utah 213, **213**
Sevier Lake, Utah 18, **213** M4
Sevier River, Utah **213** O7
Sevilleta, N. Mex. **183** J7
Seward, Alas. **237** M19
Seward Peninsula, Alas. **237** F14
Sharer, Lake, Ind. **139** F5
Shaker Heights, Ohio **143** D12
Sharon, Pa. **57** E1
Sharpe, Lake, S. Dak. **157** G11
Sharpsburg, Md. **65** C10
Shasta, Mount, Calif. **231** B4
Shasta Lake, Calif. **231** D4
Shawnee, Okla. **187** J20
Shawneetown, Ill. **135** R9

Sheboygan, Wis. **127** O14
Shelby, Mont. **201** C7
Shelbyville, Lake, Ill. **135** L8
Sheldon NWR, Nev.-Oreg. **209** B3, **227** O12
Shell Keys NWR, La. **117** P8
Shellrock River, Iowa **165** C11
Shelton, Conn. **43** K6
Shelton, Wash. **223** G4
Shenandoah NP, Va. **83** D17
Shenandoah River, Va.-W. Va. **79** G19, *80,* **83** B18
Shenandoah Valley, Va. 82, **83** D16, *84*
Shenipsit Lake, Conn. **43** C12
Shepaug River, Conn. **43** F4
Shepherdstown, W. Va. **79** F19
Sheridan, Wyo. **205** B11
Shetucket River, Conn. **43** F15
Sheyenne River, N. Dak. **149** K18
Ship Rock, N. Mex. 183, **183** B2
Shively, Ky. **75** E13
Shoshone Falls, Idaho 196, **197** R6
Shreveport, La. 116, **117** C2
Shrewsbury, Mass. **39** F14
Sidney Lanier, Lake, Ga. **109** C6
Sierra Blanca Peak, N. Mex. **183** M9
Sierra Nevada, Calif. 8, 208, **220-221,** 221, 230, **231** E6-O11
Silver City, N. Mex. **183** O3
Silver Spring, Md. **65** G15
Silverton, Colo. **217** M5
Simi Valley, Calif. **231** R10
Sinclair, Lake, Ga. **109** G8
Sioux City, Iowa 164, **165** D1
Sioux Falls, S. Dak. 156, **157** J17
Sipsey River, Ala. **105** G4
Sisseton, S. Dak. **157** B17
Sitka, Alas. **237** O25
Sitting Bull Monument, S. Dak. **157** B9
Six Mile Lake, La. **117** N10
Skagit River, Wash. **223** C7
Skagway, Alas. **237** M25
Skokomish IR, Wash. **223** G4
Skull Valley IR, Utah **213** G5
Skunk River, Iowa **165** K14
Sleeping Bear Dunes NL, Mich. **131** L9
Smith Island, Md.-Va. **65** P21, **83** F24
Smith Mountain Lake, Va. **83** L13
Smithfield, Va. **83** L23, *85*
Smithville, Tenn. **87** D14; country music contest *88*
Smoky Hill River, Kans. **169** E5
Smoky Hills, Kans. 168, 169, **169** C7
Smugglers Notch, Vt. 27, **27** E5
Smyrna, Del. **69** H3
Smyrna, Ga. **109** E4
Smyrna, Tenn. **87** D12; automobile plant 86, *89*
Snake River 10, **194-195,** 196, **197,** 198, *199,* **205** F1, 213, **223** K16, 226, **227** F17; kayaker *206*

Snake River Plain, Idaho 196, **197** Q8
Snow, Mount, Vt. **27** S4
Soda Springs, Idaho **197** R12
Solomon River, Kans. **169** C11
Somerville, Mass. **39** E18
Songsong, Northern Mariana Islands **245** J13
Sonoma, Calif. **231** J4
Sonoran Desert, Ariz. 178, **179** O5
Soo Canals, Canada-U. S. 130, **131** F12, F13
Souris River, N. Dak. **149** B9
South Bend, Ind. **139** B7
South Branch Potomac River, W. Va. **79** G15
South Cape (Ka Lae), Hawaii **241** Q22
South Carolina 112-115
South Dakota 156-159
South Hero Island, Vt. **27** D2
South Holston Lake, Tenn. **87** A26
South Loup River, Nebr. **161** F9
South Milwaukee, Wis. **127** R14
South Pass, Wyo. 204, 205, **205** K6
South Platte River, Colo.Nebr. **161** F6, **217** C15
South Portland, Me. **35** S4
Southampton, N. Y. **53** S22
Southern Ute IR, Colo. **217** O4
Spanish Fork, Utah **213** H8
Spanish Trail **179, 183,** 208, **209, 213, 217, 231**
Spartanburg, S. C. **113** B6
Spenard, Alas. **237** L19
Spirit Lake, Iowa **165** A5
Spokane, Wash. 222, **223** F18
Spokane IR, Wash. **223** E16
Spokane River, Wash. **223** E16
Spoon River, Ill. **135** H4
Spring Hill, Tenn. 86, **87** D11
Springer Mountain, Ga. **109** B5
Springfield, Ill. 124, 134, **135** K6
Springfield, Mass. **38** H7
Springfield, Mo. **173** N7
Springfield, Ohio **143** L4
Springfield, Oreg. **227** H5
Springfield, Vt. **27** P7
Spruce Knob, W. Va. **79** K13
Spruce Knob-Seneca Rocks NRA, W. Va. **79** J13
Squaw Creek NWR, Mo. **173** B2
Stamford, Conn. 42, 43 O2
Standing Rock IR, N. Dak.-S. Dak. **149** M8, **157** A7
State College, Pa. **57** G9
Staten Island, N. Y. **53** T16
Statesville, N. C. **91** D10
Staunton, Va. **83** F15
Steamboat Springs, Colo. **217** C7
Steelmaking 56, 125, 130, 134; largest producer 138; steel mills *141,* nation's oldest *59*
Steelton, Pa. **57** J13; steel mill *59*
Sterling Heights, Mich. **131** R16

Steubenville, Ohio 143 J15
Stevens Point, Wis. 127 L9
Stewart B. McKinney NWR, Conn. 43 M7, M10, O3
Stillwater NWR, Nev. 209 G4
Stilwell, Okla. 187 G27, *189*
Stockbridge IR, Wis. 127 J11
Stockton, Calif. 231 J6
Stockton Lake, Mo. 173 M6
Stone Mountain, Ga. 109 E6
Stoney Lonesome, Ind. 139 N7
Stonington, Conn 43 K17
Stoughton, Mass. 39 H18
Stowe, Vt. 27 F6
Strafford, Vt. 27 L8
Stratford, Conn. 43 M6
Stratford Point, Conn. 43 M6
Stratton Mountain, Vt. 27 R4
Strawberry Reservoir, Utah 213 G9
Strawberry River, Utah 213 H11
Strom Thurmond Lake, Ga.-S. C. 109 E11, 113 G5
Sturgeon Bay, Wis. 127 J15
Stuttgart, Ark. 97 K11
Suffolk, Va. 83 M23
Sugar Creek, Ind. 139 J5
Suitland, Md. 65 H15
Sullivans Island, S. C. 113 M14
Sulphur, La. 117 M3
Summer Lake, Oreg. 227 L9
Summersville Lake, W. Va. 79 M8
Summit Lake IR, Nev. 209 B3
Sumner, Lake, N. Mex. 183 H13
Sumter, S. C. 113 G12
Sun City, Ariz. 179 M7
Sun Valley, Idaho 197 O6, *198-199*
Sunapee Lake, N. H. 31 P4
Sunapee, Mount, N. H. 31 Q4
Sundance, Wyo. 205 C17
Sunflower, Mount, Kans. 169 D1
Sunnyvale, Calif. 231 K4
Sunset Crater NM, Ariz. 179 F10
Supawna Meadows NWR, N. J. 61 P1
Superior, Wis. 127 C3, 152
Superior, Lake, Canada-U. S. 124, 126, 127, 130, 131, 131, 147, 153; lighthouse *155*
Susitna River, Alas. 237 K20
Susquehanna NWR, Md. 65 C21
Susquehanna River, Md.-N.Y.-Pa. 50, 50-51, 53 M12, 56, 57 B-L14, *58*, 64, 65
Sutton Lake, W. Va. 79 K9
Suwannee River, Fla.-Ga. 13, 109 R11, 121 D11
Swamps and wetlands 68, 82
Swan Lake, S. Dak. 157 C10
Swan Lake NWR, Mo. 173 D7
Swan River NWR, Mont. 201 D4
Swanquarter NWR, N. C. 91 F24
Swans Island, Me. 35 Q10

Sweetwater River, Wyo. 204, 205 J7
Swinomish IR, Wash. 223 C6
Syracuse, N. Y. 52, 53 J10; lacrosse game *54*

Tacoma, Wash. *222*, 223 G6
Tahlequah, Okla. 186, 187 F26
Tahoe, Lake, Calif.-Nev. 208, 209 H1, 231 G7
Tahquamenon River, Mich. 131 F10
Taliesin, Wis. 127 Q8
Talladega, Ala. 105 G9
Tallahassee, Fla. 121 B8
Tallahatchie River, Miss. 101 E5
Tallapoosa River, Ala. 105, 105 L10
Tampa, Fla. 121 J13
Tampa Bay, Fla. 121 J13
Tanana River, Alas. 237 J21
Tangier Island, Va. 83 G25; fishermen *84*
Tanglewood, Mass. 38 F2
Taos, N. Mex. 182, 183 C10
Taos IR, N. Mex. 183 C9
Taos Mountains, N. Mex. 183 B10, *184*
Taos Pueblo, N. Mex. 183 C10
Tar River, N. C. 91 B18
Tarpon Springs, Fla. 121 H12
Taunton, Mass. 39 K18
Taunton River, Mass. 39 L18
Taylor, Mount, N. Mex. 183 G5
Telluride, Colo. 217 L4
Tempe, Ariz. 179 N9
Temple, Tex. 191 J13
Ten Thousand Islands, Fla. 121 P15
Tenkiller Lake, Okla. 187 G26
Tennessee 86-89
Tennessee NWR, Tenn. 86 B7, 87 D8
Tennessee River, Ala.-Ky.-Tenn. 74, 86, 86, 87, 87, *88*, 104, 105, 105 C8
Tennessee Valley Authority 104
Tensas River NWR, La. 117 C10
Terre Haute, Ind. 139 M3
Terrebonne Bay, La. 117 Q13
Teton Range, Wyo. 10, 204, 205, 205 E1, *206*
Teton River, Mont. 201 D7
Texarkana, Ark. 114 O2
Texarkana, Tex. 191 E18
Texas 16, 190-193
Texas City, Tex. 191 M17
Texoma, Lake, Okla.-Tex. 187 O20, 191 E15
Textiles 30, 46, 90, 108, 112; spinning mill (1908) *90*
Thames River, Conn. 43 J16, *44*
Theodore Roosevelt Lake, Ariz. 178, 179 M11
Theodore Roosevelt NP, N Dak. 149 F2, H2
Thermal springs 96
Thibodaux, La. 117 N12
The Thimbles, Conn. 43 L10
Third Lake, N. H. 31 A8

Thomasville, Ga. 109 Q6
Thomasville, N. C. 91 D13
Thompson Falls, Mont. 201 D2
Thousand Islands, N. Y. 53 D10
Thousand Springs, Idaho 197 R6
Three Sisters (peaks), Oreg. 227 H7, *228*
Ticonderoga, N. Y. 53 F18
Tiffin, Ohio 143 E6
Tillamook Bay, Oreg. 227 C3
Timbalier Bay, La. 117 Q14
Time zones 6-7
Timms Hill, Wis. 127 G8
Tims Ford Lake, Tenn. 87 G13
Tinian, Northern Mariana Islands 244, 245 L17
Tippecanoe River, Ind. 139 D7
Tishomingo, Lake, Okla. 187 O20
Titusville, Fla. 121 G16
Titusville, Pa. 57 C4
Tohono O'Odham IR, Ariz. 179 O10, P9, Q8
Toledo, Ohio 125, 143 C5
Toledo Bend Reservoir, La.-Tex. 117 G2, 191 H18
Tom, Mount, Mass. 38 G6
Tombigbee River, Ala.-Miss. 101 F11, 104, 105 M2
Tombstone, Ariz. 178, 179 S13
Toms River, N. J. 61 M8
Tonawanda IR, N. Y. 52 J4
Tongue River, Mont. 201 H15
Tonto NM, Ariz. 179 M11
Toppenish NWR, Wash. 223 L11
Topeka, Kans. 169 D17
Torch Lake, Mich. 131 K11
Torrington, Conn. 43 D6
Towson, Md. 65 D17
Trans-Alaska Pipeline, Alas. 236, 237 E20, *238*
Traverse City, Mich. 131 L10
Trees: bristlecone pines 10, *210*, 230; Douglas fir *224*; giant sequoias 230; palmetto *114*; quaking aspens *218*; redwoods *16-17*, 230; sugar maples 26, *28*
Trenton, Mich. 131 T16
Trenton, N. J. 61 K5
Trinity River, Tex. 191, 191 H15
Troy, Mich. 131 R15
Troy, N. Y. 53 K17
Truchas Peak, N. Mex. 183 D10
Truckee River, Nev. 209 G2
Trumbull, Conn. 43 L5
Truro, Mass. 39 J26
Truth or Consequences, N. Mex. 183 N5
Tsala Apopka Lake, Fla. 121 F13
Tucson, Ariz. *178*, 179 Q11; film studio (1913) *178*
Tucumcari, N. Mex. 183 G14
Tug Fork (river), Ky.-W. Va. 75 F25, 79 P3
Tulalip IR, Wash. 223 D6
Tularosa, N. Mex. 183 N9
Tule Lake NWR, Calif. 231 A5
Tule River IR, Calif. 231 N10
Tullahoma, Tenn. 87 F13
Tulsa, Okla. 187 F23; art exhibit *188*; oil refinery *188*

Tumacacori NM, Ariz. 179 S11
Tumon Bay, Guam 245 Q17, *246*
Tuolumne River, Calif. 231 J7
Tupelo, Miss. 101 D10
Tupper Lake, N. Y. 53 D15
Tuscaloosa, Ala. 105 H5
Tuscarawas River, Ohio 143 G12
Tuscarora IR, N. Y. 52 J2
Tuskegee, Ala. 105 L11, *104*
Tutuila, American Samoa 244, 245 S4
Tuzigoot NM, Ariz. 179 H8
Twelve Mile, Ind. 139 F7
Twin Falls, Idaho 197 R6
Two Rivers, Wis. 127 M14
Tybee NWR, S. C. 113 P10
Tygart Lake, W. Va. 79 G11
Tyler, Tex. 191 G16

Uinta and Ouray IR, Utah 213 G11
Uinta Mountains, Utah 212, 213 E12
Uinta River, Utah 213 F12
Umatilla IR, Oreg. 227 C14
Umatilla NWR, Oreg.-Wash. 223 M12, 227 B12
Umbagog Lake, N. H. 31 E9
Unalaska Island, Alas. 237 P10
Uncompahgre River, Colo. 217 L4
Union City, N. J. 61 F10
Union City Reservoir, Pa. 57 B3
Union Slough NWR, Iowa 165 B8
Uniontown, Pa. 57 L3
U. S. Virgin Islands 235, 244, *244*, 245; diver *247*
University City, Mo. 173 H16
Upper Arlington, Ohio 143 K7
Upper Darby, Pa. 57 K18
Upper Klamath NWR, Oreg. 227 M7
Upper Mississippi River National Wildlife and Fish Refuge 127 O4, 135 C5, 153 R1, 165 D17
Upper Ouachita NWR, La. 117 A7
Urbana, Ill. 135 J9
Utah 212-215
Utah Lake, Utah 213 G8
Ute Mountain IR, Colo. 217 O2
Ute Mountains, N. Mex. 183 A3
Utica, N. Y. 52, 53 J13
Utuado, Puerto Rico 245 C10

Vail, Colo. 217 F8
Valdez, Alas. 236, 237 L20
Valdosta, Ga. 109 Q9
Valentine NWR, Nebr. 161 B8
Valley Falls, R. I. 47 C8
Valley Forge, Pa. 57 K17
Valley of Ten Thousand Smokes, Alas. 234
Valley Station, Ky. 75 F13
Valparaiso, Ind. 139 C4
Van Wert, Ohio 143 G2
Vancouver, Wash. 222, 223 N5
Venice, Fla. 121 L13

Ventura, Calif. 231 R9
Verde River, Ariz. 179 K9
Verdigris River, Kans.-Okla. 169 H16, 187, 187 F24
Vergennes, Vt. 27 H2
Vermillion Lake IR, Minn. 153 E11
Vermont 26-29
Vernon, Conn. 43 D12
Vernon, Vt. 27 U7
Vero Beach, Fla. 121 H18
Vicksburg, Miss. 94, 101 L3, *103*
Victoria, Tex. 191 N14
Vidalia, Ga. 109 L11
Vienna, Va. 83 C20
Vieques, Puerto Rico 245 D19
Vincennes, Ind. 139 P2
Vineland, N. J. 61 Q4, *62*
Vineyard Haven, Mass. 39 O22
Virgin Islands NP, U. S. Virgin Islands 245 B4
Virgin River, Nev.-Utah 209 P12, 213 S4
Virginia 82-85
Virginia, Minn. 152, 153 F11
Virginia Beach, Va. 83 L25
Virginia City, Mont. 200, 201 K7
Virginia City, Nev. 208, 209 H1, *211*
Visalia, Calif. 231 M9
Volcanoes 177, 221, 222, 230, 234, 240, 241, *242*, 244
Voyageurs NP, Minn. 153 C10

Wabash, Ind. 139 F8
Wabash River, Ill.-Ind. 135 P11, 139 U1-G12, *140-141*
Waccamaw, Lake, N. C. 91 K18
Wachusett Reservoir, Mass. 39 F14
Waco, Tex. 190, 191 J13
Wahiawa, Hawaii 241 D10
Waialeale, Hawaii 240, 240 B5
Waikiki Beach, Hawaii 241 F11, *243*
Wailuku, Hawaii 241 G17
Wailuku River, Hawaii 241 M24
Waimea, Hawaii 240 C4
Waimea Canyon, Hawaii 240 C4
Walker Lake, Nev. 209 J3
Walker River IR, Nev. 209 J3
Walla Walla, Wash. 223 M16
Wallenpaupack, Lake, Pa. 57 D18
Wallingford, Conn. 43 J9
Wallops Island NWR, Va. 83 G26
Walnut Canyon NM, Ariz. 179 G10
Walnut Creek NWR, Iowa 165 H10
Walter F. George Reservoir, Ala.-Ga. 105 O13, 109 N3
Wampanoag IR, Mass. 39 Q21
Wanaque Reservoir, N. J. 61 D8
Wapack NWR, N. H. 31 T5
Wapakoneta, Ohio 143 H3
Wapanocca NWR, Ark. 97 F16
Wappello Lake, Mo. 173 O16

Wapsipinicon River, Iowa **165** F15

War Horse NWR, Mont. **201** E12

Warm Springs, Ga. **109** J4

Warm Springs IR, Oreg. **227** E8

Warm Springs Reservoir, Oreg. **227** J15

Warner Robins, Ga. **109** K7

Warren, Mich. **131** R16

Warren, Ohio **143** E14

Warwick, R. I. **47** G7

Wasatch Range, Utah 212, **213** B9-K8, *214*

Washington 222-225

Washington, D. C. *20-23,* 50, 73, 83 C21

Washington, Mo. **173** H14

Washington, Pa. **57** K2

Washington, Mount, N. H. 24, **25**, 30, 31, 31 J8; climate research station *33*

Washington Crossing, Pa. **57** J19

Washington Island, Wis. **127** G16

Washita NWR, Okla. **187** G12

Washita River, Okla. **187** L18

Wassaw NWR, Ga. **109** M16

Watauga Lake, Tenn. **87** B26

Watchaug Pond, R. I. **47** O3

Waterbury, Conn. **43** G7

Wateree Lake, S. C. **113** D11

Wateree River, S. C. **113** G11

Waterford, Conn. **43** K15

Waterloo, Iowa 164, **165** E12

Watertown, Conn. **43** G6

Watertown, N. Y. **53** E11

Watertown, S. Dak. **157** D16

Waterville, Me. **35** O6

Watertown, Wis. 126, **127** Q11

Waterville, Me. 34, **35** O6

Watts Bar Lake, Tenn. 87, **87** D18

Waubay NWR, S. Dak. **157** C16

Waukegan, Ill. **135** B10

Waukesha, Wis. **127** Q13

Wausau, Wis. **127** J9

Waycross, Ga. **109** P12

Weather and climate: droughts *186,* 189; rainfall: greatest 222, scarce 194, 208

Webster Groves, Mo. **173** H16

Weirton, W. Va. **79** B9

Weiss Lake, Ala. **105** D11

Wellesley, Mass. **39** F17

Wellfleet, Mass. **39** K26

Wenatchee, Wash. **223** G11

Wenatchee River, Wash. **223** E10

Wendover, Nev. **209** D13

Wentworth, Lake, N. H. **31** N9

Wertheim NWR, N. Y. **53** T20

West Allis, Wis. **127** Q13

West Bend, Iowa **165** C7; bicyclists *166-167*

West Branch Farmington River, Conn.-Mass. **38** H3, **43** C7

West Branch Susquehanna River, Pa. **57** E9

West Cote Blanche Bay, La. **117** O9

West Hartford, Conn. **43** E9

West Haven, Conn. **43** L8

West Lafayette, Ind. **139** H5

West Memphis, Ark. **97** G16, *99*

West Palm Beach, Fla. **121** M19

West Point, N. Y. **53** Q17

West Point Lake, Ga. **109** H3

West Quoddy Head, Me. 34, **35** N15; morris dancers *37*

West River, Vt. **27** S6

West Virginia 78-81

West Warwick, R. I. **47** G6

Westbrook, Me. **35** S3

Westfield, Mass. **38** H6

Westminster, Colo. **217** E11

Westport, Conn. **43** N4

Wetlands 10, 13, 68, 82, 108, 109, 116, *119; see also* Everglades

Weymouth, Mass. **39** G19

Wheeler Lake, Ala. **105** B7

Wheeler NWR, Ala. **105** C7

Wheeler Peak, Nev. **209** J12

Wheeler Peak, N. Mex. **183** C10

Wheeling, W. Va. **79** C8

Whiskeytown-Shasta-Trinity NRA, Calif. **231** D3

White Butte, N. Dak. **149** L2

White Earth IR, Minn. **153** C4

White Lake, La. **117** O6

White Mountain National Forest, N. H. 30

White Mountains, N. H. 24, 30, **31** J8, *32,* 33

White Mountains NRA, Alas. **237** G20

White Plains, N. Y. **53** S17

White River, Ark. **97** B9-M13

White River, Colo.-Utah **213** H15, **217** E4

White River, Ind. **139** N5

White River, S. Dak. **157** H10

White River, Vt. **27** L6

White River Junction, Vt. **27** M9

White River NWR, Ark. **97** L13

White Sands NM, N. Mex. **183** O8

White Sulphur Springs, Mont. **201** G8

White Sulphur Springs, W. Va. **79** O10, *81*

Whiteface Mountain, N. Y. **53** D17

Whitefish Bay, Mich. **131** E11

Whitefish Bay, Wis. **127** Q14

Whitehall, Ohio **143** L7

Whitewater River, Ind. **139** N11

Whitney, Mount, Calif. **231** M10

Whittier, Alas. **237** L19

Wichita, Kans. 146, 168, **169** H12

Wichita Falls, Tex. **191** E12

Wichita Mountains NWR, Okla. **187** L14

Wickenburg, Ariz. **179** L6

Wickford, R. I. **47** K7

Wickiup Reservoir, Oreg. **227** J7

Wickliffe, Ohio **143** C12

Wicomico River, Md. **65** M15

Wildcat Mountain, N. H.: skier *32*

Wildlife: alligators 108, *110;* bighorn sheep *202;* bison *159,* 168; brown bear *238;* elk *206;* horned lizard *193;* moose *37;* prairie dog *159;* white-tailed deer *128;* wolves 155, *155; see also* Birds

Wilkes-Barre, Pa. **57** E16

Willamette River, Oreg. **227** G4

Willamette Valley, Oreg. 226, 227; vineyard *229*

Williamsburg, Va. **83** K23; mansion *85*

Williamsport, Pa. **57** E12

Willimantic, Conn. **43** E14

Willimantic River, Conn. **43** D14

Willingboro, N. J. **61** M5

Wilmette, Ill. **135** C10

Wilmington, Del. 68, **69** B4, *70*

Wilmington, N. C. 90, **91** K20

Wilson, N. C. **91** D20; tobacco warehouse *93*

Wilson Lake, Ala. **105** B5

Wilson Lake, Kans. **169** D10

Winchester, Va. **83** B17

Wind Cave NP, S. Dak. **157** H2, *159*

Wind River, Wyo. **205** G5

Wind River IR, Wyo. **205** G6

Wind River Range, Wyo. **205** H5

Windham, Conn. **43** E15

Window Rock, Ariz. **179** E16

Windsor, Conn. **43** D10

Windsor, Vt. **27** O7

Winfield, Kans. **169** K13

Winnebago, Lake, Wis. 126, **127** N12

Winnebago IR, Wis. **127** M6

Winnibigoshish, Lake, Minn. **153** G7

Winnipesaukee, Lake, N. H. **31** O8

Winnisquam Lake, N. H. **31** O7

Winona, Miss. **101** F7

Winooski River, Vt. 26, **27** G5

Winston-Salem, N. C. **91** C12

Winter Haven, Fla. **121** J14

Winter Park, Fla. **121** G15

Winterthur (estate), Del. *71*

Wisconsin 126-129

Wisconsin Dells, Wis. **127** O9; rock formation *126*

Wisconsin Rapids, Wis. **127** L8

Wisconsin River, Wis. **127** H9

Wissota, Lake, Wis. **127** J5

Withlacoochee River, Fla. **121** F13

Woburn, Mass. **39** D18

Wolf Island NWR, Ga. **109** O15

Wolf River, Wis. **127** H11

Wood River, R. I. **47** K2

Woodall Mountain, Miss. **101** B11

Woods Hole, Mass. **39** O22

Woodstock, Vt. **27** N7

Woonasquatucket River, R. I. **47** C6

Woonsocket, R. I. **47** A6

Worcester, Mass. **39** G13

Worden Pond, R. I. **47** N5

Worthington, Ohio **143** K7

Wounded Knee, S. Dak. **157** K4

Wrangell, Alas. **237** P26

Wrangell Mountains, Alas. 236, **237** K21

Wrangell-St. Elias NP and Preserve, Alas. **237** K22

Wray, Colo. **217** D18

Wright Brothers NM, N. C. **91** C26

Wright Patman Lake, Tex. **191** F17

Writing Rock, N. Dak. **149** B1

Wupatki NM, Ariz. **179** F10

Wyandotte NWR, Mich. **131** S16

Wylie Lake, S. C. **113** A10

Wyoming 204-207

Wyoming, Mich. **131** R10

Xenia, Ohio **143** M4

Yadkin River, N. C. **91** B10

Yakima, Wash. **223** K10

Yakima IR, Wash. **223** L9

Yakima River, Wash. **223** L11

Yalobusha River, Miss. **101** E6

Yampa River, Colo. **217** C4

Yankton IR, S. Dak. **157** K14

Yazoo NWR, Miss. **101** H3

Yazoo River, Miss. **101** G5, *103*

Yellow River, Fla. **121** B2

Yellowstone Lake, Wyo. **205** C3

Yellowstone NP, Idaho-Mont.-Wyo. **197** N13, **201** L8, **205** B2; geyser *207*

Yellowstone River, Mont.-Wyo. 201, **201** H13, **205** A3

Yockanookany River, Miss. **101** G8

Yonkers, N. Y. **53** S17

York, Pa. **57** K13

York River, Va. 82, **83** J23

Yorktown, Va. 82, **83** K23

Yosemite NP, Calif. **231** J8

Youghiogheny River, Md.-Pa. **57** K4, **64** B1

Youngstown, Ohio **143** E15

Ypsilanti, Mich. **131** S15

Ysleta Del Sur IR, Tex. **191** H1

Yuba Lake, Utah **213** K7

Yucca House NM, Colo. **217** O2

Yukon Delta NWR, Alas. **237** K12, K14

Yukon Flats NWR, Alas. **237** G21

Yukon River, Canada-U. S. 8, **235**, **237** H22-H14

Yuma, Ariz. **179** P1

Zanesville, Ohio **143** L10

Zeeland, N. Dak. **149** M11

Zia IR, N. Mex. **183** E7, F7

Zion, Ill. **135** B10

Zion NP, Utah **213** S4

Zuni IR, N. Mex. **183** G2

Type composition by the Typographic section of National Geographic Production Services, Pre-Press Division. Color separations by Lanman Progressive Co., Washington, D.C.; Phototype Color Graphics, Pennsauken, N.J. Printed and bound by Ringier America, Inc., New Berlin, Wisc. Paper by Mead Paper Co., New York, N.Y.

Library of Congress CIP Data

National Geographic Society (U. S.). Book Division
National Geographic picture atlas of our fifty states/prepared by National Geographic Book Division.
p.   cm.

Includes index.
Summary: Includes maps and other pertinent information about the geography, industries, and population of each of the fifty states.
ISBN 0-87044-859-5 (regular ed. : alk. paper). — ISBN
0-87044-860-9 (lib. ed. : alk. paper)
1. United States—Maps.   [1. United States—Maps. 2. Atlases.]
I. Title. II. Title: Our fifty states.
G1200.N33 1991 [G&M]
912.73—dc20   91-28084
                                              CIP
                                        MAP AC